REA's Books Are The Best...
They have rescued lots of grades and more!
(a sample of the <u>hundreds of letters</u> REA receives each year)

"Your books are great! They are very helpful, and have upped my grade in every class. Thank you for such a great product."
Student, Seattle, WA

"Your book has really helped me sharpen my skills and improve my weak areas. Definitely will buy more."
Student, Buffalo, NY

"Compared to the other books that my fellow students had, your book was the most useful in helping me get a great score."
Student, North Hollywood, CA

"I really appreciate the help from your excelle_ _ _ _ _k. Please keep up your great wor_ _ _
*Student, Albuquerqu_*

"Your book was such a better _ _ _ _ch more complete than anything your c_ _ _ _as produced (and I have them _
Teacher, Virginia Beach, VA

(more on next page)

(continued from previous page)

"Your books have saved my GPA, and quite possibly my sanity.
My course grade is now an 'A', and I couldn't be happier."
Student, Winchester, IN

"These books are the best review books on the market.
They are fantastic!"
Student, New Orleans, LA

"Your book was responsible for my success on the exam. . . I
will look for REA the next time I need help."
Student, Chesterfield, MO

"I think it is the greatest study guide I have ever used!"
Student, Anchorage, AK

"I encourage others to buy REA because of their superiority.
Please continue to produce the best quality books on the market."
Student, San Jose, CA

"Just a short note to say thanks for the great support your book
gave me in helping me pass the test . . . I'm on my way to a B.S.
degree because of you !"
Student, Orlando, FL

UNITED STATES HISTORY

Jerome McDuffie, Ph.D.
Professor of History
University of North Carolina
at Pembroke

Gary Piggrem, Ph.D.
Professor of History
DeVry University/Columbus
Columbus, Ohio

Steven E. Woodworth, Ph.D.
Assistant Professor of History
Toccoa Falls College
Toccoa, Georgia

Edited by
Paul R. Babbitt, Ph.D.
Assistant Professor of Political Science
Southern Arkansas University
Magnolia, Arkansas

Research & Education Association
Visit our website at
www.rea.com

Research & Education Association
61 Ethel Road West
Piscataway, New Jersey 08854
E-mail: info@rea.com

SUPER REVIEW®
OF UNITED STATES HISTORY

Printed in the United States of America

Library of Congress Control Number 2009943979

ISBN-13: 978-0-7386-0070-3
ISBN-10: 0-7386-0070-9

What this **Super Review**® Will Do for You

REA's **Super Review** provides **all you need to know** to excel in class and succeed on midterms, finals, and even pop quizzes.

Think of this book as giving you access to your own private tutor. Here, right at your fingertips, is a brisk review to help you not only understand your textbook but also pick up where even some of the best lectures leave off.

Outstanding **Super Review** features include...

- Comprehensive yet concise coverage
- Targeted preparation for subject tests
- End-of-chapter quizzes that provide pretest tune-up

We think you'll agree that, whether you're prepping for your next test or want to be a stronger contributor in class, **REA's Super Review** truly provides **all you need to know!**

Larry B. Kling
Super Review Program Director

CONTENTS

Chapter 5
Jacksonian Democracy and
Westward Expansion (1824-1850)　　　　110

Chapter 6
Sectional Conflict and the Causes of
the Civil War (1850-1860)   156

Chapter 7
The Civil War and Reconstruction (1860-1877)   187

Chapter 8
Industrialism, War, and the
Progressive Era (1877-1912)   216

Chapter 13
The New Frontier, Vietnam, and
Social Upheaval (1960-1972)   **430**

Chapter 14
Watergate, Carter, and the
New Conservatism (1972-2009) **450**

Picture Credits

Page 11: Pilgrims landing at Plymouth Rock, Sarony & Major, The Landing of the Pilgrims on Plymouth Rock, Dec. 11th, 1620. 1846. U.S. Library of Congress.

Page 22: William Penn, Historical Society of Pennsylvania, copy of a 17th century portrait, possibly by Sir Peter Lely.

Page 41: Thomas Paine, copy of engraving after George Romney. U.S. National Archives & Records Administration.

Page 61: George Washington, from a portrait by Gilbert Stuart. U.S. Library of Congress.

Page 78: John Adams, from a portrait by Gilbert Stuart. U.S. Library of Congress.

Page 81: Thomas Jefferson, lithograph by Henry R. Robinson. U.S. Library of Congress.

Page 198: Lincoln at Antietam, Oct. 3, 1862. Photo by Alexander Gardner. U.S. Library of Congress.

Page 200: Lincoln campaign poster. U.S. Library of Congress.

Page 207: Impeachment of Andrew Johnson, 1868, wood engraving after T.R. Davis. U.S. Library of Congress.

Page 212: Ulysses S. Grant, photo by Matthew B. Brady. U.S. Library of Congress.

Page 224: Indian prisoners, from Black Kettle's camp, captured by General Custer, traveling through snow. Illustrated by Theodore R. Davis, *Harper's*, v. 12, 1868, p. 825. U.S. Library of Congress.

Page 228: Linotype operators at *New York World*, *New York World* photo. U.S. Library of Congress.

Page 247: Assassination of McKinley, photo of wash drawing by T. Dart Walker. U.S. Library of Congress.

Page 263: President Taft speaking at Manassas Court House, Nov. 10, 1911. U.S. Library of Congress.

Page 264: William Taft. U.S. Library of Congress.

Page 267: Woodrow Wilson. U.S. Library of Congress.

Page 298: General John J. Pershing. National Archives and Records Administration.

Page 351: Destitute peapickers. Photo by Dorothea Lange. U.S. Library of Congress.

Page 388: Attack on Pearl Harbor. U.S. Naval Historical Center Photo.

Page 392: D-Day landing at Normandy. Franklin D. Roosevelt Library.

Page 432: John F. Kennedy. U.S. Library of Congress.

Page 436: President Johnson signs Civil Rights Act of 1968. U.S. Library of Congress.

Page 437: Apollo 11's Buzz Aldrin walks on the lunar surface. Photo by Neil Armstrong, NASA.

Page 441: President Johnson awards a medal to a wounded U.S. serviceman in Cam Rahn Bay, South Vietnam (1966). Photo by Yoichi Okamoto. Lyndon Baines Johnson Library.

Page 452: Nixon departing from the White House after resigning Aug. 9, 1973. Richard Milhous Nixon Presidential Materials Project.

Page 456: Jimmy Carter, 1977. Official White House photo. U.S. Library of Congress.

Page 459: President Ronald Reagan at a political rally (1982). Photo by Michael Evans. Courtesy of Ronald Reagan Presidential Library.

Page 477: President Clinton and Russian President Yeltsin. White House photo by Bob McNeely.

Page 481: President George W. Bush and First Lady Laura Bush observe a moment of silence after the 9/11 terrorist attacks. White House photo by Eric Draper.

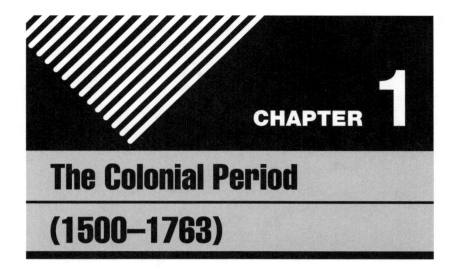

CHAPTER 1

The Colonial Period (1500–1763)

The Age of Exploration

The Treaty of Tordesillas

Excited by the gold Columbus had brought back from America (after Amerigo Vespucci, an Italian member of a Portuguese expedition to South America whose widely reprinted report suggested a new world had been found), Ferdinand and Isabella, joint monarchs of Spain, sought formal confirmation of their ownership of these new lands. They feared the interference of Portugal, which was at that time a powerful seafaring nation and had been active in overseas exploration. In 1493, at Spain's urging, the pope drew a "Line of Demarcation" 100 leagues west of the Cape Verde Islands, dividing the heathen world into two equal parts—that east of the line for Portugal and that west of it for Spain.

Because this line tended to be unduly favorable to Spain, and because Portugal had the stronger navy, the two countries worked out the Treaty of Tordesillas (1494), by which the line was moved farther west. As a result, Brazil eventually became a Portuguese colony, while Spain maintained claims to the rest of the Americas. As other European nations joined the hunt for colonies, they tended to ignore the Treaty of Tordesillas.

Spanish Explorer Ships

The Spanish Conquistadores

To conquer the Americas, the Spanish monarchs used their powerful army, led by independent Spanish adventurers known as *conquistadores*. At first the conquistadores confined their attentions to the Caribbean islands, where the European diseases they unwittingly carried with them devastated the local Indian populations, who had no immunities against such diseases.

After about 1510 the conquistadores turned their attention to the American mainland. In 1513 Vasco Nunez de Balboa crossed the isthmus of Panama and became the first European to see the Pacific Ocean. The same year Juan Ponce de Leon explored Florida in search of gold and a fabled fountain of youth. He found neither, but claimed Florida for Spain. In 1519 Hernando (Hernan) Cortes led his dramatic expedition against the Aztecs of Mexico. Aided by the fact that the Indians at first mistook him for a god, as well as by firearms, armor, horses, and (unbeknown to him) smallpox germs, all previously unknown in America, Cortes destroyed the Aztec empire and won enormous riches. By the 1550s other such fortune seekers had conquered much of South America.

In North America the Spaniards sought in vain for riches. In 1528 Panfilio de Narvaez led a disastrous expedition through the Gulf Coast region from which only four of the original 400 men returned. One of them, Cabeza de Vaca, brought with him a story of seven great cities full of gold (the "Seven Cities of Cibola") somewhere to the north. In response to this, two Spanish expeditions explored the interior of North America. Hernando de Soto led a 600-man expedition (1539–1541) through what is now the southeastern United States, penetrating as far west as Oklahoma and discovering the Mississippi River, on whose banks de Soto was buried. Francisco Vasquez de Coronado led an expedition (1540–1542) from Mexico, north across the Rio Grande and through New Mexico, Arizona, Texas, Oklahoma, and Kansas. Some of Coronado's men were the first Europeans to see the Grand Canyon. While neither expedition discovered rich Indian civilizations to plunder, both increased Europe's knowledge of the interior of North America and asserted Spain's territorial claims to the continent.

New Spain

Spain administered its new holdings as an autocratic, rigidly controlled empire in which everything was to benefit the parent country. Tight control of even mundane matters was carried out by a suffocating bureaucracy run directly from Madrid. Annual treasure fleets carried the riches of the New World to Spain for the furtherance of its military-political goals in Europe.

As population pressures were low in sixteenth-century Spain, only about 200,000 Spaniards came to America during that time. To deal with the consequent labor shortages—and as a reward to successful conquistadores—the Spaniards developed a system of large manors or estates (*encomiendas*), with Indian slaves ruthlessly managed for the benefit of the conquistadores. The encomienda system was later replaced by the similar but somewhat milder *hacienda* system. As the Indian population died from overwork and European diseases, Spaniards began importing African slaves to supply their labor needs. Society in New Spain was rigidly stratified, with the highest level reserved for natives of Spain (*peninsulares*) and the next for those of Spanish parentage born in the New World (*creoles*). Those of mixed or Indian blood occupied lower levels.

English and French Beginnings

In 1497 the Italian John Cabot (Giovanni Caboto), sailing under the sponsorship of the king of England in search of a Northwest Passage (a water route to the Orient through or around the North American continent), became the first European since the Viking voyages more than four centuries earlier to reach the mainland of North America, which he claimed for England.

In 1524 the king of France authorized another Italian, Giovanni da Verrazzano, to undertake a mission similar to Cabot's. Endeavoring to duplicate the achievement of Portuguese Ferdinand Magellan, who had five years earlier found a way around the southern tip of South America, Verrazzano followed the American coast from present-day North Carolina to Maine.

Beginning in 1534, Jacques Cartier, also authorized by the king of France, mounted three expeditions to the area of the St. Lawrence River, which he believed might be the hoped-for Northwest Passage. He explored up the river as far as the site of Montreal, where—as he saw it—rapids prevented him from continuing to China. He claimed the area for France before abandoning his last expedition and returning to France in 1542. France made no further attempts to explore or colonize in America for sixty-five years.

England showed little interest in America as well during most of the sixteenth century. But when the English finally did begin colonization, commercial capitalism in England had advanced to the point that the English efforts were supported by private rather than government funds, allowing the English colonists to enjoy a greater degree of freedom from government interference.

Partially as a result of the New World rivalries and partially through differences between Protestant and Catholic countries, the sixteenth century was a violent time both in Europe and in America. French Protestants, called Huguenots, who attempted to escape persecution in

Catholic France by settling in the New World, were massacred by the Spaniards. One such incident led the Spaniards, nervous about any possible encroachment on what they considered to be their exclusive holdings in America, to build a fort that became the beginning of a settlement at St. Augustine, Florida, the first city in North America. Spanish priests ventured north from St. Augustine, but no permanent settlements were built in the interior.

French and especially English sea captains made great sport of—and considerable profit from—plundering the Spaniards of the wealth they had first plundered from the Indians. One of the most successful English captains, Francis Drake, sailed around South America and raided the Spanish settlements on the Pacific coast of Central America before continuing on to California, which he claimed for England and named Nova Albion. Drake then returned to England by sailing around the world. England's Queen Elizabeth, sister and Protestant successor to Mary, had been quietly investing in Drake's highly profitable voyages. On Drake's return from his round-the-world voyage, Elizabeth openly showed her approval.

Angered by this, as well as by Elizabeth's support of the Protestant cause in Europe, Spain's King Philip II in 1588 dispatched a mighty fleet, the Spanish Armada, to conquer England. Instead, the Armada was defeated by the English navy and largely destroyed by storms in the North Sea. This victory established England as a great power and moved it a step closer to overseas colonization, although the war with Spain continued until 1604.

Gilbert, Raleigh, and the First English Attempts at Colonization

English nobleman Sir Humphrey Gilbert believed England should found colonies and find a Northwest Passage. In 1576 he sent English sea captain Martin Frobisher to look for such a passage. Frobisher scouted along the inhospitable northeastern coast of Canada and brought back large amounts of a yellow metal that turned out to be fool's gold. In 1578 Gilbert obtained a charter allowing him to found a colony with his own funds and guaranteeing the prospective colonists all the rights of those born and residing in England, thus setting an important precedent for future colonial charters. His attempts to found a colony in Newfoundland failed, and, while pursuing these endeavors, he was lost at sea.

With the queen's permission, Gilbert's work was taken up by his half-brother, Sir Walter Raleigh. Raleigh turned his attention to a more southerly portion of the North American coastline, which he named Virginia, in honor of England's unmarried queen. He selected as a site for the first settlement Roanoke Island just off the coast of present-day North Carolina.

After one abortive attempt, a group of 114 settlers—men, women, and children—landed in July 1587. Shortly thereafter, Virginia Dare became the first English child born in America. Later that year the expedition's leader, John White, returned to England to secure additional supplies. Delayed by the war with Spain, he did not return until 1590, when he found the colony deserted. It is not known what became of the Roanoke settlers. After this failure, Raleigh was forced by financial constraints to abandon his attempts to colonize Virginia. Hampered by unrealistic expectations, inadequate financial resources, and the ongoing war with Spain, English interest in American colonization was submerged for fifteen years.

The Beginnings of Colonization

Virginia

In the first decade of the 1600s, Englishmen, exhilarated by the recent victory over Spain and influenced by the writings of Richard Hakluyt (who urged American colonization as the way to national greatness and the spread of the gospel), once again undertook to plant colonies.

Two groups of merchants gained charters from James I, Queen Elizabeth's successor. One group of merchants was based in London and received a charter to North America between what are now the Hudson and the Cape Fear rivers. The other was based in Plymouth and was granted the right to colonize in North America from the Potomac to the northern border of present-day Maine. They were called the Virginia Company of London and the Virginia Company of Plymouth, respectively. These were joint-stock companies, which raised their capital by the sale of shares of stock. Companies of this sort had already been used to finance and carry on English trade with Russia, Africa, and the Middle East.

The Plymouth Company, in 1607, attempted to plant a colony in Maine, but after one winter the colonists became discouraged and returned to Britain. Thereafter, the Plymouth Company folded.

The Virginia Company of London, in 1607, sent out an expedition of three ships with 104 men to plant a colony some forty miles up the James River from Chesapeake Bay. Like the river on which it was located, the new settlement was named Jamestown in honor of England's king. It became the first permanent English settlement in North America, but for a time it appeared to be going the way of the earlier attempts. During the early years of Jamestown, the majority of the settlers died of starvation, various diseases, or hostile action by Indians. Though the losses were continuously replaced by new settlers, the colony's survival remained in doubt for a number of years.

There were several reasons for these difficulties. The entire colony was owned by the company, and all members shared the profits regardless of how much or how little they worked; thus, there was a lack of incentive. Many of the settlers were gentlemen, who considered themselves too good to work at growing the food the colony needed to survive. Others were simply unambitious and little inclined to work in any case. Furthermore, the settlers had come with the expectation of finding gold or other quick and easy riches and wasted much time looking for these while they should have been providing for their survival.

For purposes of defense, the settlement had been sited on a peninsula formed by a bend in the river; but this low and swampy location proved to be a breeding ground for all sorts of diseases and, at high tide, even contaminated the settlers' drinking supply with sea water. To make matters worse, relations with Powhatan, the powerful local Indian chief, were at best uncertain and often openly hostile, with disastrous results for the colonists.

In 1608 and 1609 the dynamic and ruthless leadership of John Smith kept the colony from collapsing. Smith's rule was, "He who works not, eats not." After Smith returned to England in late 1609, the condition of the colony again became critical.

In 1612, a Virginia resident named John Rolfe discovered that a superior strain of tobacco, native to the West Indies, could be grown in Virginia. There was a large market for this tobacco in Europe, and Rolfe's discovery gave Virginia a major cash crop.

To secure more settlers and boost Virginia's shrinking labor force, the company moved to make immigration possible for Britain's poor, who were without economic opportunity at home or financial means to procure transportation to America. This was achieved by means of the indenture system, by which a poor worker's passage to America was paid by an American planter (or the company itself), who, in exchange, was indentured to work for the planter (or the company) for a specified number of years. The system was open to abuse and often resulted in the mistreatment of the indentured servants.

To control the workers thus shipped to Virginia, as well as the often lazy and unruly colonists already present, the company gave its governors in America dictatorial powers. Governors such as Lord De La Warr, Sir Thomas Gates, and Sir Thomas Dale made use of such powers, imposing a harsh rule.

For such reasons, and its well-known reputation as a death trap, Virginia continued to attract inadequate numbers of immigrants. To solve this, a reform-minded faction within the company proposed a new approach, and under its leader, Edwin Sandys, made changes designed to attract more settlers. Colonists were promised the same rights they had in England. A representative assembly, the House of Burgesses, was founded in 1619—the first in America. Additionally, private ownership of land was instituted.

Despite these reforms, Virginia's unhealthy reputation kept many Englishmen away. Large numbers of indentured servants were brought in, especially young, single men. The first Africans were brought to Virginia in 1619 but were treated as indentured servants rather than slaves.

Virginia's Indian relations remained difficult. In 1622 an Indian massacre took the lives of 347 settlers. In 1644 the Indians struck again, massacring another 300 settlers. Shortly thereafter, the coastal Indians were subdued and no longer presented a serious threat.

Impressed by the potential profits from tobacco growing, King James I determined to have Virginia for himself. Using the high mortality and the 1622 massacre as a pretext, he revoked the London Company's charter in 1624 and made Virginia a royal colony. This pattern was followed throughout colonial history; both company colonies and proprietary colonies tended eventually to become royal colonies. Upon taking over Virginia, James revoked all political rights and the representative assembly—he did not believe in such things—but fifteen years later his son, Charles I, was forced, by constant pressure from the Virginians and the continuing need to attract more settlers, to restore these rights.

New France

Shortly after England returned to the business of colonization, France renewed its interest in the areas previously visited by such French explorers as Jacques Cartier. The French opened with the Indians a lucrative trade in furs, plentiful in America and much sought after in Europe.

The St. Lawrence River was the French gateway to the interior of North America. In 1608 Samuel de Champlain established a trading post in Quebec, from which the rest of what became New France eventually spread.

Relatively small numbers of Frenchmen came to America, and, partially because of this, they were generally able to maintain good relations with the Indians. French Canadians were energetic in exploring and claiming new lands for France.

French exploration and settlement spread through the Great Lakes region and the valleys of the Mississippi and Ohio rivers. In 1673 Jacques Marquette explored the Mississippi Valley, and in 1682 Sieur de la Salle followed the river to its mouth. French settlements in the Midwest were not generally real towns, but rather forts and trading posts serving the fur trade.

Throughout its history, New France was handicapped by an inadequate population and a lack of support from the parent country.

New Netherlands

Other countries also took an interest in North America. In 1609 Holland sent an Englishman named Henry Hudson to search for a Northwest Passage. In this endeavor, Hudson discovered the river that bears his name.

Arrangements were made to trade with the Iroquois for furs, especially beaver pelts for the hats then popular in Europe. In 1624 Dutch trading outposts were established on Manhattan Island (New Amsterdam) and at the site of present-day Albany (Fort Orange). A profitable fur trade was carried on and became the main source of revenue for the Dutch West India Company, the joint-stock company that ran the colony.

To encourage enough farming to keep the colony supplied with food, the Dutch instituted the patroon system, by which large landed estates would be given to wealthy men who transported at least fifty families to New Netherlands. These families would then become tenant farmers on the estate of the patroon who had transported them. As Holland's home economy was healthy, few Dutch felt desperate enough to take up such unattractive terms.

New Netherlands was, in any case, internally weak and unstable. It was poorly governed by inept and lazy governors, and its population was a mixture of people from all over Europe as well as many African slaves, forming what historians have called an "unstable pluralism."

The Pilgrims at Plymouth

Many Englishmen came from England for religious reasons. For the most part, these fell into two groups, Puritans and Separatists. Though similar in many respects to the Puritans, the Separatists believed the Church of England was beyond saving and so felt they must separate from it.

Pilgrims landing at Plymouth Rock (1620)

One group of Separatists, suffering government harassment, fled to Holland. Dissatisfied there, they decided to go to America and, thus, became the famous Pilgrims.

Led by William Bradford, they departed in 1620, having obtained from the London Company a charter to settle just south of the Hudson River. Driven by storms, their ship, the *Mayflower*, made landfall at Cape Cod in Massachusetts. They decided it was God's will for them to settle in that area. This, however, put them outside the jurisdiction of any established government, and so, before going ashore, they drew up and signed the *Mayflower Compact,* establishing a foundation for orderly government based on the consent of the governed. After a difficult first winter that saw many die, the Pilgrims went on to establish a quiet and modestly prosperous colony. After a number of years of hard work, they were able to buy out the investors who had originally financed their voyage and thus gain greater autonomy.

The Massachusetts Bay Colony

The Puritans were far more numerous than the Separatists. Contrary to stereotype, they did not dress in drab clothes and were not ignorant or bigoted. They did, however, take the Bible and their religion seriously and felt the Anglican Church still retained too many unscriptural practices left over from Roman Catholicism.

King James I had no use for the Puritans but, mindful of their growing political power, refrained from bringing on a confrontation. His son, Charles I, determined in 1629 to persecute the Puritans aggressively and to rule without the Puritan-dominated Parliament. This course would lead eventually (ten years later) to civil war, but in the meantime some of the Puritans decided to set up a community in America.

To accomplish their purpose, they sought in 1629 to charter a joint-stock company to be called the Massachusetts Bay Company. Whether because Charles was glad to be rid of the Puritans or because he did not realize the special nature of this joint-stock company, the charter was granted. Further, the charter neglected to specify where the company's headquarters should be located. Taking advantage of this unusual omission, the Puritans determined to make their headquarters in the colony itself, 3,000 miles from meddlesome royal officials.

Under the leadership of John Winthrop, who taught that a new colony should provide the whole world with a model of what a Christian society ought to be, the Puritans carefully organized their venture and, upon arriving in Massachusetts in 1630, did not undergo the "starving time" that had often plagued other first-year colonies.

The government of Massachusetts developed to include a governor and a representative assembly (called the General Court) selected by the "freemen"—adult male church members. As Massachusetts' population increased (20,000 Puritans had come by 1642 in what came to be called the Great Migration), new towns were chartered, each town being granted a large tract of land by the Massachusetts government. As in European villages, these towns consisted of a number of houses clustered around the church house and the village green. Farmland was located around the outside of the town. In each new town, the elect—those who testified of having experienced saving grace—covenanted together as a church.

Rhode Island, Connecticut, and New Hampshire

Puritans saw their colony not as a place to do whatever might strike one's fancy, but as a place to serve God and build His kingdom. Dissidents would be tolerated only insofar as they did not interfere with the colony's mission.

One such dissident was Roger Williams. A Puritan preacher, Williams was received warmly in Massachusetts in 1631; but he had a talent for carrying things to their logical (or sometimes not so logical) extreme. When his activities became disruptive, he was asked to leave the colony. To avoid having to return to England—where he would have been even less welcome—he fled to the wilderness around Narragansett Bay, bought land from the Indians, and founded the settlement of Providence (1636), soon populated by his many followers.

Another dissident was Anne Hutchinson, who openly taught things contrary to Puritan doctrine. Called before the General Court to answer for her teachings, she claimed to have had special revelations from God superseding the Bible. This was unthinkable in Puritan theology and led to Hutchinson's banishment from the colony. She also migrated to the area around Narragansett Bay and with her followers founded Portsmouth (1638). She later migrated still farther west and was killed by Indians.

In 1644 Roger Williams secured from Parliament a charter combining Providence, Portsmouth, and other settlements that had sprung up in the area into the colony of Rhode Island. Through Williams' influence, the colony granted complete religious toleration. Rhode Island tended to be populated by such exiles and troublemakers as could not find welcome in the other colonies or in Europe. It suffered constant political turmoil.

Connecticut was founded by Puritans who had slight religious disagreements with the leadership of Massachusetts. In 1636 Thomas Hooker led a group of settlers westward to found Hartford. (Hooker, though a good friend of Massachusetts Governor John Winthrop, felt he was exercising somewhat more authority than was prudent.) Others also moved into Connecticut from Massachusetts. In 1639 the *Fundamental Orders of Connecticut,* the first written constitution in America, was drawn up, providing for a representative government.

In 1637 a group of Puritans led by John Davenport founded the neighboring colony of New Haven. Davenport and his followers felt that Winthrop, far from being too strict, was not being strict enough. In 1662 a new charter combined both New Haven and Connecticut into an officially recognized colony of Connecticut.

New Hampshire's settlement did not involve any disagreement at all among the Puritans. It was simply settled as an overflow from Massachusetts. In 1677 King Charles II chartered the separate royal colony of New Hampshire. It remained economically dependent on Massachusetts.

Maryland

By the 1630s, the English crown was taking a more direct interest in exercising control over the colonies, and therefore turned away from the practice of granting charters to joint-stock companies, and toward granting such charters to single individuals or groups of individuals known as proprietors. The proprietors would actually own the colony and would be directly responsible for it to the king, in an arrangement similar to the feudalism of medieval Europe. Though this was seen as providing more opportunity for royal control and less for autonomy on the part of the colonists, in practice proprietary colonies turned out much like the company colonies because settlers insisted on self-government.

The first proprietary colony was Maryland, granted in 1632 to George Calvert, Lord Baltimore. It was to be located just north of the Potomac River and to be at the same time a reward for Calvert's loyal service to the king as well as a refuge for English Catholics, of whom Calvert was one. George Calvert died before the colony could be planted, but the venture was carried forward by his son Cecilius.

From the start, more Protestants than Catholics came. To protect the Catholic minority, Calvert approved an Act of Religious Toleration (1649) guaranteeing political rights to Christians of all persuasions. Calvert also allowed a representative assembly. Economically and socially, Maryland developed as a virtual carbon copy of neighboring Virginia.

The Carolinas

In 1663 Charles II, having recently been restored to the throne after a twenty-year Puritan revolution that had seen his father beheaded, moved to reward eight of the noblemen who had helped him regain the crown by granting them a charter for all the lands lying south of Virginia and north of Spanish Florida.

The new colony was called Carolina, after the king. In hopes of attracting settlers, the proprietors came up with an elaborate plan for a hierarchical, almost feudal, society. Not surprisingly, this proved unworkable, and despite offers of generous land grants to settlers, the Carolinas grew slowly.

The area of North Carolina developed as an overflow from Virginia with similar economic and cultural features. South Carolina was settled by English planters from the island of Barbados; they founded Charles Town (Charleston) in 1670. These planters brought with them their black slaves; thus, unlike the Chesapeake colonies of Virginia and Maryland, South Carolina had slavery as a fully developed institution from the outset.

New York and New Jersey

Charles II, though immoral and dissolute, was cunning and had an eye for increasing Britain's power. The Dutch colony of New Netherlands, lying between the Chesapeake and the New England colonies, caught his eye as a likely target for British expansion. In 1664 Charles gave his brother, James, Duke of York, title to all the Dutch lands in America, provided James conquered them first. To do this, James sent an invasion fleet under the command of Colonel Richard Nicols. New Amsterdam fell almost without a shot and became New York.

James was adamantly opposed to representative assemblies and ordered that there should be none in New York. To avoid unrest, Nicols shrewdly granted as many other civil and political rights as possible; but residents, particularly Puritans who had settled on Long Island, continued to agitate for self-government. Finally, in the 1680s, James relented, only to break his promise when he became king in 1685.

To add to the confusion in the newly renamed colony, James granted a part of his newly acquired domain to John Lord Berkeley and Sir George Carteret (two of the Carolina proprietors) who named their new proprietorship New Jersey. James neglected to tell Colonel Nicols of this, with the result that both Nicols, on the one hand, and Carteret and Berkeley, on the other, were granting titles to the same land—to different settlers. Conflicting claims of land ownership plagued New Jersey for decades, being used by the crown in 1702 as a pretext to take over New Jersey as a royal colony.

The Colonial World

Life in the Colonies

New England grew not only from immigration but also from natural increase during the seventeenth century. The typical New England family had more children than the typical English or Chesapeake family, and more of those children survived to have families of their own. A New Englander could expect to live fifteen to twenty years longer than his counterpart in the parent country and twenty-five to thirty years longer than his fellow colonist in the Chesapeake. Because of the continuity provided by these longer lifespans, because the Puritans had migrated as intact family units, and because of the homogeneous nature of the Puritan New England colonies, New England enjoyed a much more stable and well-ordered society than did the Chesapeake colonies.

Puritans placed great importance on the family, which in their society was highly patriarchal. Young people were generally subject to their parents' direction in the matter of when and whom they would marry. Few defied this system, and illegitimate births were rare. Puritans also placed great importance on the ability to read, since they believed everyone should be able to read the Bible, God's word, himself. As a result, New England was ahead of the other colonies educationally and enjoyed extremely widespread literacy.

Since New England's climate and soil were unsuited to large-scale farming, the region developed a prosperous economy based on small farming, home industry, fishing, and especially trade and a large ship-building industry. Boston became a major international port.

Life in the Chesapeake colonies was drastically different. The typical Chesapeake colonist lived a shorter, less healthy life than his New England counterpart and was survived by fewer children. As a result the Chesapeake's population steadily declined despite a constant influx of settlers. Nor was Chesapeake society as stable as that of New England. Most Chesapeake settlers came as indentured servants; and since planters desired primarily male servants for work in the tobacco fields, men largely outnumbered women in Virginia and Maryland. This hindered the development of family life. The short lifespans also contributed to the region's unstable family life, as few children reached adulthood without experiencing the death of one or both parents. Re-marriage resulted in households that contained children from several different marriages.

The system of indentured servitude was open to serious abuse, with masters sometimes treating their servants brutally or contriving through some technicality to lengthen their terms of indenture. In any case, forty percent of the Chesapeake region indentured servants failed to survive long enough to gain their freedom.

By the late seventeenth century, life in the Chesapeake was beginning to stabilize, with death rates declining and life expectancies rising. As society stabilized, an elite group of wealthy families, such as the Byrds, Carters, Fitzhughs, Lees, and Randolphs, among others, began to dominate the social and political life of the region. Aping the lifestyle of the English country gentry, they built lavish manor houses from which to rule their vast plantations. For every one of these, however, there were many small farmers who worked hard for a living, showed deference to the great planters, and hoped someday they, or their children, might reach that level.

On the bottom rung of Southern society were the black slaves. During the first half of the seventeenth century, blacks in the Chesapeake made up only a small percentage of the population and were treated more or less as indentured servants. In the decades between 1640 and 1670, this gradually changed, and blacks came to be seen and treated as lifelong chattel slaves whose status would be inherited by their children. Larger numbers of them began to be imported, and, with this and rapid natural population growth, they came by 1750 to compose thirty to forty percent of the Chesapeake population.

While North Carolina tended to follow Virginia in its economic and social development (although with fewer great planters and more small farmers), South Carolina developed a society even more dominated by large plantations and chattel slavery. By the early decades of the eighteenth century, blacks had come to outnumber whites in that colony. South Carolina's economy remained dependent on the cultivation of its two staple crops, rice and, to a lesser extent, indigo.

Mercantilism and the Navigation Acts

Beginning around 1650, British authorities began to take more interest in regulating American trade for the benefit of the mother country. A key idea that underlay this policy was the concept of mercantilism. Mercantilists believed the world's wealth was sharply limited, and therefore one nation's gain was automatically another nation's loss. Each nation's goal was to export more than it imported (i.e., to have a "favorable balance of trade"). The difference would be made up in gold and silver, which, so the theory ran, would make the nation strong both economically and militarily. To achieve their goals, mercantilists believed economic activity should be regulated by the government. Colonies could fit into England's mercantilist scheme by providing staple crops, such as rice, tobacco, sugar, and indigo, and raw materials, such as timber, that England would otherwise have been forced to import from other countries.

To make the colonies serve this purpose, Parliament passed a series of Navigation Acts (1651, 1660, 1663, and 1673). These were the foundation of England's worldwide commercial system and some of the most important pieces of imperial legislation during the colonial period. They were also intended as weapons in England's on-going struggle against its chief seventeenth-century maritime rival, Holland. The system created by the Navigation Acts stipulated that trade with the colonies was to be carried on only in ships made in Britain or

America and with at least seventy-five percent British or American crews. Additionally, when certain "enumerated" goods were shipped from an American port, they were to go only to Britain or to another American port. Finally, almost nothing could be imported to the colonies without going through Britain first.

Mercantilism's results were mixed. Though ostensibly for the benefit of all subjects of the British Empire, its provisions benefited some at the expense of others. It boosted the prosperity of New Englanders, who engaged in large-scale shipbuilding (something Britain's mercantilist policy-makers chose to encourage), while it hurt the residents of the Chesapeake by driving down the price of tobacco (an enumerated item). On the whole, the Navigation Acts, as intended, transferred wealth from America to Britain by increasing the prices Americans had to pay for British goods and lowering the prices Americans received for the goods they produced. Mercantilism also helped bring on a series of three wars between England and Holland in the late 1600s.

Charles II and his advisors worked to tighten up the administration of colonies, particularly the enforcement of the Navigation Acts. In Virginia tempers grew short as tobacco prices plunged as a result. Virginians were also angry at Royal Governor Sir William Berkeley, whose high-handed, high-taxing ways they despised and whom they believed was running the colony for the benefit of himself and his circle of cronies.

When, in 1674, an impoverished nobleman of shady past by the name of Nathaniel Bacon came to Virginia and failed to gain admittance to Berkeley's inner circle with its financial advantages, he began to oppose Berkeley at every turn and came to head a faction of like-minded persons. In 1676 disagreement over Indian policy brought the matter to the point of armed conflict. Bacon and his men burned Jamestown, but then the whole matter came to an anticlimactic ending when Bacon died of dysentery.

The British authorities, hearing of the matter, sent ships, troops, and an investigating commission. Berkeley, who had had twenty-three of the rebels hanged in reprisal, was removed. Thenceforth, Virginia's royal governors had strict instructions to run the colony for the benefit of the mother country. In response, Virginia's gentry, who had been divided over Bacon's Rebellion, united to face this new threat to their local autonomy. By political means, they consistently obstructed the governors' efforts to increase royal control.

The Half-Way Covenant

By the latter half of the seventeenth century, many Puritans were coming to fear that New England was drifting away from its religious purpose. The children and grandchildren of the first generation were displaying more concern for making money than creating a godly society.

To deal with this, some clergymen in 1662 proposed the "Half-Way Covenant," providing a sort of half-way church membership for the children of members, even though those children, having reached adulthood, did not profess saving grace as was normally required for Puritan church membership. Those who embraced the Half-Way Covenant felt that in an increasingly materialistic society it would at least keep church membership rolls full and might preserve some of the church's influence in society.

Some communities rejected the Half-Way Covenant as an improper compromise, but in general the shift toward secular values continued, though slowly.

King Philip's War

As New England's population grew, local Indian tribes felt threatened, and conflict sometimes resulted. Puritans endeavored to convert Indians to Christianity. The Bible was translated into Algonquian; four villages were set up for converted Indians, who by 1650 numbered over a thousand. Still, most Indians remained unconverted.

In 1675 a Wampanoag chief named King Philip (Metacomet) led a war to exterminate the whites. Some 2,000 settlers lost their lives before King Philip was killed and his tribe subdued. New England continued to experience Indian troubles from time to time, though not as severe as those suffered by Virginia.

The Dominion of New England

The trend toward increasing imperial control of the colonies continued. In 1684 the Massachusetts charter was revoked in retaliation for that colony's large-scale evasion of the restrictions of the Navigation Acts.

The following year Charles II died and was succeeded by his brother, James II. James was prepared to go even farther in controlling the colonies, favoring the establishment of a unified government for all of New England, New York, and New Jersey. This was to be called the Dominion of New England, and the fact that it would abolish representative assemblies and facilitate the imposition of the Church of England on Congregationalist (Puritan) New England made it still more appealing to James.

To head the Dominion, James sent the obnoxious and dictatorial Sir Edmond Andros. Arriving in Boston in 1686, Andros quickly alienated the New Englanders. When news reached America of England's 1688 Glorious Revolution, replacing the Catholic James with his Protestant daughter Mary and her husband, William of Orange, New Englanders cheerfully shipped Andros back to England.

Similar uprisings occurred in New York and Maryland. William and Mary's new government generally accepted these actions, though Jacob Leisler, leader of Leisler's Rebellion in New York, was executed for hesitating to turn over power to the new royal governor. This unfortunate incident poisoned the political climate of New York for many years.

The charter of Massachusetts, now including Plymouth, was restored in 1691, this time as a royal colony, though not as tightly controlled as others of that type.

The Salem Witch Trials

In 1692 Massachusetts was shaken by an unusual incident in which several young girls in Salem Village (now Danvers) claimed to be tormented by the occult activities of certain of their neighbors. Before the resulting Salem witch trials could be stopped by the intervention of Puritan ministers such as Cotton Mather, some twenty persons had been executed (nineteen by hanging and one crushed under a pile of rocks).

Pennsylvania and Delaware

Pennsylvania was founded as a refuge for Quakers. One of a number of radical religious sects that had sprung up about the time of the English Civil War, the Quakers held many controversial beliefs. They believed all persons had an "inner light" that allowed them to commune directly with God. They believed human institutions were, for the most part, unnecessary and, since they believed they could receive revelation directly from God, placed little importance on the Bible. They were also pacifists and declined to show customary deference to those who were considered to be their social superiors. This and their aggressiveness in denouncing established institutions brought them trouble in both Britain and America.

William Penn (age 22), 1666

William Penn, a member of a prominent British family, converted to Quakerism as a young man. Desiring to found a colony as a refuge for Quakers, in 1681 he sought and received from Charles II a grant of land in America as payment of a large debt the king had owed Penn's late father.

Penn advertised his colony widely in Europe, offered generous terms on land, and guaranteed a representative assembly and full religious freedom. He personally went to America to set up his colony, laying out the city of Philadelphia. He succeeded in maintaining peaceful relations with the Indians.

In the years that followed, settlers flocked to Pennsylvania from all over Europe. The colony grew and prospered, and its fertile soil made it not only attractive to settlers but also a large exporter of grain to Europe and the West Indies.

Delaware, though at first part of Pennsylvania, was granted by Penn a separate legislature, but until the American Revolution, Pennsylvania's proprietary governors also functioned as governor of Delaware.

The Eighteenth Century

Economy and Population

British authorities continued to regulate the colonial economy, though usually without going so far as to provoke unrest. An exception was the Molasses Act of 1733, which would have been disastrous for New England merchants. In this case, trouble was averted by the customs agents wisely declining to enforce the act stringently.

The constant drain of wealth from America to Britain, created by the mother country's mercantilistic policies, led to a corresponding drain in hard currency (gold and silver). The artificially low prices that this shortage of money created for American goods was even more advantageous to British buyers. When colonial legislatures responded by endeavoring to create paper money, British authorities blocked such moves. Despite these hindrances, the colonial American economy remained for the most part extremely prosperous.

America's population continued to grow rapidly, both from natural increases due to prosperity and a healthy environment, and from large-scale immigration, not only of English but also of such other groups as Scots-Irish and Germans.

The Germans were prompted to migrate because of wars, poverty, and religious persecution in their homeland. They found Pennsylvania especially attractive and settled there fairly close to the frontier, where land was more readily available. They eventually came to be called the "Pennsylvania Dutch."

The Scots-Irish, Scottish Presbyterians who had been living in northern Ireland for several generations, left their homes because of high rent and economic depression. In America they settled even farther west than the Germans, on or beyond the frontier in the Appalachians.

The Early Wars of the Empire

Between 1689 and 1763 Britain and its American colonies fought a series of four wars with Spain, France, and France's Indian allies, in part to determine who would dominate North America.

Though the first war, known in America as King William's War (1689–1697) but in Europe as the War of the League of Augsburg, was a limited conflict involving no major battles in America, it did bring a number of bloody and terrifying border raids by Indians. It was ended by the Treaty of Ryswick, which made no major territorial changes.

The second war was known in America as Queen Anne's War (1702–1713), but in Europe as the War of the Spanish Succession, and brought America twelve years of sporadic fighting against France and Spain. It was ended by the Treaty of Utrecht, the terms of which gave Britain major territorial gains and trade advantages.

In 1739 war once again broke out with France and Spain. Known in America as King George's war, it was called the War of Jenkins' Ear in Europe (since Captain Robert Jenkins had claimed to have lost an ear to the Spanish coast guards in the Caribbean) and later the War of the Austrian Succession. American troops played an active role, accompanying the British on several important expeditions and suffering thousands of casualties. In 1745 an all-New England army, led by William Pepperrell, captured the powerful French fortress of Louisbourg at the mouth of the St. Lawrence River. To the Americans' disgust, the British in the 1748 Treaty of Aix-la-Chapelle gave Louisbourg back to France in exchange for land in India.

Georgia

With this almost constant imperial warfare in mind, it was decided to found a colony as a buffer between South Carolina and Spanish-held Florida. A group of British philanthropists, led by General James Oglethorpe, obtained a charter for such a colony in 1732, to be located between the Savannah and Altamaha rivers and to be populated by such poor as could not manage to make a living in Great Britain.

The philanthropist trustees, who were to control the colony for twenty-one years before it reverted to royal authority, made elaborate and detailed rules to mold the new colony's society as they felt best. As a result, relatively few settlers came, and those who did complained endlessly. By 1752 Oglethorpe and his colleagues were ready to acknowledge their efforts a failure.

The Enlightenment

As the Eighteenth century progressed, Americans came to be more or less influenced by European ways of thought, culture, and society. Some Americans embraced the European intellectual movement known as the "Enlightenment."

The key concept of the Enlightenment was rationalism—the belief that human reason was adequate to solve all of mankind's problems and, correspondingly, much less faith was needed in the central role of God as an active force in the universe.

A major English political philosopher of the Enlightenment was John Locke. Writing partially to justify England's 1688 Glorious Revolution, he strove to find in the social and political world the sort of natural laws Isaac Newton had recently discovered in the physical realm. He held that such natural laws included the rights of life, liberty, and property; that to secure these rights people submit to governments; and that governments that abuse these rights may justly be overthrown. His writings were enormously influential in America, though usually indirectly, by way of early eighteenth-century English political philosophers. Americans tended to equate Locke's law of nature with the universal law of God.

The most notable Enlightenment man in America was Benjamin Franklin. While Franklin never denied the existence of God, he focused his attention on human reason and what it could accomplish.

The Great Awakening

Of much greater impact on the lives of the common people in America was the movement known as the Great Awakening. It consisted of a series of religious revivals occurring throughout the colonies from the 1720s to the 1740s. Preachers, such as the Dutch Reformed Theodore Frelinghuysen, the Presbyterians William and Gilbert Tennent, and the Congregationalist Jonathan Edwards—best known for his sermon "Sinners in the Hands of an Angry God"—proclaimed a message of personal repentance and faith in Jesus Christ for salvation from an otherwise certain eternity in hell. The most dynamic preacher of the Great Awakening was the Englishman George Whitefield, who traveled through the colonies several times, speaking to crowds of up to 30,000.

The Great Awakening had several important results. America's religious community came to be divided between the "Old Lights," who rejected the Great Awakening, and the "New Lights," who accepted it—and sometimes suffered persecution because of their fervor. A number of colleges were founded (many of them today's "Ivy League" schools), primarily for the purpose of training New-Light ministers. The Great Awakening also fostered a greater readiness to lay the claims of established authority (in this case religious) alongside a fixed standard (in this case the Bible) and to reject any claims it found wanting.

The French and Indian War

The Treaty of Aix-la-Chapelle (1748), ending King George's War, provided little more than a breathing space before the next European and imperial war. England and France continued on a collision course as France determined to take complete control of the Ohio Valley and western Pennsylvania.

British authorities ordered colonial governors to resist this, and Virginia's Robert Dinwiddie, already involved in speculation on the Ohio Valley lands, was eager to comply. George Washington, a young major of the Virginia militia, was sent to western Pennsylvania to request the French to leave. When the French declined, Washington was sent in 1754 with 200 Virginia militiamen to expel them. After success in a small skirmish, Washington was forced by superior numbers to fall back on his hastily built Fort Necessity and then to surrender.

The war these operations initiated spread to Europe two years later, where it was known as the Seven Years' War. In America it later came to be known as the French and Indian War.

While Washington skirmished with the French in western Pennsylvania, delegates of seven colonies met in Albany, New York, to discuss common plans for defense. Delegate Benjamin Franklin proposed a plan for an intercolonial government. While the other colonies showed no support for the idea, it was an important precedent for the concept of uniting in the face of a common enemy.

To deal with the French threat, the British dispatched Major General Edward Braddock with several regiments of British regular troops. Braddock marched overland toward the French outpost of Fort Duquesne, at the place where the Monongahela and Allegheny rivers join to form the Ohio. About eight miles short of his goal, he was ambushed by a small force of French and Indians. Two-thirds of the British regulars, including Braddock himself, were killed. However, Britain bounced back from this humiliating defeat and several others that followed, and under the leadership of its capable and energetic prime minister, William Pitt, had by 1760 taken Quebec and Montreal and virtually liquidated the French empire in North America.

By the Treaty of Paris of 1763, which officially ended hostilities, Britain gained all of Canada and all of what is now the United States east of the Mississippi River. France lost all of its North American holdings.

Americans at the end of the French and Indian War were proud to be part of the victorious British Empire and proud of the important role they had played in making it so. They felt affection for Great Britain, and thoughts of independence would not have crossed their minds.

CHAPTER 2

The American Revolution (1763–1787)

The Coming of the American Revolution

Writs of Assistance

While Americans' feelings toward Great Britain were pride and affection, British officials felt contemptuous of Americans and were eager to increase imperial control over them beyond anything that had previously been attempted. This drive to gain new authority over the colonies, beginning in 1763, led directly to American independence.

Even before that time, the Writs of Assistance cases had demonstrated that Americans would not accept a reduction of their freedom.

In 1761 a young Boston lawyer named James Otis argued before a Massachusetts court that Writs of Assistance (general search warrants issued to help royal officials stop evasion of Britain's mercantilist trade restrictions) were contrary to natural law. He made his point though he lost his case, and others in the colonies joined in protesting against the Writs.

Grenville and the Stamp Act

In 1763 the strongly anti-American George Grenville became prime minister and set out to solve some of the empire's more pressing problems. Chief among these was the large national debt incurred in the recent war.

Of related concern was the cost of defending the American frontier, recently the scene of a bloody Indian uprising led by an Ottawa chief named Pontiac. Goaded by French traders, Pontiac had aimed to drive the entire white population into the sea. While failing in that endeavor, he had succeeded in killing a large number of settlers along the frontier.

Grenville created a comprehensive program to deal with these problems and moved energetically to put it into effect. He sent the Royal Navy to suppress American smuggling and vigorously enforce the Navigation Acts. He also issued the Proclamation of 1763, forbidding white settlement west of the crest of the Appalachians, in hopes of keeping the Indians happy and the settlers close to the coast and thus easier to control.

Initially lampooned, George Grenville's Revenue Act begat rebellion.

In 1764, Grenville pushed through Parliament the Sugar Act (also known as the Revenue Act) aimed at raising revenue by taxes on goods imported by the Americans. It halved the duties imposed by the Molasses Act but was intended to raise revenue rather than control trade. Unlike the Molasses Act, it was stringently enforced, with accused violators facing trial in admiralty courts without benefit of jury or the normal protections of due process.

Grenville determined to maintain up to 10,000 British regulars in America to control both colonists and Indians and secure passage of the Quartering Act, requiring the colonies in which British troops were stationed to pay for their maintenance. Americans had never before been required to support a standing army in their midst.

Grenville also saw through the passage of his Currency Act of 1764, which forbade once and for all any colonial attempts to issue currency not redeemable in gold or silver, making it more difficult for Americans to avoid the constant drain of money that Britain's mercantilist policies were designed to create in the colonies.

Most important, however, Grenville got Parliament to pass the Stamp Act (1765), imposing a direct tax on Americans for the first time. The Stamp Act required Americans to purchase revenue stamps on everything from newspapers to legal documents and would have created an impossible drain on hard currency in the colonies. Because it overlooked the advantage already provided by Britain's mercantilist exploitation of the colonies, Grenville's policy was shortsighted and foolish; but few in Parliament were inclined to see this.

Americans reacted first with restrained and respectful petitions and pamphlets, in which they pointed out that "taxation without representation is tyranny." From there resistance progressed to stronger and stronger protests that eventually became violent and involved intimidation of those Americans who had contracted to be the agents for distributing the stamps.

Resistance was particularly intense in Massachusetts, where it was led first by James Otis and then by Samuel Adams, who formed the organization known as the Sons of Liberty.

Angered by the Stamp Act, protesters in Boston burn a pile of stamps.

Other colonies copied Massachusetts' successful tactics while add-ing some of their own. In Virginia, a young Burgess named Patrick Henry introduced seven resolutions denouncing the Stamp Act. Though only the four most moderate of them were passed by the House of Burgesses, newspapers picked up all seven and circulated them widely through the colonies, giving the impression all seven had been adopted. By their denial of Parliament's authority to tax the colonies, they en-couraged other colonial legislatures to issue strongly worded statements.

In October 1765, delegates from nine colonies met as the Stamp Act Congress. Called by the Massachusetts legislature at the instiga-tion of James Otis, the Stamp Act Congress passed moderate resolu-tions against the act, asserting that Americans could not be taxed without their consent, given by their representatives. They pointed out that Americans were not, and, because of their location could not practi-cally be, represented in Parliament and concluded by calling for the repeal of both the Stamp and Sugar Acts. Most important, however, the Stamp Act Congress showed that representatives of the colonies could work together and gave political leaders in the various colonies a chance to become acquainted with each other.

Most effective in achieving repeal of the Stamp Act was colonial merchants' nonimportation (boycott) of British goods. Begun as an agreement among New York merchants, the boycott spread throughout the colonies and had a powerful effect on British merchants and manufacturers, who began clamoring for the act's repeal.

Meanwhile, the fickle King George III had dismissed Grenville over an unrelated disagreement and replaced him with a Cabinet headed by Charles Lord Rockingham. In March 1766, under the leadership of the new ministry, Parliament repealed the Stamp Act. At the same time, however, it passed the Declaratory Act, claiming power to tax or make laws for the Americans "in all cases whatsoever."

Though the Declaratory Act denied exactly the principle Americans had just been at such pains to assert—that of no taxation without representation—the Americans generally ignored it in their exuberant celebration of the repeal of the Stamp Act. Americans continued to eagerly proclaim their loyalty to Great Britain.

The Townshend Acts

The Rockingham ministry proved to be even shorter lived than that of Grenville. It was replaced with a Cabinet dominated by Chancellor of the Exchequer Charles Townshend. Townshend had boasted that he could successfully tax the colonies, and in 1766 Parliament gave him his chance by passing his program of taxes on items imported into the colonies. These taxes came to be known as the Townshend Duties. Townshend mistakenly believed the Americans would accept this method while rejecting the use of direct internal taxes. The Townshend Acts also included the use of admiralty courts to try those accused of violations, the use of writs of assistance, and the paying of customs officials out of the fines they levied. Townshend also had the New York legislature suspended for noncompliance with the Quartering Act.

American reaction was at first slow. Philadelphia lawyer John Dickinson wrote an anonymous pamphlet entitled "Letters from a

Farmer in Pennsylvania," in which he pointed out in moderate terms that the Townshend Acts violated the principle of no taxation without representation and that if Parliament could suspend the New York legislature, it could do the same to others. At the same time, he urged a restrained response on the part of his fellow Americans.

In February 1768 the Massachusetts legislature, at the urging of Samuel Adams, passed the Massachusetts Circular Letter, reiterating Dickinson's mild arguments and urging other colonial legislatures to pass petitions calling on Parliament to repeal the acts. Had the British government done nothing, the matter might have passed quietly.

Instead, British authorities acted. They ordered that if the letter was not withdrawn, the Massachusetts legislature should be dissolved and new elections held. They forbade the other colonial legislatures to take up the matter, and they also sent four regiments of troops to Boston to prevent intimidation of royal officials and intimidate the populace instead.

The last of these actions was in response to the repeated pleas of the Boston customs agents. Corrupt agents had used technicalities of the confusing and poorly written Sugar and Townshend Acts to entrap innocent merchants and line their own pockets. Mob violence had threatened when agents had seized the ship *Liberty*, belonging to Boston merchant John Hancock. Such incidents prompted the call for troops.

The sending of troops, along with the British authority's repressive response to the Massachusetts Circular Letter, aroused the Americans to resistance. Nonimportation was again instituted, and soon British merchants were calling on Parliament to repeal the acts. In March 1770, Parliament, under the new prime minister Frederick Lord North, repealed all of the taxes except that on tea, which was retained to prove Parliament had the right to tax the colonies if it so desired.

By the time of the repeal, however, friction between British soldiers and Boston citizens had led to an incident in which five Bostonians were killed. Although the British soldiers had acted more or less in self-defense, Samuel Adams labeled the incident the "Boston Massacre" and publicized it widely. At their trial the British soldiers were defended by prominent Massachusetts lawyer John Adams and were acquitted on the charge of murder.

The Return of Relative Peace

Following the repeal of the Townshend duties, a period of relative peace set in. The tax on tea remained as a reminder of Parliament's claims, but it could be easily avoided by smuggling.

Much goodwill had been lost and colonists remained suspicious of the British government. Many Americans believed the events of the previous decade to have been the work of a deliberate conspiracy to take their liberty.

Occasional incidents marred the relative peace. One such was the burning, by a seagoing mob of Rhode Islanders disguised as Indians, of the *Gaspee,* a British customs schooner that had run aground offshore. The *Gaspee*'s captain and crew had alienated Rhode Islanders by their extreme zeal for catching smugglers as well as by their theft and vandalism when ashore.

In response to this incident, British authorities appointed a commission to find the guilty parties and bring them to England for trial. Though those responsible for the burning of the *Gaspee* were never found, this action on the part of the British prompted the colonial legislatures to form committees of correspondence to communicate with each other regarding possible threats from the British government.

The Tea Act

The relative peace was brought to an end by the Tea Act of 1773.

In desperate financial condition—partially because the Americans were buying smuggled Dutch tea rather than the taxed British product—the British East India Company sought and obtained from Parliament concessions allowing it to ship tea directly to the colonies rather than only by way of Britain. The result would be that East India Company tea, even with the tax, would be cheaper than smuggled Dutch tea. The colonists would thus, it was hoped, buy the tea, tax and all.

Boston Tea Party

The East India Company would be saved and the Americans would be tacitly accepting Parliament's right to tax them.

The Americans, however, proved resistant to this approach, and, rather than seem to admit Parliament's right to tax, they vigorously resisted the cheaper tea. Various methods, including tar and feathers, were used to prevent the collection of the tax on tea. In most ports Americans did not allow the tea to be landed.

In Boston, however, pro-British Governor Thomas Hutchinson forced a confrontation by ordering Royal Navy vessels to prevent the tea ships from leaving the harbor. After twenty days this would, by law, result in the cargoes being sold at auction and the tax paid. The night before the time was to expire, December 16, 1773, Bostonians thinly disguised as Indians boarded the ships and threw the tea into the harbor.

Many Americans felt this—the destruction of private property—was going too far, but the reaction of Lord North and Parliament quickly united Americans in support of Boston and opposition to Britain.

The Intolerable Acts

The British responded with four acts collectively titled the Coercive Acts. First, the Boston Port Act closed the port of Boston to all trade until local citizens would agree to pay for the lost tea (they would not). Second, the Massachusetts Government Act greatly increased the power of Massachusetts' royal governor at the expense of the legislature. Third, the Administration of Justice Act provided that royal officials accused of crimes in Massachusetts could be tried elsewhere, where chances of acquittal might be greater. Finally, a strengthened Quartering Act allowed the new governor, General Thomas Gage, to quarter his troops anywhere, including unoccupied private homes.

A further act of Parliament also angered and alarmed Americans. This was the Quebec Act, which extended the province of Quebec to the Ohio River, established Roman Catholicism as Quebec's official religion, and set up for Quebec a government without a representative assembly.

For Americans this was a denial of the hopes and expectations of westward expansion for which they had fought the French and Indian War. Also, New Englanders especially saw it as a threat that in their colonies too, Parliament could establish autocratic government and the hated Church of England.

Americans lumped the Quebec Act together with the Coercive Acts and referred to them all as the Intolerable Acts.

In response to the Coercive Acts, the First Continental Congress was called and met in Philadelphia in September 1774. It once again petitioned Parliament for relief but also passed the Suffolk Resolves (so called because they were first passed in Suffolk County, Massachusetts), denouncing the Intolerable Acts and calling for strict nonimportation and rigorous preparation of local militia companies in case the British should resort to military force.

The Congress then narrowly rejected a plan, submitted by Joseph Galloway of Pennsylvania, calling for a union of the colonies within the empire and a rearrangement of relations with Parliament. Most of the delegates felt matters had already gone too far for such a mild measure. Finally, before adjournment, it was agreed that there should be a Second Continental Congress to meet in May of the following year if the colonies' grievances had not been righted by then.

The War for Independence

Lexington and Concord

The British government paid little attention to the First Continental Congress, having decided to teach the Americans a military lesson. More troops were sent to Massachusetts, which was officially declared to be in a state of rebellion. Orders were sent to General Gage to arrest the leaders of the resistance or, failing that, to provoke any sort of confrontation that would allow him to turn British military might loose on the Americans.

Gage decided on a reconnaissance-in-force to find and destroy a reported stockpile of colonial arms and ammunition at Concord. Seven hundred British troops set out on this mission on the night of April 18, 1775. Their movement was detected by American surveillance and news was spread throughout the countryside by dispatch riders Paul Revere and William Dawes.

At the little village of Lexington, Captain John Parker and some seventy Minutemen (militiamen trained to respond at a moment's no-

Battle of Lexington

tice) awaited the British on the village green. As the British approached, a British officer shouted at the Minutemen to lay down their arms and disperse. The Minutemen did not lay down their arms but did turn to file off the green. A shot was fired, and then the British opened fire and charged. Eight Americans were killed and several others wounded, most shot in the back.

The British continued to Concord only to find that nearly all of the military supplies they had expected to find had already been moved. Attacked by growing numbers of Minutemen, they began to retreat toward Boston. As the British retreated, Minutemen, swarming from every village for miles around, fired on the column from behind rocks, trees, and stone fences. Only a relief force of additional British troops saved the first column from destruction.

Open warfare had begun, and the myth of British invincibility was destroyed. Militia came in large numbers from all the New England colonies to join the force besieging Gage and his army in Boston.

Bunker Hill

In May 1775, three more British generals, William Howe, Henry Clinton, and John Burgoyne, arrived in Boston urging Gage to further aggressive action. The following month the Americans tightened the noose around Boston by fortifying Breed's Hill (a spur of Bunker Hill), from which they could, if necessary, bombard Boston.

The British determined to remove them by a frontal attack that would demonstrate the awesome power of British arms. Twice the British were thrown back and finally succeeded as the Americans ran out of ammunition. Over a thousand British soldiers were killed or wounded in what turned out to be the bloodiest battle of the war (June 17, 1775). Yet, the British had gained very little and remained bottled up in Boston.

Meanwhile, in May 1775, American forces under Ethan Allen and Benedict Arnold took Fort Ticonderoga on Lake Champlain.

Congress, hoping Canada would join in the resistance against Britain, authorized two expeditions into Quebec. One, under General Richard Montgomery took Montreal and then turned toward the city of Quebec. It was met there by the second expedition under Benedict Arnold. The attack on Quebec (December 31, 1775) failed. Montgomery was killed, Arnold wounded, and American hopes for Canada ended.

The Second Continental Congress

While these events were taking place in New England and Canada, the Second Continental Congress met in Philadelphia in May 1775. Congress was divided into two main factions. One was composed mostly of New Englanders and leaned toward declaring independence from Britain. The other drew its strength primarily from the Middle Colonies and was not yet ready to go that far. It was led by John Dickinson of Pennsylvania.

Congress took action to deal with the difficult situation facing the colonies. It adopted the New England army around Boston, calling on the other colonies to send troops and sending George Washington to command it, adopted a "Declaration of the Causes and Necessity for Taking up Arms," and adopted the "Olive Branch Petition" pleading with King George III to intercede with Parliament to restore peace.

This last overture was ignored in Britain, where the king gave his approval to the Prohibitory Act, declaring the colonies in rebellion and no longer under his protection. Preparations were made for full-scale war against America.

Throughout 1775, Americans remained deeply loyal to Britain and King George III despite the king's proclamations declaring them to be in revolt. In Congress moderates still resisted independence.

In January 1776, Thomas Paine published a pamphlet entitled *Common Sense,* calling for immediate independence. Its arguments were extreme and sometimes illogical and its language intemperate, but it sold largely and may have had much influence in favor of independence. Continued evidence of Britain's intention to carry on the war throughout the colonies also weakened the moderates' resistance to independence. The Prohibitory Act, with its virtual declaration of war against America, convinced many that no further moral scruples need stand in the way of such a step.

Thomas Paine

On June 7, 1776, Richard Henry Lee of Virginia introduced a series of formal resolutions in Congress calling for independence and a national government. Accepting these ideas, Congress named two committees. One, headed by John Dickinson, was to work out a framework for a national government. The other was to draft a statement of the reasons for declaring independence. This statement, the Declaration of Independence, was primarily the work of Thomas Jefferson of Virginia. It was a restatement of political ideas by then commonplace in America, showing why the former colonists felt justified in separating from Great Britain. It was formally adopted by Congress on July 4, 1776.

Washington Takes Command

Britain, meanwhile, was preparing a massive effort to conquer the United States. Gage was removed for being too timid, and top command went to Howe. To supplement the British army, large numbers of troops were hired from various German principalities. Since many of these Germans came from the state of Hesse-Kassel, Americans referred to all such troops as Hessians.

Although the London authorities desired a quick and smashing campaign, General Howe and his brother, British naval commander Richard, Admiral Lord Howe, intended to move slowly, using their powerful force to cow the Americans into signing loyalty oaths.

In March 1776, Washington placed on Dorchester Heights, overlooking Boston, some of the large cannons that had been captured at Ticonderoga, forcing the British to evacuate the city.

The British shipped their troops to Nova Scotia and then, together with large reinforcements from Britain, landed that summer at New York City. They hoped to find many loyalists there and make that city the key to their campaign to subdue America.

Washington anticipated the move and was waiting at New York, which Congress had ordered should be defended. However, the under-trained, under-equipped, and badly outnumbered American army was no match for the powerful forces under the Howes. Defeated at the Battle of Long Island (August 27, 1776), Washington narrowly avoided being trapped there (an escape partially due to the Howes' slowness). Defeated again at the Battle of Washington Heights (August 29–30, 1776) on Manhattan, Washington was forced to retreat across New Jersey with the aggressive British General Lord Cornwallis, a subordinate of Howe, in pursuit. By December, what was left of Washington's army had made it into Pennsylvania.

With his victory almost complete, Howe decided to wait until spring to finish annihilating Washington's army. Scattering his troops in small detachments so as to hold all of New Jersey, he went into winter quarters.

Washington, with his small army melting away as demoralized soldiers deserted, decided on a bold stroke. On Christmas night 1776, his army crossed the Delaware River and struck the Hessians at Trenton. The Hessians, still groggy from their hard-drinking Christmas party, were easily defeated. A few days later Washington defeated a British force at Princeton (January 3, 1777).

Continental Army

Howe was so shocked by these two unexpected defeats that he pulled his outposts back close to New York. Much of New Jersey was regained. Those who had signed British loyalty oaths in the presence of Howe's army were now at the mercy of their patriot neighbors. And Washington's army was saved from disintegration.

Early in the war, France began making covert shipments of arms to the Americans. This it did, not because the French government loved freedom (it did not), but because it hated Britain and saw the war as a way to weaken Britain by depriving it of its colonies. Arms shipments from France were vital for the Americans.

Saratoga and Valley Forge

For the summer of 1777, the British home authorities adopted an elaborate plan of campaign urged on them by General Burgoyne. According to the plan, Burgoyne himself would lead an army southward from Canada along the Lake Champlain corridor while another army under Howe moved up the Hudson River to join hands with Burgoyne at Albany. This, it was hoped, would cut off New England and allow the British to subdue that region, which they considered the hotbed of the "rebellion."

Howe had other ideas and shipped his army by sea to Chesapeake Bay, hoping to capture the American capital, Philadelphia, and destroy Washington's army at the same time. At Brandywine Creek (September 1, 1777), Washington tried but failed to stop Howe's advance. Yet the American army, though badly beaten, remained intact. Howe occupied Philadelphia as the Congress fled westward to York, Pennsylvania.

In early October, Washington attempted to drive Howe out of Philadelphia; but his attack at Germantown, though at first successful, failed at least partially due to thick fog and the still imperfect level of training in the American army, both of which contributed to confusion among the troops. Thereafter, Howe settled down to comfortable winter quarters in Philadelphia, and Washington and his army to very uncomfortable ones at nearby Valley Forge, while far to the north, the British strategy that Howe had ignored was going badly awry.

Burgoyne's advance began well but slowed as the Americans placed obstructions on the rough wilderness trails by which his army, including numerous cannon, and much bulky baggage, had to advance. A diversionary force of British troops and Iroquois Indians under the command of Colonel Barry St. Leger swung east of Burgoyne's column, but although it defeated and killed American General Nicholas Herkimer at the Battle of Oriskany (August 6, 1777), it was finally forced to withdraw to Canada.

In mid-August, a detachment of Burgoyne's force was defeated by New England militia under General John Stark near Bennington in what is now Vermont. By autumn Burgoyne found his way blocked by an American army: continentals (American regular troops such as those that made up most of Washington's army, paid, in theory at least, by Congress); and New England militia, under General Horatio Gates, at Saratoga, about thirty miles north of Albany. Burgoyne's two attempts to break through (September 19 and October 7, 1777) were turned back by the Americans under the brilliant battlefield leadership of Benedict Arnold. On October 17, 1777, Burgoyne surrendered to Gates.

The American victory at Saratoga convinced the French to join openly in the war against England. Eventually, the Spanish (1779) and the Dutch (1780) joined as well, and England was faced with a world war.

The British Move South

The new circumstances brought a change in British strategy. With fewer troops available for service in America, the British would have to depend more on loyalists, and since they imagined that larger numbers of these existed in the South than elsewhere, it was there they turned their attention.

Howe was relieved and replaced by General Henry Clinton, who was ordered to abandon Philadelphia and march to New York. In doing so, he narrowly avoided defeat at the hands of Washington's army—much improved after a winter's drilling at Valley Forge under the direction of Prussian nobleman Baron von Steuben—at the Battle of Monmouth, New Jersey (June 28, 1778).

Clinton was thenceforth to maintain New York as Britain's main base in America while detaching troops to carry out the new Southern strategy. In November 1778 the British easily conquered Georgia. Late the following year, Clinton moved on South Carolina with a land and naval force, and in May 1780, U.S. General Benjamin Lincoln surrendered Charleston. Clinton then returned to New York, leaving Cornwallis to continue the Southern campaign.

Congress, alarmed at the British successes, sent General Horatio Gates to lead the forces opposing Cornwallis. Gates blundered to a resounding defeat at the Battle of Camden, in South Carolina (August 16, 1780).

The general outlook seemed bad for America at that point in the war. Washington's officers grumbled about their pay in arrears. The army was understrength and then suffered successive mutinies among the Pennsylvania and New Jersey troops. Benedict Arnold went over to the British. In short, the British seemed to be winning the contest of endurance. This outlook was soon to change.

Washington and his troops prepare to cross the Delaware.

In the West, George Rogers Clark, acting under the auspices of the state of Virginia, led an expedition down the Ohio River and into the area of present-day Illinois and Indiana, defeating a British force at Vincennes, Indiana, and securing the area north of the Ohio River for the United States.

In the South, Cornwallis began to move northward toward North Carolina, but on October 7, 1780, a detachment of his force under Major Patrick Ferguson was defeated by American frontiersmen at the Battle of Kings Mountain in northern South Carolina. To further increase the problems facing the British, Cornwallis had unwisely moved north without bothering to secure South Carolina first. The result was that the British would no sooner leave an area than American militia or guerilla bands, such as that under Francis Marion ("the Swamp Fox"), were once again in control and able to deal with those who had expressed loyalty to Britain in the presence of Cornwallis's army.

To command the continental forces in the South, Washington sent his most able subordinate, military genius Nathaniel Greene. Greene's brilliant strategy led to a crushing victory at Cowpens, South Carolina (January 17, 1781), by troops under Greene's subordinate, General Daniel Morgan of Virginia. It also led to a near victory by Greene's own force at Guilford Court House, North Carolina (March 15, 1781).

Yorktown

The frustrated and impetuous Cornwallis now abandoned the Southern strategy and moved north into Virginia. Clinton, disgusted at this departure from plan, sent instructions for Cornwallis to take up a defensive position and await further orders. Against his better judgment, Cornwallis did so, selecting Yorktown, Virginia, on a peninsula that reaches into Chesapeake Bay between the York and James rivers.

Washington now saw and seized the opportunity this presented. With the aid of a French fleet, which took control of Chesapeake Bay, and a French army that joined him in sealing off the land approaches to Yorktown, Washington succeeded in trapping Cornwallis. After three weeks of siege, Cornwallis surrendered on October 17, 1781.

The War at Sea

Britain had other problems as well. Ships of the small but daring U.S. Navy as well as privateers (privately owned vessels outfitted with guns and authorized by a warring government to capture enemy merchant ships for profit) preyed on the British merchant marine. John Paul Jones, the most famous of American naval leaders, captured ships and carried out audacious raids along the coast of Britain itself. French and Spanish naval forces also struck against various outposts of the British Empire.

The Treaty of Paris of 1783

News of the debacle at Yorktown brought the collapse of Lord North's ministry, and the new Cabinet opened peace negotiations. The extremely able American negotiating team was composed of Benjamin Franklin, John Adams, and John Jay. The negotiations continued for some time, delayed by French and Spanish maneuvering. When it became apparent that France and Spain were planning to achieve an agreement unfavorable to the United States, the American envoys negotiated a separate treaty with Britain.

The final agreement became known as the Treaty of Paris of 1783. Its terms stipulated the following: 1) The United States was recognized as an independent nation by the major European powers, including Britain; 2) Its western boundary was set at the Mississippi River; 3) Its southern boundary was set at 31° north latitude (the northern boundary of Florida); 4) Britain retained Canada but had to surrender Florida to Spain; 5) Private British creditors would be free to collect any debts owed by U.S. citizens; and 6) Congress was to recommend that the states restore confiscated loyalist property.

The Creation of New Governments

The State Constitutions

After the collapse of British authority in 1775, it became necessary to form new state governments. By the end of 1777 ten new state constitutions had been formed.

Connecticut and Rhode Island kept their colonial charters, which were republican in nature, simply deleting references to British sovereignty. Massachusetts waited until 1780 to complete the adoption of its new constitution. The constitutions ranged from such extremely democratic models as the virtually unworkable Pennsylvania constitution (soon abandoned), in which a unicameral legislature ruled with little check or balance, to more reasonable frameworks such as those of Maryland and Virginia, which included more safeguards against popular excesses.

Massachusetts voters set an important example by insisting that a constitution should be made by a special convention rather than the legislature. This would make the constitution superior to the legislature and, it was hoped, assure that the legislature would be subject to the constitution.

Most state constitutions included bills of rights—lists of things the government was not supposed to do to the people.

The Articles of Confederation

In the summer of 1776, Congress appointed a committee to begin devising a framework for a national government. When completed,

Declaration of Independence

this document was known as the Articles of Confederation. John Dickinson, who had played a leading role in writing the Articles, felt a strong national government was needed; but by the time Congress finished revising them, the Articles went to the opposite extreme of preserving the sovereignty of the states and creating a very weak national government.

The Articles of Confederation provided for a unicameral Congress in which each state would have one vote, as had been the case in the Continental Congress. Executive authority under the Articles would be vested in a committee of thirteen, one member from each state. In order to amend the Articles, the unanimous consent of all the states was required.

The Articles of Confederation government was empowered to make war, create treaties, determine the amount of troops and money each state should contribute to the war effort, settle disputes between states, admit new states to the Union, and borrow money. More importantly, however, was that it was not empowered to levy taxes, raise troops, or regulate commerce.

Ratification of the Articles of Confederation was delayed by a disagreement over the future status of the lands that lay to the west of the original thirteen states. Some states, notably Virginia, held extensive claims to these lands based on their original colonial charters. Maryland, which had no such claim, withheld ratification until in 1781 Virginia agreed to surrender its western claims to the new national government.

Meanwhile, the country was on its way to deep financial trouble. Unable to tax, Congress resorted to printing large amounts of paper money to finance the war; but these inflated "Continentals" were soon worthless. Other financial schemes fell through, and only grants and loans from France and the Netherlands staved off complete financial collapse. A plan to amend the Articles to give Congress power to tax was stopped by the lone opposition of Rhode Island. The army, whose pay was far in arrears, threatened mutiny. Some of those who favored a stronger national government welcomed this development and in what became known as the Newburgh Conspiracy (1783) consulted with army second-in-command Horatio Gates as to the possibility of using the army to force the states to surrender more power to the national government. This movement was stopped by a moving appeal to the officers by Washington himself.

The Trans-Appalachian West and the Northwest Ordinance

For many Americans the enormous trans-Appalachian frontier represented an opportunity to escape the economic hard times that followed the end of the war.

In 1775, Daniel Boone opened the "Wilderness Road" through the Cumberland Gap and on to the "Bluegrass" region of Kentucky. Others scouted down the Ohio River from Pittsburgh. By 1790, over 100,000 had settled in Kentucky and Tennessee, despite the risk of violent death at the hands of Indians. This risk was made worse by the presence of the British in northwestern military posts that should have been evacuated at the end of the war. From these posts they supplied the Indians with guns and encouraged them to use them on Americans. The Spaniards on the Florida frontier behaved in much the same way.

The settlement of Kentucky and Tennessee increased the pressure for the opening of the lands north of the Ohio River. To facilitate this, Congress passed three land ordinances in the years from 1784 to 1787.

The Land Ordinance of 1784 provided for territorial government and an orderly system by which each territory could progress to full statehood (this ordinance is sometimes considered part of the Land Ordinance of 1785).

The Land Ordinance of 1785 provided for the orderly surveying and distribution of land in townships six miles square, each composed of thirty-six one-square-mile (640 acre) sections, of which one should be set aside for the support of education. (This ordinance is sometimes referred to as the "Northwest Ordinance of 1785").

The Northwest Ordinance of 1787 provided a bill of rights for settlers and forbade slavery north of the Ohio River.

These ordinances were probably the most important legislation of the Articles of Confederation government.

The Jay-Gardoqui Negotiations

Economic depression followed the end of the war as the United States remained locked into the disadvantageous commercial system of the British Empire but without the trade advantages that this system had provided.

One man who thought he saw a way out of the economic quagmire was Congress's secretary of foreign affairs, John Jay. In 1784, Jay began negotiating with Spanish minister Gardoqui a treaty that would have granted lucrative commercial privileges—benefiting large east-coast merchants such as Jay—in exchange for U.S. acceptance of Spain's closure of the Mississippi River as an outlet for the agricultural goods of the rapidly growing settlements in Kentucky and Tennessee. This the Spanish desired because they feared that extensive settlement in what was then the western part of the United States might lead to American hunger for Spanish-held lands.

When Jay reported this to Congress in the summer of 1786, the West and South were outraged. Negotiations were broken off. Some, angered that Jay could show so little concern for the other sections of the country, talked of dissolving the Union; this helped spur to action those who desired not the dissolution but the strengthening of the Union.

Shays' Rebellion

Nationalists were further stimulated to action by Shays' Rebellion (1786). Economic hard times coupled with high taxes intended to pay off the state's war debt drove western Massachusetts farmers to desperation. Led by war veteran Daniel Shays, they shut down courts to prevent judges from seizing property or condemning people to debtors' prison for failing to pay their taxes.

The unrest created a disproportionate amount of panic in the rest of the state and the nation. The citizens of Boston subscribed money to raise an army to suppress the rebels. The success of this army together with timely tax relief caused the "rebellion" to fizzle out fairly quickly.

Amid the panic caused by the news of the uprising, many came to feel that a stronger government was needed to control such violent public outbursts as those of the western Massachusetts farmers.

Quiz: Chapters 1 and 2

1. Which of the following is true of the Stamp Act Congress?

   (A) It was the first unified government for all the American colonies.

   (B) It provided an important opportunity for colonial stamp agents to discuss methods of enforcing the act.

   (C) It was attended only by Georgia, Virginia, and the Carolinas.

   (D) It provided an important opportunity for colonial leaders to meet and establish ties with one another.

   (E) It rejected the assertion that the colonies ought to protest acts of Parliament deemed to be unconstitutional.

2. In seeking diplomatic recognition from foreign powers during the War for Independence, the American government found it necessary to

    (A) make large financial payments to the governments of France, Spain, and Holland.

    (B) promise to cede large tracts of American territory to France upon a victorious conclusion of the war.

    (C) demonstrate its financial stability and self-sufficiency.

    (D) demonstrate a determination and potential to win independence.

    (E) agree to grant France a specially favored trading status.

3. The primary motive of those who founded the British colony in Virginia during the seventeenth century was the desire

    (A) for economic gain.

    (B) for religious freedom.

    (C) to create a perfect religious commonwealth as an example to the rest of the world.

    (D) to recreate in the New World the story of feudalistic society that was fading in the Old.

    (E) to increase the power and glory of Great Britain.

4. The Molasses Act was intended to enforce England's mercantilist policies by

    (A) forcing the colonists to export solely to Great Britain.

    (B) forcing the colonists to buy sugar from other British colonies rather than from foreign producers.

(C) forbidding the colonists to engage in manufacturing activity in competition with British industries.

(D) providing a favorable market for the products of the British East India Company.

(E) creating an economic situation in which gold tended to flow from the colonies to the mother country.

5. All of the following were weaknesses of the Articles of Confederation government EXCEPT

(A) it lacked the power to levy taxes.

(B) it lacked the power to regulate commerce.

(C) it lacked the power to borrow money.

(D) it could not compel the states to abide by the terms of international treaties it had made.

(E) it lacked a strong executive.

6. Congress's most successful and effective method of financing the War of Independence was

(A) printing large amounts of paper money.

(B) obtaining grants and loans from France and the Netherlands.

(C) levying heavy direct taxes.

(D) issuing paper securities backed by the promise of western land grants.

(E) appealing to the states for voluntary contributions.

7. During the first two decades of the seventeenth century, all of the following aided in the establishment and growth of the colony at Jamestown, Virginia, EXCEPT

    (A) the establishment of the Virginia House of Burgesses.

    (B) the establishment of the ownership of private property.

    (C) the beginning of tobacco cultivation.

    (D) good relations with the local Indians.

    (E) large influxes of supplies and colonists from England.

8. The reason slavery flourished in the Southern English colonies and not in New England is

    (A) most New England farms were too small for slaves to be economically necessary or viable, whereas in the South the cultivation of staple crops such as rice and tobacco on large plantations necessitated the use of large numbers of indentured servants or slaves.

    (B) blacks from the tropical climate of Africa could not adapt to the harsh New England winters. Their high death rates made their use as slave laborers unprofitable.

    (C) a shortage of females in the Southern English colonies led to many female black Africans being imported as slaves and as potential wives for white planters in the region.

    (D) New England religious groups such as the Puritans forbade slavery on moral grounds, whereas the Anglican church which dominated the Southern English colonies encouraged the belief that blacks were inferior, thus, not deserving of equal status.

    (E) the Stono uprising in 1739 convinced New Englanders that the cost of controlling slaves was not worth their marginal economic benefits.

9. Pocahontas

    I.   was taken captive by an English trader and held as a hostage at Jamestown.

    II.   was converted to Christianity at her own request.

    III.   married John Rolfe.

    IV.   died in England.

        (A) I only

        (B) II only

        (C) I and III only

        (D) II and IV only

        (E) I, II, III, and IV

10. New York was an English colony because the

        (A) English conquered the area from the Dutch.

        (B) English settlers in the area gradually overwhelmed the French and Swedes.

        (C) England laid claim to the area by right of colonization.

        (D) Dutch and Swedes of the area petitioned the English to annex the colony.

        (E) Treaty of Tordesillas gave the area to the English.

ANSWER KEY

1.	(D)	6.	(B)
2.	(D)	7.	(D)
3.	(A)	8.	(A)
4.	(B)	9.	(E)
5.	(C)	10.	(A)

DETAILED ANSWERS

1. **(D)** One of the most important aspects of the Stamp Act Congress was the opportunity it provided for colonial leaders to meet and establish acquaintances with one another. Nine colonies—not merely Georgia, Virginia, and the Carolinas (C)—were represented at it, but far from being a unified government for all the American colonies (A), it simply passed mild resolutions protesting the Stamp Act. It was not, therefore, either a vehicle for enforcing the act (B) or opposed to American protests against the act (E).

2. **(D)** In order to gain foreign recognition during the War for Independence, it was necessary for the United States to demonstrate a determination and potential to win independence. The U.S. could not have demonstrated financial stability (C) at this time, nor could it have made financial payments (A). It did not prove necessary to make either territorial (B) or trade (E) concessions to France.

3. **(A)** The colony at Jamestown was founded primarily for economic gain, though a secondary motive was desire to increase the power and glory of Great Britain (E). Desire for religious freedom in some form (B) was the motivation of the settlers of Plymouth and some

of those who settled Maryland and Pennsylvania. Desire to create a perfect religious commonwealth as an example to the rest of the world (C) was the motive for the Massachusetts Bay colony; and the desire to recreate in the New World the sort of feudalistic society that was fading in the Old (D) was probably a motive of some of the colonial proprietors such as those of the Carolinas.

4. **(B)**   The Molasses Act was intended to force the colonists to buy sugar from more expensive British colonial sources rather than from foreign producers. Forcing the colonists to export solely to Great Britain (A), forbidding them to engage in manufacturing activity in competition with British industries (C), and creating an economic situation in which gold tended to flow from the colonies to the mother country (E) were also goals of mercantilism. Providing a favorable market for the products of the British East India Company (D) was the purpose of the Tea Act.

5. **(C)**   The Articles of Confederation government did have the power to borrow money and that is how it financed most of what it did. It did not, however, have the power to levy taxes (A), regulate commerce (B), or compel the states to abide by treaties (D), and it lacked a strong executive (E).

6. **(B)**   The most successful method of financing the War of Independence was by obtaining grants from foreign countries. Printing large amounts of paper money (A), issuing paper securities backed by the promise of western land grants (D), and appealing to the states for voluntary contributions (E) were tried with very little success. Congress did not have the power to levy direct taxes (C).

7. **(D)**   Relations with the Indians in colonial Virginia were not especially good. The colonists lived in constant fear of them and for good reason. The colony was kept alive by large influxes of supplies and recruits (E), drawn by promises of political rights represented by the House of Burgesses (A), and the hope of becoming rich through the cultivation of tobacco (C) on their own private property (B).

8.   **(A)**   Slavery never effectively established itself in New England, in large part because the economic system of the New England colonies and the large population of New England, which provided a large pool of workers, rendered the need for large numbers of slaves unnecessary. Most New England farms were relatively small, self-sufficient farms, and the members of farming communities depended on each other to keep their communities economically viable. In the Southern English colonies, there was less community cohesion among the colonists, there were fewer people, and there was a constant demand for laborers to cultivate the cash crops necessary to keep the colonies economically afloat. At first this demand was met by the use of indentured servants, but after the 1660s the supply of potential servants dwindled and the only immediate replacement labor pool was imported slave labor.

9.   **(E)**   Pocahontas was the daughter of the powerful Indian chieftan Powhatan. While being held as a hostage at Jamestown, she converted to Christianity and was baptized Rebecca. In 1614, she married John Rolfe and accompanied him to England. As Pocahontas was preparing to return to Virginia, she died suddenly.

10.   **(A)**   The Dutch founded the colony of New Netherlands on the Hudson River. Despite this, Charles II bestowed a large tract of land south of the Massachusetts Bay Colony upon his brother in 1664. Although it took three Anglo-Dutch wars to secure it, New Netherlands was under British control by the end of 1664.

CHAPTER 3

The United States Constitution (1787–1789)

Development and Ratification

Toward a New Constitution

As time went on, the inadequacy of the Articles of Confederation became increasingly apparent. Congress could not compel the states to comply with the terms of the Treaty of Paris of 1783 regarding debts and loyalists' property. The British used this as an excuse for not evacuating their Northwestern posts, hoping to be on hand to make the most of the situation when, as they not unreasonably expected, the new government fell to pieces. In any case, Congress could do nothing to force them out of the posts, nor to solve any of the nation's other increasingly pressing problems.

In these dismal straits, some called for disunion, others for monarchy. Others felt that republican government could still work if given a better constitution, and they made it their goal to achieve this.

In 1785 a meeting of representatives of Virginia, Maryland, Pennsylvania, and Delaware was held at George Washington's residence, Mt. Vernon, for the purpose of discussing current problems of interstate commerce. At their suggestion, the Virginia legislature issued a call for a convention of all the states on the same subject, to meet the following summer in Annapolis, Maryland.

The Annapolis Convention met in September of 1786, but only five states were represented. Among those present, however, were such nationalists as Alexander Hamilton, John Dickinson, and James Madison. With so few states represented, it was decided instead to call for a convention of all the states to meet the following summer in Philadelphia for the purpose of revising the Articles of Confederation.

The Constitutional Convention

The men who met in Philadelphia in 1787 were remarkably able, highly educated, and exceptionally accomplished. For the most part, they were lawyers, merchants, and planters. Though representing individual states, most thought in national terms. Prominent among them were James Madison, Alexander Hamilton, Gouverneur Morris, Robert Morris, John Dickinson, and Benjamin Franklin.

George Washington was unanimously elected to preside, and the enormous respect that he commanded helped hold the convention together through difficult times (as it had the Continental Army) and make the product of the convention's work more attractive to the rest of the nation. The delegates then voted that the convention's discussions should be secret, to avoid the distorting and confusing influence of the press and publicity.

George Washington

The delegates shared a basic belief in the innate selfishness of man, which must somehow be kept from abusing the power of government. For this purpose the document that they finally produced contained many checks and balances, designed to prevent the government, or any one branch of the government, from gaining too much power.

Madison, who has been called the "father of the Constitution," devised a plan of national government and persuaded fellow Virginian Edmund Randolph, who was more skilled at public speaking, to introduce it. Known as the "Virginia Plan," it called for an executive branch and two houses of Congress, each based on population.

Smaller states, which would thus have seen their influence decreased, objected and countered with William Paterson's "New Jersey Plan," calling for the continuation of a unicameral legislature with equal representation for the states as well as sharply increased powers for the national government.

A temporary impasse developed that threatened to break up the convention. At this point Benjamin Franklin played an important role in reconciling the often wrangling delegates, suggesting that the sessions of the convention henceforth begin with prayer (they did) and making various other suggestions that eventually helped the convention arrive at the "Great Compromise." The Great Compromise provided for a presidency, a Senate with all states represented equally (by two Senators each), and a House of Representatives with representation according to population.

Another crisis involved North-South disagreement over the issue of slavery. Here also a compromise was reached. Slavery was neither endorsed nor condemned by the Constitution. Each slave was to count as three-fifths of a person for purposes of apportioning representation and direct taxation on the states (the Three-Fifths Compromise). The federal government was prohibited from stopping the importation of slaves prior to 1808.

The third major area of compromise was the nature of the presidency. This was made easier by the virtual certainty that George Washington would be the first president and the universal trust that he would not abuse the powers of the office or set a bad example for his successors. The result was a strong presidency with control of foreign policy and the power to veto Congress's legislation. Should the president commit an actual crime, Congress would have the power to impeach him. Otherwise, the president would serve for a term of four years and be re-electable without limit. As a check to the possible excesses of democracy, the president was to be elected by an Electoral College, in which each state would have the same number of electors as it did senators and representatives combined. The person with the second highest total in the electoral college would be vice-president. If no one gained a majority in the electoral college, the President would be chosen by the House of Representatives.

The new Constitution was to take effect when nine states, through special state conventions, had ratified it.

The Struggle for Ratification

As the struggle over ratification got under way, those favoring the Constitution astutely took for themselves the name Federalists (i.e., advocates of centralized power) and labeled their opponents Antifederalists. The Federalists were effective in explaining the convention and the document it had produced. *The Federalist Papers,* written as a series of eighty-five newspaper articles by Alexander Hamilton, James Madison, and John Jay, brilliantly expounded the Constitution and demonstrated how it was designed to prevent the abuse of power from any direction. These essays are considered to be the best commentary on the Constitution by those who helped write it.

At first, ratification progressed smoothly, with five states approving in quick succession. In Massachusetts, however, a tough fight developed. By skillful maneuvering, Federalists were able to win over to their side such popular opponents of the Constitution as Samuel Adams and John Hancock. Others were won over by the promise that a bill of rights would be added to the Constitution, limiting the federal government just as the state governments were limited by their bills of rights. With such promises, Massachusetts ratified by a narrow margin.

By June 21, 1788, the required nine states had ratified, but the crucial states of New York and Virginia still held out. In Virginia, where George Mason and Patrick Henry opposed the Constitution, the influence of George Washington and the promise of a bill of rights finally prevailed and ratification was achieved there as well. In New York, where Alexander Hamilton led the fight for ratification, *The Federalist Papers,* the promise of a bill of rights, and the news of Virginia's ratification were enough to carry the day.

Only North Carolina and Rhode Island still held out, but they both ratified within the next fifteen months.

In March 1789, George Washington was inaugurated as the nation's first president.

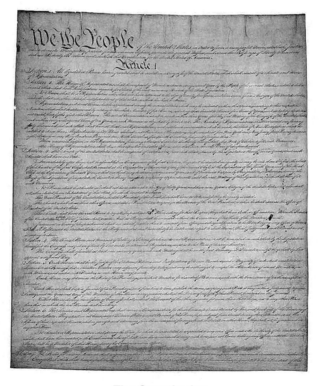

The Constitution

Outline of the United States Constitution

Articles of the Constitution

Preamble

"We the People of the United States, in order to form a more perfect Union, establish justice, insure domestic tranquility, provide for the common defense, promote the general welfare, and secure the blessings of liberty to ourselves and our posterity, do ordain and establish this Constitution for the United States of America."

Article I – Legislature

The legislature is divided into two parts—the House of Representatives (435 members currently; determined by proportional representation of the population) and the Senate (100 members currently; two from each state).

The House of Representatives may bring impeachment charges. All bills that concern money must originate in the House. Because of the size of the body, debate is limited except in special cases, where all representatives may meet as the Committee of the Whole. The Speaker of the House presides over the proceedings. Terms of representatives are two years, re-electable without limit, to persons who are at least 25 years of age.

The Senate, originally elected by state legislatures but now by direct election (Seventeenth Amendment), approves or rejects presidential nominations and treaties, and serves as the court and jury in impeachment proceedings. Debate within the Senate is unlimited. The President pro tempore usually presides, but the vice-president of the United States is the presiding officer, and may vote to break a tie. Senate elected terms are for six years, re-electable without limit, to persons who are at least 30 years of age.

Article II – Executive

The President of the United States is elected for a four-year term, originally electable without limit (the Twenty-second Amendment limits election to two terms), and must be at least 35 years old.

Responsibilities for the president as outlined in the Constitution include acting as the chief of state, the chief executive, commander-in-chief of the armed forces, the chief diplomat, and chief legislature.

Article III – Judiciary

While the Constitution describes the Supreme Court in Article III, the actual construction of the court system was accomplished by the Judiciary Act of 1789. The Supreme Court has jurisdiction for federal courts and appellate cases on appeal from lower courts.

Article IV – Interstate Relations

This article guarantees that court decisions and other legal actions (marriage, incorporation, etc.) valid in one state are valid in another. Extradition of criminals (and, originally, runaway slaves) and the exchange of citizenship benefits are likewise guaranteed. Article IV also provides for the admission of new states and guarantees federal protection against invasion and violence for each state. States admitted maintain the same status as the original states. All states are guaranteed a republican form of government.

Article V – Amendment Process

Amendments are proposed by a two-thirds vote of each house of Congress or by a special convention called by Congress upon the request of two-thirds of the state legislatures. Amendments are ratified by three-fourths of the state legislatures or state conventions.

Article VI – Supremacy Clause

Article VI sets up the hierarchy of laws in the United States. The Constitution is the "supreme law of the land" and supersedes treaties.

Treaties supercede federal laws, federal laws (later to include federal regulatory agency directives) supercede state constitutions, state laws, and local laws, respectively. All federal and state officials, including judges, must take an oath to support and defend the Constitution.

Article VII – Ratification

This article specified the ratification process necessary for the Constitution to take effect. Nine of the original thirteen states had to ratify the Constitution before it became operative.

Amendments to the Constitution

The Amendments to the Constitution guarantee certain individual rights and amend original dictates of the Constitution. The first ten amendments are known as the Bill of Rights, for which Thomas Jefferson provided the impetus.

1. Protects the freedom of religion, speech, press, assembly, as well as the right to petition the government for the redress of grievances (1791)*

2. Protects the right to bear arms in a regulated militia (on a state basis; it was not intended to guarantee an individual's rights) (1791)

3. Ensures that troops will not be housed in private citizens' homes (1791)

4. Protects against unreasonable search and seizure (need for search warrant) (1791)

5. Protects the rights for the accused, including required indictments, double jeopardy, self-incrimination, due process, and just compensation (1791)

6. Guarantees a speedy and public trial, the confrontation by witnesses, and the right to call witnesses on one's own behalf (1791)

7. Guarantees a jury trial (1791)

*In the 2008 decision, *District of Columbia v. Heller*, the Supreme Court struck down the sweeping ban on handguns in Washington, D.C. The high court had only examined the Second Amendment once before, in 1939, since the Constitution was ratified in 1791.

8. Protects against excessive bail and cruel and unusual punishment (1791)

9. Says that all rights not enumerated are nonetheless retained by the people (1791)

10. Says that all powers not specifically delegated to the federal government are retained by the states (1791)

11. Provides immunity to states from lawsuits in federal court (1795)

12. Provides that electors will cast separate ballots for president and vice-president; in the event of no clear winner, the House will select the president and the Senate the vice-president (1804)

13. Abolished slavery (1865)

14. Extends citizenship to all persons; made Confederate debt void and Confederate leaders ineligible for public office; states which denied voting rights to qualified citizens (blacks) would have their representation in Congress reduced; conferred "dual" citizenship (both of the United States and of a specific state) on all citizens (1868)

15. Extends voting rights to blacks (1870)

16. Legalized the income tax (1913)

17. Provides for the direct election of senators (1913)

18. Prohibited the general manufacture, sale, and use of alcoholic beverages (1919)

19. Extends voting rights to women (1920)

20. Changed the inauguration date from March 4 to January 20; eliminated the "lame duck" session of Congress (after the November elections) (1933)

21. Repealed the Eighteenth Amendment (1933)

22. Limits presidents to two terms (1951)

23. Gives presidential electoral votes to the District of Columbia (1961)

24. Prohibits poll taxes (1964)

25. Changed the order of the presidential line of succession and provides guidelines for presidential disability (1967)

26. Extends voting rights to eighteen-year-olds (1971)

27. Restricts the practice of congressional salary adjustment (1992)

Separation and Limitation of Powers

Powers Reserved for the Federal Government Only

- Regulate foreign commerce regulation
- Regulate interstate commerce regulation
- Mint money
- Create and establish post offices
- Regulate naturalization and immigration
- Grant copyrights and patents
- Declare and wage war, declare peace
- Admit new states
- Fix standards for weights and measures
- Raise and maintain an army and navy
- Govern the federal city (Washington, D.C.)
- Conduct relations with foreign powers
- Universalize bankruptcy laws

Powers Reserved for State Governments Only

- Conduct and monitor elections
- Establish voter qualifications
- Provide for local governments

- Ratify proposed amendments to the Constitution
- Regulate contracts and wills
- Regulate intrastate commerce
- Provide education for its citizens
- Levy direct taxes (the Sixteenth Amendment permits the federal government to levy direct taxes)
- Maintain police power over public health and safety
- Maintain integrity of state borders

Powers Shared by Federal and State Governments

- Taxing, borrowing, and spending money
- Controlling the militia
- Acting directly on individuals

Restrictions on the Federal Government

- No ex post facto laws
- No bills of attainder
- Two-year limit on appropriation for the military
- No suspension of habeas corpus (except in a crisis)
- One port may not be favored over another
- All guarantees as stated in the Bill of Rights

Restrictions on State Governments

- Treaties, alliances, or confederations may not be entered into
- Letters of marque and reprisal may not be granted
- Contracts may not be impaired
- Money may not be printed or bills of credit emitted

- No import or export taxes

- May not wage war (unless invaded)

Required Percentages of Voting

Actions that require a simple majority include raising taxes, requesting appropriations, declaring war, increasing the national debt, instituting a draft, and introducing an impeachment charge (House).

Actions that require a two-thirds majority include overriding a presidential veto, proposing amendments to the Constitution, expelling a member of Congress (in the individual house only), ratifying treaties (Senate), acting as a jury for impeachment (Senate), and ratifying presidential appointments (Senate).

The action that requires a three-fourths majority is approving a proposed constitutional amendment (states).

CHAPTER 4

The New Nation
(1789–1824)

The Federalist Era

The results of the first elections held under the new Constitution made it clear that the fledgling government was going to be managed by those who had drawn up the document and by their supporters. Few Antifederalists were elected to Congress, and many of the new legislators had served as delegates to the Philadelphia Convention two years before. This Federalist majority immediately set about to draft legislation that would fill in the gaps left by the convention and to erect the structure of a strong central government.

The New Executive

There had never been any doubt as to who would be the first president. George Washington received virtually all the votes of the presidential electors, and John Adams received the next highest number, thus becoming the vice president. After a triumphal journey from Mount Vernon, Washington was inaugurated in New York City, the temporary seat of government, on April 30, 1789.

Congress Erects the Structure of Government

The new national legislature immediately acted to honor the Federalist pledge of a bill of rights made to those voters who had hesitated to ratify the new Constitution. Twelve amendments were drafted that embodied the guarantees of personal liberties, most of which had been traditionally enjoyed by English citizens. Ten of these were ratified by the states by the end of 1791, and they became our Bill of Rights. The first nine spelled out specific guarantees of personal freedoms, such as religion, speech, press, assembly, petition, and a speedy trial by one's peers, and the Tenth Amendment reserved to the states all those powers not specifically withheld, or granted to the federal government. This last was a concession to those who feared the potential of the central government to usurp the sovereignty of the individual states.

The Establishment of the Federal Court System

The Judiciary Act of 1789 provided for a Supreme Court, with six justices, and invested it with the power to rule on the constitutional validity of state laws. It was to be the interpreter of the "supreme law of the land." A system of district courts was established to serve as courts of original jurisdiction, and three courts of appeal were also provided.

The Establishment of the Executive Departments

The Constitution had not specified the names or number of the departments of the executive branch. Congress established three—state, treasury, and war—and also the offices of attorney general and postmaster general. President Washington immediately appointed Thomas Jefferson, Alexander Hamilton, and Henry Knox, respectively, to fill the executive posts, and Edmund Randolph became attorney general. These four men were called upon regularly by the president for advice, and they later formed the nucleus of what became known as the "cabinet," although no provision for such was made in the Constitution.

Alexander Hamilton

Washington's Administration, 1789–1797

Hamilton's Financial Program

Treasury Secretary Alexander Hamilton, in his "Report on the Public Credit," proposed the funding of the national debt at face value, federal assumption of state debts, and the establishment of a national bank. In his "Report on Manufactures," Hamilton proposed an extensive program for federal stimulation of industrial development through subsidies and tax incentives. The money needed to fund these programs, proposed Hamilton, would come from an excise tax on distillers and from tariffs on imports.

Opposition to Hamilton's Program

Jefferson and others objected to the funding proposal because it obviously would benefit speculators who had bought up state and confederation obligations at depressed prices, and who would profit handsomely by their redemption at face value. The original purchasers, they claimed, should at least share in the windfall. They opposed the tax program because it would fall primarily on the small farmers. They saw Hamilton's entire program as enriching a small elite group at the expense of the more worthy common citizen.

The Appearance of Political Parties

Political parties had been considered a detrimental force by the founding fathers, since they were seen as contributing to the rise of "factions." Thus, no mention of such was made in the Constitution. But differences in philosophy very quickly began to drive the leaders of government into opposing camps—the Federalists and the Republicans.

Alexander Hamilton and the Federalists

Hamilton, as the theorist of the group who favored a strong central government, interpreted the Constitution as having vested extensive powers in the federal government. This "implied powers" stance claimed that the government was given all powers that were not expressly denied to it. This is the "broad" interpretation.

Thomas Jefferson and the Republicans

Jefferson and Madison held the view that any action not specifically permitted in the Constitution was thereby prohibited. This is the "strict" interpretation, and the Republicans opposed the establishment of Hamilton's national bank on this view of government. The Jeffersonian supporters, primarily under the guidance of James Madison, began to organize political groups in opposition to the Federalist program, and called themselves Republicans.

Sources of Partisan Support

The Federalists received their strongest support from the business and financial groups in the commercial centers of the Northeast and in the port cities of the South. The strength of the Republicans lay primarily in the rural and frontier areas of the South and West.

Foreign and Frontier Affairs

The French Revolution

When revolutionary France went to war with the European powers in 1792, Washington's response was a Proclamation of Neutrality. Citizen Genet violated that policy by trying to encourage popular support in this country for the French government and embarrassed the president. American merchants traded with both sides, though the most lucrative business was carried on with the French West Indies. This brought retaliation by the British, who began to seize American merchant ships and force their crews into service with the British navy.

Jay's Treaty with Britain (1794)

John Jay negotiated a treaty with the British that attempted to settle the conflict at sea, as well as to curtail English agitation of their Indian allies on the western borders. The agreement actually settled few of the issues and merely bought time for the new nation in the worsening international conflict. Jay was severely criticized for his efforts and was even hanged in effigy, but the Senate accepted the treaty as the best possible under the circumstances.

The Treaty with Spain (1795)

Thomas Pinckney was invited to the Spanish court to strengthen what Madrid perceived to be her deteriorating position on the American frontier. The result was the Pinckney Treaty, ratified by the Senate in 1796, in which the Spanish opened the Mississippi River to American traffic, including the right of deposit in the port city of New Orleans, and recognized the 31st parallel as the northern boundary of Florida.

Frontier Problems

Indian tribes on the northwest and southwest borders were increasingly resisting the encroachments on their lands by the American settlers. British authorities in Canada were encouraging the Indians in their depredations against frontier settlements.

In 1794, General Anthony Wayne decisively defeated the Indians at the Battle of Fallen Timbers, and the resulting Treaty of Greenville cleared the Ohio territory of Indian tribes.

Internal Problems

The Whiskey Rebellion (1794)

Western farmers refused to pay the excise tax on whiskey, which formed the backbone of Hamilton's revenue program. When a group of Pennsylvania farmers terrorized the tax collectors, President Washington sent out a federalized militia force of some 15,000 men, and the rebellion evaporated, thus strengthening the credibility of the young government.

Land Policy

As the original 13 states ceded their western land claims to the new federal government, new states were organized and admitted to the Union, thus strengthening the ties of the western farmers to the central government (Vermont, 1791; Kentucky, 1792; and Tennessee, 1796).

John Adams' Administration, 1797–1801

The Election of 1796

John Adams was the Federalist candidate, and Thomas Jefferson ran under the opposition banner of the Republicans. John Adams was elected president. Since Jefferson received the second highest number of electoral votes, he became vice president. Thus, a Federalist president and a Republican vice president served together, an obviously awkward arrangement. Adams was a brilliant lawyer and statesman, but too dogmatic and uncompromising to be an effective politician, and he endured a very frustrating and unproductive term in office.

John Adams

The XYZ Affair

A three-man delegation was sent to France in 1798 to persuade the French to stop harassing American ships. When they were solicited for a bribe by three subordinates of the French Minister Talleyrand, they indignantly refused, and their report of this insult produced outrage at home. The cry "millions for defense, but not one cent for tribute" was raised, and public feelings against the French ran high. Since Talleyrand's officials were unnamed in the dispatches, the incident became known as the "XYZ Affair."

Cartoon of the XYZ Affair depicts U.S. as a maiden victimized by the French government.

Quasi-War, 1798–1799

This uproar moved Adams to suspend all trade with the French, and American ship captains were authorized to attack and capture armed French vessels. Congress created the Department of the Navy, and war seemed imminent. In 1800, the new French government, now under Napoleon, signed a new treaty, and the peace was restored.

Repression and Protest

The Alien and Sedition Acts

The elections in 1798 had increased the Federalists' majorities in both houses of Congress, and they used their "mandate" to enact legislation to stifle foreign influences. The Alien Act raised new hurdles in the path of immigrants trying to obtain citizenship, and the Sedition Act widened the powers of the Adams administration to muzzle its newspaper critics. Both bills were aimed at actual or potential Republican opposition, and a number of editors were actually jailed for printing critical editorials.

The Kentucky and Virginia Resolutions

Republican leaders were convinced that the Alien and Sedition Acts were unconstitutional, but the process of deciding on the constitutionality of federal laws was as yet undefined. Jefferson and Madison decided that the state legislatures should have that power, and they drew up a series of resolutions, which were presented to the Kentucky and Virginia legislatures, respectively. They proposed that John Locke's "compact theory" be applied, which would empower the state bodies to "nullify" federal laws within those states. These resolutions were adopted, but only in these two states, and so the issue died. A principle, however, had now been set forth, would later bear fruit in the nullification controversy of the 1830s and ultimately in the secession crisis of 1860–1861.

The Revolution of 1800

The Election

Thomas Jefferson and Aaron Burr ran on the Republican ticket, though not together, against John Adams and Charles Pinckney for the Federalists. All ran for the presidency; the candidate winning the second-highest number of votes would become vice president. Jefferson and Burr received the same number of electoral votes, so the selection went to the House of Representatives. After a lengthy deadlock, Alexander Hamilton threw his support to Jefferson, and Burr had to accept the vice presidency, the result obviously intended by the electorate. This increased the ill-will between Hamilton and Burr and helped set the stage for their famous duel in 1804.

Packing the Judiciary

The Federalist Congress passed a new Judiciary Act early in 1801, and President Adams filled the newly created vacancies with party supporters, many of them with last-minute commissions. John Marshall was then appointed Chief Justice of the U.S. Supreme Court, thus guaranteeing continuation of Federalist policies from the bench of the high court.

The Jeffersonian Era

Thomas Jefferson and his Republican followers envisioned a society in vivid contrast to that of Hamilton and the Federalists. They dreamed of a nation of independent farmers, living under a central government that exercised a minimum of control over their lives and served merely to protect the individual liberties guaranteed by the Constitution. This agrarian paradise would be free from the industrial smoke and urban blight of Europe, and would serve as a beacon light of Enlightenment rationalism to a world searching for direction. That vision was to prove a mirage, and Jefferson was to preside over a nation that was growing more industrialized and urban, and that seemed to need an ever stronger hand at the presidential tiller.

Thomas Jefferson

The New Federal City

The city of Washington had been designed by Pierre L'Enfant and was briefly occupied by the Adams administration. When Jefferson moved in, it was still a straggling provincial town, with muddy streets and muggy summers. Most of its inhabitants moved out when Congress was not in session.

Jefferson the President

The new president tried to project an image of democratic simplicity, sometimes appearing so casually dressed as to appear slovenly. But he was a brilliant thinker and a shrewd politician. He appointed men to his cabinet who agreed with his political philosophy: James Madison as secretary of state and Albert Gallatin to the treasury.

Conflict with the Judges

Marbury v. Madison

William Marbury, one of Adams' "midnight appointments," sued Secretary of State Madison to force delivery of his commission as a justice of the peace in the federal district. John Marshall, as Supreme Court justice, refused to rule on the request, claiming that the law which gave the Supreme Court jurisdiction over such matters had exceeded the Constitutional grant of powers and thus was unconstitutional. Marshall thus asserted the power of judicial review over federal legislation, a power that has become the foundation of the Supreme Court's check on the other two branches of government.

The Impeachment Episodes

Jefferson began a campaign to remove Federalist judges by impeachment. One district judge was removed, and proceedings were begun to impeach Supreme Court Justice Samuel Chase. That effort failed, but the threat had encouraged the judiciary to be less blatantly political.

Domestic Affairs

Enforcement of the Alien and Sedition Acts was immediately suspended, and the men convicted under those laws were released.

The federal bureaucracy was reduced and expenses were drastically cut. The size of the army was reduced, and the expansion program of the Navy was cancelled.

The excise taxes were repealed and federal income was limited to land sale proceeds and customs duties. Federal land sale policy was liberalized, smaller parcels were authorized, and less cash was required—policies that benefitted small farmers.

The Twelfth Amendment was adopted and ratified in 1804, ensuring that a tie vote between candidates of the same party could not again cause the confusion of the Jefferson-Burr affair.

Following the Constitutional mandate, the importation of slaves was stopped by law in 1808.

The Louisiana Purchase

Napoleon, in an effort to regain some of France's New World empire, had obtained the old French trans-Mississippi territory from Spain by political pressure. Jefferson sent a delegation to Paris to try to buy New Orleans, lest the new French officials close it to American traffic. Napoleon's defeat in Santo Domingo persuaded him that Louisiana could not be exploited, and indeed was now subject to potential American incursions. So he offered to sell the entire territory to the United States for $15 million. The American delegation accepted the offer in April 1803, even though they had no authority to buy more than the city of New Orleans.

The Constitutional Dilemma

Jefferson's stand on the strict interpretation of the Constitution would not permit him to purchase land without Congressional approval. But he accepted his advisors' counsel that his treaty-making powers

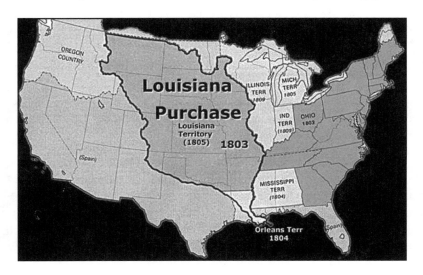

The Louisiana Purchase

included the authority to buy the land. Congress concurred, after the fact, and the purchase price was appropriated, thus doubling the territory of the nation overnight.

Exploring the West

Even before Napoleon's offer, Jefferson had authorized an expedition to explore the western territory to the Pacific. The Lewis and Clark group, with 48 men, left St. Louis in 1804, and returned two years later with a wealth of scientific and anthropological information, and having strengthened the United States' claim to the Oregon territory. At the same time, Zebulon Pike and others had been traversing the middle parts of Louisiana and mapping the land.

The Essex Junto (1804)

Some New England Federalists saw the western expansion as a threat to their position in the Union, and they tried to organize a secessionist movement. They courted Aaron Burr's support by offering to back him in a bid for the governorship of New York. Hamilton led the opposition to that campaign, and when Burr lost the election, he challenged Hamilton to a duel, which resulted in Hamilton's death.

The Burr Conspiracy

Aaron Burr was now a fugitive, without a political future. He became involved in a scheme to take Mexico from Spain and establish a new nation in the West.

In the fall of 1806, he led a group of armed men down the Mississippi River system toward New Orleans. He was arrested in Natchez and tried for treason in Richmond, Virginia. Judge John Marshall's decision for acquittal helped to narrow the legal definition of treason. Jefferson's attempts to influence and prejudice the trial were justified by his claims of "executive privilege," but they were fruitless.

John Randolph and the Yazoo Claims

Jefferson's Republican opponents, under the leadership of his cousin John Randolph of Roanoke, called themselves the "Quids." They accused the president of complicity in the Yazoo Land controversy, which had followed Georgia's cession of her western lands to the federal government. This created serious strife within the Republican party and weakened Jefferson's effectiveness in his second term.

International Involvement

The Barbary War

In 1801 Jefferson sent a naval force to the Mediterranean to break the practice of the North African Muslim rulers of exacting tribute from Western merchant ships. Intermittent undeclared war dragged on until 1805, with no decisive settlement.

The Napoleonic Wars

War continued in Europe between France under Napoleon and the European powers led by Britain. Both sides tried to prevent trade with their enemies by neutral powers, especially the United States. Napoleon's "Continental System" was answered by Britain's "Orders in Council." American ships were seized by both sides and American sailors were "impressed" into the British navy.

The Chesapeake-Leopard Affair (1807)

The British ship H.M.S. *Leopard* stopped the U.S.S. *Chesapeake* off the Chesapeake Bay, and four alleged British deserters were taken off. Public outcry for war followed, and Jefferson was hard pressed to remain neutral.

The Embargo of 1807

Jefferson's response to the cry for war was to draft a law prohibiting American ships from leaving port for any foreign destination, thus avoiding contact with vessels of either belligerent. The result was economic depression, particularly in the heavily commercial Northeast. This proved to be his most unpopular policy of both terms in office.

Madison's Administration, 1809–1817

The Election of 1808

Republican James Madison won the election over Federalist Charles Pinckney, but the Federalists gained seats in both houses of the Congress. The embargo-induced depression was obviously a heavy political liability, and Madison was to face growing pressures to deal with the international crisis. He was a brilliant man but with few social or political skills. His greatest asset was probably his wife, the vivacious and energetic Dolly.

The War of 1812

Congress had passed a modified embargo just before Madison's inauguration, known as the Non-Intercourse Act, which opened trade to all nations except France and Britain. When it expired in 1810, it was replaced by Macon's Bill No. 2, which gave the president power to prohibit trade with any nation that violated our neutrality.

The War of 1812 forced the President and the Congress to flee from Washington as the British set public buildings ablaze.

The Indian tribes of the Northwest and the Mississippi Valley were resentful of the government's policy of pressured removal to the West, and the British authorities in Canada were exploiting their discontent by encouraging border raids against the American settlements.

The Shawnee chief Tecumseh set out to unite the Mississippi Valley tribes and reestablish Indian dominance in the Old Northwest. With the help of his brother, the Prophet, and the timely New Madrid earthquake, he persuaded a sizeable force of warriors to join him. On November 11, 1811, General William Henry Harrison destroyed Tecumseh's village on Tippecanoe Creek and dashed his hopes for an Indian confederacy.

Southern frontiersmen coveted Spanish Florida, which included the southern ranges of Alabama, Mississippi, and Louisiana. They resented Spanish support of Indian depredations against the borderlands, and since Spain was Britain's ally, they saw Britain as the background cause of their problems.

The Congress in 1811 contained a strong pro-war group called the War Hawks, led by Henry Clay and John C. Calhoun. They gained control of both houses and began agitating for war with the British. On June 1, 1812, President Madison asked for a declaration of war, and Congress complied.

A three-pronged invasion of Canada met with disaster on all three fronts, and the Americans fell back to their own borders. At sea, American privateers and frigates, including "Old Ironsides," scored early victories over British warships, but were soon driven back into their home ports and blockaded by the powerful British ships-of-the-line.

Admiral Oliver Hazard Perry constructed a fleet of ships on Lake Erie and on September 10, 1813, defeated a British force at Put-In Bay and established control of the lake. His flagship flew the banner "Don't Give Up the Ship." This victory opened the way for William Henry Harrison to invade Canada in October and defeat a combination British and Indian force at the Battle of the Thames.

The War in the Southwest

Andrew Jackson led a force of frontier militia into Alabama in pursuit of Creek Indians who had massacred the white inhabitants of Fort Mims. On March 27, 1814, he crushed the Indians at Horseshoe Bend, and then seized the Spanish garrison at Pensacola.

British Strategy Changes, 1814

A British force came down Lake Champlain and met defeat at Plattsburgh, New York, in September. A British armada sailed up the Chesapeake Bay and sacked and burned Washington, D.C. It then proceeded toward Baltimore, which was guarded by Fort McHenry. That fort held firm through the British bombardment, inspiring Key's "Star Spangled Banner."

The Battle of New Orleans

The most serious British threat came at the port of New Orleans. A powerful invasion force was sent there to close the mouth of the Mississippi River, but Andrew Jackson decisively defeated it with a polyglot army of frontiersmen, blacks, Creoles, and pirates. The battle was fought on January 8, 1815, two weeks after a peace treaty had been signed at the city of Ghent, in Belgium.

The Battle of New Orleans

The Treaty of Ghent, Christmas Eve 1814

With the European wars ended, the major causes for the dispute with Britain had ceased to be important, so both sides were eager for peace. The treaty provided for the acceptance of the status quo at the beginning of hostilities, so both sides restored their wartime conquests to the other.

The Hartford Convention, December 1814

The Federalists had become increasingly a minority party. They vehemently opposed the war, and Daniel Webster and other New England congressmen consistently blocked the administration's efforts to prosecute the war effort. On December 15, 1814, delegates from the New England states met in Hartford, Connecticut, and drafted a set of resolutions suggesting nullification—and even secession—if their interests were not protected against the growing influence of the South and the West.

Soon after the convention adjourned, the news of the victory at New Orleans was announced and their actions were discredited. The Federalist party ceased to be a political force from this point on.

Postwar Developments

Protective Tariff (1816)

The first protective tariff in the nation's history was passed in 1816 to slow the flood of cheap British manufactures into the country.

Rush-Bagot Treaty (1817)

An agreement was reached in 1817 between Britain and the United States to stop maintaining armed fleets on the Great Lakes. This first "disarmament" agreement is still in effect.

Jackson's Florida Invasion (1817)

Indian troubles in the newly acquired areas of western Florida prompted General Andrew Jackson, acting under dubious authority, to invade Spanish East Florida and to hang two British subjects whom he suspected of selling guns and supplies to the Indians. Then he reoccupied Pensacola and raised the American flag, a clear violation of international law. Only wide public support prevented his arrest and prosecution by the government.

Indian Policy

The government began to systematically pressure all the Indian tribes remaining in the East to cede their lands and accept new homes west of the Mississippi, a policy that met with disappointing results. Most declined the offer.

The Barbary Wars (1815)

In response to continued piracy and extortion in the Mediterranean, Congress declared war on the Muslim state of Algiers in 1815 and dispatched a naval force to the area under Stephen Decatur. He quickly defeated the North African pirates and forced them to pay indemnities for past tribute they had exacted from American ship captains. This action finally gained the United States free access to the Mediterranean basin.

The Adams-Onis Treaty (1819)

Spain had decided to sell the remainder of the Florida territory to the Americans before they took it anyway. Under this agreement, the Spanish surrendered all their claims to the territory and drew the boundary of Mexico all the way to the Pacific. The United States in exchange agreed to assume $5 million in debts owed to American merchants.

The Monroe Doctrine

Around 1810, national revolutions had begun in Latin America, so the colonial populations refused to accept the rule of the new Napoleonic governments in Europe. Leaders like San Martin and Bolivar had declared independence for their countries and, after Napoleon's fall in 1814, were defying the restored Hapsburg and Bourbon rulers of Europe.

James Monroe

British and American leaders feared that the new European governments would try to restore the former New World colonies to their erstwhile royal owners.

In December 1823, President Monroe included in his annual message to Congress a statement that the American hemisphere was "henceforth not to be considered as subjects for future colonization by any European powers." Thus began a thirty-year period of freedom from serious foreign involvement for the United States.

Internal Development, 1820–1830

The years following the War of 1812 were years of rapid economic and social development. Too rapid, in fact, and they were followed by a severe depression in 1819. But this slump was temporary, and it became obvious that the country was moving rapidly from its agrarian origins toward an industrial, urban future. Westward expansion accelerated, and the mood of the people became very positive. In fact, these years were referred to as the "Era of Good Feelings."

The Monroe Presidency, 1817–1825

James Monroe, the last of the "Virginia Dynasty," had been hand-picked by the retiring Madison, and he was elected with only one electoral vote opposed: a symbol of national unity.

Postwar Boom

The years following the war were characterized by a high foreign demand for American cotton, grain, and tobacco; commerce flourished. The Second National Bank, through its overly liberal credit policies, proved to be an inflationary influence, and the price level rose rapidly.

The Depression of 1819

Inventories of British manufactured goods had built up during the war, and English merchants began to dump their products on the American market at cut-rate prices. American manufacturers suffered from this influx of imports. The U.S. bank tried to slow the inflationary spiral by tightening credit, and a sharp business slump resulted.

This depression was most severe in the newly expanding West, partly because of its economic dependency and partly because of heavy speculation in Western lands.

The Marshall Court

John Marshall delivered the majority opinions in a number of critical decisions in these formative years, all of which served to strengthen the power of the federal government and restrict the powers of state governments.

Marbury v. Madison (1803)

This case established the Supreme Court's power of judicial review over federal legislation.

Fletcher v. Peck (1810)

The Georgia legislature had issued extensive land grants in a shady deal with the Yazoo Land Company. A subsequent legislative session repealed that action because of the corruption that had attended the original grant. The court decided that the original action by the Georgia Assembly had constituted a valid contract, that could not be broken regardless of the corruption that had followed. This was the first time a state law was voided on the grounds that it violated a principle of the U.S. Constitution.

Dartmouth College v. Woodward (1819)

The quarrel between the president and the trustees of the New Hampshire college became a political issue when the Republicans backed the president and the Federalists supported the trustees. The president tried to change Dartmouth from a private to a public institution by having its charter revoked. The court ruled that the charter, though issued by the king during colonial days, still constituted a contract, and thus could not be arbitrarily changed or revoked without the consent of both parties. The result of this decision was to severely limit the power of state governments to control the corporation, which was the emerging form of business organization.

McCulloch v. Maryland (1819)

The state of Maryland had tried to levy a tax on the Baltimore branch of the Bank of the United States, and so protect the competitive position of its own state banks. Marshall's ruling declared that no state has the right to control an agency of the federal government. Since "the power to tax is the power to destroy," such state action violated Congress' "implied powers" to establish and operate a national bank.

Gibbons v. Ogden (1824)

The State of New York had granted a monopoly to Ogden to operate a steamboat between New York and New Jersey. Gibbons obtained a Congressional permit to operate a steamboat line in the same waters. When Ogden sued to maintain his monopoly, the New York courts ruled in his favor. Gibbons' appeal went to the Supreme Court. John Marshall ruled that commerce included navigation, and that only Congress has the right to regulate commerce among states. Thus, the state-granted monopoly was void.

Statehood: A Balancing Act

The Missouri Compromise (1820)

The Missouri Territory, the first to be organized from the Louisiana Purchase, applied for statehood in 1819. Since the Senate membership was evenly divided between slave-holding and free states at that time, the admission of a new state was obviously going to give the voting advantage either to the North or to the South. Slavery was already well-established in the new territory, so the Southern states were confident in their advantage, until Representative Tallmadge of New York proposed an amendment to the bill that would prohibit slavery in Missouri.

The Southern outcry was immediate, and the ensuing debate grew hot. The Senate was deadlocked.

Henry Clay's Compromise Solution

As the debate dragged on, the northern territory of Massachusetts applied for admission as the state of Maine. This offered a way out of the dilemma, and House Speaker Clay formulated a package that both sides could accept. The two admission bills were combined, with Maine coming in free and Missouri as a slave state. To make the package palatable for the House, a provision was added to prohibit slavery in the remainder of the Louisiana Territory, north of the southern boundary of Missouri (latitude 36° 30'). Clay guided this bill through the House and it became law, thus maintaining the balance of power.

The debates in Congress had reminded everyone of the deep division between the sections, and some saw it as evidence of trouble to come. Thomas Jefferson, in retirement at Monticello, remarked that the news from Washington was like a "fire-ball in the night."

Monroe Doctrine Editorial Cartoon

The Expanding Economy

The Growing Population

Population continued to double every twenty-five years. The migration of people to the West increased in volume, and by 1840 over one-third of all Americans lived west of the Alleghenies. Immigration from abroad was not significant until 1820; then it began to increase rapidly, mostly from the British Isles.

The Farming Sector

The growth of markets for farm products in the expanding cities, coupled with liberal land sale policies by the federal government, made the growing of staple agricultural crops more profitable. More and more land was put into cultivation, and the prevailing system of clearing and planting became more wasteful of timber as well as of the fertility of the land.

The Cotton Kingdom

The new lands in the southwest, then constituting Alabama, Mississippi, Louisiana, and Texas, proved ideal for the production of short-staple cotton. Eli Whitney's invention of the cotton gin solved the problem of separating the seeds from the fibers, and the cotton boom was under way.

The growing market for food and work animals in the cotton South provided the opportunity for the new Western farmers to specialize in those items and further stimulated the westward movement.

Fishing

New England and Chesapeake fishing proved very profitable. Deep-sea whaling became a significant enterprise, particularly from the Massachusetts/Rhode Island ports.

Lumbering

The expanding population created a need for building materials, and timber remained a profitable export item. Shipbuilding thrived in a number of Eastern Seaboard and Gulf Coast ports.

Fur Trade

John Jacob Astor and others opened up business all the way to the northwest coast. "Mountain men" probed deeper and deeper into the Rocky Mountain ranges in search of beaver.

Trade with the Spanish

The Santa Fe Trail, which ran from New Mexico northeast to Independence, Missouri, became an active trading corridor, opening up the Spanish territories to American migration and influence, and also providing the basis for future territorial claims.

The Transportation Revolution

The first half of the Nineteenth century witnessed an extraordinary sequence of inventions and innovations that produced a true revolution in transport, and communications.

River Traffic

The steamboats built by Robert Fulton, the *Clermont* in 1807 and the *New Orleans* in 1811, transformed river transport. As shipment times and freight rates both plummeted, regular steam service was established on all the major river systems.

Road Building

By 1818, the National Road, which was built with federal funds, had been completed from Cumberland, Maryland, to Wheeling, Virginia, linking the Potomac with the Ohio River. A network of privately owned toll roads (turnpikes) began to reach out from every sizeable city. They were usually built for only a few miles out, and they never accounted for a significant share of the total freight tonnage moved, but they formed the nucleus of a growing road system in the new nation.

The Canal Era

The Erie Canal, linking the Hudson River at Albany, New York, with Lake Erie, was completed in 1825 and became the first and most successful example of an artificial waterway. It was followed by a rash of construction until canals linked every major waterway system east of the Mississippi River.

Canals were the first development projects to receive large amounts of public funding. They ran east-west and so tied the new West to the old East, with later implications for sectional divisions.

The Rise of New York City

Its location as a transport hub, coupled with innovations in business practices, boosted New York City into a primary trade center and made it America's largest city by 1830. One such innovation was the packet boats, which operated on a guaranteed schedule and helped to rationalize commerce, both internal and international.

New York soon dominated the domestic market for cotton, a situation that progressively reduced the South to the status of an economic colony.

Industrialization

The Rise of the Factory System

Samuel Slater had migrated from Britain in 1789, having served as an apprentice under inventor Richard Arkwright and then as a mill manager. He used his knowledge to build the first successful cotton-spinning mill in this country. The first cotton manufacturing plant in the world to include all the elements of manufacturing under one roof was built in Boston in 1813.

Eli Whitney's development and application of the principle of interchangeable parts, first used in his firearms factories, helped to speed the growth of mass-production operations.

The expansion of markets in Latin America and the Far East, as well as domestic markets, both resulted from and helped to develop the factory system.

Eli Whitney

Manufacturers and industrialists found it necessary to organize banks, insurance companies, and real estate firms to meet the needs of their growing business organizations.

The Corporation

The corporate form, with its limited liability and its potential for raising and utilizing large amounts of capital, became the typical type of business organization. By the 1830s, most states had enacted general laws for incorporating.

The Labor Supply

In the early days, the "Lowell System" became a popular way to staff the New England factories. Young women were hired from the surrounding countryside, brought to town and housed in dormitories in the mill towns. They were paid low wages for hard work under poor conditions, but they were only working for a short time, to earn a dowry or help out with the family income, so they soon went back home. This "rotating labor supply" was ideal for the owners, since the girls were not motivated to agitate for better wages and conditions.

Labor was always in short supply in this country, so the system depended on technology to increase production. This situation always placed a premium on innovation in machinery and technique.

The Growth of Unions

The factory system separated the owners from the workers and thus depersonalized the workplace. It also made the skilled artisan less important, since the repetitive processes of the mill could be performed by relatively unskilled laborers.

Although the first organized strike took place in 1828, in Paterson, New Jersey, by child workers, periodic economic downturns helped keep workers relatively dependent and passive until the 1850s.

A major goal of early unions was the ten-hour day, and this effort sparked a period of growth in organized labor that was later effectively quenched by the depression of 1837.

Educational Development

The Growth of Public Schools

Before 1815, there were no public schools to speak of in this country. Some states had endorsed the idea of free schools for the people, but they shrank from the task of financing such a system. Jefferson had outlined such a plan for Virginia, but it came to nothing.

Schools were primarily sponsored by private institutions—corporate academies in the Northeast and religious institutions in the South and mid-Atlantic states. Most were aristocratic in orientation, training the nation's leaders, and few had any interest in schooling the children of the poor.

Women were likewise considered unfit for academic training, and those female schools that existed concentrated on homemaking skills and the fine arts that would make "ornaments" of the young ladies enrolled.

The New York Free School, one of those rare examples of a school for the poor, experimented for a time with the Lancastrian system, in which older students tutored the younger ones, thus stretching scarce budget dollars.

Higher Education

Although the number of institutions of higher learning increased sharply in the early years of the nineteenth century, none was truly public. All relied upon high tuition rates for survival, so less than one in ten young men, and no women, ever attended a college or university.

The training these schools provided was very limited as well. The only professional training was in theology, and only a scattering of colleges offered brief courses of study in law or medicine. The University of Pennsylvania, for example, offered one year of medical schooling, after which a person could obtain a license to practice the healing arts. Needless to say, medical practice was quite primitive.

The Growth of Cultural Nationalism

Jeffersonian Americans tried to demonstrate their newly won independence by championing a strong sense of cultural nationalism, a feeling that their young republic represented the "final stage" of civilization, the "last great hope of mankind."

Literary Nationalism

Although most Americans had access to one or more newspapers, the market for native authors was quite limited. Publishers preferred to print works from British authors or to import books from Europe. A few Americans who were willing to pay the costs of publishing their own works found a growing number of readers.

Significant American Authors

Washington Irving was by far the best-known native writer in America. He excelled in the telling of folk tales and local color stories, and is best remembered for his portraits of Hudson River characters.

Mercy Otis Warren, the revolutionary pamphleteer, published a multivolume *History of the Revolution* in 1805.

"Parson" Mason Weems wrote the best-seller *Life of Washington* in 1806, which was short on historical accuracy but long on nationalistic hero-worship.

Educational Literature

Early schoolbooks, like Noah Webster's *Blue Backed Speller*, as well as his dictionary of the "American" language, reflected the intense desire to promote patriotism and a feeling of national identity.

Developments in Religious Life

The Post-Revolution Years

The Revolutionary War weakened the position of the traditional, established churches. The doctrines of the Enlightenment became very popular, and its religious expression, deism, gained a considerable following among the educated classes. Rationalism, Unitarianism, and Universalism all saw a period of popularity. Thomas Paine's exposition of the rationalist posture, *The Age of Reason*, attacked the traditional Christian values and was read widely.

The Second Great Awakening

The reaction to the trend toward rationalism, the decline in church membership, and the lack of piety was a renewal of personal, heart-felt evangelicalism. A second Great Awakening began in 1801 at Cane Ridge, Kentucky, in the first "camp meeting."

As the revival spread, its characteristics became more uniform—an emphasis on personal salvation, an emotional response to God's grace, an individualistic faith. Women took a major part in the movement. Blacks were also heavily involved, and the individualistic emphasis created unrest among their ranks, particularly in the slave-holding South.

The revival produced strong nationalistic overtones, and the Protestant ideas of a "called nation" were to flourish later in some of the Manifest Destiny doctrines of expansionism. The social overtones of this religious renewal were to spark the great reform movements of the 1830s and 1840s.

Quiz: Chapters 3 and 4

1. The Republican response to the 1798 Alien and Sedition Acts included

    (A) South Carolina's nullification of the acts.

    (B) the Virginia and Kentucky Resolutions.

    (C) the Hartford Convention.

    (D) the Ostend Manifesto.

    (E) the Mulligan Letters.

2. The greatest significance of the Supreme Court's decision in *Marbury v. Madison* was that it

    (A) claimed for the first time that the Supreme Court could issue directives to the president.

    (B) claimed that the Supreme Court alone was empowered to say what the Constitution meant.

    (C) claimed for the first time that the Supreme Court could declare an act of Congress to be unconstitutional.

    (D) was openly defied by President Thomas Jefferson.

    (E) resulted in a major realignment of the first American party system.

3. The most controversial portion of Alexander Hamilton's economic program was

    (A) federal assumption of state debts.

    (B) assessment of direct taxes on the states.

    (C) creation of the Bank of the United States.

    (D) imposition of high protective tariffs.

    (E) establishment of a bimetallic system.

4. During the first two decades under the United States Constitution, the main factor that separated Federalists from Republicans was

    (A) whether they accepted the Constitution or opposed it.

    (B) whether they favored the French Revolution or opposed it.

    (C) whether they leaned more toward states' rights or national sovereignty.

    (D) their personal like or dislike for the personalities of Thomas

Jefferson and Alexander Hamilton.

(E) whether they had been patriots or loyalists during the American War of Independence.

5. All of the following contributed to the coming of the War of 1812 EXCEPT

(A) the *Chesapeake-Leopard* Incident.

(B) British impressment of American seamen from American ships on the high seas.

(C) the concerns of Western Americans that the Indian raids they suffered were being carried out with British encouragement.

(D) the Congressional "War Hawks'" desire to annex Canada.

(E) the armed confrontation between U.S. and British forces along the Maine-Canada border.

6. In the 1790s political conflict between Thomas Jefferson and Alexander Hamilton, Jefferson would have been more likely to

(A) take a narrow view of the Constitution.

(B) favor Britain over France in the European wars.

(C) favor the establishment of a national bank.

(D) win the cooperation of presidents George Washington and John Adams.

(E) oppose the efforts of Citizen Genet in America.

7. The Connecticut Compromise advocated by Roger Sherman proposed settling the issue of representation in Congress by

(A) giving each state two senators with the vote in the Senate to be by individuals and not states.

    (B)   having the members of both houses of Congress chosen by the state legislatures.

    (C)   providing for the popular election of both houses of Congress.

    (D)   apportioning representation in the House of Representatives according to population.

    (E)   Both (A) and (D).

8.   The purchase of the Louisiana territory

    I.   doubled the size of the United States.

    II.   guaranteed Western farmers access to the Mississippi River as an avenue of trade.

    III. presented Jefferson with a constitutional dilemma since he was a "strict" constructionist.

    IV. gave the United States control of the port of New Orleans.

    (A)   I and II only.

    (B)   I and III only.

    (C)   I, II, and III only.

    (D)   I, II, and IV only.

    (E)   I, II, III, and IV.

9.   The Northwest Ordinance

    I.   provided for the admission of new states to the Union on an equal footing with the original 13.

    II.   prohibited slavery in the Western territory above the Ohio River.

    III. stipulated that the land and property of the Indians "shall never be taken from them without their permission."

(A) I only.

(B) II only.

(C) I and II only.

(D) I and III only.

(E) I, II, and III.

10. *The Federalist Papers*

(A) were written anonymously by Alexander Hamilton, John Jay, and James Madison.

(B) argued that under the Constitution the states would relinquish too much sovereignty.

(C) opposed ratification of the Constitution without the addition of a bill of rights.

(D) convinced Patrick Henry to support the Constitution.

(E) stressed that the Constitutional Convention was instructed to revise the Articles of Confederation, not to write a new constitution.

ANSWER KEY

1.	(B)	6.	(A)
2.	(C)	7.	(E)
3.	(C)	8.	(E)
4.	(B)	9.	(E)
5.	(E)	10.	(A)

DETAILED ANSWERS

1.   **(B)**   The Virginia and Kentucky Resolutions were the centerpiece of the Republican response to the Alien and Sedition Acts. The 1814 Hartford Convention (C), on the other hand, was a Federalist response to Republican policies. South Carolina's nullification (A) was aimed at the highly protective Tariff of 1828. The 1854 Ostend Manifesto (D) dealt with U.S. desires to acquire Cuba from Spain, and the Mulligan Letters (E) incriminated 1884 Republican presidential candidate James G. Blaine in an unsavory stock scheme.

2.   **(C)**   *Marbury v. Madison* asserted for the first time the Supreme Court's right to declare an act of Congress unconstitutional. It did not, however, go so far as to claim that the Supreme Court alone was empowered to say what the Constitution meant (B). In the decision of this case, Chief Justice John Marshall wisely avoided issuing a directive (A) that President Thomas Jefferson would have defied (D) had it been issued. The case did not bring any major political realignment (E).

3. **(C)** Creation of the Bank of the United States was more controversial than federal assumption of state debts (A) or the imposition of protective tariffs (D), though these, too, were controversial to a degree. Neither direct taxes (B) nor establishment of a bimetallic system (E) were part of Hamilton's program, though a century later the bimetallic issue did become very controversial.

4. **(B)** Though many factors might contribute to an individual's choice of party, including, perhaps, the character of the party's leader (D), and the party's stand on such issues as states' rights (C), the chief factor during this period was acceptance or rejection of the French Revolution—Jefferson and his supporters saw it as good, Hamilton and the Federalists did not. By this time the Constitution had virtually universal acceptance in the U.S. (A). Though during the days of the fight over ratification, those favoring the Constitution were known as Federalists; they are not to be confused with the political party bearing the same name that gradually took form *after* the Constitution was in effect. Patriot and Loyalist divisions came to mean increasingly less (E).

5. **(E)** The armed confrontation—brief and bloodless—along the Maine-Canada border was the "Aroostook War" and took place in 1842, thirty years after the outbreak of the War of 1812. The other items, the *Chesapeake-Leopard* Incident (A), the British impressment of American seamen from American ships on the high seas (B), the concerns of Western Americans that the British were inciting the Indians (C), and the "War Hawks'" desire to annex Canada (D), were all real and all contributed to the coming of the war.

6. **(A)** Jefferson would have been more likely to take a narrow view of the Constitution, Hamilton a broad and permissive one. Hamilton, rather than Jefferson, also favored Britain over France in the European war (B), favored the establishment of a national bank (C), won the cooperation of presidents George Washington and John Adams most of the time (D), and opposed the efforts of Citizen Genet in America (E).

7. **(E)**   The Connecticut Compromise, advanced by Oliver Ellsworth and Roger Sherman, was submitted to the Constitutional Convention to break the deadlock created by the rejection of the Randolph Plan and Paterson Plan. The compromise provided for a bicameral legislature. One chamber of the legislature was to have equal representation from each state, and the other chamber was to be based on proportional representation.

8. **(E)**   While the Louisiana Purchase more than doubled the size of the United States, it also guaranteed Western farmers access to the Mississippi River as an avenue of trade. Importantly, the purchase of this territory gave the United States control of the port of New Orleans. Jefferson was troubled by the fact that according to his oft-repeated "strict" interpretation of the Constitution, the United States technically lacked the constitutional power to purchase the Louisiana territory. Nevertheless, Jefferson approved its purchase.

9. **(E)**   The Northwest Ordinance was a major accomplishment of the Confederation Congress. By excluding slavery from the Northwest, it ensured that the entire North would be free territory. By establishing the precedent that new states would enter the Union on an equal footing with the original 13, it ensured the continued settlement of the West. The ordinance also stipulated that the land and property of the Indians "shall never be taken from them without their permission."

10. **(A)**   *The Federalist Papers*, a collection of 85 essays, were written anonymously by Alexander Hamilton, John Jay, and James Madison. Seventy-seven of the essays originally appeared in New York newspapers under the pseudonym "Publius." These essays argued for the ratification of the Constitution by stressing the inadequacies of the Articles of Confederation.

CHAPTER 5

Jacksonian Democracy
and Westward Expansion
(1824–1850)

The Jacksonian Democracy, 1829–1841

While the "Age of Jackson" did not bring perfect political, social, or economic equality to all Americans, it did mark a transformation in the political life of the nation that attracted the notice of European travelers and observers. Alexis de Tocqueville observed an "equality of condition" here that existed nowhere else in the world, and an egalitarian spirit among the people that was unique. Certainly the electorate had become broadened so that all white males had access to the polls, even if blacks and women were still outside the system. It was, in that sense, the "age of the common man." As to whether Andrew Jackson and his party were actually working for the good of those common men is another matter.

The Election of 1824

The Expansion of the Electorate

Most states had already eliminated the property qualifications for voting before the campaigns for this election began. The new Massachusetts state constitution of 1820 had led the way in this liberalization of the franchise, and most Northern states followed soon after, usually with some conservative opposition, but not violent reactions. In Rhode Island, Thomas Dorr led a bloodless "rebellion" in an effort to expand the franchise in that state, and though he was briefly imprisoned for his efforts, the incident led the conservative legislature to relent and grant the vote to nonproperty owners. The movement for reform was much slower in the Southern states.

Free blacks were excluded from the polls across the South, and in most of the Northern states. In those areas where they had held the franchise, they were gradually excluded from the social and economic mainstream—as well as from the political arena—in the early years of this period.

National elections had never attracted much enthusiasm until 1824. Legislative caucuses had made the presidential nominations and kept the ruling cliques in power by excluding the voters from the process. But this year the system failed, and the caucuses were bypassed.

The members of the electoral college were now being almost universally elected by the people, rather than by the state legislatures, as in the early days.

The Candidates

Secretary of the Treasury William H. Crawford of Georgia was the pick of the Congressional caucus. Secretary of State John Quincy Adams held the job that traditionally had been the stepping-stone to the executive office. Speaker of the House Henry Clay presented the only coherent program to the voters, the "American System," which provided a high tariff on imports to finance an extensive internal improvement package. Andrew Jackson of Tennessee presented himself as a war hero from the 1812 conflict. All four candidates claimed to be Republicans.

The Election

Jackson won 43% of the popular vote, but the four-way split meant that he only received 38% of the electoral votes. Under the provisions of the Twelfth Amendment, the top three candidates were voted on by

Andrew Jackson

the House of Representatives. This left Henry Clay out of the running, and he threw his support to Adams. The votes had no sooner been counted when the new president, Adams, appointed Henry Clay his secretary of state.

Andrew Jackson and his supporters immediately cried "foul!" and accused Clay of making a deal for his vote. The rallying cry of "corrupt bargain" became the impetus for their immediate initiation of the campaign for the 1828 election.

The Adams Administration

The new president pushed for an active federal government in areas like internal improvements and Native American affairs. These policies proved unpopular in an age of increasing sectional jealousies and conflicts over states' rights.

Adams was frustrated at every turn by his Jacksonian opposition, and his unwillingness, or inability, to compromise further antagonized his political enemies. For example, his refusal to endorse and enforce the Creek Native Americans' land cession to the state of Georgia was negated by their re-cession of their lands under pressure from Georgia's Jacksonian government.

John C. Calhoun and Nullification

In 1828, Congress passed a new tariff bill that was originally supported by Southern congressmen in order to embarrass the administration. The finished bill, however, included higher import duties for many goods that were bought by Southern planters, so they bitterly denounced the law as the "Tariff of Abominations."

John C. Calhoun was serving as Adams' vice president, so to protest the tariff and still protect his position, he anonymously published the "South Carolina Exposition and Protest," which outlined his theory of the "concurrent majority": that a federal law which was deemed harmful to the interests of an individual state could be declared null and void within that state by a convention of the people. Thus, a state holding a minority position could ignore a law enacted by the majority which they considered unconstitutional (shades of Thomas Jefferson).

The Election of 1828

Adams' supporters now called themselves the National Republicans, and Jackson's party ran as the Democratic Republicans. Andrew Jackson had aggressively campaigned since his defeat in the House in 1825.

It was a dirty campaign. Adams' people accused Jackson of adultery and of the murder of several militiamen who had been executed for desertion during the War of 1812. Jackson's followers in turn defamed Adams and his programs and accused him of extravagance with public funds.

When the votes were counted, Jackson had won 56% of the popular vote and swept 178 of the 261 electoral votes. John C. Calhoun was elected vice president.

Andrew Jackson as President

Jackson was popular with the common man. He seemed to be the prototype of the self-made Westerner: rough-hewn, violent, vindictive, with few ideas but strong convictions. He ignored his appointed Cabinet officers and relied instead on the counsel of his "Kitchen Cabinet," a group of partisan supporters who had the ear and the confidence of the president.

Jackson expressed the conviction that government operations could be performed by untrained, common folk, and he threatened the dismissal of large numbers of government employees, to replace them with his supporters. Actually, he talked more about this "spoils system" than he acted on it.

He exercised his veto power more than any other president before him. A famous example was the Maysville Road, a project in Kentucky that would require a federal subsidy. Jackson opposed it because it would exist only within the boundaries of a single state.

Jacksonian Indian Policy

Jackson supported the removal of all Indian tribes to west of the Mississippi River. The Indian Removal Act in 1830 provided for federal enforcement of that process.

The portion of the Cherokee Nation which occupied northern Georgia claimed to be a sovereign political entity within the boundaries of that state. The Supreme Court supported that claim in its decision in

Political cartoon depicting Jackson's Native American policy.

Worcester v. Georgia (1832), but President Jackson refused to enforce the court's decision.

The result of this policy was the Trail of Tears, the forced march, under U.S. Army escort, of thousands of Cherokees to the West. A quarter or more of the Indians, mostly women and children, perished on the journey.

The Webster-Hayne Debate (1830)

Federal Land Policy

The method of disposing of government land raised sectional differences. Westerners wanted cheap lands available to the masses. Northeasterners opposed this policy because it would lure away their labor supply and drive up wages. Southerners supported the West, hoping to weaken the ties between East and West.

The Senate Confrontation

Senator Robert Hayne of South Carolina made a speech in support of cheap land, and he used Calhoun's anti-tariff arguments to support his position. In his remarks, he referred to the possibility of nullification.

Daniel Webster's famous replies to this argument moved the debate from the issue of land policy to the nature of the Union and states' rights within it. Webster argued for the Union as indissoluble and sovereign over the individual states. His concluding statements have become a part of our rhetorical heritage: "It is, Sir, the people's Constitution, the people's government, made for the people, made by the people, and answerable to the people....Liberty and Union, now and for ever, one and inseparable!"

The Second Nullification Crisis

The final split between Andrew Jackson and his vice president, John C. Calhoun, came over the new Tariff of 1832, and over Mrs. Calhoun's snub of Peggy Eaton, the wife of Secretary of War John Eaton.

Mrs. Eaton was a commoner, and the aristocratic Mrs. Calhoun refused to include her on the guest lists for the Washington parties. Jackson, no doubt remembering the slights to his own dear Rachel, defended his friends Peggy and John, and demanded that they be included in the social life of the capital.

Jackson was a defender of states' rights, but within the context of a dominant Union. When he supported the higher rates of the new tariff, Calhoun resigned his office in a huff and went home to South Carolina. There he composed an Ordinance of Nullification, which was duly approved by a special convention, and the customs officials were ordered to stop collecting the duties at the port of Charleston.

Jackson's response was immediate and decisive. He obtained a Force Bill from Congress (1833), which empowered him to use federal troops to enforce the collection of the taxes. And he suggested the possibility of hanging Calhoun. At the same time, he offered a gradual reduction in the levels of the duties. Calhoun backed down, both sides claimed victory, and the crisis was averted.

The War on the Bank

The Controversy

The Bank of the United States had operated under the direction of Nicholas Biddle since 1823. He was a cautious man, and his conservative economic policy enforced conservatism among the state and private banks—which many bankers resented. Many of the bank's enemies opposed it simply because it was big and powerful. Many still disputed its constitutionality.

The Election of 1832

Andrew Jackson freely voiced his antagonism toward the bank and his intention to destroy it. During the campaign for the presidency in 1832, Henry Clay and Daniel Webster promoted a bill to recharter the bank, even though its charter did not expire until 1836. They feared that Jackson would gain support over time and could kill the bank as a parting shot as he retired. The Congress passed the recharter bill, but Jackson vetoed it. This left that institution a lame duck agency.

Jackson soundly defeated Henry Clay in the presidential race and he considered his victory a mandate from the people to destroy the bank. His first move was to remove the federal government's deposits from Biddle's vaults and distribute the funds to various state and local banks, called by his critics the "pet banks." Biddle responded by tightening up on credit and calling in loans, hoping to embarrass the government and force a withdrawal by Jackson. Jackson stood firm and the result was a financial recession.

The Panic of 1837

When Biddle was forced to relent through pressure from business interests, the economy immediately rebounded. With credit policies relaxed, inflation began to pick up. The government contributed to this expansion by offering millions of acres of western land for sale to settlers at low prices.

In 1836, Jackson ordered a distribution of surplus funds and thus helped to further fuel the inflationary rise in prices. Finally, even Jackson recognized the danger and tried to slow the spiral by issuing the Specie Circular, which required payment for public land in hard money; no more paper or credit. Depression quickly followed this move.

The business recession lasted well into the 1840s. Our national economy was by this time so tied in with international business and finance that the downturn affected the entire Atlantic community, and was in turn worsened by the global impact. But most Americans blamed everyone in power, including Jackson, and our institutions and business practices. This disillusionment helped to initiate and intensify the reform movement that so occupied this nation in the nineteenth century's second quarter.

The Election of 1836

Jackson had handpicked his Democratic successor, Martin Van Buren of New York. The Whigs ran three regional candidates in hopes of upsetting the Jacksonians. The Whig Party had emerged from the ruins of the National Republicans and other groups who opposed Jackson's policies. The name was taken from the British Whig tradition, which simply refers to the "opposition."

Van Buren's Presidency

Van Buren, known as Old Kinderhook (O.K.), inherited all the problems and resentments generated by his mentor. He spent most of his term in office dealing with the financial chaos left by the death of the Second Bank. The best he could do was to eventually persuade Congress to establish an Independent Treasury to handle government funds. It began functioning in 1840.

The Election of 1840

The Candidates

The Whigs nominated William Henry Harrison, "Old Tippecanoe," a Western Indian fighter. Their choice for vice president was John Tyler, a former Democrat from Virginia. The Democrats put up Van Buren again, but they could not agree on a vice presidential candidate, so they ran no one.

The Campaign

This election saw the largest voter turnout to date. The campaign was a dramatic one. The Whigs stressed the depression and the opulent lifestyle of the incumbent in contrast to the simple "log cabin" origins of their candidate.

Harrison won a narrow popular victory, but swept 80% of the electoral vote. Unfortunately for the Whigs, President Harrison died only a month after the inauguration, having served the shortest term in presidential history.

The Meaning of Jacksonian Politics

The Party System

The Age of Jackson was the beginning of the modern party system. Popular politics, based on emotional appeal, became the accepted style. The practice of meeting in mass conventions to nominate national candidates for office was established during these Jackson years.

The Strong Executive

Jackson, more than any president before him, used his office to dominate his party and the government to such an extent that he was called "King Andrew" by his critics.

The Changing Emphasis Towards States' Rights

Andrew Jackson supported the authority of the states against the national government, but he drew the line at the concept of nullification. He advocated a strong union made up of sovereign states, and this created some dissonance in his political thinking.

The Supreme Court reflected this shift in thinking in its decision on the *Charles River Bridge* case in 1837, delivered by Jackson's new Chief Justice, Roger Taney. He ruled that a state could abrogate a grant of monopoly if that original grant had ceased to be in the best interests of the community. This was clearly a reversal of the *Dartmouth College* principle of the sanctity of contracts, in a case where the general welfare was perceived as being involved.

Party Philosophies

The Democrats opposed big government and the requirements of modernization: urbanization and industrialization. Their support came from the working classes, small merchants, and small farmers.

The Whigs promoted government participation in commercial and industrial development, the encouragement of banking and corporations, and a cautious approach to westward expansion. Their support came largely from northern business and manufacturing interests, and from large southern planters. Calhoun, Clay, and Webster dominated the Whig party during these early decades of the nineteenth century.

Tocqueville's *Democracy in America*

Alexis de Tocqueville, a French civil servant, traveled to this country in the early 1830s to study the American prison system, which was one of the more innovative systems in the world. His book, *Democracy in America*, published in 1835, was the result of his observations, and it reflected a broad interest in the entire spectrum of the American democratic process and the society in which it had developed. His insightful commentary on the American way of life has proven to be almost prophetic in many respects, and provides the modern reader with an outsider's objective view of what this country was like in the Age of Jackson.

Antebellum Culture: An Age of Reform

The American people in 1840 found themselves living in an era of transition and instability. The society was changing and traditional values were being challenged. The responses to this uncertainty were twofold: a movement toward reform and a rising desire for order and control.

We have a fairly vivid picture of what Americans were like in this period of time, from accounts by hundreds of foreign visitors who came to this country to observe our society-in-the-making. These observers noted a restless population, always on the move, compulsive joiners of associations, committed to progress, hard-working and hard-playing, driven relentlessly by a desire for wealth. They believed in and talked about equality, but the reality was that the system was increasingly creating a class society. Americans seemed to lean toward violence, and mob incidents were common.

The Reform Impulse: Major Sources of Reform

Romanticism held a belief in the innate goodness of man, thus in his improvability. This movement had its roots in turn-of-the-century

Europe, and it emphasized the emotions and feelings over rationality. It appeared as a reaction against the excesses of the Enlightenment, which had put strong emphasis on reason, to the exclusion of feelings.

There was also a growing need perceived for a stable social order and control over the forces that were threatening the traditional values.

Both of these major streams of reform activity were centered in the Northeast, especially in New England.

The Flowering of Literature

Northern Writers and Themes

James Fenimore Cooper's *Leatherstocking Tales* emphasized the independence of the individual and also the importance of a stable social order.

Walt Whitman's *Leaves of Grass* likewise celebrated the importance of individualism.

Henry Wadsworth Longfellow's epic poems *Evangeline* and *Hiawatha* spoke of the value of tradition and the impact of the past on the present.

Herman Melville's classic stories—*Typee, Billy Budd, Moby Dick*—all lashed out at the popular optimism of his day. He believed in the Puritan doctrine of original sin and his characters spoke of the mystery of life.

Historian and nationalist Francis Parkman vividly portrayed the struggle for empire between France and Britain in his *Montcalm and Wolfe. The Oregon Trail* described the opening frontier of the Rocky Mountains and beyond.

James Russell Lowell, poet and editor, wrote the *Bigelow Papers* and the *Commemoration Ode*, honoring Civil War casualties of Harvard.

A writer of romances and tales, Nathaniel Hawthorne is best remembered for his criticism of Puritan bigotry in *The Scarlet Letter*.

Southern Writers and Themes

Author of *The Raven*, *Tamerlane*, and many tales of terror and darkness, Edgar Allan Poe explored the world of the spirit and the emotions.

South Carolina poet William Gilmore Simms changed from a staunch nationalist to a defender of the slave system and the uniqueness of the Southern way of life.

A Georgia storyteller, Augustus Longstreet used vulgar, earthy language and themes to paint the common folk of the South.

The Fine Arts

Artists and Themes

The Hudson River School was a group of landscape painters who portrayed the awesomeness of nature in America, the new world. George Catlin painted the American Indian, whom he saw as a vanishing race. John James Audubon painted the wide array of American birds and animals.

Music and the Theater

The theater was popular, but generally condemned by the church and conservatives as a "vagabond profession." The only original American contribution was the blackface minstrel show.

The Transcendentalists

Major Themes

This movement had its origins in Concord, Massachusetts. The basic objective of these thinkers was to transcend the bounds of the intellect and to strive for emotional understanding, to attain unity with God, without the help of the institutional church, which they saw as reactionary and stifling to self-expression.

Major Writers

Ralph Waldo Emerson, essayist and lecturer, authored "Nature" and "Self-Reliance." Henry David Thoreau, best known for his *Walden*, repudiated the repression of society and preached civil disobedience to protest unjust laws.

The Utopians

Their Purpose

The cooperative community was their attempt to improve the life of the common man in the face of increasing impersonal industrialism.

The Utopian Communities

Brook Farm, in Massachusetts, was the earliest commune in America, and it was short-lived. Nathaniel Hawthorne was a short-term resident, and his *Blithedale Romance* was drawn from that experience. This work and *The Scarlet Letter* were both condemnations of the life of social isolation.

New Harmony, Indiana, was founded by Robert Owen, of the New Lanark experiment in Wales, but it failed after two years. He attacked religion, marriage, and the institution of private property, so he encountered resistance from neighboring communities.

Nashoba was in the environs of Memphis, Tennessee, established by the free-thinking Englishwoman Frances Wright as a communal haven for freed slaves. Needless to say, her community experiment encountered fierce opposition from her slaveholding neighbors and it survived only briefly.

Oneida Community in New York was based on free love and open marriages.

The Shakers were directed by Mother Ann Lee. The communities were socialistic experiments that practiced celibacy, sexual equality, and social discipline. The name was given to them by onlookers at their community dancing sessions.

Amana Community, in Iowa, was another socialist experiment, with a rigidly ordered society.

The Mormons

The Origins of the Religion

Joseph Smith received the "sacred" writings in New York state in 1830, and organized the Church of Jesus Christ of Latter Day Saints. They were not popular with their neighbors, primarily because of their practice of polygamy, and so were forced to move about, first to Missouri, then to Nauvoo, Illinois. There Smith was killed by a mob, and in 1847 the community was led to the valley of the Great Salt Lake by their new leader, Brigham Young, in one of the great epic migrations to the West.

The Church

They established a highly organized, centrally controlled system, which provided security and order for the faithful. They held a strong belief in human perfectability, and so were in the mainstream of romantic utopians.

Remaking Society: Organized Reform

Sources of Inspiration

Transcendentalism, as a branch of European Romanticism, spawned a great deal of interest in remaking society into more humane forms.

Protestant Revivalism was a powerful force for the improvement of society. Evangelist Charles G. Finney, through his "social gospel," offered salvation to all. A strong sectarian spirit split the Protestant movement into many groups (e.g., the Cumberland Presbyterians). Also evident was a strong anti-Catholic element, which was strengthened by the new waves of immigration from Catholic Ireland and southern Germany after 1830.

Temperance

The American Society for Promotion of Temperance was organized in 1826. It was strongly supported by Protestants, but just as strongly opposed by the new Catholic immigrants.

Public Schools

The motivations for the free school crusade were mixed. Some wanted to provide the opportunity for all children to learn the skills for self-fulfillment and success in a republic. Others wanted to use schools as agencies for social control—to Americanize the new immigrant children as well as to Protestantize the Catholics, and to defuse the growing problems of urbanization. The stated purpose of the public schools was to instill social values: thrift, order, discipline, democracy.

Public apathy and even opposition met the early reformers: Horace Mann, the first secretary of the Massachusetts Board of Education, and Henry Barnard, his counterpart in Connecticut and Rhode Island.

The movement picked up momentum in the 1830s, but progress was very spotty. Few public schools were available in the West, fewer still for Southern whites, and none at all for Southern blacks.

Higher Education

In 1839, the first state-supported school for women, Troy Female Seminary, was founded in Troy, New York. Oberlin College in Ohio was the nation's first coeducational college. The Perkins School for the Blind in Boston was the first of its kind in the United States.

Asylums for the Mentally Ill

Dorothea Dix led the fight for these institutions, advocating more humane treatment for the mentally incompetent.

Prison Reform

The purpose of the new penitentiaries was not to just punish, but to rehabilitate. The first was built in Auburn, New York, in 1821.

Feminism

The Seneca Falls, New York, meeting in 1848, and its "Declaration of Sentiments and Resolutions," was the beginning of the modern feminist movement. The Grimké sisters, Elizabeth Cady Stanton, and Harriet Beecher Stowe were active in these early days. The movement was linked with that of the abolitionists, but suffered because it was considered to be of secondary importance.

The Abolitionist Movement

The early antislavery movement was benign, advocating only the purchase and transportation of slaves to free states in Africa. The American Colonization Society was organized in 1817 and established the colony of Liberia in 1830, but by that time the movement had reached a dead end.

In 1831, William Lloyd Garrison started his paper *The Liberator* and began to advocate total and immediate emancipation, thus giving new life to the movement. He founded the New England Antislavery

Abolitionist Cartoon

Society in 1832 and the American Antislavery Society in 1833. Theodore Weld pursued the same goals, but advocated more gradual means.

Frederick Douglass, having escaped from his Maryland owner, became a fiery orator for the movement and published his own newspaper, the *North Star*.

There were frequent outbursts of anti-abolition violence in the 1830s against the fanaticism of the radicals. Abolitionist editor Elijah Lovejoy was killed by a mob in Illinois.

The movement split into two wings: Garrison's radical followers, and the moderates who favored "moral suasion" and petitions to Congress. In 1840, the Liberty Party, the first national antislavery party, fielded a presidential candidate on the platform of "free soil," nonexpansion of slavery into the new western territories.

The literary crusade continued with Harriet Beecher Stowe's *Uncle Tom's Cabin* being the most influential among the many books that presented the abolitionist message.

Educating the Public

This was the golden age of oratory. Speechmaking drew huge and patient crowds, and four-hour-long orations were not uncommon, especially at public events like Fourth of July celebrations.

Newspapers and magazines multiplied and were available to everyone.

More and more magazines became oriented to the interests of women. Periodicals like *Godey's Ladies Book* reached mass circulation figures.

Colleges sprang up everywhere, the products of religious sectarianism as well as local pride, which produced "booster colleges" in every new community as the population moved west. Many of these were poorly funded and managed, and thus did not survive.

Diverging Societies—Life in the North

Although the United States was a political entity, with all of the institutions of government and society shared among the peoples of the various states, there had always been a wide diversity of cultural and economic goals among the various states of the union. As the nineteenth century progressed, that diversity seemed to grow more pronounced, and the collection of states seemed to polarize more into the two sections we call the North and the South, with the expanding West becoming ever more identified with the North.

Population Growth, 1790–1860

The new West was the fastest growing area of the country, with the population tending to move along parallels westward. From four million in 1790, the population had reached 32 million in 1860 with one-half living in states and territories that did not even exist in Washington's administration.

Increase in Median Age

Birth rates began to drop after 1800 more rapidly in the cities than in the rural areas. Families who had averaged six children in 1800 only had five in 1860. Some of the reasons were economic: children were becoming liabilities rather than assets. The new "cult of domesticity" reflected a shift in family responsibilities. Father was out of the home working, and the burden of child-rearing fell more heavily on mother. Primitive birth control methods were used, and abortion was becoming common enough that several states passed laws restricting it. One result of all this was an aging population, with the median age rising from 16 to 20 years.

Immigration

The influx of immigrants had slowed during the conflicts with France and England, but the flow increased between 1815 and 1837, when the economic downturn again sharply reduced their numbers. Thus, the overall rise in population during these years was due more to incoming foreigners than to natural increase. Most of the newcomers were from Britain, Germany, and southern Ireland. The Germans usually fared best, since they brought more money and more skills. Discrimination was common in the job market, primarily directed against the Catholics. "Irish Need Not Apply" signs were common. However, the persistent labor shortage prevented the natives from totally excluding the foreign elements. These newcomers huddled in ethnic neighborhoods in the cities, or those who could moved west to try their hand at farming.

Growth of the Cities

In 1790, five percent of the U.S. population lived in cities of 2,500 or more. By 1860, that figure had risen to twenty-five percent. This rapid urbanization created an array of problems.

Problems of Urbanization

The rapid growth in urban areas was not matched by the growth of services. Clean water, trash removal, housing, and public transportation all lagged behind, and the wealthy got them first. Bad water and poor sanitation produced poor health, and epidemics of typhoid fever, typhus, and cholera were common. Police and fire protection were usually inadequate and the development of professional forces was resisted because of the cost and the potential for political patronage and corruption.

Social Unrest

Rapid growth helped to produce a wave of violence in the cities. In New York City in 1834, the Democrats fought the Whigs with such vigor that the state militia had to be called in. New York and Philadelphia witnessed race riots in the mid-1830s, and a New York mob sacked a Catholic convent in 1834. In the 1830s, 115 major incidents of mob violence were recorded. Street crime was common in all the major cities.

The Role of Women and Minorities

Women

Women were treated as minors before the law. In most states a woman's property became her husband's with marriage. Political activity was limited to the formation of associations in support of various pious causes, such as abolition, and religious and benevolent activity. Professional employment was largely limited to schoolteaching; that occupation became dominated by women. The women's rights movement focused on social and legal discrimination, and women like Lucretia Mott and Sojourner Truth became well-known figures on the speakers' circuit.

Blacks

By 1850, 200,000 free blacks lived in the North and West. Their lives were restricted everywhere by prejudice, and "Jim Crow" laws separated the races. Black citizens organized separate churches and fraternal orders. The African Methodist Episcopal Church, for example, had been organized in 1794 in Philadelphia and flourished in the major Northern cities. Black Masonic and Odd Fellows lodges were likewise established. The economic security of the free blacks was constantly threatened by the newly arrived immigrants, who were willing to work at the least desirable jobs for less wages. Racial violence was a daily threat.

The Northeast Leads the Way

The Growth of Industry

By 1850, the value of industrial output had surpassed that of agricultural production. The Northeastern states led the way in this movement. Over one-half of the manufacturing establishments and most of the larger enterprises were located there. Seventy percent of the workers who were employed in manufacturing lived in New England and the middle states, and the Northeast produced more than two-thirds of the manufactured goods.

Inventions and Technology

The level of technology used in American manufacturing already exceeded that of European industry. Eli Whitney's applications of interchangeable parts were being introduced into a wide variety of manufacturing processes. Coal was replacing water as the major source of industrial power. Machine tools were reaching a high level of sophistication. Much of this progress was due to the contributions of America's inventors. Between 1830 and 1850 the number of patents issued for industrial inventions almost doubled. Charles Goodyear's process of vulcanizing rubber was put to 500 different uses and formed the basis for an entire new industry. Elias Howe's sewing machine was to revolutionize the clothing industry. The mass production of iron, with its new techniques and uses, created a new array of businesses, of which the new railroad industry was the largest consumer. Samuel B. Morse's new electric telegraph was first used in 1840 to transmit business news and information.

The Rise of Unions

The growth of the factory system was accompanied by the growth of the corporate form of business ownership, which in turn further separated the owners from the workers. One result was the organization of worker groups to fight for benefits, an early example of which was the ten-hour workday. In 1835, Boston construction craftsmen struck for seven months to win a ten-hour workday, and Paterson, New Jersey, textile workers became the first factory workers to strike for shorter hours. The federal government's introduction of the 10-hour workday for federal projects, in 1840, helped to speed the acceptance of this goal. The influx of immigrants who were willing to work for low wages helped to spur the drive for unions, and, in turn, their numbers helped to weaken the bargaining position of union members.

The Revolution in Agriculture

Farm and industry reinforced each other and developed simultaneously. As more urban workers became dependent on food grown by others, the potential profits of farming increased. Many of the technological developments and inventions were applied to farm machinery, which in turn enabled farmers to produce more food more cheaply for the urban workers. As in industry, specialization and mechanization became the rule in agriculture, particularly on the newly opening western prairies of Illinois, Iowa, and Kansas.

Inventions and Technology

Large-scale farming on the prairies spurred critical inventions. McCormick's mechanical reaper, patented in 1834, enabled a crew of six men to harvest in one day as much wheat as fifteen men could using older methods. John Deere's steel plow, patented in 1837, provided a more durable tool to break the heavy prairie sod. Jerome Case's threshing machine multiplied the bushels of grain that could be separated from the stalk in a day's time.

The New Market Economy

These developments not only made large-scale production possible—they also shifted the major emphasis from corn to small grain production, and made farming for the international market feasible, which in turn made the Western farmer dependent on economic forces over which he had no control. This dependence produced the rising demand for government provision of free land and the agricultural colleges that later were provided by the Homestead and Morrill bills during the Civil War.

In the East, the trend was toward truck farming for the nearby burgeoning urban areas, and the production of milk, fruits, and berries. Here, as in the West, there was much interest in innovative practices that could increase production efficiency and profits.

The Revolution in Commerce

Before the coming of the railroad, coastal sailing ships practically monopolized domestic trade. The canal construction boom of the 1830s had taken commercial traffic from the river systems, but by 1840 the railroad had begun to emerge as the carrier of the future. Pennsylvania and New York State contained most of the 3,328 miles of track, but the rail system was rapidly expanding across the northern tier of states, tying the industrializing East to the expanding, agricultural West.

Everyday Life in the North

Between 1800 and 1860 output of goods and services increased twelve-fold, and the purchasing power of the average worker doubled. The household labor system was breaking down, and the number of wage-earners exceeded for the first time the number of independent, self-employed Americans. Even so, everyday living was still quite primitive. Most people bathed infrequently, and washed clothes and dishes even less. Housing was primitive for most, consisting of one- or two-room cabins heated by open fireplaces, with water carried in from springs or public faucets. For the working man, rural or urban, life was hard.

Diverging Societies—Life in the South

The Southern states experienced dramatic growth in the second quarter of the nineteenth century. The economy grew more productive and more prosperous, but still the South was basically agrarian, with few important cities and scattered industry. The plantation system, with its cash crop production driven by the use of slave labor, remained the dominant institution. In the words of one historian, "The South grew, but it did not develop." The South grew more unlike the North, and it became more defensive of its distinctive way of life.

The Cotton Kingdom

The most important economic phenomenon of the early decades of the nineteenth century was the shift in population and production from the old "upper South" of Virginia and the Carolinas to the "lower South" of the newly opened Gulf States of Alabama, Mississippi, and Louisiana. This shift was the direct result of the increasing importance of cotton. In the older Atlantic states, tobacco retained its importance, but had shifted westward to the Piedmont, and was replaced in the east by food grains. The southern Atlantic coast continued to produce rice and southern Louisiana and east Texas retained their emphasis on sugar cane. But the rich black soil of the new Gulf states proved ideal for the production of short-staple cotton, especially after the invention of the gin, and cotton became the center of the Southern economy. Nearly three million bales were being produced annually by 1850.

By 1860, cotton was to account for two-thirds of the value of U.S. exports. In the words of a Southern legislator of that era, "Cotton is King!"

Classes in the South

Although the large plantation with its white-columned mansion and its aristocratic owner is frequently seen as typical of Southern life, the truth is quite different.

The Planter Class

Owners of large farms who also owned fifty or more slaves actually formed a small minority of the Southern population. Three-fourths of Southern whites owned no slaves at all, almost half of slave-owning families owned fewer than six, and twelve percent owned twenty or more. But this minority of large slave owners exercised political and economic power far beyond what their numbers would indicate. They became a class to which all others paid deference, and they dominated the political and social life of their region.

The Yeoman Farmers

The largest group of Southern whites was the independent small farmers who worked their land with their family, sometimes side-by-side with one or two slaves, to produce their own food, with sometimes enough surplus to sell for a little extra cash. These simple folk predominated in the upland South and constituted a sizeable element even in the lower cotton-producing states. Their major crop was corn, and indeed the South's corn crop was more valuable than its cotton the corn was used at home for dinner and for animal feed. However, and so ranked behind cotton as an item of export. These people were generally poorer than their Northern counterparts.

The Poor Whites

Perhaps a half-million white Southerners lived on the edge of the agrarian economy, in varying degrees of poverty. These "crackers," or "sandhillers," occupied the barren soils of the red hills or sandy bottoms, and they lived in squalor worse than the slaves. They formed a true underclass.

The Institution of Slavery

As the necessary concomitant of this expanding plantation system, the "Peculiar Institution" of black slavery fastened itself upon the Southern people, even as it isolated them from the rest of the world.

"Inspection and Sale of a Negro" depicts an African man being inspected for sale into slavery.

Slavery as a Labor System

The utilization of slave labor varied according to the region and the size of the growing unit. The large plantations growing cotton, sugar or tobacco used the gang system, in which white overseers directed black drivers, who supervised large groups of workers in the fields, all performing the same operation. In the culture of rice, and on the smaller farms, slaves were assigned specific tasks, and when those tasks were finished, the worker had the remainder of the day to himself.

House servants usually were considered the most favored since they were spared the hardest physical labor and enjoyed the most intimate relationship with the owner's family. This could be considered a drawback, since they were frequently deprived of the social communion of the other slaves, enjoyed less privacy, and were more likely to suffer the direct wrath of a dissatisfied master or mistress.

It is still debated as to whether the living conditions of the Southern plantation slaves were better or worse than the Northern wage laborers. Certainly their lot was better than their counterparts in South America and the Caribbean.

Urban Slavery in the Southern City

A sizeable number of black slaves worked in the towns, serving as factory hands, domestics, artisans, and construction workers. They lived fairly independent lives and indeed a good number purchased their freedom with their savings, or quietly crossed the color line and disappeared into the general population. As the nineteenth century progressed, these people were increasingly seen as a bad model and a threat to the institution, and so urban slavery practically disappeared.

The Slave Trade

The most significant demographic shift in these decades was the movement of blacks from the Old South to the new Southwest. Traders shipped servants by the thousands to the newly opened cotton lands of the Gulf states. A prime field hand fetched an average price of $800, as high as $1,500 in peak years. Families were frequently split apart by this miserable traffic. Planters freely engaged in this trade, but assigned very low status to the traders who carried it out.

Although the importation of slaves from abroad had been outlawed by Congress since 1808, they continued to be smuggled in until the 1850s. The import ban kept the price up and encouraged the continuation of the internal trade.

Slaves' Reaction to Slavery

Blacks in bondage suffered varying degrees of repression and deprivation. The harsh slave codes were comprehensive in their restrictions on individual freedom, but they were unevenly applied, and so there was considerable variety in the severity of life. The typical slave probably received a rough but adequate diet and enjoyed crude but sufficient housing and clothing.

But the loss of freedom and the injustice of the system produced a variety of responses. Many "soldiered" on the job and refused to work hard, or they found ways to sabotage the machinery or the crops. There was an underground system of ridicule toward the masters that was nurtured, as reflected in such oral literature as the "Br'er Rabbit" tales.

Violent reaction to repression was not uncommon. Gabriel Prosser in Richmond (1800), Denmark Vesey in Charleston (1822), and Nat Turner in coastal Virginia (1831) all plotted or led uprisings of blacks against their white masters. Rumors of such uprisings kept whites in a state of constant apprehension.

The ultimate rebellion was to simply leave, and many tried to run away, some successfully. Especially from the states bordering the North, an ever increasing number of slaves fled to freedom, many with the aid of the "underground railroad" and smugglers such as Harriet Tubman, who led over 300 of her family and friends to freedom after she herself had escaped.

Most of those in bondage, however, were forced simply to adapt, and they did. A rich culture was developed within the confines of the system, and included distinctive patterns of language, music, and religion.

Commerce and Industry

The lack of manufacturing and business development has frequently been blamed for the South's losing its bid for independence in 1861–1865. Actually, the South was highly industrialized for its day and compared favorably with most European nations in the development of manufacturing capacity. Obviously, it trailed far behind the North, so much so that when war erupted in 1861, the Northern states owned eighty-one percent of the factory capacity in the United States.

Manufacturing

The Southern states saw considerable development in the 1820s and 1830s in textiles and iron production and in flour milling. Richmond's Tredegar Iron Works compared favorably with the best in the North. Montgomery Bell's forges in Tennessee produced a good proportion of the ironware used in the upper South. Even so, most of the goods manufactured in these plants were for plantation consumption rather than for export, and they never exceeded two percent of the value of the cotton crop.

Commercial Activity

The businessmen of the South worked primarily with the needs and products of the plantation, and the factors of New Orleans and Charleston had to serve as bankers and insurance brokers as well as the agents for the planters. An organized network of commerce never developed in the South, even though the planters themselves must be recognized as businessmen, since they operated large, complex staple-producing units.

Voices for Change

There were those who saw their native South sinking ever more into the position of dependency upon Northern bankers and businessmen, and they cried out for reform. James B.D. DeBow's *Review* advocated commercial development and agricultural diversification, but his cries fell largely on deaf ears.

Why were Southerners so wedded to the plantation system, in the face of much evidence that it was retarding development? Certainly one reason is that cotton was profitable. Over the long run, capital return on plantation agriculture was at least as good as on Northern industrial capital. Even though skilled slaves abounded and could have manned factories, they were more profitable in the field.

Since most of the planter's capital was tied up in land and slaves, there was little left to invest in commerce or manufacturing. Most important, perhaps, was the value system of the Southern people, who put great store in traditional rural ideals: chivalry, leisure, genteel elegance. Even the yeoman farmer held these values and hoped someday to attain to the position the planters held.

Life in the Southern States

The Role of Women

The position of the Southern woman was similar in many ways to her Northern counterpart, but also very different. She had fewer opportunities for anything but home life. The middle-class wife was heavily involved in the operation of the farm, and served as supervisor and nurse for the servants, as well as manager of the household, while the upper-class women served merely as ornaments. Education was rare and centered on the "domestic arts." High birth and death rates took their toll on childbearing women, and many men outlived several wives. The half-breed slave children were constant reminders of the planters' dalliances and produced constant tension and frustration among plantation wives.

Education

Schooling beyond literacy training was available only to the sons of the well-to-do. Academics and colleges abounded, but not for the working classes, and the public schools that existed were usually inferior and ill-supported. By 1860, one-half of all the illiterates in the United States lived in the South.

Daily Life in the South

The accounts of travelers in the Southern states provide us with vivid pictures of living conditions on the average homestead. Housing was primitive, one- or two-room cabins being the rule. Corn, sweet potatoes, and pork formed the staples of the Southern diet, and health problems reflected the resulting vitamin deficiencies. Rickets and pellagra were common ailments.

Although the prevalence of violence has probably been overstated, it certainly existed and the duel remained an accepted avenue for settling differences well into the nineteenth century.

Southern Response to the Antislavery Movement

As the crusade for abolition intensified in the North, the South assumed an ever more defensive position. Biblical texts were used to justify the enslavement of an "inferior race." Scientific arguments were advanced to prove the inherent inferiority of the black African. Southern postal authorities refused to deliver any mail that contained information antagonistic to the slave system. Any kind of dissent was brutally suppressed, and the South became more and more a closed society. Literature and scholarship shriveled, and creative writers like Edgar Allan Poe and William Gilmore Simms became the rare exception.

The last serious Southern debate over the institution of slavery took place in the Virginia legislature in 1832, in the aftermath of Nat Turner's revolt. That discussion squelched any move toward emancipation. In 1836 Southern members of the U.S. House of Representatives pushed through the infamous "gag rule," which forbade any discussion on the question of slavery on the floor of the House. That rule remained in effect until 1844.

The most elaborate product of this ferment was John C. Calhoun's theory of the "concurrent majority," in which a dual presidency would insure a South independent of Northern dominance, and would forever keep majority rule at bay.

Depiction of Manifest Destiny.

Beginning in 1837, regular conventions were held across the South to discuss ways to escape Northern economic and political hegemony.

As the decade of the 1840s opened, the two sections were becoming more and more estranged, and the channels of compromise were becoming more and more poisoned by the emotional responses to black slavery. The development that contributed most to keeping the sore festering was westward expansion.

Manifest Destiny and Westward Expansion

Although the term "Manifest Destiny" was not actually coined until 1844, the belief that the American nation was destined to eventually expand all the way to the Pacific Ocean, and to possibly embrace Canada to the north, and Mexico to the south, had been voiced for years by many who believed that American liberty and ideals should be shared with everyone possible, by force if necessary. The rising sense of nationalism that followed the War of 1812 was fed by the rapidly expanding population, the reform impulse of the 1830s, and the desire to acquire new markets and resources for the burgeoning economy of "Young America."

Louisiana and the Far West Fur Trade

The Lewis and Clark expedition had scarcely filed its reports before a variety of adventurous entrepreneurs began to penetrate the newly acquired territory and the lands beyond. "Mountain men" like Jim Bridges trapped the Rocky Mountain streams and the headwaters of the Missouri River system for the greatly prized beaver pelts, while explorers like Jedediah Smith mapped the vast territory that stretched from the Rockies to the Sierra Nevada range and on into California. John Jacob Astor established a fur post at the mouth of the Columbia River, which he named Astoria, and challenged the British claim to the northwest. Though he was forced to sell his establishment to the British, he lobbied Congress to pass trade restrictions against British furs, and eventually became the first American millionaire from the profits of the American Fur Company. The growing trade with the Orient in furs and other specialty goods was sharpening the desire of many businessmen for American ports on the Pacific coast.

The Oregon Country

The Adams-Onis Treaty of 1819 had set the northern boundary of Spanish possessions near the present northern border of California. The territory north of that line and west of the vague boundaries of the Louisiana Territory had been claimed over the years by Spain, England, Russia, France, and the United States. By the 1820s, all these claims had been yielded to Britain and the United States. The Hudson's Bay Company had established a fur trading station at Fort Vancouver and claimed control south to the Columbia. The United States claimed all the way north to the 54°40' parallel. Unable to settle the dispute, they had agreed on a joint occupation of the disputed land.

In the 1830s American missionaries followed the traders and trappers to the Oregon country, and began to publicize the richness and beauty of the land, sending back official reports on their work which were published in the new, inexpensive "penny press" papers. Everyone read these reports, and the result was the "Oregon Fever" of the 1840s, as thousands of settlers trekked across the Great Plains and the Rocky Mountains to settle the new Shangri-La.

The Texas Question: 1836–1845

Texas had been a state in the Republic of Mexico since 1822, following the Mexican revolution against Spanish control. The United States had offered to buy the territory at the time, since it had renounced its claim to the area in the Adams-Onis Treaty of 1819. The new Mexican government indignantly refused to sell, but immediately began to invite immigration from the north by offering land grants to Stephen Austin and other Americans. They needed to increase the population of the area and to produce revenue for the infant government. The Americans responded in great numbers, and by 1835 approximately 35,000 "gringos" were homesteading on Texas land.

The Mexican officials saw their power base eroding as the foreigners flooded in, so they moved to tighten control, through restrictions on new immigration, and through tax increases. The Texans responded in 1836 by proclaiming independence and establishing a new republic. The ensuing war was short-lived. The Mexican dictator Antonio López de Santa Anna advanced north and annihilated the Texan garrisons at the Alamo and at Goliad. On April 23, 1836, Sam Houston defeated him at San Jacinto, and the Mexicans were forced to let Texas go its way.

Houston immediately asked the American government for recognition and annexation, but President Andrew Jackson feared the revival of the slavery issue since the new state would come in on the slave-holding side of the political balance, and he also feared war with Mexico, so he did nothing. When Van Buren followed suit, the new republic sought foreign recognition and support, which the European nations eagerly provided, hoping thereby to create a counterbalance to the rising American power and influence in the Southwest. France and England both quickly concluded trade agreements with the Texans.

New Mexico and California

The district of New Mexico had, like Texas, encouraged American immigration, and for the same reasons. Soon that state was more American than Mexican. The Santa Fe Trail—from Independence, Missouri, to the town of Santa Fe—created a prosperous trade in mules, gold and silver, and furs, which moved north in exchange for manufactured goods that went south. American settlements sprung up all along the route.

Though the Mexican officials in California had not encouraged it, American immigration nevertheless had been substantial. First traders and whaling crews, then merchants, arrived to set up stores and developed a brisk trade. As the decade of the 1830s passed, the number of newcomers increased. Since the Missouri Compromise had established the northern limits for slavery at the 36° 30' parallel, most of this Mexican territory lay in the potential slave-holding domain, and many of the settlers had carried their bondsmen with them.

Manifest Destiny and Sectional Stress

The question of expansion was universally discussed. Although the strongest sentiment was found in the North and West, the South had its own ambitions, and they usually involved the extension of their "peculiar institution."

The Democrats generally favored the use of force, if necessary, to extend American borders. The Whigs favored more peaceful means, through diplomacy. Some Whigs, like Henry Clay, feared expansion under any circumstances because of its potential for aggravating the slavery issue.

Clay was closest to the truth. As the decade of the 1840s opened, the questions of Texas, California, and the New Mexican territory were increasingly prominent, and the sectional tension that they produced was destined to light the fires of civil war.

Tyler, Polk, and Continued Westward Expansion

Tyler and the Whigs

When William Henry Harrison became president, he immediately began to rely on Whig leader Henry Clay for advice and direction, just as Clay had planned and expected he would. He appointed to his Cabinet those whom Clay suggested, and at Clay's behest he called a special session of Congress to vote the Whig legislative program into action. To the Whigs' dismay, Harrison died of pneumonia just one month into his term, to be replaced by Vice President John Tyler.

A states' rights Southerner and a strict constitutionalist who had been placed on the Whig ticket to draw Southern votes, Tyler rejected the entire Whig program of a national bank, high protective tariffs, and federally funded internal improvements (roads, canals, etc.). Clay stubbornly determined to push the program through anyway. In the resulting legislative confrontations, Tyler vetoed a number of Whig-sponsored bills.

The Whigs were furious. Every Cabinet member but one resigned in protest. Tyler was officially expelled from the party and made the target of the first serious impeachment attempt. (It failed.) In opposition to Tyler over the next few years, the Whigs, under the leadership of Clay, transformed themselves from a loose grouping of diverse factions to a coherent political party with an elaborate organization.

One piece of important legislation that did get passed during Tyler's administration was the Preemption Act (1841), allowing settlers who had squatted on unsurveyed federal lands first chance to buy the land (up to 160 acres at low prices) once it was put on the market.

The Webster-Ashburton Treaty

The member of Tyler's Cabinet who did not immediately resign in protest was Secretary of State Daniel Webster. He stayed on to negotiate the Webster-Ashburton Treaty with Great Britain.

There were at this time several causes of tension between the U.S. and Great Britain:

1. The Canada-Maine boundary in the area of the Aroostook Valley was disputed. British efforts to build a military road through the disputed area led to reaction by Maine militia in a bloodless confrontation known as the "Aroostook War" (1838).

2. The Caroline Affair (1837) involved an American ship, the *Caroline*, that had been carrying supplies to Canadian rebels. It was burned by Canadian loyalists who crossed the U.S. border in order to do so.

3. In the Creole Incident, Britain declined to return escaped slaves who had taken over a U.S. merchant ship, the *Creole*, and sailed to the British-owned Bahamas.

4. British naval vessels, patrolling the African coast to suppress slave-smuggling, sometimes stopped and searched American ships.

The Webster-Ashburton Treaty (1842) dealt with these problems in a spirit of mutual concession and forbearance:

1. Conflicting claims along the Canada-Maine boundary were compromised.

2. The British expressed regret for the destruction of the *Caroline*.

3. The British promised to avoid "officious interference" in freeing slaves in cases such as that of the *Creole*.

4. Both countries agreed to cooperate in patrolling the African coast to prevent slave-smuggling.

The Webster-Ashburton Treaty was also important in that it helped create an atmosphere of compromise and forbearance in U.S.-British relations.

After negotiating the treaty, Webster too resigned from Tyler's Cabinet.

The Texas Issue

Rejected by the Whigs and without ties to the Democrats, Tyler was a politician without a party but not without ambitions. Hoping to gather a political following of his own, he sought an issue with powerful appeal and believed he had found it in the question of Texas annexation.

The Republic of Texas had gained its independence from Mexico in 1836 and, since most of its settlers had come from the U.S., immediately sought admission as a state. It was rejected because antislavery forces in Congress resented the presence of slavery in Texas and because Mexico threatened war should the U.S. annex Texas.

To excite American jealousy and thus hasten annexation, Texas President Sam Houston made much show of negotiating for closer relations with Great Britain. Southerners feared that Britain, which opposed slavery, might bring about its abolition in Texas and then use Texas as a base from which to undermine slavery in the American South. Other Americans were disturbed at the possibility of a British presence in Texas because of the obstacle it would present to what many Americans were coming to believe—and what New York journalist John L. O'Sullivan would soon express—as America's "manifest destiny to overspread the continent."

Tyler's new secretary of state, John C. Calhoun, negotiated an annexation treaty with Texas. Calhoun's identification with extreme proslavery forces and his insertion in the treaty of proslavery statements brought the treaty's rejection by the Senate (1844). Nevertheless, the Texas issue had been injected into national politics and could not be made to go away.

The Election of 1844

Democratic front-runner Martin Van Buren and Whig front-runner Henry Clay agreed privately that neither would endorse Texas annexation and that it would not become a campaign issue, but expansionists at the Democratic convention succeeded in dumping Van Buren in favor of James K. Polk. Polk, called "Young Hickory" by his supporters, was a staunch Jacksonian who opposed protective tariffs and a national bank but, most important, favored territorial expansion, including not only annexation of Texas but also occupation of all the Oregon country (up to latitude 54° 40') hitherto jointly occupied by the U.S. and Britain. The latter claim was expressed in his campaign slogan, "Fifty-four forty or fight."

Tyler, despite his introduction of the issue that was to decide that year's presidential campaign, was unable to build a party of his own and withdrew from the race.

The Whigs nominated Clay, who continued to oppose Texas annexation but, sensing the mood of the country was against him, began to equivocate. His wavering cost him votes among those Northerners who were extremely sensitive to the issue of slavery and believed that the settlement, independence, and proposed annexation of Texas was a gigantic plot to add slave states to the Union. Some of these voters shifted to the Liberty Party.

The antislavery Liberty Party nominated James G. Birney. Apparently because of Clay's wavering on the Texas issue, Birney was able to take enough votes away from Clay in New York to give that state, and thus the election, to Polk.

Tyler, as a lame-duck president, made one more attempt to achieve Texas annexation before leaving office. By means of a joint resolution, which unlike a treaty required only a simple majority rather than a two-thirds vote, he was successful in getting the measure through Congress. Texas was finally admitted to the Union (1845).

Polk as President

Though a relatively unknown "dark horse" at the time of his nomination for the presidency, Polk had considerable political experience within his home state of Tennessee and was an adept politician. He turned out to be a skillful and effective president.

As a good Jacksonian, Polk favored a low, revenue-only tariff rather than a high, protective tariff. This he obtained in the Walker Tariff (1846). He also opposed a national debt and a national bank and re-established Van Buren's Independent Sub-Treasury system, which then remained in effect until 1920.

The Settlement of Oregon

A major issue in the election campaign of 1844, Oregon at this time comprised all the land bounded on the east by the Rockies, the west by the Pacific, the south by latitude 42°, and the north by the boundary of Russian-held Alaska at 54° 40'. Oregon had been visited by Lewis and Clark and in later years by American fur traders and especially missionaries such as Jason Lee and Marcus Whitman. Their reports sparked interest in Oregon's favorable soil and climate. During the first half of the 1840s, some 6,000 Americans had taken the 2,000-mile, six-month journey on the Oregon Trail, from Independence, Missouri, across the plains along the Platte River, through the Rockies at South Pass, and down the Snake River to their new homesteads. Most of them settled in the Willamette Valley, south of the Columbia River.

The area had been under the joint occupation of the U.S. and Great Britain since 1818, but Democrats in the election of 1844 had called for U.S. ownership of all of Oregon. Though this stand had helped him win the election, Polk had little desire to fight the British for land he considered unsuitable for agriculture and unavailable for slavery, which he favored. This was all the more so since trouble seemed to be brewing with Mexico over territory Polk considered far more desirable.

The British, for their part, hoped to obtain the area north of the Columbia River, including the natural harbor of Puget Sound (one of only three on the Pacific coast), with its adjoining Strait of Juan de Fuca.

By the terms of the Oregon Treaty (1846), a compromise solution was reached. The existing U.S.-Canada boundary east of the Rockies (49°) was extended westward to the Pacific, thus securing Puget Sound and shared use of the Strait of Juan de Fuca for the U.S. Some northern Democrats were angered and felt betrayed by Polk's failure to insist on all of Oregon, but the Senate readily accepted the treaty.

The Mormon Migration

Aside from the thousands of Americans who streamed west on the Oregon Trail during the early 1840s, and the smaller number who migrated to what was then Mexican-held California, another large group of Americans moved west to a different destination and for different reasons. These were the Mormons.

Mormonism is a unique religion founded in 1832 by Joseph Smith at Palmyra, New York. Mormons were often in trouble with their neighbors and had been forced to migrate to Kirtland, Ohio, then Clay County,

Missouri and finally, Nauvoo, Illinois. There, on the banks of the Mississippi River, they built the largest city in the state, had their own militia, and were a political force to be reckoned with.

In 1844 Mormon dissidents published a newspaper critical of church leader Smith and his newly announced doctrine of polygamy. Smith had their printing press destroyed. Arrested by Illinois authorities, Smith and his brother were confined to a jail in Carthage, Illinois, but were later killed by a crowd of hostile non-Mormons who forced their way into the jail.

The Mormons then decided to migrate to the Far West, preferably someplace outside U.S. jurisdiction. Their decision to leave was hastened by pressure from their non-Mormon neighbors, among whom anti-Mormon feelings ran high as a response to polygamy and the Mormons' monolithic social and political structure.

Under the leadership of their new church leader Brigham Young, some 85,000 Mormons trekked overland in 1846 to settle in the valley of the Great Salt Lake in what is now Utah (but was then owned by Mexico). Young founded the Mormon republic of Deseret and openly preached (and practiced) polygamy.

After Deseret's annexation by the U.S. as part of the Mexican Cession, Young was made territorial governor of Utah. Nevertheless, friction developed with the federal government. By 1857 public outrage over polygamy prompted then-President James Buchanan to replace Young with a non-Mormon governor. Threats of Mormon defiance led Buchanan to send 2,500 army troops to compel Mormon obedience to federal law. Young responded by calling out the Mormon militia and blocking the passes through which the army would have to advance. This standoff, known as the "Mormon War," was resolved in 1858, with the Mormons accepting the new governor and Buchanan issuing a general pardon.

The Coming of War with Mexico

For some time American interest had been growing in the far western lands then held by Mexico:

1. Since the 1820s, Americans had been trading with Santa Fe and other Mexican settlements along the Rio Grande by means of the Santa Fe Trail. Though not extensive enough to be of economic importance, the trade aroused further American interest in the area.

2. Also, since the 1820s, American "mountain men," trappers who sought beaver pelts in the streams of the Rockies, had explored the mountains of the Far West, opening new trails and discovering fertile lands. They later served as guides for settlers moving west.

3. At the same time, whaling ships and other American vessels had carried on a thriving trade with the Mexican settlements on the coast of California.

4. Beginning in 1841, American settlers came overland to California by means of the California Trail, a branch from the Oregon Trail that turned southwest in the Rockies and crossed Nevada along the Humboldt River. By 1846, several hundred Americans lived in California.

The steady flow of American pioneers into Mexican-held areas of the Far West led to conflicting territorial desires and was thus an underlying cause of the Mexican War. Several more immediate causes existed:

1. Mexico's ineffective government was unable to protect the lives and property of American citizens in Mexico during the country's frequent and recurring revolutions, and repeatedly declined to pay American claims for damages even when such claims were supported by the findings of mutually agreed upon arbitration.

2. Mexico had not reconciled itself to the loss of Texas and considered its annexation by the U.S. a hostile act.

3. The southern boundary of Texas was disputed. First the independent Republic of Texas and now the U.S. claimed the Rio Grande as the boundary; however, Mexico claimed the Nueces River, 130 miles farther north, because it had been the boundary of the province of Texas when it had been part of Mexico.

4. Mexican suspicions had been aroused regarding U.S. designs on California when, in 1842, a U.S. naval force under Commodore Thomas Catsby Jones had seized the province in the mistaken belief that war had broken out between the U.S. and Mexico. When the mistake was discovered, the province was returned and apologies made.

5. Mexican politicians had so inflamed the Mexican people against the U.S. that no Mexican leader could afford to take the risk of appearing to make concessions to the U.S. for fear of being overthrown.

Though Mexico broke diplomatic relations with the U.S. immediately upon Texas' admission to the Union, there still seemed to be some hope of a peaceful settlement. In the fall of 1845, Polk sent John Slidell to Mexico City with a proposal for a peaceful settlement of the differences between the two countries. Slidell was empowered to cancel the damage claims and pay $5,000,000 for the disputed land in southern Texas. He was also authorized to offer $25,000,000 for California and $5,000,000 for other Mexican territory in the Far West. Polk was especially eager to obtain California because he feared the British would snatch it from Mexico's extremely weak grasp.

Nothing came of these attempts at negotiation. Racked by coup and countercoup, the Mexican government refused even to receive Slidell.

Polk thereupon sent U.S. troops into the disputed territory in southern Texas. A force under General Zachary Taylor (who was nicknamed "Old Rough and Ready") took up a position just north of the Rio Grande. Eight days later, on April 5, 1846, Mexican troops attacked an American patrol. When news of the clash reached Washington, Polk sought and received from Congress a declaration of war against Mexico, on May 13, 1846.

The Mexican War

Americans were sharply divided about the war. Some favored it because they felt Mexico had provoked the war or because they felt it was the destiny of America to spread the blessings of freedom to oppressed peoples. Others opposed the war. Some, primarily Polk's po-

The Mexican War

litical enemies the Whigs, accused the president of having provoked it. Others, generally Northern abolitionists, saw in the war the work of a vast conspiracy of Southern slaveholders greedy for more slave territory.

In planning military strategy, Polk showed genuine skill. American strategy consisted originally of a three-pronged attack, consisting of a land movement westward through New Mexico into California, a sea movement against California, and a land movement southward into Mexico.

The first prong of this three-pronged strategy, the advance through New Mexico and into California, was led by Colonel Stephen W. Kearny. Kearny's force easily secured New Mexico, entering Santa Fe on August 16, 1846, before continuing west to California. There American settlers, aided by an army exploring party under John C. Fremont, had already revolted against Mexico's weak rule in what was called the Bear Flag Revolt.

As part of the second prong of U.S. strategy, naval forces under Commodore John D. Sloat had seized Monterey and declared California to be part of the United States. Forces put ashore by Commodore Robert Stockton joined with Kearny's troops to defeat the Mexicans at the Battle of San Gabriel in January 1847 and complete the conquest of California.

The third prong of the American strategy, an advance southward into Mexico, was itself divided into two parties:

1. Troops under Colonel Alexander W. Doniphan defeated Mexicans at El Brazito (December 25–28, 1846) to take El Paso, and then proceeded southward, winning the Battle of Sacramento (February 28, 1847) to take the city of Chihuahua, the capital of the Mexican province of that name.

2. The main southward thrust, however, was made by a much larger American army under General Zachary Taylor. After badly defeating larger Mexican forces at the battles of Palo Alto (May 7, 1846) and Resaca de la Palma (May 8, 1846), Taylor advanced into Mexico and defeated an even larger Mexican force at the Battle of Monterey (September 20–24, 1846). Then, after substantial numbers of his troops had been transferred to other sectors of the war, he successfully withstood, though badly outnumbered, an attack by a Mexican force under Antonia Lopez de Santa Anna at the Battle of Buena Vista, February 22–23, 1847.

Despite the success of all three parts of the American strategy, the Mexicans refused to negotiate. Polk, therefore, ordered U.S. forces under General Winfield Scott to land on the east coast of Mexico, march inland, and take Mexico City.

Scott landed at Veracruz on March 9, 1847, and by March 27 had captured the city with the loss of only twenty American lives. He advanced from there, being careful to maintain good discipline and avoid atrocities in the countryside. At Cerro Cord (April 18, 1847), in what has been called "the most important single battle of the war," Scott outflanked and soundly defeated a superior enemy force in a seemingly impregnable position. After beating another Mexican army at Churubusco (August 19–20, 1847), Scott paused outside Mexico City to offer the Mexicans another chance to negotiate. When they declined, U.S. forces stormed the fortress of Chapultepec (September 13, 1847) and the next day entered Mexico City. Still Mexico refused to negotiate a peace and instead carried on guerilla warfare.

Negotiated peace finally came about when the State Department clerk Nicholas Trist, though his authority had been revoked and he had been ordered back to Washington two months earlier, negotiated and signed the Treaty of Guadalupe-Hidalgo (February 2, 1848), ending the Mexican War. Under the terms of the treaty Mexico ceded to the U.S. the territory Polk had originally sought to buy, this time in exchange for a payment of $15,000,000 and the assumption of $3,250,000 in American citizens' claims against the Mexican government. This territory, the Mexican Cession, included the natural harbors at San Francisco and San Diego, thus giving the U.S. all three of the major west coast natural harbors.

Despite the appropriation of vast territories, many, including Polk, felt the treaty was far too generous. There had been talk of annexing all of Mexico or of forcing Mexico to pay an indemnity for the cost of the war. Still, Polk felt compelled to accept the treaty as it was, and the Senate subsequently ratified it.

On the home front many Americans supported the war enthusiastically and flocked to volunteer. Some criticized the war, among them Henry David Thoreau, who, to display his protest, went to live at Walden Pond and refused to pay his taxes. Jailed for this, he wrote "Civil Disobedience."

Although the Mexican War increased the nation's territory by one-third, it also brought to the surface serious political issues that threatened to divide the country, particularly the question of slavery in the new territories.

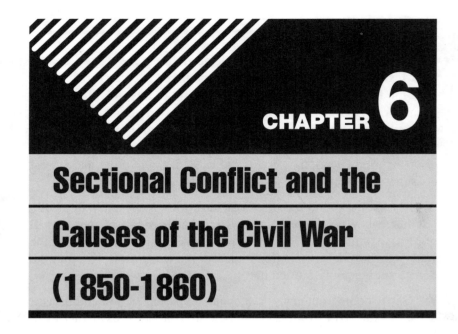

CHAPTER 6

Sectional Conflict and the Causes of the Civil War (1850-1860)

The Crisis of 1850 and America at Mid-Century

The Wilmot Proviso

The Mexican War had no sooner started when, on August 8, 1846, freshman Democratic Congressman David Wilmot of Pennsylvania introduced his Wilmot Proviso as a proposed amendment to a war appropriations bill. It stipulated that "neither slavery nor involuntary servitude shall ever exist" in any territory to be acquired from Mexico. It was passed by the House, and though rejected by the Senate, it was reintroduced again and again amid increasingly acrimonious debate.

The Wilmot Proviso aroused intense sectional feelings. Southerners, who had supported the war enthusiastically, felt they were being treated unfairly. Northerners, some of whom had been inclined to see the war as a slaveholders' plot to extend slavery, felt they saw their worst suspicions confirmed by the Southerners' furious opposition to the Wilmot Proviso. There came to be four views regarding the status of slavery in the newly acquired territories.

The Southern position was expressed by John C. Calhoun, now serving as senator from South Carolina. He argued that the territories were the property not of the U.S. federal government, but of all the states together, and therefore Congress had no right to prohibit in any territory any type of "property" (by which he meant slaves) that was legal in any of the states.

Antislavery Northerners, pointing to the Northwest Ordinance of 1787 and the Missouri Compromise of 1820 as precedents, argued that Congress had the right to make what laws it saw fit for the territories, including, if it so chose, laws prohibiting slavery.

A compromise proposal favored by President Polk and many moderate Southerners called for the extension of the 36° 30' line of the Missouri Compromise westward through the Mexican Cession to the Pacific, with territory north of the line to be closed to slavery and territory south of it open to slavery.

Another compromise solution, favored by Northern Democrats such as Lewis Cass of Michigan and Stephen A. Douglas of Illinois, was known as "squatter sovereignty" and later as "popular sovereignty." It held that the residents of each territory should be permitted to decide for themselves whether or not to allow slavery, but it was vague as to when they might exercise that right.

The Election of 1848

Both parties sought to avoid as much as possible the hot issue of slavery in the territories as they prepared for the 1848 election campaign.

The Democrats nominated Lewis Cass, and their platform endorsed his middle-of-the-road popular sovereignty position with regard to slavery in the territories.

The Whigs dodged the issue even more effectively by nominating General Zachary Taylor, whose fame in the Mexican War made him a strong candidate. Taylor knew nothing of the current political issues, had never voted, and liked to think of himself as above politics. He took no position at all with respect to slavery in the territories.

Some anti slavery Northern Whigs and Democrats, disgusted with their parties' failure to take a clear stand against the spread of slavery, deserted the party ranks to form another antislavery third party. They were known as "Conscience" Whigs (because they voted their conscience) and "Barnburner" Democrats (because they were willing to burn down the whole Democratic "barn" to get rid of the pro slavery "rats"). Their party was called the Free Soil Party, since it stood for keeping the soil of new western territories free of slavery. Its candidate was Martin Van Buren.

The election excited relatively little public interest. Taylor won a narrow victory, apparently because Van Buren took enough votes from Cass in New York and Pennsylvania to throw those states into Taylor's column.

Gold in California

The question of slavery's status in the Western territories was made more immediate when, on January 24, 1848, gold was discovered at Sutter's Mill, not far from Sacramento, California. The next year gold-seekers from the eastern U.S. and from many foreign countries swelled California's population from 14,000 to 100,000.

Once in the gold fields, these "forty-niners" proved to contain some rough characters, and that fact, along with the presence, or at least the expectation, of quick and easy riches, made California a wild and lawless place. No territorial government had been organized since the U.S. had received the land as part of the Mexican Cession, and all that existed was an inadequate military government. In September 1849, having more than the requisite population and being much in need of better government, California petitioned for admission to the Union as a state.

Since few slaveholders had chosen to risk their valuable investments in human property in the turbulent atmosphere of California, the people of the area not surprisingly sought admission as a free state, touching off a serious sectional crisis back east.

Zachary Taylor

The Compromise of 1850

President Zachary Taylor, though himself a Louisiana slaveholder, opposed the further spread of slavery. Hoping to sidestep the dangerously divisive issue of slavery in the territories, he encouraged California, as well as the rest of the Mexican Cession, to organize and seek admission directly as states, thus completely bypassing the territorial stage.

Southerners were furious. They saw the admission of California as a free state as a backdoor implementation of the hated Wilmot Proviso they had fought so hard to turn back in Congress. They were also growing increasingly alarmed at what was becoming the minority status of their section within the country. Long outnumbered in the House of Representatives, the South would now find itself, should California be admitted as a free state, also outvoted in the Senate.

Other matters created friction between the North and South. A large tract of land was disputed between Texas, a slave state, and the as-yet-unorganized New Mexico Territory, where slavery's future was at best uncertain. Southerners were angered by the small-scale but much-talked-of efforts of Northern abolitionists' "underground railroad" to aid escaped slaves in reaching permanent freedom in Canada. Northerners were disgusted by the presence of slave pens and slave markets in the nation's capital. Radical southerners talked of secession and scheduled an all-Southern convention to meet in Nashville in June 1850 to propose ways of protecting Southern interests, inside or outside the Union.

At this point, the aged Henry Clay attempted to compromise the various matters of contention between the North and South. He proposed an eight-part package deal that he hoped would appeal to both sides.

For the North, the package contained these aspects: California would be admitted as a free state; the land in dispute between Texas and New Mexico would go to New Mexico; New Mexico and Utah Territories (all of the Mexican Cession outside of California) would not be specifically reserved for slavery, but its status there would be decided by popular sovereignty; and, slave trade would be abolished in the District of Columbia.

For the South, the package offered the following: A tougher Fugitive Slave Law would be enacted; the federal government would pay Texas' $10,000,000 pre-annexation debt; Congress would declare that it did not have jurisdiction over the interstate slave trade; and Congress would promise not to abolish slavery itself in the District of Columbia.

What followed the introduction of Clay's compromise proposal was eight months of heated debate, during which Clay, Calhoun, and Daniel Webster, the three great figures of Congress during the first half of the nineteenth century—all three aged and none of them with more than two years to live—made some of their greatest speeches. Clay called for compromise and "mutual forbearance." Calhoun gravely warned that the only way to save the Union was for the North to grant all the South's demands and keep quiet on the issue of slavery. Webster abandoned his previous opposition to the spread of slavery (as well as most of his popularity back in his home state of Massachusetts) to support the Compromise in an eloquent speech.

The opponents of the Compromise were many and powerful and ranged from President Taylor, who demanded admission of California without reference to slavery, to Northern extremists such as Senator

William Seward of New York, who spoke of a "higher law" than the Constitution, forbidding the spread of slavery, to Southern extremists such as Calhoun or Senator Jefferson Davis of Mississippi. By mid-summer all seemed lost for the Compromise, and Clay left Washington exhausted and discouraged.

Then the situation changed dramatically. President Taylor died (apparently of gastroenteritis) on July 9, 1850, and was succeeded by Vice President Millard Fillmore, a quiet but efficient politician and a strong supporter of compromise. In Congress the fight for the Compromise was taken up by Senator Stephen A. Douglas of Illinois. Called the "Little Giant" for his small stature and large political skills, Douglas broke Clay's proposal into its component parts so that he could use varying coalitions to push each part through Congress. This method proved successful, and the Compromise was adopted.

The Compromise of 1850 was received with joy by most of the nation. Sectional harmony returned, for the most part, and the issue of slavery in the territories seemed to have been permanently settled. That this was an illusion became apparent within a few years.

The Election of 1852

The 1852 Democratic convention was deadlocked between Cass and Douglas and so instead settled on dark horse Franklin Pierce of New Hampshire. The Whigs, true to form, chose General Winfield Scott, a war hero with no political background.

The result was an easy victory for Pierce, largely because the Whig Party, badly divided along North-South lines as a result of the battle over the Compromise of 1850, was beginning to come apart. The Free Soil Party's candidate, John P. Hale of New Hampshire, fared poorly, demonstrating the electorate's weariness with the slavery issue.

Pierce and "Young America"

Americans eagerly turned their attention to railroads, cotton, clipper ships, and commerce. The world seemed to be opening up to American trade and influence.

President Pierce expressed the nation's hope that a new era of sectional peace was beginning. To assure this, he sought to distract the nation's attention from the slavery issue to an aggressive program of foreign economic and territorial expansion known as "Young America."

In 1853 Commodore Matthew Perry led a U.S. naval force into Tokyo Bay on a mission to open Japan—previously closed to the outside world—to American diplomacy and commerce.

By means of the Reciprocity Treaty (1854), Pierce succeeded in opening Canada to greater U.S. trade. He also sought to annex Hawaii, increase U.S. interest in Central America, and acquire territories from Mexico and Spain.

From Mexico he acquired in 1853 the Gadsden Purchase, a strip of land in what is now southern New Mexico and Arizona along the Gila River. The purpose of this purchase was to provide a good route for a transcontinental railroad across the southern part of the country.

Pierce sought to buy Cuba from Spain. When Spain declined, three of Pierce's diplomats, meeting in Ostend, Belgium, sent him the Ostend Manifesto urging military seizure of Cuba should Spain remain intransigent.

Pierce was the first "doughface" president—"a northern man with southern principles"—and his expansionist goals, situated as they were in the South, aroused suspicion and hostility in antislavery northerners. Pierce's administration appeared to be dominated by southerners, such as Secretary of War Jefferson Davis, and whether in seeking a southern route for a transcontinental railroad or seeking to annex potential slave territory such as Cuba, it seemed to be working for the good of the South.

Economic Growth

The chief factor in the economic transformation of America during the 1840s and 1850s was the dynamic rise of the railroads. In 1840 America had less than 3,000 miles of railroad track. By 1860 that number had risen to over 30,000 miles. Railroads pioneered big-business techniques, and by improving transportation, helped create a nationwide market. They also helped link the Midwest to the Northeast rather than the South, as would have been the case had only water transportation been available.

Water transportation during the 1850s saw the heyday of the steamboat on inland rivers and the clipper ship on the high seas. The period also saw rapid and sustained industrial growth. The factory system began in the textile industry, where Elias Howe's invention of the sewing machine (1846) and Isaac Singer's improved model (1851) aided the process of mechanization, and spread to other industries.

Agriculture varied according to region. In the South, large plantations and small farms existed side by side for the most part, and both prospered enormously during the 1850s from the production of cotton. Southern leaders referred to the fiber as "King Cotton," an economic power that no one would dare fight against.

In the North the main centers of agricultural production shifted from the Middle Atlantic states to the more fertile lands of the Midwest. The main unit of agriculture was the family farm, and the main products were grain and livestock. Unlike the South, where 3,500,000 slaves provided abundant labor, the North faced incentives to introduce labor-saving machines. Cyrus McCormick's mechanical reaper came into wide use, and by 1860 over 100,000 were in operation on Midwestern farms. Mechanical threshers also came into increasing use.

Decline of the Two-Party System

Meanwhile, ominous developments were taking place in politics. America's second two-party system, which had developed during the 1830s, was in the process of breaking down. The Whig Party, whose dismal performance in the election of 1852 had signaled its weakness, was now in the process of complete disintegration. Partially this was the result of the issue of slavery, which tended to divide the party along North-South lines. Partially, though, it may have been the result of the nativist movement.

The nativist movement and its political party, the American, or, as it was called, the Know-Nothing Party, grew out of alarm on the part of native-born Americans at the rising tide of German and Irish immigration during the late 1840s and early 1850s. The Know-Nothing Party, so called because its members were told to answer "I know nothing" when asked about its secret proceedings, was anti-foreign and, since many of the foreigners were Catholic, also anti-Catholic. It surged briefly to become the country's second-largest party by 1855 but faded even more quickly due to the ineptness of its leaders and the growing urgency of the slavery question, which, though ignored by the Know-Nothing Party, was rapidly coming to overshadow all other issues. To some extent the Know-Nothing movement may simply have benefitted from the already progressing disintegration of the Whig Party, but it may also have helped to complete that disintegration.

All of this was ominous because the collapse of a viable nationwide two-party system made it much more difficult for the nation's political process to contain the explosive issue of slavery.

The Return of Sectional Conflict

Continuing Sources of Tension

While Americans hailed the apparent sectional harmony created by the Compromise of 1850 and enjoyed the rapid economic growth of the decade that followed, two items that continued to create tension centered on the issue of slavery.

The Strengthened Fugitive Slave Law

The more important of these was a part of the Compromise itself, the strengthened federal Fugitive Slave Law. The law enraged Northerners, many of whom believed it was little better than a legalization of kidnapping. Under its provisions, blacks living in the North and claimed by slave catchers were denied trial by jury and many of the other protections of due process. Even more distasteful to antislavery Northerners was the provision that required all U.S. citizens to aid, when called upon, in the capture and return of alleged fugitives. So violent was Northern feeling against the law that several riots erupted as a result of attempts to enforce it. Some Northern states passed personal liberty laws in an attempt to prevent the working of the Fugitive Slave Law.

The effect of all this was to polarize the country even further. Many Northerners who had not previously taken an interest in the slavery issue now became opponents of slavery as a result of having its injustices forcibly brought home to them by the Fugitive Slave Law. Southerners saw in Northern resistance to the law further proof that the North was determined to tamper with the institution of slavery.

Uncle Tom's Cabin

One Northerner who was outraged by the Fugitive Slave Act was Harriet Beecher Stowe. In response, she wrote *Uncle Tom's Cabin*, a fictional book depicting what she perceived as the evils of slavery. Furiously denounced in the South, the book became an overnight bestseller in the North, where it turned many toward active opposition to slavery. This, too, was a note of harsh discord among the seemingly harmonious sectional relations of the early 1850s.

The Kansas-Nebraska Act

All illusion of sectional peace ended abruptly when in 1854 Senator Stephen A. Douglas of Illinois introduced a bill in Congress to organize the area west of Missouri and Iowa as the territories of Kansas and Nebraska. Douglas, who apparently had no moral convictions on slavery one way or the other, hoped organizing the territories would facilitate the building of a transcontinental railroad on a central route, something that would benefit him and his Illinois constituents.

Though he sought to avoid directly addressing the touchy issue of slavery, Douglas was compelled by pressure from Southern senators such as David Atchison of Missouri to include in the bill an explicit repeal of the Missouri Compromise (which banned slavery in the areas in question) and a provision that the status of slavery in the newly organized territories would be decided by popular sovereignty.

The bill was opposed by most Northern Democrats and a majority of the remaining Whigs, but with the support of the Southern-dominated Pierce administration, it was passed and signed into law.

The Republican Party

The Kansas-Nebraska Act aroused a storm of outrage in the North, where the repeal of the Missouri Compromise was seen as the breaking of a solemn agreement. It hastened the disintegration of the Whig Party and divided the Democratic Party along North-South lines.

In the North, many Democrats left the party and were joined by former Whigs and Know-Nothings in the newly created Republican Party. Springing to life almost overnight as a result of Northern fury at the Kansas-Nebraska Act, the Republican party included diverse elements whose sole unifying principle was the firm belief that slavery should be banned from all the nation's territories, confined to the states where it already existed, and allowed to spread no further.

Though its popularity was confined almost entirely to the North, the Republican Party quickly became a major power in national politics.

Bleeding Kansas

With the status of Kansas (Nebraska was never in much doubt) to be decided by the voters there, the North and South began competing to see which could send the greatest number. Northerners formed the New England Emigrant Aid Company to promote the settling of anti-slavery men in Kansas, and Southerners responded in kind. Despite these efforts, the majority of Kansas settlers were Midwesterners who were generally opposed to the spread of slavery but were more concerned with finding good farm land than deciding the national debate over slavery in the territories.

Despite this large antislavery majority, large-scale election fraud, especially on the part of heavily armed Missouri "border ruffians" who crossed into Kansas on election day to vote their proslavery principles early and often, led to the creation of a virulently proslavery territorial government. When the presidentially appointed territorial governor protested this gross fraud, Pierce removed him from office.

Free-soil Kansans responded by denouncing the proslavery government as illegitimate and forming their own free-soil government in an election that the proslavery faction boycotted. Kansas now had two rival governments, each claiming to be the only lawful one.

Both sides began arming themselves and soon the territory was being referred to in the Northern press as "Bleeding Kansas" as full-scale guerilla war erupted. In May 1856, Missouri border ruffians sacked the free-soil town of Lawrence, killing two, and destroying homes, businesses, and printing presses. Two days later a small band of antislavery zealots under the leadership of fanatical abolitionist John Brown retaliated by killing and mutilating five unarmed men and boys at a proslavery settlement on Pottawatomie Creek. In all, some 200 died in the months of guerilla fighting that followed.

Meanwhile, violence had spread even to Congress itself. In the same month as the Sack of Lawrence and the Pottawatomie Massacre, Senator Charles Sumner of Massachusetts made a two-day speech entitled "The Crime Against Kansas," in which he not only denounced slavery but also made degrading personal references to aged South Carolina Senator Andrew Butler. Two days later Butler's nephew, Congressman Preston Brooks, also of South Carolina, entered the Senate chamber and, coming on Sumner from behind, beat him about the head and shoulders with a cane, leaving him bloody and unconscious.

Once again the North was outraged, while in the South, Brooks was hailed as a hero. New canes were sent to him to replace the one he had broken over Sumner's head. Denounced by Northerners, he resigned his seat and was overwhelmingly re-elected. Northerners were further incensed and bought thousands of copies of Sumner's inflammatory speech.

The Election of 1856

The election of 1856 was a three-way contest that pitted Democrats, Know-Nothings, and Republicans against each other.

The Democrats dropped Pierce and passed over Douglas to nominate James Buchanan of Pennsylvania. Though a veteran of forty years of politics, Buchanan was a weak and vacillating man whose chief qualification for the nomination was that during the slavery squabbles of the past few years he had been out of the country as American minister to Great Britain and therefore had not been forced to take public positions on the controversial issues.

The Know-Nothings, including the remnants of the Whigs, nominated Millard Fillmore. However, choice of a Southerner for the nomination of vice president so alienated Northern Know-Nothings that many shifted their support to the Republican candidate.

The Republicans nominated John C. Frémont of California. A former officer in the army's Corps of Topographical Engineers, Frémont was known as "the Pathfinder" for his explorations in the Rockies and the Far West. The Republican platform called for high tariffs, free Western homesteads (160 acres) for settlers, and, most important, no further spread of slavery. Their slogan was "Free Soil, Free Men, and Frémont." Southerners denounced the Republican Party as an abolitionist organization and threatened secession should it win the election.

Against divided opposition Buchanan won with apparent ease. However, his victory was largely based on the support of the South, since Frémont carried most of the Northern states. Had the Republicans won Pennsylvania and either Illinois or Indiana, Frémont would have been elected. In the election the Republicans demonstrated surprising strength for a political party only two years old and made clear that they, and not the Know-Nothings, would replace the moribund Whigs as the other major party along with the Democrats.

The Dred Scott Case

Meanwhile, there had been, rising through the court system, a case that would give the Supreme Court a chance to state its opinion on the question of slavery in the territories. The case was *Dred Scott v. Sanford*, which involved a Missouri slave, Dred Scott, who had been encouraged by abolitionists to sue for his freedom on the basis that his owner, an Army doctor, had taken him for a stay of several years in a free state, Illinois, and then in a free territory, Wisconsin. By 1856 the case had made its way to the Supreme Court, and by March of the following year, the court was ready to render its decision.

Press coverage of Dred Scott Case.

The justices were at first inclined to rule simply that Scott, as a slave, was not a citizen and could not sue in court. Buchanan, however, shortly before his inauguration, urged the justices to go farther and attempt to settle the whole slavery issue once and for all, thus removing it from the realm of politics where it might prove embarrassing to the president.

The court obliged. Under the domination of aging pro-Southern Chief Justice Roger B. Taney of Maryland, it attempted to read the extreme Southern position on slavery into the Constitution, ruling not only that Scott had no standing to sue in federal court, but also that temporary residence in a free state, even for several years, did not make a slave free, and that the Missouri Compromise (already a dead letter by that time) had been unconstitutional all along because Congress did not have the authority to exclude slavery from any territory whatsoever. Nor did territorial governments, which were considered to receive their power from Congress, have the right to prohibit slavery.

Far from settling the sectional controversy, the *Dred Scott* case only made it worse. Southerners were encouraged to take an extreme position and refuse compromise, while antislavery Northerners became more convinced than ever that there was a proslavery conspiracy controlling all branches of government, and expressed an unwillingness to accept the court's dictate as final.

Buchanan and Kansas

Later in 1857 the proslavery government in Kansas, through largely fraudulent means, arranged for a heavily proslavery constitutional convention to meet at the town of Lecompton. The result was a state constitution that allowed slavery. To obtain a pretense of popular approval for this constitution, the convention provided for a referendum in which the voters were to be given a choice only to prohibit the entry of additional slaves into the state.

Disgusted free-soilers boycotted the referendum, and the result was a constitution that put no restrictions at all on slavery. Touting this Lecompton constitution, the proslavery territorial government petitioned Congress for admission to the Union as a slave state. Meanwhile, the free-soilers drafted a constitution of their own and submitted it to Congress as the legitimate one for the prospective state of Kansas.

Eager to appease the South, which had started talking of secession again, and equally eager to suppress antislavery agitation in the North, Buchanan vigorously backed the Lecompton constitution. Douglas, appalled at this travesty of popular sovereignty, broke with the administration to oppose it. He and Buchanan became bitter political enemies, with the president determined to use all the power of the Democratic organization to crush Douglas politically.

After extremely bitter and acrimonious debate, the Senate approved the Lecompton constitution, but the House insisted that Kansans be given a chance to vote on the entire document. Southern congressmen did succeed in managing to apply pressure to the Kansas voters by adding the stipulation that, should the Lecompton constitution be approved, Kansas would receive a generous grant of federal land, but should it be voted down, Kansas would remain a territory.

Nevertheless, Kansas voters, when given a chance to express themselves in a fair election, turned down the Lecompton constitution by an overwhelming margin, choosing to remain a territory rather than become a slave state. Kansas was finally admitted as a free state in 1861.

The Panic of 1857

In 1857 the country was struck by a short but severe depression. There were three basic causes for this "Panic of 1857": several years of overspeculation in railroads and lands, faulty banking practices, and an interruption in the flow of European capital into American investments as a result of the Crimean War. The North blamed the Panic on low tariffs, while the South, which had suffered much less than the industrial North, saw the Panic as proof of the superiority of the Southern economy in general and slavery in particular.

The Lincoln-Douglas Debates

The 1858 Illinois senatorial campaign produced a series of debates that got to the heart of the issues that were threatening to divide the nation. In that race incumbent Democratic senator and front-runner for the 1860 presidential nomination Stephen A. Douglas was opposed by

Lincoln–Douglas Campaign Cartoon

a Springfield lawyer, little known outside the state, by the name of Abraham Lincoln.

Though Douglas had been hailed in some free-soil circles for his opposition to the Lecompton constitution, Lincoln, in a series of seven debates that the candidates agreed to hold during the course of the campaign, stressed that Douglas's doctrine of popular sovereignty failed to recognize slavery for the moral wrong it was. Again and again Lincoln hammered home the theme that Douglas was a secret defender of slavery because he did not take a moral stand against it.

Douglas, for his part, maintained that his guiding principle was democracy, not any moral standard of right or wrong with respect to slavery. The people could, as far as he was concerned, "vote it up or vote it down." At the same time, he strove to depict Lincoln as a radical and an abolitionist who believed in racial equality and race mixing.

At the debate held in Freeport, Illinois, Lincoln pressed Douglas to reconcile the principle of popular sovereignty with the Supreme Court's decision in the *Dred Scott* case. How could the people "vote it up or vote it down," if, as the Supreme Court said, no territorial government could prohibit slavery? Douglas, in what came to be called his "Freeport Doctrine," replied that the people of any territory could exclude slavery simply by declining to pass any of the special laws that slave jurisdictions usually passed for their protection.

Douglas's answer was good enough to win him re-election to the Senate, although by the narrowest of margins, but hurt him in the coming presidential campaign. The Lecompton fight had already destroyed Douglas's hopes of uniting the Democratic Party and defusing the slave issue. It had also damaged his 1860 presidential hopes by alienating the South. Now his Freeport Doctrine hardened the opposition of Southerners already angered by his anti-Lecompton stand.

For Lincoln, despite the failure to win the Senate seat, the debates were a major success, propelling him into the national spotlight and strengthening the backbone of the Republican Party to resist compromise on the free-soil issue.

The Coming of the Civil War

John Brown's Raid

On the night of October 16, 1859, John Brown, the Pottawatomie Creek murderer, led eighteen followers in seizing the federal arsenal at Harpers Ferry, Virginia (now West Virginia), taking hostages, and endeavoring to incite a slave uprising. Brown, supported and bankrolled by several prominent Northern abolitionists (later referred to as "the Secret Six"), planned to arm local slaves and then spread his uprising across the South. His scheme was ill-conceived and had little chance of success. Quickly cornered by Virginia militia, he was eventually captured by a force of U.S. Marines under the command of Army Colonel Robert E. Lee. Ten of Brown's eighteen men were killed in the fight, and Brown himself was wounded.

Charged under Virginia law with treason and various other crimes, Brown was quickly tried, convicted, sentenced, and, on December 2, 1859, hanged. Throughout his trial and at his execution, he conducted himself with fanatical resolution, making eloquent and grandiose state-

Trial of John Brown

ments that convinced many Northerners that he was a martyr rather than a criminal. His death was marked in the North by signs of public mourning.

Though responsible Northerners such as Lincoln denounced Brown's raid as a criminal act that deserved to be punished by death, many Southerners became convinced that the entire Northern public approved of Brown's action and that the only safety for the South lay in a separate Southern confederacy. This was all the more so because Brown, in threatening to create a slave revolt, had touched on the foremost fear of white Southerners.

Hinton Rowan Helper's Book

The second greatest fear of Southern slaveholders was that Southern whites who did not own slaves, by far the majority of the Southern population, would come to see the continuation of slavery as not being in their best interest. This fear was touched on by a book, *The Impending Crisis in the South*, by a North Carolinian named Hinton Rowan Helper. In it Helper argued that slavery was economically harmful to the South and that it enriched the large planter at the expense of the yeoman farmer.

Southerners were enraged, and more so when the Republicans re-issued a condensed version of the book as campaign literature. When the new House of Representatives met in December 1859 for the first time since the 1858 elections, angry Southerners determined that no Republican who had endorsed the book should be elected speaker.

The Republicans were the most numerous party in the House although they did not hold a majority. Their candidate for speaker, John Sherman of Ohio, had endorsed Helper's book. A rancorous two-month battle ensued in which the House was unable even to organize itself, let alone transact any business. Secession was talked of openly by Southerners, and as tensions rose congressmen came to the sessions carrying revolvers and Bowie knives. The matter was finally resolved by the withdrawal of Sherman and the election of a moderate Republican as speaker. Tensions remained fairly high.

The Election of 1860

In this mood the country approached the election of 1860, a campaign that eventually became a four-man contest.

The Democrats met in Charleston, South Carolina. Douglas had a majority of the delegates, but at that time a party rule required a two-thirds vote for the nomination. Douglas, faced with the bitter opposition of the Southerners and the Buchanan faction, could not gain this majority. Finally, the convention split up when Southern "fire-eaters" led by William L. Yancey walked out in protest of the convention's refusal to include in the platform a plank demanding federal protection of slavery in all the territories.

A second Democratic convention several weeks later in Baltimore also failed to reach a consensus, and the sundered halves of the party nominated separate candidates. The Southern wing of the party nominated Buchanan's vice president, John C. Breckinridge of Kentucky, on a platform calling for a federal slave code in all the territories. What was left of the national Democratic Party nominated Douglas on a platform of popular sovereignty.

A third presidential candidate was added by the Constitutional Union Party, a collection of aging former Whigs and Know Nothings from the southern and border states as well as a handful of moderate Southern Democrats. It nominated John Bell of Tennessee on a platform that sidestepped the issues and called simply for the Constitution, the Union, and the enforcement of the laws.

The Republicans met in Chicago, confident of victory and determined to do nothing to jeopardize their favorable position. Accordingly, they rejected as too radical front-running New York Senator William H. Seward in favor of Illinois' favorite son Abraham Lincoln. The platform was designed to have something for all Northerners, including the provisions of the 1856 Republican platform as well as a call for federal support of a transcontinental railroad. Once again its centerpiece was a call for the containment of slavery.

Douglas, believing only his victory could reconcile the North and South, became the first U.S. presidential candidate to make a vigorous nationwide speaking tour. In his speeches he urged support for the Union and opposition to any extremist candidates who might endanger its survival, by which he meant Lincoln and Breckinridge.

On election day, the voting went along strictly sectional lines. Breckinridge carried the Deep South; Bell, the border states; and Lincoln, the North. Douglas, although second in popular votes, carried only a single state and part of another. Lincoln led in popular votes, and though he was short of a majority in that category, he did have the needed majority in electoral votes and was elected.

The Secession Crisis

Lincoln had declared he had no intention of disturbing slavery where it already existed, but many Southerners thought otherwise. They also feared further raids of the sort John Brown had attempted and felt their pride injured by the election of a president for whom no Southerner had voted.

On December 20, 1860, South Carolina, by vote of a special convention made up of delegates elected by the people of the state, declared itself out of the Union. By February 1, 1861, six more states (Alabama, Georgia, Florida, Mississippi, Louisiana, and Texas) had followed suit.

Representatives of the seven seceded states met in Montgomery, Alabama, in February 1861 and declared themselves to be the Confederate States of America. They elected former Secretary of War and U.S. Senator Jefferson Davis of Mississippi as president and Alexander Stephens of Georgia as vice president. They also adopted a constitution for the Confederate States that, while similar to the U.S. Constitution in many ways, contained several important differences:

1. Slavery was specifically recognized, and the right to move slaves from one state to another was guaranteed.

2. Protective tariffs were prohibited.

3. The president was to serve for a single non-renewable six-year term.

4. The president was given the right to veto individual items within an appropriations bill.

5. State sovereignty was specifically recognized.

In the North reaction was mixed. Some, such as prominent Republican Horace Greeley of the *New York Tribune*, counseled, "Let erring sisters go in peace." President Buchanan, now a lame duck, seemed to be of this mind, since he declared secession to be unconstitutional but at the same time stated his belief that it was unconstitutional for the federal government to do anything to stop states from seceding. Taking his own advice, he did nothing.

Others, led by Senator John J. Crittenden of Kentucky, strove for a compromise that would preserve the Union. Throughout the period of several weeks as the Southern states one by one declared their secession, Crittenden worked desperately with a congressional compromise committee in hopes of working out some form of agreement.

The compromise proposals centered on the passage of a constitutional amendment forever prohibiting federal meddling with slavery in the states where it existed as well as the extension of the Missouri Compromise line (36° 30') to the Pacific, with slavery specifically protected in all the territories south of it.

Some Congressional Republicans were inclined to accept this compromise, but President-elect Lincoln urged them to stand firm for no further spread of slavery. Southerners would consider no compromise that did not provide for the spread of slavery, so talks broke down.

Quiz: Chapters 5 and 6

1. President Andrew Jackson's Specie Circular stipulated that

    (A) inefficient employees of the federal government should be immediately dismissed regardless of their political affiliation.

    (B) federal government deposits should be withdrawn from the Second Bank of the United States.

    (C) no federal funds should be spent on internal improvements.

    (D) paper money should not be accepted in payment for federal government lands sold.

    (E) the government would use force if necessary to collect the tariff in South Carolina.

2. When President Andrew Jackson's enemies spoke of the "Kitchen Cabinet," they were referring to

    (A) a group of old friends and unofficial advisors of the president.

    (B) a number of persons of low social standing, including a former cook, who were appointed by Jackson to high cabinet positions.

    (C) a suggestion as to where Jackson might keep the federal government's money if he removed it from the Bank of the United States.

    (D) a coterie of Jackson supporters in the U.S. Senate.

    (E) several state governors who supported Jackson.

3.   The 1840s Pre-emption Act, signed by President John Tyler, provided that

    (A)   the status of slavery in a territory was to be decided by the settlers there.

    (B)   slave law pre-empted free law in disputes involving escaped slaves.

    (C)   settlers who had squatted on government land would have first chance to buy it.

    (D)   the vice president automatically became president upon the death of the president.

    (E)   federal law pre-empted state law in matters pertaining to slavery.

4.   The paternalistic view of slavery held that slavery was

    (A)   a necessary evil that should be phased out as soon as it was economically possible.

    (B)   a totally unjustifiable abuse of humanity demanding immediate abolition.

    (C)   an artifact of a more primitive past that would eventually fade out on its own.

    (D)   necessary to protect blacks from the mistreatment and abuse they would receive if they were freed.

    (E)   necessary to keep blacks from developing their superior potential and eventually dominating the white race.

5.   The Mexican War of 1846 was fought primarily to

    (A)   avenge the slaughter of 186 Texans at the Alamo by Santa Anna's Mexican forces.

    (B)   drive the Spanish from Mexico and establish Mexican freedom once and for all.

    (C)   stop raids by Mexican "bandits" into U.S. territory in Texas and Arkansas.

    (D)   acquire California, New Mexico, and disputed territory along Texas' southern and western borders from Mexico.

    (E)   depose the Mexican dictator Santa Anna and replace his regime with a democratically elected government friendly to the United States.

6.   John Brown's raid on the federal arsenal at Harper's Ferry and his subsequent trial and execution had the effect of

    (A)   making a martyr of John Brown and convincing many Southerners that secession from the Union was the only way they could prevent the increasingly abolitionist North from interfering with slavery in the South.

    (B)   discrediting the abolitionist movement in the eyes of most people and convincing most Southerners that the North would not support forceful efforts to end slavery, despite verbal attacks on slavery by Northern abolitionists.

    (C)   inciting a series of slave revolts that resulted in the deaths of thousands of Southern slaves, further enraging both Northern abolitionists and Southern slaveholders.

    (D)   sparking a virtual civil war in the state of Nebraska over the issue of slavery.

    (E)   exposing a proslavery plot to assassinate the leaders of several abolitionist groups and discrediting the prosecution despite Brown being found guilty.

7. The doctrine of nullification put forth by John C. Calhoun in *The South Carolina Exposition and Protest*, published anonymously in 1828, held that

    (A) federal laws could be nullified only by amending the Constitution.

    (B) the Supreme Court had the sole power to nullify state and federal laws through the process of judicial review.

    (C) state and federal laws could be nullified only by the legislative bodies passing them.

    (D) the citizens of a state in a called convention could nullify state laws if these laws contradicted federal policies.

    (E) if a state judged a federal law to violate the Constitution, the state could declare the law null and void within its borders.

8. William Lloyd Garrison persuaded the American Anti-Slavery Society to endorse the concept of

    (A) compensated emancipation.

    (B) gradual emancipation.

    (C) immediate emancipation.

    (D) colonization.

    (E) violent revolution.

9. At the Seneca Falls Woman's Rights Convention organized by Lucretia Mott and Elizabeth Cady Stanton in 1848, the delegates

    (A) organized a political party to nominate candidates for public office.

(B) unanimously endorsed the ratification of an amendment to the Constitution giving women the right to vote in national elections.

(C) accepted the prevailing notion that women were endowed with weaker intellectual abilities than men.

(D) issued the pamphlet *Treatise on Domestic Economy*, instructing women on how to make their homes more efficient and more moral.

(E) declared that "all men and women are created equal" and that "the history of mankind is a history of repeated injuries and usurpations on the part of man toward woman . . ."

10. In 1831, Nat Turner organized and led a slave insurrection in Southhampton County, Virginia, that resulted in

(A) the gradual and compensated emancipation of the majority of slaves in Virginia.

(B) increased miscegenation between the white and slave populations of the slave states.

(C) the immediate emancipation and eventual transportation of Nat Turner and his followers to Santo Domingo.

(D) Congress passing a stringent fugitive slave law.

(E) the Southern states expanding their militia systems and strengthening the slave codes.

ANSWER KEY

1.	(D)	6.	(A)
2.	(A)	7.	(E)
3.	(C)	8.	(C)
4.	(D)	9.	(E)
5.	(D)	10.	(E)

DETAILED ANSWERS

1. **(D)** The Specie Circular forbade the purchase of federal lands with anything but "specie"—hard money. Jackson's determination to rid the federal bureaucracy of inefficient and corrupt workers (A) is generally associated with his so-called "spoils system." His determination to collect the tariff in South Carolina (E) is associated with the Nullification Controversy. He also withdrew federal funds from the Bank of the United States (B) and opposed the spending of federal funds for internal improvements (C).

2. **(A)** The "Kitchen Cabinet" was a group of old friends and unofficial advisors to Andrew Jackson, so called by his political enemies from the derisive suggestion that they entered the White House through the kitchen, or servants' entrance. Jackson's cabinet may not have been socially acceptable among some of Jackson's aristocratic critics, but it certainly included no former cooks (B). It was not suggested that government funds be kept on the premises of the White House (C).

3.   **(C)**   The Pre-emption Act provided that those who settled on government land would have first chance to buy it. Tyler did set a precedent for the vice president's becoming a full-fledged (rather than merely acting) president when the incumbent dies (D). The idea that the status of slavery in a territory should be decided by the settlers there (A) was popular sovereignty. Slave law pre-empted free law in disputes involving escaped slaves (B) by means of the Fugitive Slave Law, and that was the only case in which federal law pre-empted state law in matters pertaining to slavery (E).

4.   **(D)**   The paternalistic view of slavery, held by most Southern plantation owners, held that blacks were inferior, mentally weak and ignorant, requiring "protection" from the evils that could befall them if they were left on their own. In this view, slaveowners were benevolent protectors who took care of their black slaves almost as parents take care of children. This was a comforting myth that most slaveholders really appear to have believed. It was comforting in that if they were really protectors of their poor black "children," then holding slaves wasn't sinful at all. It was, rather, a social service providing a good for everybody involved. Unfortunately, this twisted rationalization denied the fact that slaves were horribly mistreated and often abused or killed for little or no provocation. If they were ignorant or childlike, it is only because they were denied educational opportunities, and many slaves learned that acting with childlike deference to their "master" often got them better treatment. In other words, their childishness was often an act based on a powerful instinct to survive rather than any limitations of mental capacity.

5.   **(D)**   When the independent Republic of Texas asked to be admitted to the United States, the government of Mexico threatened war if Texas was admitted. When the U.S. admitted Texas, a confrontation between the U.S. and Mexico rapidly developed over the southwestern border of Texas. President Polk sent American forces to guard the disputed lands claimed by Texas. Mexican forces attacked a small contingent of those forces. America retaliated by declaring war.

6.   **(A)**   John Brown's raid climaxed the growing hostility between proslavery Southerners and antislavery Northerners. His execution made him a martyr in many people's eyes. Despite the condemnations of Brown's tactics issued by several Northern leaders, such as Abraham Lincoln, most Southerners were convinced that Northerners agreed with Brown's goals and were upset only because he had failed. After John Brown's raid, both sides' views polarized further and many Southerners became convinced that the North would not rest until slavery had been abolished. Therefore, the only way they could preserve their "peculiar institution" was to secede from the Union and establish their own confederacy where slavery could continue unimpeded.

7.   **(E)**   The doctrine of nullification was based on the contention that the Constitution was a compact among the sovereign states. When the states entered into the compact, they retained their essential sovereignty and delegated limited and clearly specified powers to the federal government. If a state judged a federal law to violate the compact, it could nullify the law within its borders.

According to the doctrine of nullification/interposition, each state could be the judge of the legality or constitutionality of national action and could "interpose" its sovereignty to nullify invalid federal action. Southern leaders reactivated the theory in opposition to the desegregation rulings of the Supreme Court. The federal courts have rejected the doctrine as contrary to the national supremacy clause of Article VI of the Constitution.

8.   **(C)**   William Lloyd Garrison was the most vehement of the Massachusetts abolitionists. From 1831 to 1865, he advocated the immediate and complete emancipation of slaves. Garrison edited a militantly abolitionist weekly paper, the *Liberator*. In its pages, he attacked moderate abolitionists, advocated Northern secession, and castigated slaveholders. On July 4, 1854, Garrison publicly burned a copy of the Constitution and informed the holiday gathering: "So perish all compromises with tyranny."

9. **(E)** The convention adopted a "Declaration of Sentiments and Resolutions" modelled after the Declaration of Independence in form and language. The ninth resolution of this document demanded that women be given the right to vote, but many delegates believed this demand was too controversial. When the delegates voted on the resolutions, only the ninth resolution was not adopted unanimously.

10. **(E)** The ferocity of the Nat Turner insurrection surprised the planters. After the uprising, the slave states reacted by expanding their militia systems, passing new slave codes, strengthening existing slave codes, and severely restricting the activities of slaves.

CHAPTER 7

The Civil War and Reconstruction (1860–1877)

Hostilities Begin

Fort Sumter

Lincoln did his best to avoid angering the slave states that had not yet seceded. In his inaugural address, he urged Southerners to reconsider their actions but warned that the Union was perpetual, that states could not secede, and that he would therefore hold the federal forts and installations in the South.

Of these only two remained in federal hands: Fort Pickens, off Pensacola, Florida; and Fort Sumter, in the harbor of Charleston, South Carolina. Lincoln soon received word from Major Robert Anderson, commanding the small garrison at Sumter, that supplies were running low. Desiring to send in the needed supplies, Lincoln informed the governor of South Carolina of his intention but promised that no attempt would be made to send arms, ammunition, or reinforcements unless Southerners initiated hostilities.

Not satisfied, Southerners determined to take the fort. Confederate General P. G. T. Beauregard, acting on orders from President Davis, demanded Anderson's surrender. Anderson said he would if not resupplied. Knowing supplies were on the way, the Confederates opened fire at 4:30 a.m. on April 12, 1861. The next day the fort surrendered.

Abraham Lincoln

On the day following Sumter's surrender, Lincoln declared the existence of an insurrection and called for the states to provide 75,000 volunteers to put it down. In response to this, Virginia, Tennessee, North Carolina, and Arkansas declared their secession.

The remaining slave states, Delaware, Kentucky, Maryland, and Missouri, wavered to varying degrees but stayed with the Union. Delaware, which had few slaves, gave little serious consideration to the idea of secession. Kentucky declared itself neutral and then sided with the North when the South failed to respect this neutrality. Maryland's incipient secession movement was crushed by Lincoln's timely imposition of martial law. Missouri was saved for the Union by the quick and decisive use of federal troops as well as the sizeable population of pro-Union, antislavery German immigrants living in St. Louis.

Relative Strengths at the Outset

An assessment of available assets at the beginning of the war would not have looked favorable for the South.

The North enjoyed at least five major advantages over the South. It had overwhelming preponderance in wealth and thus was better able to finance the enormous expense of the war. The North was also vastly superior in industry and thus capable of producing the needed war materials; the South, as a primarily agricultural society, often had to improvise or do without.

Furthermore, the North had an advantage of almost three-to-one in manpower, and over one-third of the South's population was composed of slaves, whom Southerners would not use as soldiers. Unlike the South, the North received large numbers of immigrants during the war. The North retained control of the U.S. Navy, and thus would command the sea and be able, by blockading, to cut the South off from outside sources of supply.

Finally, the North enjoyed a far superior system of railroads, while the South's relatively sparse railroad net was composed of a number of smaller railroads, often not interconnected and with varying gauges of track. They were more useful for carrying cotton from the interior to port cities than for moving large amounts of war supplies or troops around the country.

The South did, however, have several advantages of its own. It was vast in size, and this would make it difficult to conquer; it did not need to conquer the North, but only resist being conquered itself. Its troops would also be fighting on their own ground, a fact that would give them the advantage of familiarity with the terrain, as well as the added motivation of defending their homes and families. Its armies would often have the opportunity of fighting on the defensive, a major advantage in the warfare of that day.

At the outset of the war, the South drew a number of highly qualified senior officers, such as Robert E. Lee, Joseph E. Johnston, and Albert Sidney Johnston, from the U.S. Army. By contrast, the Union command structure was already set when the war began, with the aged

Winfield Scott, of Mexican War fame, at the top. It took young and talented officers, such as Ulysses S. Grant and William T. Sherman, time to work up to high rank. Meanwhile, Union armies were often led by inferior commanders as Lincoln experimented while in search of good generals.

At first glance, the South might also have seemed to have an advantage in its president. Jefferson Davis had extensive military and political experience and was acquainted with the nation's top military men and, presumably, with their relative abilities. On the other hand, Lincoln had been, up until his election to the presidency, less successful politically and had virtually no military experience. In fact, Lincoln was much superior to Davis as a war leader, showing firmness, flexibility, mental toughness, great political skill, and, eventually, an excellent grasp of strategy.

Opposing Strategies

Both sides were full of enthusiasm for the war. In the North the battle cry was "On to Richmond," the new Confederate capital established after the secession of Virginia. In the South it was "On to Washington." Yielding to popular demand, Lincoln ordered General Irvin McDowell to advance on Richmond with his army. At a creek called Bull Run near the town of Manassas Junction, Virginia, just southwest of Washington, D.C., they met a Confederate force under Generals P. G. T. Beauregard and Joseph E. Johnston, on July 21, 1861. In the First Battle of Bull Run (called First Battle of Manassas in the South) the Union army was forced to retreat in confusion back to Washington.

Bull Run demonstrated the unpreparedness and inexperience of both sides. It also demonstrated that the war would be long and hard, and, particularly in the North, that greater efforts would be required. Lincoln would need an overall strategy. To supply this, Winfield Scott suggested his Anaconda Plan to squeeze the life out of the Confederacy. This plan included a naval blockade to shut out supplies from Europe, a campaign to take the Mississippi River, thereby splitting the South in two, and the taking of several strategic points, then waiting for pro-Union sentiment in the South to overthrow the secessionists.

Lincoln liked the first two points of Scott's strategy but considered the third point unrealistic.

He ordered a naval blockade, an overwhelming task considering the South's long coastline. Yet under Secretary of the Navy Gideon Welles the Navy was expanded enormously and the blockade, derided in the early days as a "paper blockade," became increasingly effective.

Lincoln also ordered a campaign to take the Mississippi River. A major step in this direction was taken when naval forces under Captain David G. Farragut took New Orleans in April 1862.

Rather than waiting for pro-Unionists in the South to gain control, Lincoln hoped to raise huge armies and apply overwhelming pressure from all sides at once until the Confederacy collapsed. The strategy was good; the problem was finding good generals to carry it out.

The Union Preserved

Lincoln Tries McClellan

To replace the discredited McDowell, Lincoln chose General George B. McClellan. McClellan was a good trainer and organizer and was loved by the troops, but was unable to effectively use the powerful army (now called the Army of the Potomac) he had built up. Despite much prodding from Lincoln, McClellan hesitated to advance, badly overestimating his enemy's numbers.

Finally, in the spring of 1862, he took the Army of the Potomac by water down Chesapeake Bay to land between the York and James rivers in Virginia. His plan was to advance up the peninsula formed by these rivers directly to Richmond.

The operations that followed were known as the Peninsula Campaign. McClellan advanced slowly and cautiously toward Richmond, while his equally cautious Confederate opponent, General Joseph E. Johnston, drew back to the outskirts of the city before turning to fight at the Battle of Seven Pines, May 31–June 1, 1862. In this inconclusive battle, Johnston was wounded. To replace him Jefferson Davis appointed his military advisor, General Robert E. Lee.

Lee summoned General Thomas J. "Stonewall" Jackson and his army from the Shenandoah Valley (where Jackson had just finished defeating several superior federal forces, causing consternation in Washington), and with the combined forces attacked McClellan.

After two days of bloody but inconclusive fighting, McClellan lost his nerve and began to retreat. In the remainder of what came to be called the Battle of the Seven Days, Lee continued to attack McClellan, forcing him back to his base, though at great cost in lives. McClellan's army was loaded back onto its ships and taken back to Washington.

Before McClellan's army could reach Washington and be completely deployed in northern Virginia, Lee saw and took an opportunity to thrash Union General John Pope, who was operating in northern Virginia with another Northern army, at the Second Battle of Bull Run.

Union Victories in the West

In the western area of the war's operations (essentially everything west of the Appalachian Mountains), matters were proceeding in a much different fashion. The Northern commanders there, Henry W. Halleck and Don Carlos Buell, were no more enterprising than McClellan, but Halleck's subordinate, Ulysses S. Grant, definitely was.

Seeking and obtaining permission from Halleck, Grant mounted a combined operation—army troops and navy gunboats—against two vital Confederate strongholds, Forts Henry and Donelson, which guarded the Tennessee and Cumberland rivers in northern Tennessee, and which were the weak point of the thin-stretched Confederate line under General Albert Sidney Johnston. When Grant captured the forts in February 1862, Johnston was forced to retreat to Corinth in northern Mississippi.

Grant pursued but, ordered by Halleck to wait until all was in readiness before proceeding, Grant halted his troops at Pittsburg Landing on the Tennessee River, twenty-five miles north of Corinth. On April 6, 1862, Johnston, who had received reinforcements and been joined by General P. G. T. Beauregard, surprised Grant there, but in the two-day battle that followed (Shiloh) failed to defeat him. Johnston himself was among the many killed in what was, up to this point, the bloodiest battle in American history.

Grant was severely criticized in the North for having been taken by surprise. Yet with other Union victories and Farragut's capture of New Orleans, the North had taken all of the Mississippi River except for a 110-mile stretch between the Confederate fortresses of Vicksburg, Mississippi, and Port Hudson, Louisiana.

The Success of Northern Diplomacy

Many Southerners believed Britain and France would rejoice in seeing a divided and weakened America. The two countries would likewise be driven by the need of their factories for cotton and thus intervene on the Confederacy's behalf. So strongly was this view held that during the early days of the war, when the Union blockade was still too weak to be very effective, the Confederate government itself prohibited the export of cotton in order to hasten British and French intervention.

This view proved mistaken for several reasons. Britain already had on hand large stocks of cotton from the bumper crops of the years immediately prior to the war. During the war, the British were successful in finding alternative sources of cotton, importing the fiber from India and Egypt. British leaders may also have weighed their country's need to import wheat from the northern United States against its desire for cotton from the Southern states. Finally, British public opinion opposed slavery.

Skillful Northern diplomacy had a great impact. In this, Lincoln had the extremely able assistance of Secretary of State William Seward, who took a hard line in warning Europeans not to interfere, and of Ambassador to Great Britain Charles Francis Adams. Britain, therefore, remained neutral and other European countries, France in particular, followed its lead.

One incident nevertheless came close to fulfilling Southern hopes for British intervention. In November 1861, Captain Charles Wilkes of the U.S.S. *San Jacinto* stopped the British mail and passenger ship *Trent* and forcibly removed Confederate emissaries James M. Mason and John Slidell. News of Wilkes' action brought great rejoicing in the North but outrage in Great Britain, where it was viewed as a violation of Britain's rights on the high seas. Lincoln and Seward, faced with British threats of war at a time when the North could ill afford it, wisely chose to release the envoys and smooth things over with Britain.

The Confederacy was able to obtain some loans and to purchase small amounts of arms, ammunition, and even commerce-raiding ships such as the highly successful C.S.S. *Alabama.* However, Union naval superiority kept such supplies to a minimum.

The War at Sea

The Confederacy's major bid to challenge the Union's naval superiority was based on the employment of a technological innovation, the ironclad ship. The first and most successful of the Confederate ironclads was the C.S.S. *Virginia.* Built on the hull of the abandoned Union frigate *Merrimac*, the *Virginia* was protected from cannon fire by iron plates bolted over her sloping wooden sides. In May 1862 she destroyed two wooden warships of the Union naval force at Hampton Roads, Virginia, and was seriously threatening to destroy the rest of the squadron before being met and fought to a standstill by the Union ironclad U.S.S. *Monitor.*

The Home Front

The war on the home front dealt with the problems of maintaining public morale, supplying the armies of the held, and resolving constitutional questions regarding authority and the ability of the respective governments to deal with crises.

For the general purpose of maintaining public morale but also as items many Republicans had advocated even before the war, Congress in 1862 passed two highly important acts dealing with domestic affairs in the North.

The Homestead Act granted 160 acres of government land free of charge to any person who would farm it for at least five years. Much of the West was eventually settled under the provisions of this act. The

Morrill Land Grant Act offered large amounts of the federal government's land to states that would establish "agricultural and mechanical" colleges. Many of the nation's large state universities were founded in later years under the provisions of this act.

Keeping the people relatively satisfied was made more difficult by the necessity, apparent by 1863, of imposing conscription in order to obtain adequate manpower for the huge armies that would be needed to crush the South. Especially hated by many working class Northerners was the provision of the conscription act that allowed a drafted individual to avoid service by hiring a substitute or paying $300. Resistance to the draft led to riots in New York City in which hundreds were killed.

The Confederacy, with its much smaller manpower pool on which to draw, had instituted conscription in 1862. Here, too, it did not always meet with cooperation. Some Southern governors objected to it on doctrinaire states' rights grounds, doing all they could to obstruct its operation. A provision of the Southern conscription act allowing one man to stay home as overseer for every twenty slaves led the non-slaveholding whites who made up most of the Southern population to grumble that it was a "rich man's war and a poor man's fight." Draft-dodging and desertion became epidemic in the South by the latter part of the war.

Scarcity of food and other consumer goods in the South as well as high prices led to further desertion as soldiers left the ranks to care for their starving families. Discontent also manifested itself in the form of a "bread riot" in Richmond.

Supplying the war placed an enormous strain on both societies, but one the North was better able to bear.

To finance the Northern side of the war, high tariffs and an income tax (the nation's first) were resorted to, yet even more money was needed. The Treasury Department, under Secretary of the Treasury Salmon P. Chase, issued "greenbacks," an unbacked fiat currency that nevertheless fared better than the Southern paper money because of greater confidence in Northern victory. To facilitate the financing of the war through credit expansion, the National Banking Act was passed in 1863.

The South, with its scant financial resources, found it all but impossible to cope with the expense of war. Excise and income taxes were levied and some small loans were obtained in Europe, yet the Southern Congress still felt compelled to issue paper money in such quantities that it became virtually worthless. That, and the scarcity of almost everything created by the war and its disruption of the economy, led to skyrocketing prices.

The Confederate government responded to the inflation it created by imposing taxes-in-kind and impressment, the seizing of produce, livestock, etc., by Confederate agents in return for payment according to an artificially set schedule of prices. Since payment was in worthless inflated currency, this amounted to confiscation and soon resulted in goods of all sorts becoming even scarcer than otherwise when a Confederate impressment agent was known to be in the neighborhood.

Questions of constitutional authority to deal with crises plagued both presidents.

To deal with the emergency of secession, Lincoln stretched the presidential powers to the limit, or perhaps beyond the limit, of the Constitution. To quell the threat of secession in Maryland, Lincoln suspended the writ of *habeas corpus* and imprisoned numerous suspected secessionists without charges or trial, ignoring the insistence of pro-Southern Chief Justice Roger B. Taney in *ex Parte Merryman* (1861) that such action was unconstitutional.

"Copperheads," Northerners such as Clement L. Vallandigham of Ohio who opposed the war, denounced Lincoln as a tyrant and would-be dictator but remained a minority. Though occasionally subject to arrest and/or deportation for their activities, they were generally allowed a considerable degree of latitude.

Davis encountered obstructionism from various state governors, the Confederate Congress, and even his own vice president, who denounced him as a tyrant for assuming too much power and failing to respect states' rights. Hampered by such attitudes, the Confederate government proved less effective than it might have been.

Lincoln issuing the Emancipation Proclamation

The Emancipation Proclamation

By mid-1862, Lincoln, under pressure from radical elements of his own party and hoping to create a favorable impression on foreign public opinion, determined to issue the Emancipation Proclamation, declaring free, as of January 1, 1863, all slaves in areas still in rebellion. In order that this not appear an act of panic and desperation in view of the string of defeats the North had recently suffered on the battlefields of Virginia, Lincoln, at Seward's recommendation, waited to announce the proclamation until the North should win some sort of victory. This was provided by the Battle of Antietam on September 17, 1862.

Though the Radical Republicans, prewar abolitionists for the most part, had for some time been urging Lincoln to take such a step, Northern public opinion as a whole was less enthusiastic, as the Republicans suffered major losses in the November 1862 congressional elections.

The Turning Point in the East

After his victory of the Second Battle of Bull Run, August 27–30, 1862, Lee moved north and crossed into Maryland, where he hoped to win a decisive victory that would force the North to recognize Southern independence.

He was confronted by the Army of the Potomac, once again under the command of General George B. McClellan. Through a stroke of good fortune early in the campaign, detailed plans for Lee's entire audacious operation fell into McClellan's hands, but the Northern general, by extreme caution and slowness, threw away this incomparable chance to annihilate Lee and win—or at least shorten—the war.

The armies finally met along Antietam Creek, just east of the town of Sharpsburg in western Maryland. In a bloody but inconclusive day-long battle, known as Antietam in the North and as Sharpsburg in the South, McClellan's timidity led him to miss another excellent chance to destroy Lee's cornered and badly outnumbered army. After the battle Lee retreated to Virginia, and Lincoln, besides issuing the Emancipation Proclamation, removed McClellan from command.

To replace him, Lincoln chose General Ambrose E. Burnside, who promptly demonstrated his unfitness for command by blundering into a lopsided defeat at Fredericksburg, Virginia, on December 13, 1862.

Lincoln then replaced Burnside with General Joseph "Fighting Joe" Hooker. Handsome and hard-drinking, Hooker had bragged of what he would do to "Bobby Lee" when he got at him; but when he took his army south, "Fighting Joe" quickly lost his nerve. He was out-generaled

Lincoln at Antietam, October 3, 1862,
after the bloodiest single day of the Civil War.

and soundly beaten at the Battle of Chancellorsville, May 5–6, 1863. At this battle, the brilliant Southern General "Stonewall" Jackson was accidentally shot by his own men and died several days later.

Lee, anxious to shift the scene of the fighting out of his beloved Virginia, sought and received permission from President Davis to invade Pennsylvania. He was pursued by the Army of the Potomac, now under the command of General George G. Meade, whom Lincoln had selected to replace the discredited Hooker. They met at Gettysburg, and in a three-day battle (July 1–3,1863) that was the bloodiest of the entire war, Lee, who sorely missed the services of Jackson and whose cavalry leader, the normally reliable J. E. B. Stuart, failed to provide him with timely reconnaissance, was defeated. However, he was allowed by the victorious Meade to retreat to Virginia with his battered army intact, much to Lincoln's disgust. Still, Lee would never again have the strength to mount such an invasion.

Lincoln Finds Grant

Meanwhile, Grant undertook to take Vicksburg, one of the two last Confederate bastions on the Mississippi River. In a brilliant campaign, he bottled up the Confederate forces of General John C. Pemberton inside the city and placed them under siege. After six weeks of siege, the defenders surrendered on July 4, 1863. Five days later Port Hudson surrendered as well, giving the Union complete control of the Mississippi.

After Union forces under General William Rosecrans suffered an embarrassing defeat at the Battle of Chickamauga in northwestern Georgia, September 19–20, 1863, Lincoln named Grant overall commander of the Union forces in the West.

Grant went to Chattanooga, Tennessee, where Confederate forces under General Braxton Bragg were virtually besieging Rosecrans, and immediately took control of the situation. Gathering Union forces from other portions of the western theater and combining them with reinforcements from the East, Grant won a resounding victory at the Battle of Chattanooga (November 23–25, 1863), in which federal forces stormed seemingly impregnable Confederate positions on Lookout

Mountain and Missionary Ridge. This victory put Union forces in position for a drive into Georgia, which began the following spring.

Early in 1864 Lincoln made Grant commander of all Union armies. Grant devised a coordinated plan for constant pressure on the Confederacy. General William T. Sherman would lead a drive toward Atlanta, Georgia, with the goal of destroying the Confederate army under General Joseph E. Johnston (who had replaced Bragg). Grant himself would accompany Meade and the Army of the Potomac in advancing toward Richmond with the goal of destroying Lee's Confederate army.

In a series of bloody battles (the Wilderness, Spotsylvania, Cold Harbor) in May and June of 1864, Grant drove Lee to the outskirts of Richmond. Still unable to take the city or get Lee at a disadvantage, Grant circled around to try to take both by way of the back door, attacking Petersburg, Virginia, an important railroad junction just south of Richmond and the key to that city's—and Lee's—supply lines. Once again turned back by entrenched Confederate troops, Grant settled down to besiege Petersburg and Richmond in a stalemate that lasted some nine months.

Sherman had been advancing simultaneously in Georgia. He maneuvered Johnston back to the outskirts of Atlanta with relatively little fighting. At that point Confederate President Davis lost patience with Johnston and replaced him with the aggressive General John B. Hood.

Poster from Lincoln's 1864 presidential campaign in New York.

Hood and Sherman fought three fierce but inconclusive battles around Atlanta in late July, then settled down to a siege of their own during the month of August.

The Election of 1864 and Northern Victory

In the North discontentment grew with the long casualty lists and seeming lack of results. Yet the South could stand the grinding war even less. By late 1864 Jefferson Davis had reached the point of calling for the use of blacks in the Confederate armies, though the war ended before black troops could see action for the Confederacy. The South's best hope was that Northern war-weariness would bring the defeat of Lincoln and the victory of a peace candidate in the election of 1864.

Lincoln ran on the ticket of the National Union Party, essentially the Republican party with loyal or "War" Democrats. His vice presidential candidate was Andrew Johnson, a loyal Democrat from Tennessee.

The Democratic Party's presidential candidate was General George B. McClellan, who, with some misgivings, ran on a platform labeling the war a failure and calling for a negotiated peace settlement even if that meant Southern independence.

The outlook was bleak for a time, and even Lincoln himself believed that he would be defeated. Then, in September 1864, came word that Sherman had taken Atlanta. The capture of this vital Southern rail and manufacturing center brought an enormous boost to northern morale. Along with other Northern victories that summer and fall, it insured a resounding election victory for Lincoln and the continuation of the war to complete victory for the North.

To speed that victory, Sherman marched through Georgia from Atlanta to the sea, arriving at Savannah in December 1864 and turning north into the Carolinas, leaving behind a 60-mile-wide swath of destruction. His goal was to impress on Southerners that continuation of the war could mean only ruin for all of them. He and Grant planned that his army should press on through the Carolinas and into Virginia to join Grant in finishing off Lee.

Lincoln's Assassination

Before Sherman's troops could arrive, Lee abandoned Richmond (April 3, 1865) and attempted to escape with what was left of his army. Pursued by Grant, he was cornered and forced to surrender at Appomattox, Virginia, on April 9, 1865. Other Confederate armies still holding out in various parts of the South surrendered over the next few weeks.

Lincoln did not live to receive news of the final surrenders. On April 14, 1865, he was shot in the back of the head while watching a play at Ford's Theater in Washington. His assassin, pro-Southern actor John Wilkes Booth, injured his ankle in making his escape. Hunted down by Union cavalry several days later, he died of a gunshot wound, apparently self-inflicted. Several other individuals were tried, convicted, and hanged by a military tribunal for participating with Booth in a conspiracy to assassinate not only Lincoln, but also Vice President Johnson and Secretary of State Seward.

The Ordeal of Reconstruction

Lincoln's Plan of Reconstruction

Reconstruction began well before the fighting of the Civil War came to an end. It brought a time of difficult adjustments in the South.

Among those who faced such adjustments were the recently freed slaves, who flocked into Union lines, followed advancing Union armies, or whose plantations were part of the growing area of the South that came under Union military control. Some slaves had left their plantations, and thus their only means of livelihood, in order to obtain freedom within Union lines. Many felt they had to leave their plantations in order to be truly free, and some sought to find relatives separated during the days of slavery. Some former slaves also seemed to misunderstand the meaning of freedom, thinking they need never work again.

To ease the adjustment for these recently freed slaves, Congress in 1865 created the Freedman's Bureau to provide food, clothing, and education, and generally look after the interests of former slaves.

Even before the need to deal with this problem had forced itself on the Northern government's awareness, steps had been taken to deal with another major adjustment of Reconstruction, the restoration of loyal governments to the seceded states. By 1863 substantial portions of several Southern states had come under Northern military control, and Lincoln had set forth a policy for re-establishing governments in those states.

Lincoln's policy, known as the Ten Percent Plan, stipulated that Southerners, except for high-ranking rebel officials, could take an oath promising future loyalty to the Union and acceptance of the end of slavery. When the number of those who had taken this oath within any one state reached ten percent of the number who had been registered to vote in that state in 1860, a loyal state government could be formed. Only those who had taken the oath could vote or participate in the new government.

Tennessee, Arkansas, and Louisiana met the requirements and formed loyal governments but were refused recognition by Congress, which was dominated by Radical Republicans.

The Radical Republicans, such as Thaddeus Stevens of Pennsylvania, believed Lincoln's plan did not adequately punish the South, restructure Southern society, and boost the political prospects of the Republican Party. The loyal southern states were denied representation in Congress and electoral votes in the election of 1864.

Instead, the Radicals in Congress drew up the Wade-Davis Bill. Under its stringent terms, a majority of the number who had been alive and registered to vote in 1860 would have to swear an "ironclad" oath stating that they were now loyal and had never been disloyal. This was obviously impossible in any former Confederate state unless blacks were given the vote, something Radical Republicans desired but Southerners definitely did not. Unless the requisite number swore the "ironclad" oath, Congress would not allow the state to have a government.

Lincoln killed the Wade-Davis Bill with a "pocket veto," and the Radicals were furious. When Lincoln was assassinated, the Radicals rejoiced, believing Vice President Andrew Johnson would be less generous to the South or at least easier to control.

Johnson's Attempt at Reconstruction

To the dismay of the Radicals, Johnson followed Lincoln's policies very closely, making them only slightly more stringent by requiring ratification of the Thirteenth Amendment (officially abolishing slavery), repudiation of Confederate debts, and renunciation of secession. He also recommended the vote be given to blacks.

Southern states proved reluctant to accept these conditions, some declining to repudiate Confederate debts or ratify the Thirteenth Amendment (it nevertheless received the ratification of the necessary number of states and was declared part of the Constitution in December 1865). No Southern state extended the vote to blacks (at this time no Northern state did, either). Instead, the Southern states promulgated Black Codes, imposing various restrictions on the freedom of the former slaves.

Foreign Policy Under Johnson

On coming into office, Johnson had inherited a foreign policy problem involving Mexico and France. The French Emperor, Napoleon III, had made Mexico the target of one of his many grandiose foreign adventures. In 1862, while the U.S. was occupied with the Civil War and therefore unable to prevent this violation of the Monroe Doctrine, Napoleon III had Archduke Maximilian of Austria installed as a puppet emperor of Mexico, supported by French troops. The U.S. had protested but for the time could do nothing.

With the war over, Johnson and Secretary of State Seward were able to take more vigorous steps. General Philip Sheridan was sent to the Rio Grande with a military force. At the same time Mexican revolutionary leader Benito Juarez was given the tacit recognition of the U.S. government. Johnson and Seward continued to invoke the Monroe Doctrine and to place quiet pressure on Napoleon III to withdraw his troops. In May 1866, facing difficulties of his own in Europe, the French emperor did so, leaving the unfortunate Maximilian to face a Mexican firing squad.

Johnson's and Seward's course of action in preventing the extension of the French Empire into the Western Hemisphere strengthened America's commitment to and the rest of the world's respect for the Monroe Doctrine.

In 1866 the Russian minister approached Seward with an offer to sell Alaska to the U.S. The Russians desired to sell Alaska because its fur resources had been largely exhausted and because they feared that in a possible war with Great Britain (something that seemed likely at the time) they would lose Alaska anyway.

Seward, who was an ardent expansionist, pushed hard for the purchase of Alaska, known as "Seward's Folly" by its critics, and it was largely through his efforts that it was pushed through Congress. It was urged that purchasing Alaska would reward the Russians for their friendly stance toward the U.S. government during the Civil War, at a time when Britain and France had seemed to favor the Confederacy.

In 1867 the sale went through and Alaska was purchased for $7,200,000.

Congressional Reconstruction

Southern intransigence in the face of Johnson's relatively mild plan of Reconstruction manifested in the refusal of some states to repudiate

Reconstruction of the South

the Confederate debt and ratify the Thirteenth Amendment. The refusal to give the vote to blacks, the passage of black codes, and the election of many former high-ranking Confederates to Congress and other top positions in the Southern states played into the hands of the Radicals, who were anxious to impose harsh rule on the South. They could now assert that the South was refusing to accept the verdict of the war.

Once again, Congress excluded the representatives of the Southern states. Determined to reconstruct the South as it saw fit, Congress passed a Civil Rights Act and extended the authority of the Freedman's Bureau, giving it both quasi-judicial and quasi-executive powers.

Johnson vetoed both bills, claiming they were unconstitutional; but Congress overrode the vetoes. Fearing that the Supreme Court would agree with Johnson and overturn the laws, Congress approved and sent on to the states for ratification (June 1866) the Fourteenth Amendment, making constitutional the laws Congress had just passed. The Fourteenth Amendment defined citizenship and forbade states to deny various rights to citizens, reduced the representation in Congress of states that did not allow blacks to vote, forbade the paying of the Confederate debt, and made former Confederates ineligible to hold public office.

With only one Southern state, Tennessee, ratifying, the amendment failed to receive the necessary approval of three-fourths of the states. But the Radicals in Congress were not finished. Strengthened by victory in the 1866 elections, they passed, over Johnson's veto, the Military Reconstruction Act, dividing the South into five military districts to be ruled by military governors with almost dictatorial powers. Tennessee, having ratified the Fourteenth Amendment, was spared the wrath of the Radicals. The rest of the Southern states were ordered to produce constitutions giving the vote to blacks and to ratify the Fourteenth Amendment before they could be "readmitted." In this manner, the fourteenth Amendment was ratified.

Realizing the unprecedented nature of these actions, Congress moved to prevent any check or balance from the other two branches of government. Steps were taken toward limiting the jurisdiction of the Supreme Court so that it could not review cases pertaining to congressional Reconstruction policies. This proved unnecessary as the court, now headed by Chief Justice Salmon P. Chase in place of the deceased Taney, readily acquiesced and declined to overturn the Reconstruction acts.

Impeachment of Andrew Johnson, 1868

To control the president, Congress passed the Army Act, reducing the president's control over the army. In obtaining the cooperation of the army, the Radicals had the aid of General Grant, who already had his eye on the 1868 Republican presidential nomination. Congress also passed the Tenure of Office Act, forbidding Johnson to dismiss Cabinet members without the Senate's permission. In passing the latter act, Congress was especially thinking of Radical Secretary of War Edwin M. Stanton, a Lincoln holdover whom Johnson desired to dismiss.

Johnson obeyed the letter but not the spirit of the Reconstruction acts, and Congress, angry at his refusal to cooperate, sought in vain for grounds to impeach him, until in August 1867, Johnson violated the Tenure of Office Act (by dismissing Stanton) in order to test its constitutionality. The matter was not tested in the courts, however, but in Congress, where Johnson was impeached by the House of Representatives and came within one vote of being removed by the Senate. For the remaining months of his term, he offered little further resistance to the Radicals.

The Election of 1868 and the Fifteenth Amendment

In 1868 the Republican convention, dominated by the Radicals, drew up a platform endorsing Radical Reconstruction. For president, the Republicans nominated Ulysses S. Grant, who had no political record and whose views—if any—on national issues were unknown. The vice presidential nominee was Schuyler Colfax.

Though the Democratic nomination was sought by Andrew Johnson, the party knew he could not win and instead nominated former Governor Horatio Seymour of New York for president and Francis P. Blair, Jr. of Missouri for vice president. Both had been Union generals during the war. The Democratic platform mildly criticized the excesses of Radical Reconstruction and called for continued payment of the war debt in greenbacks, although Seymour himself was a hard-money man.

Grant, despite his enormous popularity as a war hero, won by only a narrow margin, drawing only 300,000 more popular votes than Seymour. Some 700,000 blacks had voted in the Southern states under the auspices of army occupation, and since all of these had almost certainly voted for Grant, it was clear that he had not received a majority of the white vote.

The narrow victory of even such a strong candidate as Grant prompted Republican leaders to decide that it would be politically expedient to give the vote to all blacks, North as well as South. For this purpose the fifteenth Amendment was drawn up and submitted to the states. Ironically, the idea was so unpopular in the North that it won the necessary three-fourths approval only with its ratification by Southern states required to do so by Congress.

Post War Life in the South

Reconstruction was a difficult time in the South. During the war approximately one in ten Southern men had been killed. Many more were maimed for life. Those who returned from the war found destruction and poverty. Property of the Confederate government was confiscated by the federal government, and dishonest Treasury agents confiscated private property as well. Capital invested in slaves or in Confederate war bonds was lost. Property values fell to one-tenth of their pre war level. The economic results of the war stayed with the South for decades.

The political results were less long-lived but more immediately disturbing to Southerners. Southerners complained of widespread corruption in governments sustained by federal troops and composed of "carpetbaggers," "scalawags" (the Southern names for Northerners who came to the South to participate in Reconstruction governments and for Southerners who supported the Reconstruction regimes, respectively), and recently freed blacks.

Under the Reconstruction governments, social programs were greatly expanded, leading to higher taxes and growing state debts. Some of the financial problems were due to corruption, a problem in both, North and South in this era when political machines, such as William Marcy "Boss" Tweed's Tammany Hall machine in New York, dominated many Northern city governments and grew rich.

Southern whites sometimes responded to Reconstruction governments with violence, carried out by groups such as the Ku Klux Klan, aimed at intimidating blacks and white Republicans out of voting. The activities of these organizations were sometimes a response to those of the Union League, an organization used by Southern Republicans to control the black vote. The goal of Southerners not allied with the Reconstruction governments, whether members of the Ku Klux Klan or not, was "redemption" (i.e., the end of the Reconstruction governments).

By 1876 Southern whites had been successful, by legal means or otherwise, in "redeeming" all but three Southern states.

Reconstruction ended primarily because the North lost interest. Corruption in government, economic hard times brought on by the Panic of 1873, and general weariness on the part of Northern voters with the effort to remake Southern society all sapped the will to continue. Diehard Radicals such as Thaddeus Stevens and Charles Sumner were dead.

Corruption Under Grant

Having arrived in the presidency with no firm political positions, Grant found that the only principle he had to guide his actions was his instinctive loyalty to his old friends and the politicians who had propelled him into office. This principle did not serve him well as president. Though personally of unquestioned integrity, he naively placed his faith in a number of thoroughly dishonest men. His administration was rocked by one scandalous revelation of government corruption after another. Not every scandal involved members of the executive branch, but together they tended to taint the entire period of Grant's administration as one of unparalleled corruption.

The "Black Friday" Scandal

In the "Black Friday" scandal, two unscrupulous businessmen, Jim Fiske and Jay Gould, schemed to corner the gold market. To further their designs, they got Grant's brother-in-law to persuade the president that stopping government gold sales would be good for farmers. Grant naively complied, and many businessmen were ruined as the price of gold was bid up furiously on "Black Friday." By the time Grant realized what was happening, much damage had already been done.

The Credit Mobilier Scandal

In the Credit Mobilier scandal, officials of the Union Pacific Railroad used a dummy construction company called Credit Mobilier to skim off millions of dollars of the subsidies the government was paying the Union Pacific for building a transcontinental railroad. To ensure that Congress would take a benevolent attitude toward all this, the officials bribed many of its members lavishly. Though much of this took place before Grant came into office, its revelation in an 1872 congressional investigation created a general scandal.

The "Salary Grab Act"

In the "Salary Grab Act" of 1873, Congress voted a 100% pay raise for the president and a 50% increase for itself and made both retroactive two years. Public outrage led to a Democratic victory in the next congressional election and the law was repealed.

The Sanborn Contract Fraud

In the Sanborn Contract fraud, a politician named Sanborn was given a contract to collect $427,000 in unpaid taxes for a 50% commission. The commission found its way into Republican campaign funds.

The Whiskey Ring Fraud

In the Whiskey Ring fraud, distillers and treasury officials conspired to defraud the government of large amounts of money from the excise tax on whiskey. Grant's personal secretary was in on the plot, and Grant himself naively accepted gifts of a questionable nature. When the matter came under investigation, Grant endeavored to shield his secretary.

The Bribing of Belknap

Grant's secretary of war, W. W. Belknap, accepted bribes from corrupt agents involved in his department's administration of Indian affairs. When the matter came out, he resigned to escape impeachment.

The Liberal Republicans

Discontentment within Republican ranks with regard to some of the earlier scandals as well as with the Radicals' vindictive Reconstruction policies led a faction of the party to separate and constitute itself as the Liberal Republicans. Besides opposing corruption and favoring sectional harmony, the Liberal Republicans favored hard money and a laissez-faire approach to economic issues. For the election of 1872, they nominated *New York Tribune* editor Horace Greeley for president. Eccentric, controversial, and ineffective as a campaigner, Greeley proved a poor choice. Though nominated by the Democrats as well as the Liberal Republicans, he was easily defeated by Grant, who was again the nominee of the Radicals.

Ulysses S. Grant

Economic Issues Under Grant

Many of the economic difficulties the country faced during Grant's administration were caused by the necessary readjustments from a wartime economy back to a peacetime economy.

The central economic question was deflation versus inflation or, more specifically, whether to retire the unbacked paper money, greenbacks, printed to meet the wartime emergency, or to print more.

Economic conservatives, creditors, and business interests usually favored retirement of the greenbacks and an early return to the gold standard.

Debtors, who had looked forward to paying off their obligations in depreciated paper money worth less than the gold-backed money they had borrowed, favored a continuation of currency inflation through the use of more greenbacks. The deflation that would come through the retirement of existing greenbacks would make debts contracted during or immediately after the war much harder to pay.

Generally, Grant's policy was to let the greenbacks float until they were on par with gold and could then be retired without economic dislocation.

Early in Grant's second term the country was hit by an economic depression known as the Panic of 1873. Brought on by the overexpansive tendencies of railroad builders and businessmen during the immediate postwar boom, the Panic was triggered by economic downturns in Europe and, more immediately, by the failure of Jay Cooke and Company, a major American financial firm.

The financial hardship brought on by the Panic led to renewed clamor for the printing of more greenbacks. In 1874 Congress authorized a small new issue of greenbacks, but it was vetoed by Grant. Pro-inflation forces were further enraged when Congress in 1873 demonetized silver, going to a straight gold standard. Silver was becoming more plentiful due to Western mining and was seen by some as a potential source of inflation. Pro-inflation forces referred to the demonetization of silver as the "Crime of '73."

In 1875 Congress took a further step toward retirement of the greenbacks and return to a working gold standard when, under the leadership of John Sherman, it passed the Specie Resumption Act, calling for the resumption of specie payments (i.e., the redeemability of the nation's paper money in gold) by January 1, 1879.

Disgruntled proponents of inflation formed the Greenback Party and nominated Peter Cooper for president in 1876. However, they gained only an insignificant number of votes.

The Disputed Election of 1876

In the election of 1876, the Democrats campaigned against corruption and nominated New York Governor Samuel J. Tilden, who had broken the Tweed political machine of New York City.

The Republicans passed over Grant, who was interested in another term and had the backing of the remaining hard-core Radicals, and turned instead to Governor Rutherford B. Hayes of Ohio. Like Tilden, Hayes was decent, honest, in favor of hard money and civil service reform, and opposed to government regulation of the economy. In their campaigning, the Republicans resorted to a tactic known as "waving the bloody shirt." Successfully used in the last two presidential elections, this meant basically playing on wartime animosities, urging Northerners to vote the way they had shot, and suggested that a Democratic victory and a Confederate victory would be about the same thing.

This time the tactic was less successful. Tilden won the popular vote and led in the electoral vote 184 to 165. However, 185 electoral votes were needed for election, and 20 votes from the three Southern states still occupied by Federal troops and run by Republican governments were disputed.

Though there had been extensive fraud on both sides, Tilden undoubtedly deserved at least the one vote he needed to win. Congress created a special commission to decide the matter. It was to be composed of five members each from the Senate, the House, and the Supreme Court. Of these, seven were to be Republicans, seven Democrats, and one an independent. The Republicans arranged, however, for the independent justice's state legislature to elect him to the Senate. When the justice resigned to take his Senate seat, it left all the remaining Supreme Court justices Republican. One of them was chosen, and in a series of eight-to-seven votes along straight party lines, the commission voted to give all 20 disputed votes—and the election—to Hayes.

When outraged congressional Democrats threatened to reject these obviously fraudulent results, a compromise was worked out. In the Compromise of 1877, Hayes promised to show consideration for Southern interests, end Reconstruction, and withdraw the remaining Federal troops from the South in exchange for Democratic acquiescence in his election.

Reconstruction would probably have ended anyway, since the North had already lost interest in it.

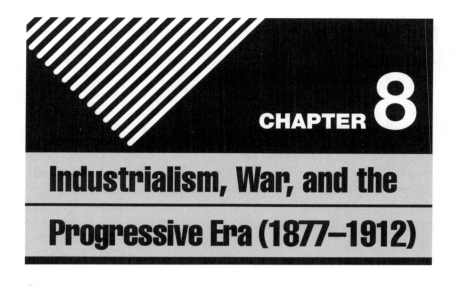

CHAPTER 8

Industrialism, War, and the Progressive Era (1877–1912)

The New Industrial Era, 1877–1882

The structure of modern American society was erected by democratic, capitalistic, and technological forces in the post-Civil War era. Between the 1870s and 1890s, "Gilded Age" America emerged as the world's leading industrial and agricultural producer.

Politics of the Period, 1877–1882

The presidencies of Abraham Lincoln and Theodore Roosevelt mark the boundaries of a half century of relatively weak executive leadership and legislative domination by Congress and the Republican Party.

The Compromise of 1877

With Southern Democratic acceptance of Rutherford B. Hayes' Republican presidency, the last remaining Union troops were withdrawn from the Old Confederacy (South Carolina, Florida, Louisiana), and the country was at last reunified as a modern nation-state led by corporate and industrial interests. The Hayes election arrangement also marked the government's abandonment of its earlier vague commitment to African-American equality.

T. A. EDISON.
Electric-Lamp.

No. 223,898. Patented Jan. 27. 1880.

Thomas Edison's Patent Application for the Light Bulb (1880)

Republican Factions

"Stalwarts," led by New York Senator Roscoe Conkling, favored the old spoils system of political patronage. "Half-Breeds," headed by Maine Senator James G. Blaine, pushed for civil service reform and merit appointments to government posts.

Election of 1880

James A. Garfield of Ohio, a Half-Breed, and his vice presidential running mate Chester A. Arthur of New York, a Stalwart, defeated the Democratic candidate General Winfield S. Hancock of Pennsylvania and former Indiana congressman William English. Tragically, the Garfield administration was but an interlude, for the president was assassinated in 1881 by a mentally disturbed patronage seeker, Charles Guiteau. Although without much executive experience, the Stalwart

Arthur had the courage to endorse reform of the political spoils system by supporting passage of the Pendleton Act (1883), which established open competitive examinations for civil service positions.

The Greenback-Labor Party

The Greenback-Labor Party movement polled over one million votes in 1878, and elected 14 members to Congress in an effort to promote the inflation of farm prices and the cooperative marketing of agricultural produce. In 1880, the party's presidential candidate, James Weaver of Iowa, advocated public control and regulation of private enterprises such as railroads in the common interest of more equitable competition. Weaver theorized that because railroads were so essential, they should be treated as a public utility. He polled only three percent of the vote.

The Economy, 1877–1882

Industrial expansion and technology assumed major proportions in this period. Between 1860 and 1894 the United States moved from the fourth-largest manufacturing nation to the world's leader through capital accumulation, natural resources (especially in iron, oil, and coal), an abundance of labor helped by massive immigration, railway transportation and communications (the telephone was introduced by Alexander Graham Bell in 1876), and major technical innovations such as the development of the modern steel industry by Andrew Carnegie, and electrical energy by Thomas Edison. In the petroleum industry, John D. Rockefeller controlled ninety-five percent of the U.S. oil refineries by 1877.

The New South

By 1880, Northern capital erected the modern textile industry in the New South by bringing factories to the cotton fields. Birmingham, Alabama, emerged as the South's leading steel producer, and the introduction of machine-made cigarettes propelled the Duke family to prominence as tobacco producers.

Standard of Living

An elite class rose during this period, which accumulated vast family fortunes, while many Americans, especially immigrants and newly freed slaves, suffered from crushing poverty.

Social Darwinism

Many industrial leaders used the doctrines associated with the "Gospel of Wealth" to justify the unequal distribution of national wealth. Self-justification by the wealthy was based on the notion that God had granted wealth as He had given grace for material and spiritual salvation of the select few. These few, according to William Graham Sumner, relied heavily on the survival-of-the-fittest philosophy associated with Charles Darwin.

Labor Unrest

When capital overexpansion and overspeculation led to the economic panic of 1873, massive labor disorders spread through the country leading to the paralyzing railroad strike of 1877. Unemployment and salary reductions caused major class conflict. President Hayes used federal troops to restore order after dozens of workers were killed. Immigrant workers began fighting among themselves in California where Irish and Chinese laborers fought for economic survival.

Labor Unions

The depression of the 1870s undermined national labor organizations. The National Labor Union (1866) had a membership of 600,000 but failed to withstand the impact of economic adversity. The Knights of Labor (1869) managed to open its membership to not only white native American workers, but immigrants, women, and African-Americans as well. Although they claimed one million members, they too could not weather the hard times of the 1870s and eventually went under in 1886 in the wake of the bloody Haymarket Riot in Chicago.

Agricultural Militancy

Agrarian discontent expressed through the activities of the National Grange and the Farmers' Alliances in the West and South showed greater lasting power. During the Civil War, many farmers had overexpanded their operations, purchased more land and machinery, and gone heavily into debt. When the relatively high wartime agricultural prices collapsed in the decades after the war, farmers worked collectively to promote currency inflation, higher farm prices, silver and gold bimetalism, debt relief, cooperative farm marketing ventures, and regulation of monopolies and railroads by the federal and state governments. Although not very successful in the 1870s, farmer militancy continued to be a powerful political and economic force in the decades of the 1880s and 1890s.

Social and Cultural Developments, 1877–1882

Urbanization was the primary social and cultural phenomenon of the period. Both internal and external migrations contributed to an industrial urban state that grew from 40 million people in 1870 to almost 80 million in 1900. New York, Chicago, and Philadelphia emerged as cities with over one million people.

Skyscrapers and Immigrants

Cities grew both up and out as the skyscraper made its appearance after the introduction of the mechanical elevator by Elisha Otis. The city also grew outward into a large, impersonal metropolis divided into various business, industrial, and residential sectors, usually segregated by ethnic group, social class, and race. Slums and tenements sprang up within walking distance of department stores and townhouses. Two million immigrants from northern Europe poured into the U.S. during the 1870s. In the 1880s, another five million entered the country, but by this time they were coming from southern and eastern Europe.

Lack of Government Policy

There were few programs to deal with the vast influx of humanity other than the prohibition of the criminal and the insane. City governments soon developed the primary responsibility for immigrants—often trading employment, housing, and social services for political support.

Social Gospel

In time, advocates of the "social gospel" such as Jane Addams and Washington Gladden urged the creation of settlement houses and better health and education services to accommodate the new immigrants. New religions also appeared, including the Salvation Army and Mary Baker Eddy's Church of Christian Science in 1879.

Education

Public education continued to expand, especially on the secondary level. Private Catholic parochial schools and teaching colleges grew in number as well. Adult education and English instruction became important functions of both public and private schooling.

African-American Leaders

Booker T. Washington emerged in 1881 as the president of Tuskegee Institute in Alabama, a school devoted to teaching and vocational education for African-Americans with a mission to encourage self-respect and economic equality of the races. It was at Tuskegee that George Washington Carver emerged in subsequent years as an agricultural chemist who did much to find industrial applications for agricultural products.

Feminism

The new urban environment encouraged feminist activism. Millions of women worked outside the home, and continued to demand voting rights. Many women became active in social reform movements such as the prohibitionist Women's Christian Temperance Movement, planned parenthood, humane societies, antiprostitution crusades, and equal rights for all regardless of gender, race, or class.

Literature

Important books appeared such as Henry George's *Progress and Poverty* (1879), a three million-copy seller that advocated one single tax on land as the means to redistribute wealth for greater social and economic justice. In fiction Lew Wallace's *Ben Hur* (1880) and the many Horatio Alger stories promoting values such as hard work, honesty, and a touch of good fortune sold many millions of copies. Other famous works of the era included Mark Twain's *The Gilded Age* (1873) and *The Adventures of Tom Sawyer* (1876), Bret Harte's stories of the Old West, William Dean Howell's social commentaries, and Henry James's *Daisy Miller* (1879) and *Portrait of a Lady* (1881).

Foreign Relations, 1877–1882

The United States gradually became involved in the "new imperialism" of the 1870s geared to finding markets for surplus industrial production, access to needed raw materials, and opportunities for overseas investment during a time of domestic economic depression. Unlike European territorial colonialism, however, the United States preferred market expansion without the political liability of military occupation.

Latin America

President Hayes recognized the government of dictator Porfirio Diaz in Mexico, thus encouraging not only trade expansion, but U.S. investment in railroads, mines, agriculture, and oil.

Pan Americanism

In 1881 Secretary of State James G. Blaine advocated the creation of an International Bureau of American Republics to promote a customs union of trade and political stability for the Western Hemisphere. The assassination of President Garfield temporarily kept Blaine from forming this organization until 1889. The Bureau subsequently evolved into the Pan American Union in 1910 and the Organization of American States in 1948.

Mediation of Border Disputes

The United States offered its good offices to promote the peaceful resolution of border conflicts between a number of states: in 1876 between Argentina and Paraguay; in 1880 between Colombia and Chile; and in 1881 between Mexico and Guatemala, Argentina and Chile, and Peru and Chile. The United States also worked to bring an end to the War of the Pacific (1879–1884) fought between Chile and the alliance of Peru and Bolivia.

Canal Project

In 1876 the Interoceanic Canal Commission recommended a Nicaraguan route for a canal to link the Atlantic and Pacific oceans. In the 1880s, the U.S. officially took a hostile position against the French Panama Canal project.

The Pacific

In 1878, the United States ratified a treaty with Samoa, giving the U.S. trading rights and a naval base at Pago Pago.

Japan

In 1878, the United States was the first country to negotiate a treaty granting tariff autonomy to Japan, and set a precedent for ending the practice by Western nations of controlling customs house collections in Asian states.

Korea

Commodore Robert Wilson Shufeldt opened trade and diplomatic relations with the Hermit Kingdom in 1882. The United States promoted the principles of equal opportunity of trade, and the sovereignty of Korea (later known as open door policies), which had earlier been advocated as desirable in China.

Native Americans

Westward expansion and the discovery of gold in South Dakota in the early 1870s led to the Sioux War, 1876–1877, and George A. Custer's "last stand." In 1877 the Nez Perce War in Idaho resulted from similar causes. The Apache in Arizona and New Mexico fought as well.

Reservations

The Indian tribes were eventually vanquished and compelled to live on isolated reservations. In addition to superior U.S. military force, disease, railway construction, alcoholism, and the virtual extermination of the bison contributed to their defeat. In 1881 Helen Hunt Jackson's *A Century of Dishonor* chronicled the tragic policy pursued against Native Americans.

Indian prisoners, from Black Kettle's camp, captured by General Custer, traveling through snow.

The Reaction to Corporate Industrialism, 1882–1887

The rise of big business and monopoly capitalism—especially in banking, railroads, mining, and the oil and steel industries—generated a reaction on the part of working class Americans in the form of new labor organizations and collective political action. Most Americans, however, were not opposed to free enterprise economics, but simply wanted an opportunity to share in the profits.

Politics of the Period, 1882–1887

The only Democrat elected president in the half century after the Civil War was Grover Cleveland.

Election of 1884

The Republicans nominated James G. Blaine (Maine) for president and John Logan (Illinois) for vice president. The Democrats chose New York governor Grover Cleveland and Thomas A. Hendricks (Indiana). The defection of Independent Republicans supporting civil service reforms, known as "Mugwumps" (such as E.L. Godkin and Carl Schurz), to the Cleveland camp cost Blaine, the former Speaker of the House, the election. The Democrats held control of the House and the Republicans controlled the Senate.

Presidential Succession Act of 1886

The death of Vice President Hendricks in 1885 led to a decision to change the line of succession (established in 1792) from the president *pro tempore* of the Senate to the Cabinet officers in order of creation of their departments to maintain party leadership. This system lasted until 1947 when the Speaker of the House was declared third in line.

Executive Appointments

President Cleveland insisted that executive appointments and removals were the prerogative of the executive and not the Senate. This was the first time since Andrew Johnson that a president had strengthened the independence of his office.

The Economy, 1882–1887

Large, efficient corporations prospered. Captains of industry, or robber barons, such as John D. Rockefeller in oil, J.P. Morgan in banking, Gustavus Swift in meat processing, Andrew Carnegie in steel, and E.H. Harriman in railroads, put together major industrial empires.

Big Business

The concentration of wealth and power in the hands of a relatively small number of giant firms in many industries led to monopoly capitalism that minimized competition. This process, in turn, led to a demand by smaller businessmen, farmers, and laborers for government regulation of the economy in order to promote capital competition for the salvation of free enterprise economics.

The Interstate Commerce Act (1887)

Popular resentment of railroad abuses, such as price fixing, kickbacks, and discriminatory freight rates, created demands for state regulation of the railway industry. When the Supreme Court ruled individual state laws unconstitutional (*Wabash* case, 1886) because only Congress had the right to control interstate commerce, the Interstate Commerce Act was passed providing that a commission be established to oversee fair and just railway rates, prohibit rebates, end discriminatory practices, and require annual reports and financial statements. The Supreme Court, however, remained a friend of special interests and often undermined the work of the I.C.C.

Expanding Cultivation

Agrarians and ranchers continued their westward expansion. The amount of land under cultivation between 1870 and 1890 more than doubled from 408 to 840 million acres. Transcontinental railroads, modern farm machinery, and soil conservation practices contributed to national prosperity.

Low Farm Prices

Despite success, many farmers were concerned about capital indebtedness, low farm prices resulting from surplus production, railroad rate discrimination, and the lack of sufficient silver currency to promote price inflation. Agrarian groups such as the National Grange and the Farmers' Alliances called for government of the economy to redress their grievances. To a certain extent, however, many of these problems were determined by participation of American agriculture in global markets. Farmers did not completely understand all the risks in an international free market economy.

American Federation of Labor, 1886

Confronted by big business, Samuel Gompers and Adolph Strasser put together a combination of national craft unions to represent the material interests of labor in the matter of wages, hours, and safety conditions. The American Federation of Labor philosophy was pragmatic and not directly influenced by the dogmatic Marxism of some European labor movements. Although militant in its use of the strike and its demand for collective bargaining in labor contracts with large corporations such as those in railroads, mining, and manufacturing, the American Federation of Labor did not intend violent revolution or political radicalism.

Scientific Management

Frederick W. Taylor, an engineer credited as the father of scientific management, introduced modern concepts of industrial engineering, plant management, and time and motion studies. This gave rise to efficiency experts and a separate class of managers in industrial manufacturing.

Social and Cultural Developments, 1882–1887

The continued growth of urban America contributed to the dissemination of knowledge and information in many fields.

Newspapers and Magazines

The linotype machine (1886) invented by Otto Mergenthaler cut printing costs dramatically. Press associations flourished and publishing became big business. In 1884, Joseph Pulitzer, a Hungarian-born immigrant, was the first publisher to reach a mass audience selling 100,000 copies of the *New York World*. New magazines such as *Forum* appeared in 1886 with a hard-hitting editorial style that emphasized investigatory journalism and controversial subjects.

Linotype compositors working at *New York Herald* (1902).

Higher Education

Colleges and universities expanded and introduced a more modern curriculum. Graduate study emphasized meticulous research and the seminar method as pioneered in the United States at Johns Hopkins University.

Women's Colleges

Bryn Mawr (1885) was established and soon found a place among such schools as Vassar, Wellesley, and Mount Holyoke in advancing education for women.

Natural Science

Albert Michelson at the University of Chicago, working on measuring the speed of light, contributed in the 1880s to theories that helped prepare the way for Einstein's Theory of Relativity. In 1907, Michelson was the first American to win a Nobel Prize.

The New Social Science

Richard T. Ely studied the ethical implications of economic problems. Henry C. Adams and Simon Patten put forth theories to justify government regulation and planning in the economy. In sociology, Lester Frank Ward's *Dynamic Sociology* (1883) stressed intelligent planning and decision making over genetic determinism as promoted by Social Darwinists such as William Graham Sumner. Woodrow Wilson's *Congressional Government* was a critique of the committee system in Congress and called for a better working relationship between the executive and legislative branches of government. After winning the presidency in 1912, Wilson would be in a position to put his ideas into practice.

Literary Realism

Romanticism declined in favor of a more realistic approach to literature. Novelists explored social problems such as crime and political corruption, urban ghetto life, class conflict, evolution, and the environment. Mark Twain's masterpiece *Huckleberry Finn* appeared in 1884. In 1885, William Dean Howell's *The Rise of Silas Lapham* presented the theme of business ethics in a competitive society. *The Bostonians* (1886) by Henry James attempted a complex psychological study of female behavior.

Art

Realism could also be seen in the artistic works of Thomas Eakins, Mary Cassatt, Winslow Homer, and James Whistler. Museums and art schools expanded. Wealthy patrons spent fortunes on personal art collections.

Foreign Relations, 1882–1887

Contrary to popular belief, the United States was not an isolationist nation in the 1880s. Trade expansion and the protection of markets were primary concerns.

Modern Navy

In 1883 Congress authorized the construction of new steel ships that would take the U.S. Navy in a twenty-year period from twelfth to third in world naval ranking. In 1884, the U.S. Naval War College was established in Newport, Rhode Island—the first of its kind.

Europe

Problems existed with Britain over violence in Ireland and England. In 1886, the U.S. refused to extradite an Irish national accused of terrorist activity in London.

Diseased meat products in the European market led to British and German bans against uninspected American meat exports. Congress soon provided for government regulation and inspection of meat for export. This action would set a precedent for systematic food and drug inspection in later years.

Africa

The United States participated in the Berlin Conference (1884) concerning trade in the Congo. The U.S. also took part in the Third International Red Cross Conference.

Asia and the Pacific

In 1882, Congress passed a law suspending Chinese immigration to the U.S. for ten years. The act reflected racist attitudes and created friction with China.

In 1886, the U.S. obtained by treaty with Hawaii the Pearl Harbor Naval Base.

Missionaries

American Christian missionaries were active in the Pacific, Asia, Africa, Latin America, and the Middle East. Missionaries not only brought religion to many Third World regions, but also Western education, exposure to science and technology, and commercial ventures. Some missionaries also took with them racist concepts of white supremacy.

Latin America

In 1884, the U.S. signed a short-lived pact with Nicaragua for joint ownership of an isthmian canal in Central America.

The Emergence of Regional Empire, 1887–1892

Despite a protective tariff policy, the United States became increasingly international as it sought to export surplus manufactured and agricultural goods. Foreign markets were viewed as a safety valve for labor employment problems and agrarian unrest. The return of Secretary of State James G. Blaine in 1889 marked a major attempt by the United States to promote a regional empire in the Western Hemisphere and reciprocal trade programs.

Politics of the Period, 1887–1892

National politics became more controversial and turbulent in this era.

Election of 1888

Although the Democrat Grover Cleveland won the popular vote by about 100,000 over the Republican Benjamin Harrison, Harrison carried the electoral college 233 to 168 and was declared president after waging a vigorous campaign to protect American industrial interests with a high protective tariff. In Congress, Republicans won control of both the House and Senate.

Benjamin Harrison

House Rules of Operation

Republican Thomas B. Reed became Speaker of the House in 1890, and changed the rules of operation to make himself a veritable tsar with absolute control in running the House.

Force Bill (1890)

Senate objections kept Congress from protecting African-American voters in the South through federal supervision of state elections.

Dependent Pensions Act (1890)

Congress granted service pensions to Union veterans and their dependents for the first time.

The Economy, 1887–1892

Antimonopoly measures, protective tariffs and reciprocal trade, and a billion dollar budget became the order of the day.

Sherman Anti-Trust Act, 1890

Corporate monopolies (trusts) that controlled whole industries were subject to federal prosecution if they were found to be combinations or conspiracies in restraint of trade. Although supported by smaller businesses, labor unions, and farm associations, the Sherman Anti-Trust Act was in time interpreted by the Supreme Court to apply to labor unions and farmers' cooperatives as much as to large corporate combinations.

Sherman Silver Purchase Act, 1890

Pro-silver interests passed legislation authorizing Congress to buy 4.5 million ounces of silver each month at market prices, and issue Treasury notes redeemable in gold and silver. This act created inflation and lowered gold reserves.

McKinley Tariff, 1890

This compromise protective tariff promised by the Republicans in 1888 and introduced by William McKinley of Ohio was passed and extended to industrial and agricultural goods. The act also included reciprocal trade provisions that allowed the president to retaliate against nations that discriminated against U.S. products and reward states that opened their markets to American goods. Subsequent price increases led to a popular backlash and a Democratic House victory in the 1890 congressional elections.

Billion-Dollar Budget

Congress depleted the Treasury surplus with the first peacetime billion-dollar appropriation of funds for state tax refunds, infrastructure improvements, Navy modernization, and pension payments. The loss of Treasury reserves put the economy in a precarious position when an economic panic occurred in 1893.

Social and Cultural Developments, 1887–1892

Entertainment for the masses became increasingly differentiated.

Popular Amusements

In addition to the legitimate stage, vaudeville shows presenting variety acts became immensely popular. The circus expanded when Barnum and Bailey formed a partnership to present "the greatest show on earth." Distinctively American Wild West shows toured North America and Europe. To record these activities, George Eastman's newly invented roll-film camera became popular with spectators.

Sports

In 1888, professional baseball sent an all-star team to tour the world. Boxing adopted leather gloves in 1892. Croquet and bicycle racing were new crazes. Basketball was invented in 1891 by James Naismith, a Massachusetts Y.M.C.A. instructor. Organized intercollegiate sports such as football, basketball, and baseball created intense rivalries between colleges that attracted mass spectator interest.

Childrearing Practices

Parents became more supportive and sympathetic to their children and less authoritarian and restrictive. The 1880s were something of a golden age in children's literature. Mary Wells Smith depicted an agrarian ideal; Sidney Lanier wrote tales of heroic boys and girls; Howard Pyle's *Robin Hood* gained wide readership, and Joel Chandler Harris' characters Br'er Rabbit, Br'er Fox, and Uncle Remus became very popular.

Religion

Many churches took issue with the growing emphasis on materialism in American society. Dwight Lyman Moody introduced Urban revivalism comparable to earlier rural movements among Protestant denominations. In addition, the new immigrants generated significant growth for Roman Catholicism and Judaism. By 1890, there were about 150 religious denominations in the United States.

Foreign Relations, 1887–1892

Following in the footsteps of William Seward as a major architect of American foreign policy, James G. Blaine promoted hemispheric solidarity with Latin America and economic expansionism.

Pan Americanism

As Secretary of State, Blaine was concerned with international trade, political stability, and excessive militarism in Latin America. His international Bureau of American Republics was designed to promote a Pan American customs union and peaceful conflict resolution. To achieve his aims, Blaine opposed U.S. military intervention in the hemisphere.

To a certain extent, his policies were in the tradition of President James Monroe and his Secretary of State, John Quincy Adams.

Haiti

After the Haitian revolution of 1888–1889, Blaine resisted pressure for U.S. intervention to establish a naval base near Port-au-Prince. The noted African-American Frederick Douglas played a key role in advising Blaine as U.S. minister to Haiti.

Chilean Revolution

When American sailors from the U.S.S. *Baltimore* were killed in Valparaiso (1891), President Harrison threatened war with the anti-American revolutionary government of President Balmaceda. Secretary Blaine helped to bring about a Chilean apology and preserve his Pan American policy.

Asia and the Pacific

The medical missionary/diplomat Horace Allen promoted peaceful American investment and trade with Korea.

In 1889, the United States upheld its interests against German expansion in the Samoan Islands by establishing a three-party protectorate over Samoa with Britain and Germany. The United States retained the port of Pago Pago.

In 1891, Queen Lydia Kamekeha Liliuokalani resisted American attempts to promote a protectorate over Hawaii. By 1893, pro-American sugar planters overthrew the native Hawaiian government and established a new government friendly to the United States.

Africa

The United States refused (1890) naval bases in the Portuguese colonies of Angola and Mozambique when Portugal was looking for allies against British expansion in Africa. Blaine opposed territorial expansion for the U.S. in Africa, but favored the development of commercial markets.

Theoretical Works

In 1890, naval Captain Alfred Thayer Mahan published *The Influence of Sea Power on History* which argued that control of the seas was the means to world power. Josiah Strong's *Our Country* presented the thesis that Americans had a mission to fulfill by exporting the word of God around the world, especially to non-white populations. Frederick Jackson Turner's "Frontier Thesis" (1893) justified overseas economic expansion as a way to secure political power and prosperity. In *The Law of Civilization and Decay* (1895), Brooks Adams postulated that a nation must expand or face inevitable decline.

Europe

The murders of eleven Italian citizens in New Orleans (1891) brought the United States and Italy into confrontation. The United States defused the situation by compensating the families of the victims.

Economic Depression and Social Crisis, 1892–1897

The economic depression that began in 1893 brought about a collective response from organized labor, militant agriculture, and the business community. Each group called for economic safeguards and a more humane free enterprise system that would expand economic opportunities in an equitable manner.

Election of 1892

Democrat Grover Cleveland (New York) and his vice presidential running mate, Adlai E. Stevenson (Illinois), regained the White House by defeating the Republican President Benjamin Harrison (Indiana) and Vice President Whitelaw Reid (New York). Voters generally reacted against the inflationary McKinley Tariff. Cleveland's conservative economic stand in favor of the gold standard brought him the support of various business interests. The Democrats won control of both houses of Congress.

Populist Party

The People's Party (Populist) nominated James Weaver (Iowa) for president and James Field (Virginia) for vice president in 1892. The party platform put together by such Populist leaders as Ignatius Donnally (Minnesota), Thomas Watson (Georgia), Mary Lease (Kansas), and "Sockless" Jerry Simpson (Kansas) called for the enactment of a program espoused by agrarians, but also for a coalition with urban workers and the middle class. Specific goals were the coinage of silver to gold at a ratio of 16 to 1; federal loans to farmers; a graduated income tax; postal savings banks; public ownership of railroads, telephone, and telegraph systems; prohibition of alien land ownership; immigration restriction; a ban on private armies used by corporations to break up strikes; an eight-hour working day; a single six-year term for president and direct election of senators; the right of initiative and referendum; and the use of the secret ballot.

Although the Populists were considered radical by some, they actually wanted to reform the system from within and allow for a fairer distribution of wealth. In a society with vast differences in income and wealth, the Populists were able to garner about one million votes (out of 11 million votes cast) and 22 electoral votes. By 1894, Populists had elected 4 senators, 4 congressmen, 21 state executive officials, 150 state senators, and 315 state representatives, primarily in the West and South. After the 1893 depression, the Populists planned a serious bid for national power in the 1896 election.

Repeal of Sherman Silver Purchase Act (1893)

After the economic panic of 1893, Cleveland tried to limit the outflow of gold reserves by asking Congress to repeal the Sherman Silver Act, which had provided for notes redemptive in either gold or silver. Congress did repeal the act, but the Democratic Party split over the issue.

Pennsylvania state militia arrive to quell violent Homestead strike (1892).

Election of 1896

The Republicans nominated William McKinley (Ohio) for president and Garrett Hobart (New Jersey) for vice president on a platform calling for maintaining the gold standard and protective tariffs. The Democratic Party repudiated Cleveland's conservative economics and nominated William Jennings Bryan (Nebraska) and Arthur Sewell (Maine) for president and vice president on a platform similar to the Populists: 1) coinage of silver at a ratio of 16 to 1; 2) condemnation of monopolies, protective tariffs, and anti-union court injunctions; and 3) criticism of the Supreme Court's removal of a graduated income tax from the Wilson-Gorman tariff bill (1894). Bryan delivered one of the most famous speeches in American history when he declared that the people must not be "crucified upon a cross of gold."

The Populist Party also nominated Bryan, but chose Thomas Watson (Georgia) for vice president. Having been outmaneuvered by the Silver Democrats, the Populists lost the opportunity to become a permanent political force.

McKinley won a hard-fought election by only about one-half million votes as Republicans succeeded in creating fear among business groups and middle-class voters that Bryan represented a revolutionary challenge to the American system. The manipulation of higher farm prices, and the warning to labor unions that they would face unemployment if Bryan won the election helped to tilt the vote in favor of McKinley. An often forgotten issue in 1896 was the Republican promise to stabilize the ongoing Cuban revolution. This pledge would eventually lead the U.S. into war with Spain (1898) for Cuban independence. The Republicans retained control over Congress, which they had gained in 1894.

The Economy, 1892–1897

The 1890s was a period of economic depression and labor agitation.

Homestead Strike, 1892

Iron and steel workers went on strike in Pennsylvania against the Carnegie Steel Company to protest salary reductions. Carnegie employed strike-breaking Pinkerton security guards. Management-labor warfare led to a number of deaths on both sides.

Depression of 1893

The primary causes for the Depression of 1893 were the dramatic growth of the federal deficit; withdrawal of British investments from the American market and the outward transfer of gold; and loss of business confidence. The bankruptcy of the National Cordage Company was the first among thousands of U.S. corporations that closed banks and businesses. As a consequence, twenty percent of the workforce was eventually unemployed. The depression would last four years. Recovery would be helped by war preparation.

March of Unemployed (1894)

The Populist businessman Jacob Coxey led a march on Washington of hundreds of unemployed workers asking for a government work relief program. The government met the marchers with force and arrested their leaders.

Pullman Strike (1894)

Eugene V. Debs' American Railway Union struck the Pullman Palace Car Co. in Chicago over wage cuts and job losses. President Cleveland broke the violent strike with federal troops. Popular opinion deplored violence and militant labor tactics.

Wilson-Gorman Tariff (1894)

This protective tariff did little to promote overseas trade as a way to ease the depression. A provision amended to create a graduated income tax was stricken by the Supreme Court as unconstitutional (*Pollack v. Farmers' Loan and Trust Co.*, 1895).

Dingley Tariff (1897)

The Dingley Tariff raised protection to new highs for certain commodities.

Surplus Production and Foreign Trade

Anxiety over domestic class warfare and the desire to sell surplus manufactured goods overseas led many business interests to encourage the U.S. government to find new international markets. Carnegie Steel and Standard Oil lobbied the State Department for better trade promotion policies as a way to recover from the depression and provide jobs for American workers. Ironically, special business interests often undercut efforts to establish reciprocal trade agreements and free trade in favor of politically motivated tariff protection.

Social and Cultural Developments, 1892–1897

Economic depression and war dominated thought and literature in the decade of the 1890s.

Literature

Lester Frank Ward of Brown University presented a critique of excessive competition in favor of social planning in *The Psychic Factors of Civilization*, 1893. William Dean Howells' *A Hazard of New Fortunes*, 1890, was a broad attack on urban living conditions in industrial America and on the callous treatment of workers by wealthy tycoons. Stephen Crane wrote about society's abuse of women in *Maggie, A Girl of the Streets*, 1892, and the pain of war in *The Red Badge of Courage*, 1895. Edward Bellamy's *Looking Backward* presented a science fiction look into a prosperous, but regimented future.

Americans also began to read such European realists as Dostoevsky, Ibsen, Tolstoy, and Zola.

William James' *Principles of Psychology* introduced the discipline to American readers as a modern science of the human mind.

Prohibition of Alcohol

The Anti-Saloon League was formed in 1893. Women were especially concerned about the increase of drunkenness during the depression.

Immigration

Immigration declined by almost 400,000 during the depression. Jane Addams' Hull House in Chicago continued to function as a means of settling poor immigrants from Greece, Germany, Italy, Poland, Russia, and elsewhere into American society. Lillian Wald's Henry Street Settlement in New York, and Robert Wood's South End House in Boston performed similar functions. Such institutions also lobbied against sweatshop labor conditions and for bans on child labor.

Chautauqua Movement

Home study courses growing out of the Chautauqua Movement in New York State became popular.

Thomas Edison, the "Wizard of Menlo Park."

Chicago World's Fair (1893)

Beautifying the cities was the fair's main theme. One lasting development was the expansion of urban public parks.

Radio and Film

Nathan Stubblefield transmitted voice over the air without wires in 1892. Thomas Edison's kinetoscope permitted the viewing of motion pictures in 1893.

Foreign Relations, 1892–1897

In addition to the economic depression, three international events in 1895 that propelled the United States foreign policy were the Cuban war for independence against Spain, Britain's boundary dispute with Venezuela, and the settlement of the Sino-Japanese War.

Cuba and Spain

The Cuban revolt against Spain in 1895 impacted the U.S. in that Americans had about $50 million invested in the Cuban economy and did an annual business of over $100 million in Cuba. During the election of 1896, McKinley promised to stabilize the situation and work for an end to hostilities. Sensational "yellow" journalism and nationalistic statements from officials such as Assistant Secretary of the Navy Theodore Roosevelt encouraged popular support for direct American military intervention on behalf of Cuban independence. President McKinley, however, proceeded cautiously through 1897.

Britain and Venezuela (1895)

The dispute over the border of Britain's colony of Guiana threatened war with Venezuela, especially after gold was discovered in the area. Although initially at odds with Britain, the United States eventually came to support British claims against Venezuela when Britain agreed to recognize the Monroe Doctrine in Latin America. Britain also sought U.S. cooperation in its dispute with Germany in South Africa. This rivalry would in time lead to the Boer War. The realignment of the United States and Britain would play a significant role during World War I.

The Sino-Japanese War, 1894–1895

Japan's easy victory over China signaled to the United States and other nations trading in Asia that China's weakness might result in its colonization by industrial powers, and the closing of the China market. The U.S. resolved to seek a naval base in the Pacific to protect its interests. The opportunity to annex the Philippines after the war with Spain was in part motivated by the desire to protect America's trade and future potential in Asia. This concern would also lead the U.S. to announce the Open Door policy with China in 1899 and 1900. It was designed to protect equal opportunity of trade and China's political independence.

Latin America

When revolutions broke out in 1894 in both Brazil and Nicaragua, the United States supported the existing governments in power to maintain political stability and favorable trade treaties. Secretaries of State Walter Q. Gresham, Richard Olney, and John Sherman continued to support James G. Blaine's Pan American policy.

The Pacific

The United States intervened in the Hawaiian revolution (1893) to overthrow the anti-American government of Queen Liliuokalani. President Cleveland rejected American annexation of Hawaii in 1894, but President McKinley agreed to annex it in 1898.

War and the Americanization of the World, 1897–1902

In 1900, an Englishman named William T. Stead authored a book entitled *The Americanization of the World* in which he predicted that American productivity and economic strength would propel the United States to the forefront of world leadership in the twentieth century. The Spanish-American War and the events following it indicated that the U.S. would be a force in the global balance of power for years to come. Few, however, would have predicted that as early as 1920 the U.S. would achieve the pinnacle of world power as a result of the debilitating policies pursued by European political leaders during World War I (1914–1919). One question remained: Would the American people be prepared to accept the responsibility of world leadership?

Politics of the Period, 1897–1902

President McKinley's wartime leadership and tragic assassination closed one door in American history, but opened another door to the leadership of Theodore Roosevelt, the first "progressive" president.

Election of 1900

The unexpected death of Vice President Garrett Hobart led the Republican Party to choose the war hero and reform governor of New York, Theodore Roosevelt, as President William McKinley's vice presidential running mate. Riding the crest of victory against Spain, the G.O.P. platform called for upholding the gold standard for full economic recovery, promoting economic expansion and power in the Caribbean and the Pacific, and building a canal in Central America. The Democrats once again nominated William Jennings Bryan and Adlai Stevenson on a platform condemning imperialism and the gold standard. McKinley easily won reelection by about 1 million votes (7.2 million to 6.3 million), and the Republicans retained control of both houses of Congress.

Other Parties

The fading Populists nominated Wharton Barker (Pennsylvania) and Ignatius Donnelly (Minnesota) on a pro-inflation platform but only received 50,000 votes. The Socialist Democratic Party nominated Eugene V. Debs (Indiana) and Job Harriman (California) on a platform urging the nationalization of major industries. Debs received 94,000 votes. The Prohibition Party nominated John Woolley (Illinois) and Henry Metcalf (Rhode Island) and called for a ban on alcohol production and consumption. They received 209,000 votes.

McKinley's Assassination (1901)

While attending the Pan American Exposition in Buffalo, New York, the president was shot on September 6 by Leon Czolgosz, an anarchist sworn to destroy all governments. The president died on September 14 after many officials had said they thought he would recover. Theodore Roosevelt became the nation's twenty-fifth president and—at age 42— its youngest to date.

Assassination of President McKinley, Sept. 6, 1901.

The Economy, 1897–1902

The war with Spain provided the impetus for economic recovery. President Roosevelt promised a "square deal" for all Americans, farmers, workers, consumers, and businessmen. Progressive economic reform was geared to the rejuvenation of free enterprise capitalism following the 1893 depression and the destruction of illegal monopolies. In this way, radicals would be denied an audience for more revolutionary and violent change.

War with Spain (1898)

The financial cost of the war was $250,000,000. Eastern and Midwestern industrial cities tended to favor war and benefit from it. Northeastern financial centers were more cautious about war until March 1898, and questioned the financial gains of wartime production at the expense of peacetime expansion and product/market development.

Federal Bankruptcy Act (1898)

This act reformed and standardized procedures for bankruptcy, along with the responsibilities of creditors and debtors.

Erdman Act (1898)

The Erdman Act provided for mediation by the chair of the Interstate Commerce Commission and the commissioner of the Bureau of Labor in unresolved railroad labor controversies.

Currency Act (1900)

The United States standardized the amount of gold in the dollar at 25.8 grains, 9/10s fine. A separate gold reserve was set apart from other general funds, and government bonds were sold to maintain the reserve.

Technology

Between 1860 and 1900 railroad trackage grew from 36,800 miles to 193,350 miles. U.S. Steel Corp. was formed in 1901 and the Standard Oil Company of New Jersey in 1899.

Social and Cultural Developments, 1897–1902

Debates about the war and territorial acquisitions, and the state of the economy, tended to dominate thought and literature.

Yellow Journalism

Joseph Pulitzer's *New York World* and William Randolph Hearst's *New York Journal* competed fiercely to increase circulation through exaggeration of Spanish atrocities in Cuba. Such stories whipped up popular resentment of Spain and helped to create a climate of opinion receptive to war.

DeLôme Letter and Sinking of the Maine

On February 9, 1898, the newspapers published a letter written by the Spanish minister in Washington, *Depuy de Lôme*, personally criticizing President McKinley in insulting terms. On February 15, the battleship U.S.S. *Maine* was blown up in Havana harbor with a loss of 250 Americans. The popular demand for war with Spain grew significantly even though it was likely that the *Maine* was blown up by accident when spontaneous combustion in a coal bunker caused a powder magazine to explode.

U.S. Military

Facing its first war since the Civil War, the U.S. Army was not prepared for a full-scale effort in 1898. Although 245,000 men served in the war (with over 5,000 deaths), the Army at the outset consisted of only 28,000 troops. The volunteers who signed up in the early stages were surprised to be issued winter uniforms to train in the tropics for war in Cuba. Cans of food stockpiled since the Civil War were reissued. After getting past these early problems, the War Department settled down to a more effective organizational procedure. Sadly, more deaths resulted from disease and food poisoning than from battlefield casualties. The U.S. Navy (26,000 men) was far better prepared for war as a result of past years of modernization.

Territories

After the United States had defeated Spain (see "Foreign Policy"), it was faced with the issue of what to do with such captured territories as the Philippines, Puerto Rico, the Isle of Pines, and Guam. A major public debate ensued with critics of land acquisition forming the Anti-Imperialist League with the support of Mark Twain, William James, William Jennings Bryan, Grover Cleveland, Charles Francis Adams, Carl Schurz, Charles W. Eliot, David Starr Jordan, Andrew Carnegie, and Samuel Gompers among others. Supporters of colonialism included Theodore Roosevelt, Mark Hanna, Alfred Thayer Mahan, Henry Cabot

Theodore Roosevelt and the Rough Riders

Lodge, Albert Beveridge, President McKinley, and many others. Ironically, many individuals in both camps favored U.S. economic expansion, but had difficulty with the idea that a democracy would actually accept colonies and overseas armies of occupations.

Literature

Thorstein Veblen's *Theory of the Leisure Class* (1899) attacked the "predatory wealth" and "conspicuous consumption" of the new rich in the gilded age. Veblen added evidence and argument to a critique begun by Jacob Riis in *How the Other Half Lives* (1890), documenting the gnawing poverty, illness, crime and despair of New York's slums. Frank Norris's *McTeague* (1899) chronicled a man's regression to brutish animal behavior in the dog-eat-dog world of unbridled and unregulated capitalist competition. His novel *The Octopus* (1901) condemned monopoly.

Foreign Policy, 1897–1902

The summer war with Spain and the expansion of American interests in Asia and the Caribbean were dominant factors.

Decision for War (1898)

Loss of markets, threats to Americans in Cuba, and the inability of both Spain and Cuba to resolve the Cuban revolution either by force or diplomacy led to McKinley's request of Congress for a declaration of war. The sinking of the *Maine* in February 1898 and the return of Vermont Senator Redfield Proctor from a fact-finding mission on March 17, 1898, revealed how poor the situation was in Cuba.

McKinley's Ultimatum

On March 27, President McKinley asked Spain to call an armistice, accept American mediation to end the war, and end the use of concentration camps in Cuba. When Spain refused to comply, McKinley requested Congress to declare war. On April 21, Congress declared war on Spain with the objective of establishing Cuban independence (Teller Amendment).

Cuba

After the first U.S. forces landed in Cuba on June 22, 1898, the United States proceeded to victories at El Caney and San Juan Hill. By July 17, Admiral Sampson's North Atlantic Squadron destroyed the Spanish fleet, Santiago surrendered, and American troops quickly went on to capture Puerto Rico.

The Philippines

As early as December 1897, Commodore Perry's Asiatic Squadron was alerted to a possible war with Spain. On May 1, 1898, the Spanish fleet in the Philippines was destroyed and Manila surrendered on August 13. Spain agreed to a peace conference to be held in Paris in October 1898.

Treaty of Paris

Secretary of State William Day led the American negotiating team, which secured Cuban independence, the ceding of the Philippines, Puerto Rico, and Guam to the U.S., and the payment of $20 million to Spain for the Philippines. The treaty was ratified by the Senate on February 6, 1900.

Philippines Insurrection

Filipino nationalists under Emilio Aguinaldo rebelled against the United States (February 1899) when they learned the Philippines would not be given independence. The United States used 70,000 men to suppress the revolutionaries by June 1902. A special U.S. commission recommended eventual self-government for the Philippines.

Hawaii and Wake Island

During the war with Spain, the U.S. annexed Hawaii on July 7, 1898. In 1900 the U.S. claimed Wake Island, 2,000 miles west of Hawaii.

China

Fearing the break-up of China into separate spheres of influence, Secretary of State John Hay called for acceptance of the Open Door Notes by all nations trading in the China market to guarantee equal opportunity of trade (1899) and the sovereignty of the Manchu government of China (1900). With Manila as a base of operations, the United States was better able to protect its economic and political concerns in Asia. Such interests included the American China Development Co. (1898), a railway and mining concession in south China, and various oil, timber, and industrial investments in Manchuria.

Boxer Rebellion (1900)

Chinese nationalists ("Boxers") struck at foreign settlements in China and at the Ch'ing dynasty Manchu government in Beijing for allowing foreign industrial nations such as Britain, Japan, Russia, France, Germany, Italy, Portugal, Belgium, The Netherlands, and the United States large concessions within Chinese borders. An international army helped to put down the rebellion and aided the Chinese government to remain in power.

Platt Amendment (1901)

Although Cuba was granted its independence, the Platt Amendment provided that Cuba become a virtual protectorate of the United States. Cuba could not 1) make a treaty with a foreign state impairing its independence or 2) contract an excessive public debt. Cuba was required to 1) allow the U.S. to preserve order on the island and 2) lease a naval base for 99 years to the U.S. at Guantanamo Bay.

Hay-Pauncefote Treaty (1901)

This treaty between the U.S. and Britain abrogated an earlier agreement (1850, Clayton-Bulwer Treaty) to build jointly an isthmian canal. The United States was free unilaterally to construct, fortify, and maintain a canal that would be open to all ships.

Insular Cases (1901–1903)

The Supreme Court decided that constitutional rights did not extend to territorial possessions, thus the Constitution did not follow the flag. Congress had the right to administer each island possession without constitutional restraint. Inhabitants of those possessions did not have the same rights as American citizens.

Theodore Roosevelt and Progressive Reforms, 1902–1907

As a Republican progressive reformer committed to honest and efficient government designed to serve all social classes in America, Theodore Roosevelt restored the presidency to the high eminence it had held through the Civil War era, and redressed the balance of power with old guard leaders in Congress.

Theodore Roosevelt

Politics of the Period, 1902–1907

President Roosevelt did much to create a bipartisan coalition of liberal reformers whose objective was to restrain corporate monopoly and promote economic competition at home and abroad. Roosevelt won the support of enlightened business leaders, the middle class, consumers, and urban and rural workers with his promise of a "square deal" for all.

Roosevelt's Anti-Trust Policy, 1902

The president pledged strict enforcement of the Sherman Anti-Trust Act (1890) to break up illegal monopolies and regulate large corporations for the public good through honest federal government administration.

Progressive Reform in the States

Taking their cue from Washington, many states enacted laws creating honest and efficient political and economic regulatory standards.

Political reforms included enacting laws establishing primary elections (Mississippi, Wisconsin), initiative and referendum (South Dakota, Oregon), and the rooting out of political bosses on the state and municipal levels (especially in New York, Ohio, Michigan, and California).

Commission Form of Government, 1903

After a hurricane and tidal wave destroyed much of Galveston, Texas, progressive businessmen and Texas state legislators removed the ineffective and corrupt mayor and city council and established a city government of five elected commissioners who were experts in their fields to rebuild Galveston. Numerous other cities adopted the commission form of government to replace the mayor/council format.

State Leaders

Significant state reformers in the period were Robert LaFollette of Wisconsin, Albert Cummins of Iowa, Charles Evans Hughes of New York, James M. Cox of Ohio, Hiram Johnson of California, William S. Wren of Oregon, Albert Beveridge of Indiana, and Woodrow Wilson of New Jersey.

City Reformers

Urban leaders included John Purroy Mitchell of New York City, Tom L. Johnson and Newton Baker of Cleveland, Hazen Pingree of Detroit, Sam Jones of Toledo, and Joseph Folk of St. Louis.

Election of 1904

Having assured Republican Party leaders that he wished to reform corporate monopolies and railroads, but not interfere with monetary policy or tariffs, Roosevelt was nominated for president along with Charles Fairbanks (Indiana) for vice president. The Democratic Party nominated New York judge Alton B. Parker for president and Henry G. Davis (West Virginia) for vice president on a platform that endorsed Roosevelt's "trust-busting," which called for even greater power for such regulatory agencies as the Interstate Commerce Commission, and accepted the conservative gold standard as the basis for monetary policy. Roosevelt easily defeated Parker by about two million votes, and the Republicans retained control of both houses of Congress.

Hepburn Act, 1906

Membership of the Interstate Commerce Commission was increased from five to seven. The I.C.C. could set its own fair freight rates, had its regulatory power extended over pipelines, bridges, and express companies, and was empowered to require a uniform system of accounting by regulated transportation companies. This act and the Elkins Act (1903 —reiterated illegality of railroad rebates) gave teeth to the original Interstate Commerce Act of 1887.

Pure Food and Drug Act (1906)

Prohibited the manufacture, sale, and transportation of adulterated or fraudulently labeled foods and drugs in accordance with consumer demands to which Theodore Roosevelt was especially sensitive.

Meat Inspection Act (1906)

Provided for federal and sanitary regulations and inspections in meat packing facilities. Wartime scandals in 1898 relating to spoiled canned meats were a powerful force for reform.

Immunity of Witness Act (1906)

Corporate officials could no longer make a plea of immunity to avoid testifying in cases involving their corporation's illegal activities.

Conservation Laws

From 1902 to 1908, a series of laws and executive actions were enacted to create federal irrigation projects, national parks and forests, develop water power (Internal Waterways Commission), and establish the National Conservation Commission to oversee the nation's resources.

The Economy, 1902–1907

Antitrust policy and government regulation of the economy gave way to a more lenient enforcement of federal laws after the panic of 1907. Recognition of the rights of labor unions was enhanced.

Antitrust Policy (1902)

In order to restore free competition, President Roosevelt ordered the Justice Department to prosecute corporations pursuing monopolistic practices. Attorney General P.C. Knox first brought suit against the Northern Securities Company, a railroad holding corporation put together by J.P. Morgan; then he moved against Rockefeller's Standard Oil Company. By the time he left office in 1909, Roosevelt brought indictments against 25 monopolies.

Department of Commerce and Labor (1903)

A new Cabinet position was created to address the concerns of business and labor. Within the department, the Bureau of Corporations was empowered to investigate and report on the illegal activities of corporations.

Coal Strike (1902)

Roosevelt interceded with government mediation to bring about negotiations between the United Mine Workers union and the anthracite mine owners after a bitter strike over wages, safety conditions, and union recognition. This was the first time that the government intervened in a labor dispute without automatically siding with management.

Panic of 1907

A brief economic recession and panic occurred in 1907 as a result, in part, of questionable bank speculations, a lack of flexible monetary and credit policies, and a conservative gold standard. This event called attention to the need for banking reform that would lead to the Federal Reserve System in 1913. Although Roosevelt temporarily eased the pressure on antitrust activity, he made it clear that reform of the economic system to promote free-enterprise capitalism would continue.

St. Louis World's Fair (1904)

The World's Fair of 1904 celebrated the centennial of the Louisiana Purchase and brought the participation of Asian nations to promote foreign trade.

Social and Cultural Developments, 1902–1907

Debate and discussion over the expanding role of the federal government commanded the attention of the nation.

Progressive Reforms

There was not one unified progressive movement, but a series of reform causes designed to address specific social, economic, and political problems. Middle-class men and women were especially active in attempting to correct the excessive powers of giant corporations, and the radical extremes of Marxist revolutionaries and radicals among intellectuals and labor activists. However, mainstream business and labor leaders were moderate in their desire to preserve economic opportunities and the free enterprise system.

Varieties of Reform

Progressive reform goals included not only honest government, economic regulation, environmental conservation, labor recognition, and new political structures. Reformers also called for gender equality for men and women in the workforce (Oregon Ten Hour Law), an end to racial segregation (National Association for the Advancement of Colored People), child labor laws, prison reform, regulation of the stock market, direct election of senators, and a more efficient foreign service among other reform activities.

Muckrakers

Muckrakers (a term coined by Roosevelt) were investigative journalists and authors who were often the publicity agents for reforms. Popular magazines included *McClure's*, *Collier's*, *Cosmopolitan*, and *Everybody's*. Famous articles that led to reforms included "The Shame of the Cities" by Lincoln Steffens, "History of Standard Oil Company" by Ida Tarbell, "The Treason of the Senate" by David Phillips, and "Frenzied Finance" by Thomas Lawson.

Literature

Works of literature with a social message included *Following the Color Line* by Ray Stannard Baker, *The Bitter Cry of the Children* by John Spargo, *Poverty* by Robert Hunter, *The Story of Life Insurance* by Burton Hendrick, *The Financier* by Theodore Dreiser, *The Jungle* by Upton Sinclair, *The Boss* by Henry Lewis, *Call of the Wild*, *The Iron Heel,* and *The War of the Classes* by Jack London, *A Certain Rich Man* by William Allen White, and *The Promise of American Life* by Herbert Croly.

Inventions

The Wright brothers made the first piloted flight of a heavier-than-air machine at Kitty Hawk, North Carolina, in 1903. News of their feat traveled slowly and was widely doubted.

Foreign Relations, 1902–1907

Theodore Roosevelt's "Big Stick" diplomacy and economic foreign policy were characteristics of the administration.

Panama Canal

Roosevelt used executive power to engineer the separation of Panama from Colombia, and the recognition of Panama as an independent country. The Hay-Bunau-Varilla Treaty of 1903 granted the United

States control of the Canal Zone in Panama for $10 million and an annual fee of $250,000 beginning nine years after ratification of the treaty by both parties. Construction of the canal began in 1904 and was completed in 1914.

Roosevelt Corollary to the Monroe Doctrine

The U.S. reserved the right to intervene in the internal affairs of Latin American nations to keep European powers from using military force to collect debts in the Western Hemisphere. The U.S. eventually intervened in the affairs of Venezuela, Haiti, the Dominican Republic, Nicaragua, and Cuba by 1905 as an international policeman brandishing the "big stick" against Europeans and Latin Americans.

Rio de Janeiro Conference (1906)

Secretary of State Elihu Root attempted to de-emphasize U.S. military and political intervention in order to promote political goodwill, economic development, trade, and finances in Latin America. President Roosevelt was actually moving away from "big stick" diplomacy and toward "dollar diplomacy" before he left office. The United States also promoted the Pan American Railway project at the meeting of the International Bureau of American Republics.

China

In pursuit of the Open Door policy of equal opportunity of trade and the guaranteed independence of China, the United States continued to promote its trade interests in Asia. Segregation and restrictions of Chinese immigrants in California and other states led Chinese national leaders to call for a boycott in 1905 of U.S. goods and services in both China and the United States. The boycott ended in 1906 without significant changes in state laws.

Russo-Japanese War (1904–1905)

With American encouragement and financial loans, Japan pursued and won a war against tsarist Russia. Roosevelt negotiated the Treaty of Portsmouth, New Hampshire, which ended the war, and for which the president ironically received the Nobel Peace Prize in 1906. Japan, however, was disappointed at not receiving more territory and financial compensation from Russia and blamed the United States.

Taft-Katsura Memo, 1905

The United States and Japan pledged to maintain the Open Door principles in China. Japan recognized American control over the Philippines, and the United States granted a Japanese protectorate over Korea.

Gentleman's Agreement with Japan, 1907

After numerous incidents of racial discrimination against Japanese in California, Japan agreed to restrict the emigration of unskilled Japanese workers to the U.S.

Great White Fleet, 1907

In order to show American strength to Japan and China, Roosevelt sent the great white naval fleet to Asian ports.

Algeciras Conference, 1906

The United States participated in the Algeciras Conference with eight European states to guarantee equal opportunity of trade for Morocco. The independence granted the sultan of Morocco was reminiscent of the Open Door policy initiated by the U.S. with China at the turn of the century. The conference (held at Algeciras, Spain, January 16–April 7, 1906), however, created tension between Germany and France, which would end up at war in the next decade.

The Second Hague Conference, 1907

Forty-six nations, including the United States, met in the Netherlands to discuss disarmament and the creation of an international court of justice. Little was accomplished except for the adoption of a resolution banning the use of military force for the collection of foreign debts.

The Regulatory State and the Ordered Society, 1907–1912

The progressive presidencies of Roosevelt, Taft, and Wilson brought the concept of big government to fruition. A complex corporate society needed rules and regulations as well as powerful agencies to enforce those measures necessary to maintain and enhance democratic free enterprise competition. The search for political, social, and economic standards designed to preserve order in American society while still guaranteeing political, social, and economic freedom was a difficult, but primary task. The nation increasingly looked to Washington to protect the less powerful segments of the republic from the special interests that had grown up in the late nineteenth century. A persistent problem for the federal government was how best to preserve order and standards in a complex technological society while not interfering with the basic liberties Americans came to cherish in the Constitution and throughout their history. The strain of World War I after 1914 would further complicate the problem.

Politics of the Period, 1907–1912

The continuation of progressive reforms by both Republican and Democratic leaders helped to form a consensus for the establishment of regulatory standards.

Election 1908

Deciding not to run for re-election, Theodore Roosevelt opened the way for William H. Taft (Ohio) and James S. Sherman (New York) to run on a Republican platform calling for a continuation of antitrust enforcement, environmental conservation, and a lower tariff policy to promote international trade. The Democrats nominated William Jennings Bryan for a third time with John Kern (Indiana) for vice president on an antimonopoly and low tariff platform. The Socialists once again nominated Eugene V. Debs. Taft easily won by over a million votes, and the Republicans retained control of both houses of Congress. For the first time, the American Federation of Labor entered national politics officially with an endorsement of Bryan. This decision began a long alliance between organized labor and the Democratic Party in the twentiethth century.

Taft's Objectives

The president had two primary political goals in 1909. One was the continuation of Roosevelt's trust-busting policies, and the other was the reconciliation of the old guard conservatives and young progressive reformers in the Republican Party.

Antitrust Policy

In pursuing antimonopoly law enforcement, Taft chose as his Attorney General George Wickersham, who brought 44 indictments in antitrust suits.

Political Rift

Taft was less successful in healing the Republican split between conservatives and progressives over such issues as tariff reform, conservation, and the almost dictatorial power held by the reactionary Republican Speaker of the House Joseph Cannon (Illinois). Taft's inability

President Taft speaking at Manassas (Va.) Court House, Nov. 10, 1911.

to bring both wings of the party together led to the hardened division that would bring about a complete Democratic victory in the 1912 elections.

The Anticannon Crusade

In 1910, Republican progressives joined with Democrats to strip Speaker Cannon of his power to appoint the Committee on Rules and serve on it himself. Critical of Cannon, Taft failed to align himself with the progressives. Democrats gained control of the House in the 1910 elections, and a Republican Democratic coalition ran the Senate.

William Taft

Ballinger-Pinchot Dispute (1909–1910)

Progressives backed Gifford Pinchot, chief of the U.S. Forest Service, in his charge that the conservative Secretary of the Interior Richard Ballinger was giving away the nation's natural resources to private corporate interests. A congressional investigatory committee found that Ballinger had done nothing illegal, but did act in a manner contrary to the government's environmental policies. Taft had supported Ballinger through the controversy, but negative public opinion forced Ballinger to resign in 1911. Taft's political standing with progressive Republicans was hurt going into the election of 1912.

The Sixteenth Amendment

In 1909, Congress passed a graduated income tax amendment to the Constitution which was ratified in 1913.

Mann-Elins Act (1910)

This act extended the regulatory function of the Interstate Commerce Commission over cable and wireless companies, and telephone and telegraph lines; gave the I.C.C. power to begin its own court proceedings and suspend questionable rates; and set up a separate but temporary commerce court to handle rate-dispute cases.

Election of 1912

This election was one of the most dramatic in American history. President Taft's inability to maintain party harmony led Theodore Roosevelt to return to national politics. When denied the Republican nomination, Roosevelt and his supporters formed the Progressive Party (Bull Moose) and nominated Roosevelt for president and Hiram Johnson (California) for vice president on a political platform nicknamed "The New Nationalism." It called for stricter regulation of large corporations, creation of a tariff commission, women's suffrage, minimum wages and benefits, direct election of senators, initiative, referendum and recall, presidential primaries, and prohibition of child labor. Roosevelt also called for a Federal Trade Commission to regulate the broader economy, a stronger executive, and more government planning. Theodore Roosevelt did not see big business as evil, but a permanent development that was necessary in a modern economy.

The Republicans

President Taft and Vice President Sherman retained control of the Republican Party after challenges by Roosevelt and Robert LaFollette, and were nominated on a platform of "Quiet Confidence," calling for a continuation of progressive programs pursued by Taft over the past four years.

The Democrats

After forty-five ballots without a nomination, the Democratic convention finally worked out a compromise whereby William Jennings Bryan gave his support to New Jersey Governor Woodrow Wilson on the forty-sixth ballot. Thomas Marshall (Indiana) was chosen as the vice presidential candidate. Wilson called his campaign the "New Freedom" based on progressive programs similar to those in the Progressive and Republican parties. Wilson, however, did not agree with Roosevelt on the issue of big business, which Wilson saw as morally evil. Therefore, Wilson called for breaking up large corporations rather than just regulating them. He differed from the other two-party candidates by favoring independence for the Philippines and the exemption from prosecution of labor unions under the Sherman Anti-Trust Act. Wilson also supported such measures as lower tariffs, a graduated income tax, banking reform, and direct election of senators. Philosophically, Wilson was skeptical of big business and big government. In some respects, he hoped to return to an earlier and simpler concept of a free enterprise republic. After his selection, however, he would modify his views to conform more with those of Theodore Roosevelt.

Election Results

The Republican split clearly paved the way for Wilson's victory. Wilson received 6.2 million votes, Roosevelt 4.1 million, Taft 3.5 million, and the Socialist Debs 900,000 votes. In the electoral college, Wilson received 435 votes, Roosevelt 88, Taft 8. Although a minority president, Wilson garnered the largest electoral majority in American history to that time. Democrats won control of both houses of Congress.

The Wilson Presidency

The Wilson administration brought together many of the policies and initiatives of the previous Republican administrations, and reform efforts in Congress by both parties. Before the outbreak of World War I in 1914, President Wilson, working with cooperative majorities in both houses of Congress, achieved much of the remaining progressive agenda including lower tariff reform (Underwood-Simmons Act, 1913), the sixteenth Amendment (graduated income tax, 1913), the seventeenth Amendment (direct election of senators, 1913), Federal Reserve Banking System (which provided regulation and flexibility to monetary policy, 1913), Federal Trade Commission (to investigate unfair business practices, 1914), and the Clayton Anti-Trust Act (improving the old Sherman Act and protecting labor unions and farm cooperatives from prosecution, 1914).

Woodrow Wilson

Other goals such as the protection of children in the workforce (Keating-Owen Act, 1916), credit reform for agriculture (Federal Farm Loan Act, 1916), and an independent tariff commission (1916) came later. By the end of Wilson's presidency, the New Freedom and the New Nationalism merged into one government philosophy of regulation, order, and standardization in the interest of an increasingly diverse and pluralistic American nation.

The Economy, 1907–1912

The short-lived panic of 1907 revealed economic weaknesses in U.S. banking and currency policy addressed by Presidents Roosevelt, Taft, and Wilson, and by Congress. Fortunately, the American economy was strengthened just in time to meet the challenges of World War I.

National Monetary Commission, 1908

Chaired by Senator Nelson Aldrich of Rhode Island, the 18-member National Monetary Commission recommended what later became the basis for the Federal Reserve System in 1913 with a secure Treasury reserve and branch banks to add and subtract currency from the monetary supply to accommodate the needs of the economy.

Payne-Aldrich Tariff, 1909

Senate amendments added to the Payne-Aldrich Tariff of 1909 turned the bill, originally intended to lower the tariff, into a protective measure. Progressive reformers felt betrayed by special interests opposed to consumer-price concerns. President Taft made the political mistake of endorsing the tariff.

Postal Savings Banks, 1910

On the recommendation of President Taft, certain U.S. post offices were authorized to receive deposits and pay interest. This was an idea that had been championed early on by the Populist Party.

New Battleship Contract, 1910

The State Department arranged for Bethlehem Steel Corporation to receive a large contract to build battleships for Argentina. This was an example of Taft's "dollar diplomacy" in action.

Antitrust Proceedings

Although a friend to the business community, President Taft ordered 90 legal proceedings against monopolies and 44 antitrust suits, including the one that broke up the American Tobacco Trust (1911). It was also under Taft that the government succeeded with its earlier suit against Standard Oil.

Canadian Reciprocity, 1911

A reciprocal trade agreement between the United States and Canada was repudiated by the Canadian legislature which feared economic and political domination by the United States.

New Cabinet Posts, 1913

The Department of Commerce and Labor was divided into two separate autonomous Cabinet-level positions.

Automobiles

In 1913 Henry Ford introduced the continuous-flow process on the automobile assembly line.

Social and Cultural Developments, 1907–1912

Progressive reform and government activism were important themes in American society.

Social Programs

States led the way with programs such as public aid to mothers of dependent children (Illinois, 1911) and the first minimum wage law (Massachusetts, 1912).

Race and Ethnic Attitudes

Despite the creation of the NAACP in 1909, many progressive reformers tended to be Anglo-Saxon elitists critical of the lack of accomplishments of Native American Indians, African-Americans, Asians, and Southern and Eastern European immigrants. In 1905, the African-American intellectual militant W.E.B. DuBois founded the Niagara Movement calling for federal legislation to protect racial equality and full rights of citizenship.

Radical Labor

Although moderate labor unions as represented by the A.F. of L. functioned within the American system, a radical labor organization called the Industrial Workers of the World (I.W.W. or Wobblies, 1905–1924) was active in promoting violence and revolution. Led by colorful figures such as Carlo Tresca, Elizabeth Gurley Flynn (the Red Flame), Daniel DeLeon, "Mother" Mary Harris Jones, the maverick priest Father Thomas Hagerty, and "Big Bill" Haywood, among others, the I.W.W. organized effective strikes in the textile industry in 1912, and among a few Western miners groups, but generally had little appeal to the average American worker. After the Red Scare of 1919, the government worked to smash the I.W.W. and deport many of its immigrant leaders and members.

White Slave Trade

In 1910, Congress made interstate prostitution a federal crime with passage of the Mann Act.

Literature

Enthused by the self-confidence exuded by political reformers, writers remained optimistic in their realism and put their faith in the American people to solve social and economic problems with honest and efficient programs.

Motion Pictures

By 1912 Hollywood had replaced New York and New Jersey as the center for silent film production. There were 13,000 movie houses in the United States, and Paramount Pictures had just been formed as a large studio resembling other large corporations. Serials, epic features, and Mack Sennett comedies were in production. All of these developments contributed to the "star system" in American film entertainment.

Science

The X-ray tube was developed by William Coolidge in 1913. Robert Goddard patented liquid rocket fuel in 1914. Plastics and synthetic fibers such as rayon were developed in 1909 by Arthur Little and Leo Baekeland, respectively. Adolphus Busch applied the Diesel engine to the submarine in 1912.

Foreign Relations, 1907–1912

The expansion of American international interests through Taft's "dollar diplomacy" and world tensions foreshadowing the First World War were dominant themes.

Dollar Diplomacy

President Taft sought to avoid military intervention, especially in Latin America, by replacing "big stick" policies with "dollar diplomacy" in the expectation that American financial investments would encourage economic, social, and political stability. This idea proved an illusion as investments never really filtered through all levels of Latin American societies, nor did such investments generate democratic reforms.

Mexican Revolution (1910)

Francisco I. Madero overthrew dictator Porfirio Diaz (1911) declaring himself a progressive revolutionary akin to reformers in the United States. American and European corporate interests (especially oil and mining) feared national interference with their investments in Mexico. President Taft recognized Madero's government, but stationed 10,000 troops on the Texas border (1912) to protect Americans from the continuing fighting. In 1913 Madero was assassinated by General Victoriano Huerta. Wilson urged Huerta to hold democratic elections and adopt a constitutional government. When Huerta refused his advice, Wilson invaded Mexico with troops at Vera Cruz in 1914. A second U.S. invasion came in northern Mexico in 1916. War between the U.S. and Mexico might have occurred had not World War I intervened.

Latin American Interventions

Although Taft and Secretary of State P.C. Knox created the Latin American Division of the State Department in 1909 to promote better relations, the United States kept a military presence in the Dominican Republic and Haiti, and intervened militarily in Nicaragua (1911) to quiet fears of revolution and help manage foreign financial problems.

Arbitration Treaties

Taking a page from Roosevelt's book, Taft promoted arbitration agreements as an alternative to war in Latin America and in Asia.

Lodge Corollary to the Monroe Doctrine, 1911

When a Japanese syndicate moved to purchase a large tract of land in Mexico's Lower California, Senator Lodge introduced a resolution to block the Japanese investment. The Corollary went further to exclude non-European powers from the Western Hemisphere under the Monroe Doctrine.

Bryan's Arbitration Treaties (1913–1915)

Wilson's Secretary of State, William Jennings Bryan, continued the policies of Roosevelt and Taft to promote arbitration of disputes in Latin America and elsewhere. Bryan negotiated about thirty such treaties.

Root-Takahira Agreement (1908)

This agreement reiterated the status quo in Asia established by the United States and Japan by the Taft-Katsura Memo (1905).

China Consortium (1909)

American bankers and the State Department demanded entry into an international banking association with Britain, France, and Germany to build a railway network (Hukuang) in southern and central China. Wilson withdrew the U.S. from participation in 1913 as the Chinese revolution deteriorated into greater instability.

Manchuria

President Taft and Secretary Knox attempted to force the sale of Japanese and Russian railroad interests in Manchuria to American investment interests. When this diplomacy failed, Knox moved to construct a competing rail system. The Chinese government, however, refused to approve the American plan. Both Japan and Russia grew more suspicious of United States interests in Asia.

Chinese Revolution, 1911

Chinese nationalists overthrew the Manchu Dynasty and the last emperor of China, Henry Pu Yi. Although the military war lord Yuan Shih-Kai seized control, decades of factionalism, revolution, and civil war destabilized China and its market potential for American and other foreign investors.

Quiz: Chapters 7 and 8

1. Which of the following statements is true of Lincoln's Ten Percent Plan?

   (A) It stipulated that at least ten percent of former slaves must be accorded the right to vote within a given Southern state before that state could be readmitted to the Union.

   (B) It allowed the rights of citizenship only to those Southerners who could take an oath that they had never been disloyal to the Union.

   (C) It allowed high-ranking rebel officials to regain the right to vote and hold office by simply promising future good behavior.

   (D) It was silent on the issue of slavery.

   (E) It provided for the restoration of loyal governments for the erstwhile Confederate states now under Union control.

2. All of the following were parts of Andrew Johnson's plan for reconstruction EXCEPT

   (A) recommending to the Southern states that the vote be extended to the recently freed slaves.

   (B) requiring ratification of the Thirteenth Amendment.

   (C) requiring payment of monetary reparations for the damage caused by the war.

   (D) requiring renunciation of secession.

   (E) requiring repudiation of the Confederate debt.

3. In response to southern intransigence in the face of President Andrew Johnson's mild reconstruction plan, Congress did all of the following EXCEPT

    (A) exclude Southern representatives and senators from participating in Congress.

    (B) pass the Civil Rights Act of 1866.

    (C) order the arrest and imprisonment of former Confederate leaders.

    (D) approve and send on to the states the Fourteenth Amendment.

    (E) divide the South into five districts to be ruled by military governors with almost dictatorial powers.

4. In speaking of "scalawags," white Southerners of the Reconstruction era made reference to

    (A) former slaves who had risen to high positions within the Reconstruction governments of the Southern states.

    (B) Northerners who had come south to take high positions within the Reconstruction governments of the Southern states.

    (C) the U.S. Army generals who served as military governors in the South.

    (D) the Radical Republicans in Congress who imposed the Reconstruction regimes on the South.

    (E) Southerners who supported or participated in the Reconstruction regimes.

5. Which of the following factors came closest to giving the Confederacy what could have been a decisive foreign policy success during the Civil War?

   (A) The U.S. Navy's seizure of Confederate emissaries James M. Mason and John Slidell from the British mail steamer *Trent*

   (B) French objections to the Union blockade

   (C) The acute economic dislocation in Britain and France caused by the cut-off of cotton imports from the South

   (D) The concerns of French financial interests that had loaned large amounts of money to the Confederacy

   (E) The skillful negotiating of Confederate diplomats in Europe

6. The Spanish-American War spurred building of the Panama Canal by

   (A) demonstrating the need to shift naval forces quickly from the Atlantic to the Pacific.

   (B) demonstrating the ease with which Latin American countries could be overcome by U.S. military force.

   (C) discrediting congressional opponents of the project.

   (D) removing the threat that any possible canal could be blockaded by Spanish forces based in Cuba and Puerto Rico.

   (E) demonstrating that such tropical diseases as malaria and yellow fever could be controlled.

7. The main reason that President Grant's administration is considered a failure is

    (A) his failure to retreat from the radical Reconstruction policies of his predecessors.

    (B) his failure to effectively quell the Indian uprisings in the Western territories.

    (C) his failure to control the corruption permeating his administration.

    (D) his attempts to destroy the Democratic Party and return the country to a one-party system.

    (E) his failure to be reelected after serving his first term in office.

8. U.S. presidents between 1876 and 1900 were considered among the weakest in American history. A major reason for this was that

    (A) none of them served more than one term in office.

    (B) they considered themselves caretakers, not dynamic initiators of new legislation.

    (C) Congress enacted several new laws restricting presidential power during this period.

    (D) they were the products of machine politics, political followers who were typically incompetent leaders.

    (E) they were limited in their actions by the overwhelming Populist sentiment of their time.

9. The most important factor in the destruction of the Plains Indians' societies by whites in the late nineteenth century was

    (A) the use of modern weapons by white soldiers and cavalrymen.

    (B) the destruction of the Buffalo herds by whites.

    (C) the introduction of alcohol by whites to Indian society.

    (D) the encroachment of railroads onto Indian lands.

    (E) the use of reservations by whites to limit the movements of Indians.

10. The only dominant, broad-based labor union in the United States from 1870–1890 was the

    (A) National Labor Union.

    (B) Industrial Workers of the World (IWW).

    (C) American Federation of Labor (AFL).

    (D) Congress of Industrial Organization (CIO).

    (E) Knights of Labor.

ANSWER KEY

1.	(E)	6.	(A)
2.	(C)	7.	(C)
3.	(C)	8.	(B)
4.	(E)	9.	(B)
5.	(A)	10.	(E)

DETAILED ANSWERS

1. **(E)** Lincoln's Ten Percent Plan provided for the restoration of loyal government in states formerly in rebellion. It did not require that any of the former slaves be given the right to vote (A). It allowed Southerners to participate in the political process provided they would take an oath of future, not past (B), loyalty to the Union and acceptance of the abolition of slavery (D). High-ranking Confederates were excepted from this provision (C) and had to apply separately to the president for a pardon.

2. **(C)** Johnson did not require former Confederate states to pay reparations. He did, however, recommend they extend the franchise to blacks (A), and he did require them to ratify the Thirteenth Amendment (B), renounce secession (D), and repudiate the Confederate debt (E).

3. **(C)** Congress did not order the arrest and imprisonment of former Confederate leaders, often because many of them were protected by presidential pardons or the terms of their surrenders. It did, however,

exclude Southern representatives (A), pass the Civil Rights Act (B), approve and send on to the states the Fourteenth Amendment (D), and put the South under army occupation and military rule (E).

4. **(E)** Scalawags were Southerners who supported or participated in the Reconstruction regimes. Northerners who came south to take up positions with the Reconstruction governments (B) were called carpetbaggers. Blacks in high positions in the Reconstruction governments (A) were simply referred to by the common vulgar racial expression. There is no record of what Southerners called the Reconstruction military governors (C) or the Radical Republicans (D), but there was probably a variety of expressions.

5. **(A)** The U.S. Navy's seizure of Confederate emissaries James M. Mason and John Slidell from the British mail steamer *Trent* came closest to giving the Confederacy the foreign help it needed by nearly bringing on a war between Great Britain and the United States. Confederate diplomats were not, on the whole, very skillful negotiatiors (E). There was some objection in Europe to the Union blockade (B), but Britain, the only country that could have done anything about it, favored permissive rules for blockading. Large prewar stocks of cotton in Britain and France, along with the discovery of alternate sources of cotton, prevented the economic dislocation in those countries that Confederate leaders had hoped would bring their aid (C). Some French financiers did float a bond issue for the Confederacy, but they slyly made sure they got their money first, assuring that if anyone got bilked it would be the small, uninfluential investors (D).

6. **(A)** The Spanish-American War showed the need of shifting naval forces rapidly between the Atlantic and the Pacific. There had never been much doubt about overcoming Latin American countries if that were necessary (B), or of dealing with any (highly unlikely) threat from Spain (D). The war did nothing to discredit opponents of the project (C), and such tropical diseases as malaria and yellow fever were not dealt with successfully (E) until during the actual building of the canal.

7.   **(C)**   Grant was an intensely loyal man who was, sadly, not the best judge of character in choosing his administrative appointees. During his first term in office, his administration was beset with financial scandals involving the vice president, Grant's brother-in-law, and a well-known financial entrepreneur named Jay Gould. In his second term, the "whiskey ring" scandal implicated Grant's private secretary. His secretary of war was implicated in a bribery scandal. While few believed Grant to be corrupt, Grant's loyalty to his corrupt associates tarnished his image in virtually everyone's eyes. It also crippled the effectiveness of his administration.

8.   **(B)**   The years between 1876–1900 were years of relative political equality between the Republicans and Democrats. It was also a time when most Americans were rejecting or resisting the cries for reform by political activists. Most people wanted the federal government to remain inactive and uninvolved as much as possible. The concept of laissez-faire leadership was flourishing. This resulted in little significant reform legislation from the Congress. It also led to the election of presidents who saw themselves as political caretakers of the office of the presidency, rather than advocates of social or political reform. The equality between the two parties at this time also made it difficult for any president to push for major changes, because the political base of support was too evenly divided to provide the necessary votes in Congress for effective action. While none of these presidents were incompetent (as asserted by choice [D]), they just didn't see the presidency as an office appropriate for taking strong initiatives. They believed their major job was to insure Congressional legislation was effectively carried out and to veto any legislation in which they felt Congress had exceeded its powers. Such an attitude does not tend to lead to inspirational, dynamic leadership. Their style was such that they believed the LESS they were noticed the better they were doing their job. This has left the long-term impression of them being "weak" presidents.

9.   **(B)**   The Plains Indians depended upon buffalo for almost every aspect of their survival. When they killed a buffalo, they used virtually every part of it, from the hide to the bones. In 1850, over 13 million Buffalo meandered along their migration routes in the Great Plains. By 1890, fewer than 1,000 remained. Without the buffalo, the Plains Indians could not live according to their traditional ways. They were forced to either adapt to white rules (usually on reservations) or fight for their survival, as the Sioux and Cheyenne did in the 1870s. Fighting the whites was hopeless, but to many Indians, it was more honorable than dying in subjugation. While they managed a few victories such as at Little Big Horn, they were too badly outmanned and outgunned to have a long-term chance at victory. Without the buffalo, the entire Indian way of life was undermined and it led directly to the destruction of the Plains Indians' societies in a much broader way than any of the other choices listed in the question.

10.   **(E)**   The Knights of Labor were founded in 1869 by workers in Philadelphia's garment district. They were the only broad-based union to survive the economic depression of 1873. They were also the only major union of their time to extend membership to blacks, women, and unskilled workers. They preached a long-term philosophy of achieving a society where employees and managers would work together cooperatively for all society's benefit. They reached the peak of their success in the mid-1880s, but following a series of failed strikes culminating in the disastrous Haymarket Square riot in 1886, the Knights began to splinter into smaller crafts unions and various other more radical workers groups. They never regained their dominance and were eventually supplanted and replaced by the AFL in the 1890s as America's major labor union.

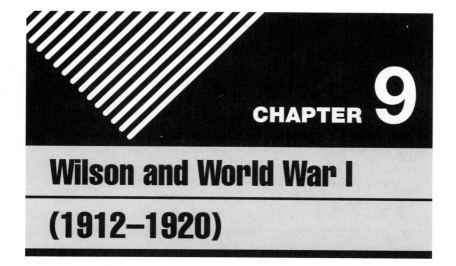

CHAPTER 9

Wilson and World War I (1912–1920)

Implementing the New Freedom: The Early Years of the Wilson Administration

The New President

Woodrow Wilson was only the second Democrat (Cleveland was the first) elected president since the Civil War. He was born in Virginia in 1856, the son of a Presbyterian minister, and was reared and educated in the South. After earning a doctorate at Johns Hopkins University, he taught history and political science at Princeton University, and in 1902 became president of that university. In 1910 he was elected governor of New Jersey as a reform, or progressive, Democrat.

The Cabinet

The key appointments were William Jennings Bryan as secretary of state and William Gibbs McAdoo as secretary of the treasury.

The Inaugural Address

Wilson called the Congress, now controlled by Democrats, into a special session beginning April 7, 1913, to consider three topics: reduction of the tariff, reform of the national banking and currency laws, and improvements in the antitrust laws. On April 8 he appeared personally before Congress, the first president since John Adams to do so, to promote his program.

The Underwood-Simmons Tariff Act of 1913

Average rates were reduced to about twenty-nine percent as compared with thirty-seven to forty percent under the previous Payne-Aldrich Tariff. A graduated income tax was included in the law to compensate for lost tariff revenue. It ranged from a tax of one percent on personal and corporate incomes over $4,000, a figure well above the annual income of the average worker, to seven percent on incomes over $500,000. The Sixteenth Amendment to the Constitution, ratified in February 1913, authorized the income tax.

The Federal Reserve Act of 1913

Following the Panic of 1907, it was generally agreed that there was need for more stability in the banking industry and for a currency supply that would expand and contract to meet business needs.

Three points of view on the subject developed. Most Republicans backed the proposal of a commission headed by Senator Nelson W. Aldrich for a large central bank controlled by private banks. Bryanite Democrats, pointing to the Wall Street influence exposed by the 1913 Pujo Committee investigation of the money trust, wanted a reserve system and currency owned and controlled by the government. Conservative Democrats favored a decentralized system privately owned and controlled but free from Wall Street.

The bill that finally passed in December 1913 was a compromise measure. The law divided the nation into twelve regions with a Federal Reserve bank in each region. Commercial banks in the region owned the Federal Reserve Bank by purchasing stock equal to six percent of their capital and surplus, and elected the directors of the bank. National banks were required to join the system, and state banks were invited to join. The Federal Reserve Banks held the gold reserves of their members. Federal Reserve Banks loaned money to member banks by rediscounting their commercial and agricultural paper; that is, the money was loaned at interest rates less than the public paid to the member banks, and the notes of indebtedness of businesses and farmers to the member banks were held as collateral. This allowed the Federal Reserve to control interest rates by raising or lowering the discount rate.

The money loaned to the member banks was in the form of a new currency, Federal Reserve Notes, which was backed sixty percent by commercial paper and forty percent by gold. This currency was designed to expand and contract with the volume of business activity and borrowing. Checks on member banks were cleared through the Federal Reserve System.

The Federal Reserve System serviced the financial needs of the federal government. The system was supervised and policy was set by a national Federal Reserve Board composed of the secretary of the Treasury, the comptroller of the currency, and five other members appointed by the president of the United States.

The Clayton Antitrust Act of 1914

This law supplemented and interpreted the Sherman Antitrust Act of 1890. Under its provisions, stock ownership by a corporation in a competing corporation was prohibited. Interlocking directorates of competing corporations were prohibited; that is, the same persons could not manage competing corporations. Price discrimination (charging less in some regions than in others to undercut the competition) and exclusive contracts that reduced competition were prohibited. Officers of corporations could be held personally responsible for violations of antitrust laws. Lastly, labor unions and agricultural organizations were not to be considered "combinations or conspiracies in restraint of trade" as defined by the Sherman Antitrust Act.

The Federal Trade Commission Act of 1914

The law prohibited all unfair trade practices without defining them, and created a commission of five members appointed by the president.

The commission was empowered to issue cease and desist orders to corporations to stop actions considered to be in restraint of trade, and to bring suit in the courts if the orders were not obeyed. Firms could also contest the orders in court. Under previous antitrust legislation, the government could act against corporations only by bringing suit.

Evaluation

The Underwood-Simmons Tariff, the Federal Reserve Act, and the Clayton Act were clearly in accord with the principles of the New Freedom, but the Federal Trade Commission reflected a move toward the kind of government regulation advocated by Roosevelt in his New Nationalism. Nonetheless, in 1914 and 1915 Wilson continued to oppose federal government action in such matters as loans to farmers, child labor regulation, and woman suffrage.

The Triumph of New Nationalism

Political Background

The Progressive Party dissolved rapidly after the election of 1912. The Republicans made major gains in Congress and in the state governments in the 1914 elections, and their victory in 1916 seemed probable. Early in 1916 Wilson and the Democrats abandoned most of their limited government and states' rights positions in favor of a legislative program of broad economic and social reforms designed to win the support of the former Progressives for the Democratic Party in the election of 1916. The urgency of their concern was increased by the fact that Theodore Roosevelt intended to seek the Republican nomination in 1916.

The Brandeis Appointment

Wilson's first action marking the adoption of the new program was the appointment on January 28, 1916, of Louis D. Brandeis, considered by many to be the principal advocate of social justice in the nation, as an associate justice of the Supreme Court.

The Federal Farm Loan Act of 1916

The law divided the country into twelve regions and established a Federal Land Bank in each region. Funded primarily with federal money, the banks made farm mortgage loans available at reasonable interest rates. Wilson had threatened to veto similar legislation in 1914.

The Child Labor Act of 1916

This law, earlier opposed by Wilson, forbade shipment in interstate commerce of products that were produced using the labor of children under fourteen or sixteen, depending on the products. The legislation was especially significant because it was the first time that Congress regulated labor within a state using the interstate commerce power. The law was declared unconstitutional by the Supreme Court in 1918 on the grounds that it interfered with the powers of the states.

The Adamson Act of 1916

This law mandated an eight-hour day for workers on interstate railroads with time and a half for overtime and a maximum of sixteen hours in a shift. Its passage was a major victory for railroad unions and averted a railroad strike in September 1916.

The Kerr-McGillicuddy Act of 1916

This law initiated a program of workmen's compensation for federal employees.

The Election of 1916

The Democrats

The minority party nationally in terms of voter registration, the Democrats nominated Wilson and adopted his platform calling for continued progressive reforms and neutrality in the European war. "He kept us out of war" became the principal campaign slogan of Democratic politicians.

President Wilson throws out the first pitch on Opening Day, 1916.

The Republicans

The convention bypassed Theodore Roosevelt, who had decided not to run as a Progressive and had sought the Republican nomination. On the first ballot, it chose Charles Evans Hughes, an associate justice of the Supreme Court and formerly a progressive Republican governor of New York. Hughes, an ineffective campaigner, avoided the neutrality issue because of divisions among the Republicans, and found it difficult to attack the progressive reforms of the Democrats. He emphasized what he considered the inefficiency of the Democrats and failed to find a popular issue.

The Election

Wilson won the election with 277 electoral votes and 9,129,000 popular votes, almost three million more than he received in 1912. Hughes received 254 electoral votes and 8,538,221 popular votes. The Democrats controlled Congress by a narrow margin. While Wilson's victory seemed close, the fact that he had increased his popular vote by almost fifty percent over the previous four years was remarkable. It appears that most of his additional votes came from people who had voted for the Progressive or Socialist tickets in 1912.

Social Issues in the First Wilson Administration

Blacks

In 1913 Treasury Secretary William G. McAdoo and Postmaster General Albert S. Burleson segregated workers in some parts of their departments with no objection from Wilson. Many Northern blacks and whites protested, especially black leader W. E. B. DuBois, who had supported Wilson in 1912. William Monroe Trotter, militant editor of the *Boston Guardian*, led a protest delegation to Washington and clashed verbally with the president. No further segregation in government agencies was initiated, but Wilson had gained a reputation for being inimical to civil rights.

Women

The movement for woman suffrage, led by the National American Woman Suffrage Association, was increasing in momentum at the time Wilson became president, and several states had granted the vote to women. Wilson opposed a federal woman suffrage amendment, maintaining that the franchise should be controlled by the states. Later he changed his view and supported the Nineteenth Amendment.

Immigration

Wilson opposed immigration restrictions that were proposed by labor unions and some reformers. He vetoed a literacy test for immigrants in 1915, but in 1917 Congress overrode a similar veto.

Wilson's Foreign Policy and the Road to War

Wilson's Basic Premise: New Freedom Policy

Wilson promised a more moral foreign policy than that of his predecessors, denouncing imperialism and dollar diplomacy, and advocating the advancement of democratic capitalist governments throughout the world.

Conciliation Treaties

Secretary Bryan negotiated treaties with 29 nations under which they agreed to submit disputes to international commissions for conciliation, not arbitration. They also included provisions for a cooling-off period, usually one year, before the nations would resort to war. While the treaties probably had no practical effect, they illustrated the idealism of the administration.

Dollar Diplomacy

Wilson signaled his repudiation of Taft's dollar diplomacy by withdrawing American involvement from the six-power loan consortium of China.

Japan

In 1913 Wilson failed to prevent passage of a California law prohibiting land ownership by Japanese aliens. The Japanese government and people were furious, and war seemed possible. Relations were smoothed over, but the issue was unresolved. In 1915 American diplomatic pressure made Japan back off from its 21 demands on China, but in 1917 the Lansing-Ishii Agreement was signed wherein Japan recognized the Open Door in China but the United States recognized Japan's special interest in that nation.

The Caribbean

Like his predecessors, Wilson sought to protect the Panama Canal, which opened in 1914, by maintaining stability in the area. He also wanted to encourage diplomacy and economic growth in the underdeveloped nations of the region. In applying his policy, he became as interventionist as Roosevelt and Taft.

In 1912 American marines had landed in Nicaragua to maintain order, and an American financial expert had taken control of customs. The Wilson administration kept the marines in Nicaragua and negotiated the Bryan-Chamorro Treaty of 1914, which gave the United States an option to build a canal through the country. In effect, Nicaragua became an American protectorate, although treaty provisions authorizing such action were not ratified by the Senate.

Claiming that political anarchy existed in Haiti, Wilson sent marines in 1915 and imposed a treaty making the country a protectorate, with American control of its finances and constabulary. The marines remained until 1934.

In 1916 Wilson sent marines to the Dominican Republic to stop a civil war, and established a military government under an American naval commander.

Wilson feared in 1915 that Germany might annex Denmark and its Caribbean possession, the Danish West Indies or the Virgin Islands. After extended negotiations, the United States purchased the islands from Denmark by treaty on August 4, 1916 for $25 million and took possession of them on March 31, 1917.

In 1913 Wilson refused to recognize the government of Mexican military dictator Victoriano Huerta, and offered unsuccessfully to mediate between Huerta and his Constitutionalist opponent, Venustiano Carranza. When the Huerta government arrested several American seamen in Tampico in April 1914, American forces occupied the port of Veracruz, an action condemned by both Mexican political factions. In July 1914, Huerta abdicated his power to Carranza, who was soon opposed by his former general Francisco "Pancho" Villa. Seeking American intervention as a means of undermining Carranza, Villa shot sixteen Americans on a train in northern Mexico in January 1916 and burned the border town of Columbus, New Mexico, in March 1916, killing nineteen people. Carranza reluctantly consented to Wilson's request that the United States be allowed to pursue and capture Villa in Mexico, but did not expect the force of about 6,000 Army troops under the command of General John J. Pershing which crossed the Rio Grande on March 18. The force advanced over 300 miles into Mexico, failed to capture Villa, and became, in effect, an army of occupation. The Carranza government demanded an American withdrawal and several clashes with Mexican troops occurred. War threatened, but in January 1917 Wilson removed the American forces.

Pan American Mediation, 1914

John Barrett, head of the Pan American Union (formerly Blaine's International Bureau of American Republics), called for multilateral mediation to bring about a solution to Mexico's internal problems and to extract the United States from its military presence in Mexico. Although Wilson initially refused, Argentina, Brazil, and Chile did mediate among the Mexican factions and Wilson withdrew American troops. Barrett hoped to replace the unilateral Monroe Doctrine with a multilateral Pan American policy to promote collective responses and mediation to difficult hemispheric problems. Wilson, however, refused to share power with Latin America.

The Road to War in Europe

American Neutrality

When World War I broke out in Europe, Wilson issued a proclamation of American neutrality on August 4, 1914. Despite that action, the United States drifted toward closer ties with the Allies, especially Britain and France. While many Americans were sympathetic to the Central Powers, the majority, including Wilson, hoped for an Allied victory. Although British naval power effectively prevented American trade with the Central Powers and European neutrals, often in violation of international law, the United States limited itself to formal diplomatic protests. The value of American trade with the Central Powers fell from $169 million in 1914 to almost nothing in 1916, but trade with the Allies rose from $825 million to $3.2 billion during the same period. In addition, the British and French had borrowed about $3.25 billion from American sources by 1917. The United States had become a major supplier of Allied munitions, food, and raw materials.

The Submarine Crisis of 1915

The Germans began the use of submarines in 1915, announced a submarine blockade of the Allies on February 4, and began to attack unarmed British passenger ships in the Atlantic. Wilson insisted to the

Germans that Americans had a right as neutrals to travel safely on such ships, and that international law required a war ship to arrange for the safe removal of passengers before attacking such a ship. The sinking of the British liner *Lusitania* off the coast of Ireland on May 7, 1915 with the loss of 1,198 lives, including 128 Americans, brought strong protests from Wilson. Secretary of State Bryan, who believed Americans should stay off belligerent ships, resigned rather than insist on questionable neutral rights and was replaced by Robert Lansing. Following the sinking of another liner, the *Arabic*, on August 19, the Germans gave the "Arabic pledge" to stop attacks on unarmed passenger vessels.

The Gore-McLemore Resolution

During the latter part of 1915, the British began to arm their merchant ships. Many Americans thought it was in the interest of United States neutrality that Americans not travel on the vessels of belligerents. Early in 1916 the Gore-McLemore Resolution to prohibit American travel on armed ships or on ships carrying munitions was introduced in Congress, but it was defeated in both houses after intensive politicking by Wilson.

The Sussex Pledge

When the unarmed French channel steamer *Sussex* was torpedoed but not sunk on March 24, 1916 with seven Americans injured, Wilson threatened to sever relations unless Germany ceased all surprise submarine attacks on all shipping, whether belligerent or neutral, armed or unarmed. Germany acceded with the "Sussex pledge" at the beginning of May, but threatened to resume submarine warfare if the British did not stop their violations of international law.

The House-Grey Memorandum

Early in 1915 Wilson sent his friend and adviser, Colonel Edward M. House, on an unsuccessful visit to the capitals of the belligerent nations on both sides to offer American mediation in the war. Late in the year, House returned to London to propose that Wilson call a peace conference, and, if Germany refused to attend or was uncooperative at the conference, the United States would probably enter the war on the Allied side. An agreement to that effect, called the House-Grey Memorandum, was signed by the British foreign secretary, Sir Edward Grey, on February 22, 1916.

Preparedness

In November 1915 Wilson proposed a major increase in the army and the abolition of the National Guard as a preparedness measure. Americans divided on the issue, with organizations like the National Security League proposing stronger military forces, and others like the League to Enforce Peace opposing. After opposition by Southern and Western antipreparedness Democrats, Congress passed a modified National Defense Act in June 1916 that increased the army from about 90,000 to 220,000 and enlarged the National Guard under federal control. In August over $500 million was appropriated for naval construction. The additional costs were met by increased taxes on the wealthy.

The Election of 1916

Wilson took the leadership on the peace issue, charging that the Republicans were the war party and that the election of Charles Evans Hughes would probably result in war with Germany and Mexico. His position was popular with many Democrats and progressives, and the slogan "He kept us out of war" became the principal theme of Democratic campaign materials, presumably contributing to his election victory.

Wilson's Final Peace Efforts, 1916–1917

On December 12, 1916, the Germans, confident of their strong position, proposed a peace conference, a step that Wilson previously had advocated. When Wilson asked both sides to state their expectations, the British seemed agreeable to reasonable negotiations, but the Germans were evasive and stated that they did not want Wilson at the conference. In an address to Congress on January 22, 1917, Wilson made his last offer to serve as a neutral mediator. He proposed a "peace without victory," based not on a "balance of power" but on a "community of power," alluding to his proposal of May 1916 for an "association of nations."

Unlimited Submarine Warfare

Germany announced on January 31, 1917, that it would sink all ships, belligerent or neutral, without warning in a large war zone off the coasts of the Allied nations in the eastern Atlantic and the Mediterranean. The Germans realized that the United States might declare war, but they believed that, after cutting the flow of supplies to the Allies, they could win the war before the Americans could send any sizable force to Europe. Wilson broke diplomatic relations with Germany on February 3. During February and March, several American merchant ships were sunk by submarines.

The Zimmerman Telegram

The British intercepted a secret message from the German foreign secretary, Arthur Zimmerman, to the German minister in Mexico, and turned it over to the United States on February 24, 1917. The Germans proposed that, in the event of a war between the United States and Germany, Mexico attack the United States. After the war, the "lost territories" of Texas, New Mexico, and Arizona would be returned to Mexico. In addition, Japan would be invited to join the alliance against the United States. When the telegram was released to the press on March 1, many Americans became convinced that war with Germany was necessary.

The Declaration of War

Wilson, on March 2, 1917, called Congress to a special session beginning April 2. When Congress convened, he requested a declaration of war against Germany. The declaration was passed by the Senate on April 4 by a vote of 82 to 6, by the House on April 6 by a vote of 373 to 50, and signed by Wilson on April 6.

Wilson's Reasons

Wilson's decision to ask for a declaration of war seems to have been based primarily on four considerations. He believed that the Zimmerman Telegram showed that the Germans were not trustworthy and would eventually go to war against the United States. He also felt that armed neutrality could not adequately protect American shipping. The democratic government established in Russia after the revolution in March 1917 also proved more acceptable as an ally than the Tsarist government. Finally, he was convinced that the United States could hasten the end of the war and insure for itself a major role in designing a lasting peace.

World War I: The Military Campaign

Raising an Army

Despite the enlistment of many volunteers, it was apparent that a draft would be necessary. The Selective Service Act was passed on May 18, 1917, after bitter opposition in the House led by the speaker, "Champ" Clark. Only a compromise outlawing the sale of liquor in or near military camps secured passage. Originally including all males 21 to 30, the limits were later extended to 17 and 46. The first drawing of 500,000 names was made on July 20, 1917. By the end of the war, 24,231,021 men had been registered and 2,810,296 had been inducted. In addition, about two million men and women volunteered.

Women and Minorities in the Military

Some women served as clerks in the navy or in the Signal Corps of the army. Originally nurses were part of the Red Cross, but eventually some were taken into the army. About 400,000 black men were drafted or enlisted, despite the objections of Southern political leaders. They were kept in segregated units, usually with white officers, which were used as labor battalions or for other support activities. Some black units did see combat, and a few blacks became officers but did not command white troops.

The War at Sea

In 1917 German submarines sank 6.5 million tons of Allied and American shipping, while only 2.7 million tons were built. German hopes for victory were based on the destruction of Allied supply lines. The American navy furnished destroyers to fight the submarines, and, after overcoming great resistance from the British navy, finally began the use of the convoy system in July 1917. Shipping losses fell from almost 900,000 tons in April 1917 to about 400,000 tons in December 1917, and remained below 200,000 tons per month after April 1918. The American navy transported over 900,000 American soldiers to France, while British transports carried over one million. Only two of the well-guarded troop transports were sunk. The navy had over 2,000 ships and over half a million men by the end of the war.

The American Expeditionary Force

The soldiers and marines sent to France under the command of Major General John J. Pershing were called the American Expeditionary Force, or the AEF. From a small initial force, which arrived in France in June 1917, the AEF increased to over two million by November 1918. Pershing resisted efforts by European commanders to amalgamate the Americans with the French and British armies, insisting that he maintain a separate command. American casualties included 112,432 dead, about half of whom died of disease, and 230,024 wounded.

Major Military Engagements

The American force of about 14,500, which had arrived in France by September 1917, was assigned a quiet section of the line near Verdun. As numbers increased, the American role became more significant. When the Germans mounted a major drive toward Paris in the spring of 1918, the Americans experienced their first important engagements. In June they prevented the Germans from crossing the Marne at

General John J. Pershing (1918)

Chateau-Thierry and cleared the area of Belleau Woods. In July, eight American divisions aided French troops in attacking the German line between Reims and Soissons. The American First Army with over half a million men under Pershing's immediate command was assembled in August 1918, and began a major offensive at St. Mihiel on the southern part of the front on September 12. Following the successful operation, Pershing began a drive against the German defenses between Verdun and Sedan, an action called the Meuse-Argonne offensive, and reached Sedan on November 7. During the same period, the English in the north and the French along the central front also broke through the German lines. The fighting ended with the armistice on November 11, 1918.

Mobilizing the Home Front

Industry

The Council of National Defense, comprised of six cabinet members and a seven-member advisory commission of business and labor leaders, was established in 1916 before American entry into the war to coordinate industrial mobilization, but it had little authority. In July 1917 the council created the War Industries Board to control raw materials, production, prices, and labor relations. The military forces refused to cooperate with the civilian agency in purchasing their supplies, and the domestic war effort seemed on the point of collapse in December 1917 when a Congressional investigation began. In 1918 Wilson took stronger action under his emergency war powers, which were reinforced by the Overman Act of May 1918. In March 1918, Wilson appointed Wall Street broker Bernard M. Baruch to head the WIB, assisted by an advisory committee of 100 businessmen. The WIB allocated raw materials, standardized manufactured products, instituted strict production and purchasing controls, and paid high prices to businesses for their products. Even so, American industry was just beginning to produce heavy armaments when the war ended. Most heavy equipment and munitions used by the American troops in France were produced in Britain or France.

Food

The United States had to supply not only its own food needs but those of Britain, France, and some of the other Allies as well. The problem was compounded by bad weather in 1916 and 1917, which had an adverse effect on agriculture. The Lever Act of 1917 gave the president broad control over the production, price, and distribution of food and fuel. Herbert Hoover was appointed by Wilson to head a newly created Food Administration. Hoover fixed high prices to encourage the production of wheat, pork, and other products, and encouraged the conservation of food through such voluntary programs as "Wheatless Mondays" and "Meatless Tuesdays." Despite the bad harvests in 1916 and 1917, food exports by 1919 were almost triple those of the prewar years, and real farm income was up almost thirty percent.

Fuel

The Fuel Administration under Harry A. Garfield was established in August 1917. It was concerned primarily with coal production and conservation because coal was the predominant fuel of the time and was in short supply during the severe winter of 1917–1918. "Fuelless Mondays" in nonessential industries to conserve coal and "Gasless Sundays" for automobile owners to save gasoline were instituted. Coal production increased about thirty-five percent from 1914 to 1918.

Railroads

The American railroad system, which provided most of the inter-city transportation in the country, seemed near collapse in December 1917 because of the wartime demands and heavy snows that slowed service. Wilson created the United States Railroad Administration under William G. McAdoo, the secretary of the treasury, to take over and operate all the railroads in the nation as one system. The government paid the owners rent for the use of their lines, spent over $500 million on improved tracks and equipment, and achieved its objective of an efficient railroad system.

Maritime Shipping

The United States Shipping Board was authorized by Congress in September 1916, and in April 1917 it created a subsidiary, the Emergency Fleet Corporation, to buy, build, lease, and operate merchant ships for the war effort. Edward N. Hurley became the director in July 1917, and the corporation constructed several large shipyards that were just beginning to produce vessels when the war ended. By seizing German and Dutch ships, and by the purchase and requisition of private vessels, the board had accumulated a large fleet by September 1918.

Labor

To prevent strikes and work stoppages in war industries, the War Labor Board was created in April 1918 under the joint chairmanship of former president William Howard Taft and attorney Frank P. Walsh with members from both industry and labor. In hearing labor disputes, the WLB in effect prohibited strikes, but it also encouraged higher wages, the eight-hour day, and unionization. Union membership doubled during the war from about 2.5 million to about 5 million.

War Finance and Taxation

The war is estimated to have cost about $33.5 billion by 1920, excluding such future costs as veterans' benefits and debt service. Of that amount, at least $7 billion was loaned to the Allies, with most of the money actually spent in the United States for supplies. The government raised about $10.5 billion in taxes and borrowed the remaining $23 billion. Taxes were raised substantially in 1917 and again in 1918. The Revenue Act of 1918, which did not take effect until 1919, imposed a personal income tax of six percent on incomes up to $4,000 and twelve percent on incomes above that amount. In addition, a graduated surtax went to a maximum of sixty-five percent on large incomes, for a total of seventy-seven percent. Corporations paid an excess profits tax of sixty-five percent, and excise taxes were levied on luxury items. Much public, peer, and employer pressure was exerted on citizens to buy Liberty Bonds, which covered a major part of the borrowing. An inflation of about one hundred percent from 1915 to 1920 contributed substantially to the cost of the war.

The Committee on Public Information

The committee, headed by journalist George Creel, was formed by Wilson in April 1917. Creel established a successful system of voluntary censorship of the press, and organized about 150,000 paid and volunteer writers, lecturers, artists, and other professionals in a propaganda campaign to build support for the American cause as an idealistic crusade, and to portray the Germans as barbaric and bestial Huns. The CPI set up volunteer Liberty Leagues in every community, and urged their members, and citizens at large, to spy on their neighbors, especially those with foreign names, and to report any suspicious words or actions to the Justice Department.

War Hysteria

A number of volunteer organizations sprang up around the country to search for draft dodgers, enforce the sale of bonds, and report any opinion or conversation considered suspicious. Perhaps the largest such organization was the American Protective League with about 250,000 members, which claimed the approval of the Justice Department. Such groups publicly humiliated people accused of not buying war bonds and persecuted, beat, and sometimes killed people of German descent. As a result of the activities of the CPI and the vigilante groups, German language instruction and German music were banned in many areas, German measles became "liberty measles," pretzels were prohibited in some cities, and the like. The anti-German and anti-subversive war hysteria in the United States far exceeded similar public moods in Britain and France during the war.

The Espionage and Sedition Acts

The Espionage Act of 1917 provided for fines and imprisonment for persons who made false statements that aided the enemy, incited rebellion in the military, or obstructed recruitment or the draft. Printed matter advocating treason or insurrection could be excluded from the mails. The Sedition Act of May 1918 forbade any criticism of the government, flag, or uniform, even if there were no detrimental consequences, and expanded the mail exclusion. The laws sounded reasonable, but they were applied in ways that trampled on civil liberties. Eugene V. Debs, the perennial Socialist candidate for president, was given a ten-year prison sentence for a speech at his party's convention in which he was critical of American policy in entering the war and warned of the dangers of militarism. Movie producer Robert Goldstein released the movie *The Spirit of '76* about the Revolutionary War. It naturally showed the British fighting the Americans. Goldstein was fined $10,000 and sentenced to ten years in prison because the film depicted the British, who were now fighting on the same side as the United States, in an unfavorable light. The Espionage Act was upheld by the Supreme Court in the case of *Shenk v. United States* in 1919. The opinion, written by Justice Oliver Wendell Holmes, Jr., stated that Congress could limit free speech when the words represented a "clear and present danger," and that, in effect, a person cannot cry "fire" in a crowded theater. The Sedition Act was similarly upheld in *Abrams v. United States* a few months later. Ultimately, 2,168 persons were prosecuted under the laws, and 1,055 were convicted, of whom only ten were charged with actual sabotage.

Wartime Social Trends

Women

With approximately sixteen percent of the normal labor force in uniform and demand for goods at a peak, large numbers of women, mostly white, were hired by factories and other enterprises in jobs never before open to them. They were often resented and ridiculed by male workers. When the war ended, almost all returned to traditional "women's jobs" or to homemaking. Returning veterans replaced them in the labor market. Women continued to campaign for woman suffrage. In 1917 six states, including the large and influential states of New York, Ohio, Indiana, and Michigan, gave the vote to women. Wilson changed his position in 1918 to advocate woman suffrage as a war measure. In January 1918 the House of Representatives adopted a suffrage amendment to the constitution, which was defeated later in the year by Southern forces in the Senate. The way was paved for the victory of the suffragists after the war.

Racial Minorities

The labor shortage opened industrial jobs to Mexican-Americans and to blacks. W. E. B. DuBois, among the most prominent black leaders of the time, supported the war effort in the hope that a war to make the world safe for democracy would bring a better life for blacks in the United States. About half a million rural Southern blacks migrated to cities, mainly in the North and Midwest, to obtain employment in war and other industries, especially in steel and meatpacking. Some white Southerners, fearing the loss of labor when cotton prices were high, tried forceably to prevent their departure. Some white Northerners, fearing job competition and encroachment on white neighborhoods, resented their arrival. In 1917 there were race riots in twenty-six cities in the North and South, with the worst in East St. Louis, Illinois. Despite the opposition and their concentration in entry-level positions, there is evidence that the blacks who migrated generally improved themselves economically.

Prohibition

Proponents of prohibition stressed the need for military personnel to be sober and the need to conserve grain for food, and depicted the hated Germans as disgusting beer drinkers. In December 1917 a constitutional amendment to prohibit the manufacture and sale of alcoholic beverages in the United States was passed by Congress and submitted to the states for ratification. While alcohol consumption was being attacked, cigarette consumption climbed from 26 billion in 1916 to 48 billion in 1918.

Peacemaking and Domestic Problems, 1918–1920

The Fourteen Points

From the time of the American entry into the war, Wilson had maintained that the war would make the world safe for democracy. He insisted that there should be peace without victory, meaning that the victors would not be vindictive toward the losers, so that a fair and stable international situation in the postwar world would insure lasting peace. In an address to Congress on January 8, 1918, he presented his specific peace plan in the form of the Fourteen Points. The first five points called for open rather than secret peace treaties, freedom of the seas, free trade, arms reduction, and a fair adjustment of colonial claims. The next eight points were concerned with the national aspirations of various European peoples and the adjustment of boundaries, as, for example, in the creation of an independent Poland. The fourteenth point, which he considered the most important and had espoused as early as 1916, called for a "general association of nations" to preserve the peace. The reception of the Fourteen Points was mixed in Europe, as there was a great desire to punish Germany. In the United States, however, many people opposed a peace plan that risked American involvement in another European war.

The Election of 1918

On October 25, 1918, a few days before the congressional elections, Wilson appealed to the voters to elect a Democratic Congress, saying that to do otherwise would be a repudiation of his leadership in European affairs. Republicans, who had loyally supported his war programs, were affronted. The voters, probably influenced more by domestic and local issues than by foreign policy, gave the Republicans a slim margin in both houses in the election. Wilson's statement had undermined his political support at home and his stature in the eyes of world leaders.

The Armistice

On October 3, 1918, German Chancellor Prince Max of Baden asked Wilson to begin peace negotiations based on his concepts of a just peace and the Fourteen Points. Wilson insisted that the Germans must evacuate Belgium and France and form a civilian government. By early November, the Allied and American armies were advancing rapidly, and Germany was on the verge of collapse. The German Emperor fled to the Netherlands and abdicated. Representatives of the new German republic signed the armistice on November 11, 1918, to be effective at 11:00 A.M. that day, and agreed to withdraw German forces to the Rhine and to surrender military equipment, including 150 submarines.

The Versailles or Paris Peace Conference

Wilson decided that he would lead the American delegation to the peace conference, which opened in Paris on January 12, 1919. In doing so, he became the first president to leave the country during his term of office. The other members of the delegation were Secretary of State Robert Lansing, General Tasker Bliss, Colonel Edward M. House, and attorney Henry White. Wilson made a serious mistake in not appointing any leading Republicans to the commission and in not consulting the Republican leadership in the Senate about the negotiations. In Paris, Wilson joined Prime Minister David Lloyd George of Great Britain, Premier Georges Clemenceau of France, and Prime Minister Vittorio Orlando of Italy to form the "Big Four", which dominated the conference. In the negotiations, which continued until May 1919, Wilson found it necessary to make many compromises in forging the text of the treaty.

The Soviet Influence

Russia was the only major participant in the war that was not represented at the peace conference. Following the Communist Revolution of 1917, Russia had made a separate peace treaty with Germany in March 1918. Wilson had resisted Allied plans to send major military forces to Russia to oust the Communists and bring Russia back into the war. An American force of about 5,000 was sent to Murmansk in the summer of 1918 in association with British and French troops to prevent the Germans from taking military supplies, and was soon active in assisting Russian anti-Bolsheviks. It remained in the area until June 1919. In July 1918 Wilson also sent about 10,000 soldiers to Siberia where they took over the operation of the railroads to assist a Czech army that was escaping from the Germans by crossing Russia. They were also to counterbalance a larger Japanese force in the area and remained until April 1920. Wilson believed that the spread of communism was the greatest threat to peace and international order. His concern made him reluctant to dispute too much with the other leaders at the Versailles Conference and more agreeable to compromise, because he believed it imperative that the democracies remain united in the face of the communist threat.

Important Provisions of the Versailles Treaty

In the drafting of the treaty, Wilson achieved some of the goals in the Fourteen Points, compromised on others, and failed to secure freedom of the seas, free trade, reduction of armaments, or the return of Russia to the society of free nations. Some major decisions were as follows:

1. The League of Nations was formed, implementing the point which Wilson considered the most important. Article X of the Covenant, or charter, of the League called on all members to protect the "territorial integrity" and "political independence" of all other members.

2. Germany was held responsible for causing the war and was required to agree to pay the Allies for all civilian damage and veterans' costs, which eventually were calculated at $33 billion; the German army and navy were limited to tiny defensive forces; and the west bank of the Rhine was declared a military-free zone forever and occupied by the French for fifteen years. These decisions were clearly contrary to the idea of peace without victory.

3. New nations of Yugoslavia, Austria, Hungary, Czechoslovakia, Poland, Lithuania, Latvia, Estonia, and Finland partially fulfilled the idea of self-determination for all nationalities, but the boundaries drawn at the conference left many people under the control of other nationalities.

4. German colonies were made mandates of the League of Nations and given in trusteeship to France, Japan, and Britain and its Dominions.

Germany and the Signing of the Treaty

The German delegates were allowed to come to Versailles in May 1919 after the completion of the treaty document. They expected to negotiate on the basis of the draft, but were told to sign it "or else," probably meaning an economic boycott of Germany. They protested, but signed the Versailles Treaty on June 28, 1919.

The Senate and the Treaty

Following a protest by thirty-nine senators in February 1919, Wilson obtained some changes in the League structure to exempt the Monroe Doctrine and domestic matters from League jurisdiction. Then, on July 26, 1919, he presented the treaty with the League within it to the

Senate for ratification. Almost all of the 47 Democrats supported Wilson and the treaty, but the forty-nine Republicans were divided. About a dozen were "irreconcilables" who thought that the United States should not be a member of the League under any circumstances. The remainder included 25 "strong" and 12 "mild" reservationists who would accept the treaty with some changes. The main objection centered on Article X of the League Covenant, where the reservationists wanted it understood that the United States would not go to war to defend a League member without the approval of Congress. The leader of the reservationists was Henry Cabot Lodge of Massachusetts, the chairman of the Foreign Relations Committee. More senators than the two-thirds necessary for ratification favored the treaty either as written or with reservations.

Wilson and the Senate

On September 3, 1919, Wilson set out on a national speaking tour to appeal to the people to support the treaty and the League, and to influence their senators. He collapsed after a speech in Pueblo, Colorado, on September 25, and returned to Washington where he suffered a severe stroke on October 2, which paralyzed his left side. He was seriously ill for several months and never fully recovered. In a letter to the Senate Democrats on November 18, Wilson urged them to oppose the treaty with the Lodge reservations. In votes the next day, the treaty failed to get a two-thirds majority either with or without the reservations.

The Final Vote

Many people, including British and French leaders, urged Wilson to compromise with Lodge on reservations, including the issue of Article X. Wilson, instead, wrote an open letter to Democrats on January 8, 1920, urging them to make the election of a Democratic president in 1920 a "great and solemn referendum" on the treaty as written. Such partisanship only acerbated the situation. Many historians think that Wilson's ill health impaired his judgment, and that he would have worked out a compromise had he not had the stroke. The Senate took up the treaty again in February 1920, and on March 19 it was again defeated both with and without the reservations. The United States officially ended the war with Germany by a resolution of Congress signed on July 2, 1921, and a separate peace treaty was ratified on July 25. The United States did not join the League.

Consequences of War

The impact of the war was far-reaching in the twentieth century. The United States emerged as the economic and political leader of the world—even if the American people were not prepared to accept the responsibility. The Russian revolution overthrew the tsar and inaugurated a communist dictatorship. Britain, France, Austria, and Turkey went into various states of decline. Germany was devastated at the Versailles Peace Conference. Revenge and bitterness would contribute to the rise of Adolph Hitler and the Nazi movement. The European industrial nations would never recover from the cost of the war. Lingering economic problems would contribute to the Crash of 1929 and the Great Depression of the 1930s. The seeds of World War II had been planted.

Domestic Problems and the End of the Wilson Administration

Demobilization

The AEF was brought home as quickly as possible in early 1919, and members of the armed forces were rapidly discharged. Congress provided for wounded veterans through a system of veteran's hospitals under the Veteran's Bureau and funded relief, especially food supplies, for war-torn Europe. The wartime agencies for the control of the economy, such as the War Industries Board, were soon disbanded. During 1919 Congress considered various plans to nationalize the railroads or continue their public operation, but then passed the Esch-Cummings or Transportation Act of 1920 that returned them to private ownership and operation. It did extend Interstate Commerce Commission control over their rates and financial affairs, and allowed supervised pooling. The fleet of ships accumulated by the Shipping Board during the war was sold to private owners at attractive prices.

Final Reforms of the Progressive Era

In January 1919 the Eighteenth Amendment to the Constitution prohibiting the manufacture, sale, transportation, or importation of intoxicating liquors was ratified by the states, and it became effective in January 1920. The Nineteenth Amendment providing for woman suffrage, which had been defeated in the Senate in 1918, was approved by Congress in 1919. It was ratified by the states in time for the election of 1920.

The Postwar Economy

Despite fear of unemployment with the return of veterans to the labor force and the end of war purchases, the American economy boomed during 1919 and the first half of 1920. Consumers had money from high wages during the war, and the European demand for American food and manufactured products continued for some months after the war. The demand for goods resulted in a rapid inflation. Prices in 1919 were seventy-seven percent above the prewar level, and in 1920 they were 105 percent above that level.

Strikes

The great increase in prices prompted 2,655 strikes in 1919 involving about four million workers or twenty percent of the labor force. Unions were encouraged by the gains they had made during the war and thought they had the support of public opinion. However, the Communist Revolution in Russia in 1917 soon inspired in many Americans, including government officials, a fear of violence and revolution by workers. While most of the strikes in early 1919 were successful, the tide of opinion gradually shifted against the workers.

Four major strikes received particular attention. In January 1919 all unions in Seattle declared a general strike in support of a strike for higher pay by shipyard workers. The action was widely condemned, the federal government sent marines, and the strike was soon abandoned.

In September 1919 Boston police struck for the right to unionize. Governor Calvin Coolidge called out the National Guard and stated that there was "no right to strike against the public safety by anybody, anywhere, anytime." The police were fired and a new force was recruited.

The American Federation of Labor attempted to organize the steel industry in 1919. When Judge Elbert H. Gary, the head of U.S. Steel, refused to negotiate, the workers struck in September. After much violence and the use of federal and state troops, the strike was broken by January 1920.

The United Mine Workers of America under John L. Lewis struck for shorter hours and higher wages on November 1, 1919. Attorney General A. Mitchell Palmer obtained injunctions and the union called off the strike. An arbitration board later awarded the miners a wage increase.

The Red Scare

Americans feared the spread of the Russian Communist Revolution to the United States, and many interpreted the widespread strikes of 1919 as communist-inspired and the beginning of the revolution. Bombs sent through the mail to prominent government and business leaders in April 1919 seemed to confirm their fears, although the origin of the bombs has never been determined. The membership of the two communist parties founded in the United States in 1919 was less than 100,000, but many Americans were sure that many workers, all foreign-born persons, radicals, and members of the International Workers of the World (also known as "Wobblies"), a radical union in the western states, were communists. The anti-German hysteria of the war years was transformed into the anticommunist and antiforeign hysteria of 1919 and 1920, and continued in various forms through the twenties.

The Palmer Raids

Attorney General A. Mitchell Palmer was one of the targets of the anonymous bombers in the spring of 1919. He was also an aspirant for the Democratic nomination for president in 1920, and he realized that many Americans saw the threat of a communist revolution as a grave danger. In August 1919 he named J. Edgar Hoover to head a new Intelligence Division in the Justice Department to collect information about radicals. In November 1919 Palmer's agents arrested almost 700 persons, mostly anarchists, and deported forty-three of them as undesirable aliens. On January 2, 1920 Justice Department agents, local police, and vigilantes in thirty-three cities arrested about 4,000 people accused of being communists. It appears that many people caught in the sweep were neither communists nor aliens. Eventually, 556 were shown to be communists and aliens, and were deported. Palmer then announced that huge communist riots were planned for major cities on May Day, May 1, 1920. Police and troops were alerted, but the day passed with no radical activity. Palmer was discredited and the Red Scare subsided.

The Race Riots of 1919

During the war, about half a million blacks had migrated from the South to industrial cities, mostly in the North and Midwest, to find employment. After the war, white hostility based on competition for lower-paying jobs and black encroachment into neighborhoods led to race riots in twenty-five cities with hundreds killed or wounded and millions of dollars in property damage. Beginning in Longview, Texas, the riots spread, among other places, to Washington, D.C., and Chicago. The Chicago riot in July was the worst, lasting thirteen days and leaving thirty-eight dead, 520 wounded, and 1,000 families homeless. Fear of resuming black veterans in the South lead to an increase of lynchings from thirty-four in 1917 to sixty in 1918 and seventy in 1919. Some of the victims were veterans still in uniform.

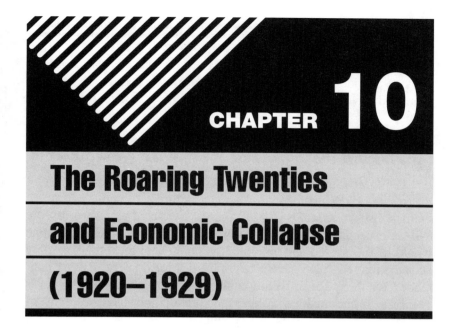

CHAPTER 10

The Roaring Twenties and Economic Collapse (1920–1929)

The Election of 1920

The Political Climate

It seemed to many political observers in 1920 that the Republicans had an excellent chance of victory. The Wilson administration was blamed by many for the wartime civil liberties abuses, the League of Nations controversy, and the strikes and inflation of the postwar period.

The Republican Convention

The principal contenders for the nomination were General Leonard Wood, who had the support of the followers of the deceased Theodore Roosevelt, and Governor Frank O. Lowden of Illinois, the pick of many of the party bosses. When the convention seemed to deadlock, Henry Cabot Lodge, the convention chairman, and several other leaders arranged for the name of Senator Warren G. Harding of Ohio to be introduced as a dark-horse candidate. Harding was nominated on the tenth ballot, and Governor Calvin Coolidge of Massachusetts was chosen as the vice presidential nominee. The platform opposed the League and promised low taxes, high tariffs, immigration restriction, and aid to farmers.

The Democratic Convention

The front-runners were William Gibbs McAdoo, the secretary of the treasury and Wilson's son-in-law, and Attorney General A. Mitchell Palmer. Governor James Cox of Ohio was entered as a favorite son. Wilson expected the convention to deadlock, at which point his name would be introduced and he would be nominated for a third term by acclamation. His plan never materialized. McAdoo and Palmer contended for thirty-seven ballots with neither receiving the two-thirds necessary for nomination. Palmer then released his delegates, most of whom turned to Cox. Cox was nominated on the forty-fourth ballot, and Franklin D. Roosevelt, an assistant secretary of the navy and distant cousin of Theodore, was selected as his running mate. The platform endorsed the League, but left the door open for reservations.

The Campaign

Harding's managers decided that he should speak as little as possible, but he did address visiting delegations from his front porch in Marion, Ohio. It was impossible to tell where he stood on the League issue, but he struck a responsive chord in many people when he urged that the nation should abandon heroics, nostrums, and experiment, and return to what he called normalcy. Cox and Roosevelt travelled extensively, speaking mostly in support of the League. Many found neither presidential candidate impressive.

The Election

Harding received 16,152,200 popular votes, 61 percent of the total, for 404 electoral votes. Cox received 9,147,353 popular votes for 127 electoral votes. Socialist candidate Eugene V. Debs, in federal prison in Atlanta for an Espionage Act conviction, received 919,799 votes. The Democrats carried only states in the Solid South, and even there

lost Tennessee. It appears that people voted Republican more as a repudiation of Wilson's domestic policies than as a referendum on the
League. Wilson had alienated German-Americans, Irish-Americans,
antiwar progressives, civil libertarians, and Midwestern farmers, all
groups that had given the Democrats considerable support in 1916.

The Twenties: Economic Advances and Social Tensions

The Recession of 1920–1921

The United States experienced a severe recession from mid-1920
until the end of 1921. Europe returned to normal and reduced its purchases in America, and domestic demand for goods not available in
wartime was filled. Prices fell, and unemployment exceeded twelve
percent in 1921.

Prosperity and Industrial Productivity

Though overall the economy was strong between 1922 and 1929,
certain segments of the economy—notably agriculture—did not share
in the nation's general prosperity. Improved industrial efficiency, which
resulted in lower prices for goods, was primarily responsible. Manufacturing output increased about sixty-five percent, and productivity,
or output per hour of work, increased about forty percent. The number
of industrial workers actually decreased from 9 million to 8.8 million
during the decade. The increased productivity resulted from improved
machinery, which in turn came about for several reasons. Industry
changed from steam to electric power, allowing the design of more
intricate machines that replaced the work of human hands. By 1929,
seventy percent of industrial power came from electricity. The moving
assembly line, first introduced by Henry Ford in the automobile industry in 1913 and 1914, was widely adopted. Scientific management, exemplified by the time and motion studies pioneered by Frederick W.
Taylor before the war, led to more efficient use of workers and lower
labor costs. Larger firms began, for the first time, to fund major research and development activities to find new and improved products,
reduce production costs, and utilize by-products, and the like.

The Automobile

The principal driving force of the economy of the 1920s was the automobile. There were 8,131,522 motor vehicles registered in the United States in 1920 and 26,704,825 in 1929. Annual output of automobiles reached 3.6 million in 1923 and remained at about that level throughout the decade. By 1925 the price of a Ford Model T had been reduced to $290, less than three months' pay for an average worker. Ford plants produced 9,000 Model Ts per day, and Henry Ford cleared about $25,000 a day throughout the decade. Automobile manufacturing stimulated supporting industries such as steel, rubber, and glass, as well as gasoline refining and highway construction. It was during the 1920s that the United States became a nation of paved roads. Mileage of paved roads increased from 387,000 miles in 1921, most of which was in urban areas, to 662,000 in 1929. Highway construction costs averaged over one billion dollars a year in the late 1920s, in part due to the Federal Highway Act of 1916 that started the federal highway system and gave matching funds to the states for construction. One estimate stated that the automobile industry directly or indirectly employed 3.7 million people in 1929.

Other Leading Industries

The electrical industry also expanded rapidly during the 1920s. The demand for power for industrial machinery as well as for business and some lighting increased dramatically, and a host of electrical appliances such as stoves, vacuum cleaners, refrigerators, toasters, and radios became available. About two-thirds of American homes had electricity by 1929, leaving only those in rural areas without it. Home and business construction also experienced a boom from 1922 until 1928. Other large industries that grew rapidly were chemicals and printing. Also, the movie industry expanded rapidly, especially after the introduction of sound films, it employed about 325,000 people by 1930. New industries that began in the period were radio and commercial aviation.

Consumer Credit and Advertising

Unlike earlier boom periods that had involved large expenditures for capital investments such as railroads and factories, the prosperity of the 1920s depended heavily on the sale of consumer products. Purchases of "big ticket" items such as automobiles, refrigerators, and furniture were made possible by installment or time payment credit. The idea was not new, but the availability of consumer credit expanded tremendously during the 1920s. Consumer interest and demand was spurred by the great increase in professional advertising using newspapers, magazines, radio, billboards, and other media. By 1929 advertising expenditures reached $3.4 billion, more than was spent on education at all levels.

The Dominance of Big Business

There was a trend toward corporate consolidation during the 1920s. By 1929 the 200 largest corporations held forty-nine percent of the corporate wealth and received forty-three percent of corporate income. The top 5 percent of the corporations in the nation received about eighty-five percent of the corporate income. Corporate profits and dividends increased about sixty-five percent during the decade. In most fields an oligopoly of two to four firms dominated, exemplified by the automobile industry, where Ford, General Motors, and Chrysler produced eighty-three percent of the nation's vehicles in 1929. Firms in many fields formed trade associations that represented their interests to the public and the government, and that claimed to stabilize each industry. Government regulatory agencies such as the Federal Trade Commission and the Interstate Commerce Commission were passive and generally controlled by persons from the business world. The public generally accepted the situation and viewed the businessmen with respect. Illustrating the attitudes of the time, *The Man Nobody Knows*, a book by advertising executive Bruce Barton published in 1925, became a best-seller. It described Jesus as the founder of modern business and his apostles as an exemplary business management team.

Banking and Finance

As with other industries, there was a trend toward consolidation in banking. Bank assets increased about sixty-six percent from 1919 to 1929. There was a growth in branch banking, and in 1929 the 3.2 percent of the banks with branch operations controlled forty-six percent of the banking resources. Because corporations were raising much of their money through the sale of stocks and bonds, the demand for business loans declined. Commercial banks then put more of their funds into real estate loans, loans to brokers against stocks and bonds, and the purchase of stocks and bonds themselves. By doing so they made themselves vulnerable to economic disaster when the depression began in late 1929. Even during the prosperous 1920s, 5,714 banks failed, most of them in rural areas or in Florida. Banks in operation in 1929 numbered 25,568.

Labor

The National Association of Manufacturers and its state affiliates began a drive in 1920 to restore the "open shop" or nonunion workplace. As an alternative, firms sought to provide job satisfaction so that the workers would not want a union. Company-sponsored pension and insurance plans, stock purchase plans, efforts to insure worker safety and comfort, social and sporting events, and company magazines were undertaken. Company unions, designed to give workers some voice with management under company control, were organized by 317 firms. The American Federation of Labor and other unions, which had prospered during World War I, found themselves on the defensive. Leaders, especially William Green, president of the American Federation of Labor after 1924, were conservative and nonaggressive. Union membership dropped about twenty percent, from five million to about four million, during the decade. The most violent labor confrontations occurred in the mining and southern textile industries. The United Mine Workers of America, headed by John L. Lewis, was involved in bitter strikes in Pennsylvania, West Virginia, Kentucky, and Illinois, but by 1929 had lost most of its power. The United Textile Workers failed to organize southern textile workers in a campaign from 1927 to 1929, but violent strikes occurred in Tennessee, North Carolina, and Virginia.

The Farm Problem

Farmers did not share in the prosperity of the twenties. Farm prices had been high during World War I because of European demand and government price fixing. By 1920 the European demand dropped considerably, and farm prices were determined by a free market. Farm income dropped from $10 billion annually in 1919 to about $4 billion in 1921, and then leveled off at about $7 billion a year from 1923 through 1929. During the same period, farm expenses rose with the cost of more sophisticated machinery and a greater use of chemical fertilizers.

American Society in the 1920s

Population

During the 1920s the population of the United States increased by 16.1 percent from 105,710,620 in 1920 to 122,775,046 in 1930, a slower percentage of growth than in previous decades. The birthrate was also lower than in former times, dropping from 27.7 per 100,000 in 1920 to 21.3 per 100,000 in 1930. About eighty-eight percent of the people were white.

Urbanization

In 1920 for the first time a majority of Americans, fifty-one percent, lived in an urban place with a population of 2,500 or more. By 1930 the figure had increased to fifty-six percent. In terms of Standard Metropolitan Areas, which are defined as areas with central cities of at least 50,000 population, forty-four percent of the people lived in an SMA in 1920 and fifty percent in 1930. Farm residents dropped from twenty-six percent of the total population in 1920 to twenty-one percent in 1930. A new phenomenon of the 1920s was the tremendous growth of suburbs and satellite cities, which grew more rapidly than the central cities. Streetcars, commuter railroads, and automobiles contributed to the process, as well as the easy availability of financing for home construction. The suburbs had once been the domain of the wealthy, but the technology of the twenties opened them to working-class families.

The Standard of Living

Improved technology and urbanization led to a sharp rise in the standard of living. Urban living improved access to electricity, natural gas, telephones, and piped water. Two-thirds of American homes had electricity by 1929. The use of indoor plumbing, hot water, and central heating increased dramatically. Conveniences such as electric stoves, vacuum cleaners, refrigerators, washing machines, toasters, and irons made life less burdensome. Improved machinery produced better-fitting and more comfortable ready-made clothing and shoes. Diet improved as the consumption of fresh vegetables increased forty-five percent and canned vegetables thirty-five percent. Sales of citrus fruit and canned fruit were also up. Correspondingly, per capita consumption of wheat, corn, and potatoes fell. Automobiles, radios, phonographs, and commercial entertainment added to the enjoyment of life. Yet enjoyment of the new standard of living was uneven. The one-third of the households that still did not have electricity in 1929 lacked access to many of the new products. For those who had access, the new standard of living required more money than had been necessary in former times. Despite heavy sales of appliances, by 1929 only twenty-five percent of American families had vacuum cleaners, and only twenty percent had electric toasters. The real income of workers increased about eleven percent during the decade, but others suffered a decline in real income, including farmers who still comprised about one-fourth of the population. It is estimated that the bottom ninety-three percent of the population had an average increase in real income of six percent during the 1920s. In 1929 about twelve million families, or forty-three percent of the total, had annual incomes under $1,500, which was considered by many to be the poverty line. About 20 million families, or seventy-two percent, had incomes under $2,500, the family income deemed necessary for a decent standard of living with reasonable comforts.

The Sexual Revolution

Traditional American moral standards regarding premarital sex and marital fidelity were widely questioned for the first time during the 1920s. There was a popular misunderstanding by people who had not read his works that Sigmund Freud had advocated sexual promiscuity.

Movies, novels, and magazine stories were more sexually explicit and sensational. The "flaming youth" of the "Jazz Age" emphasized sexual promiscuity and drinking, as well as new forms of dancing considered erotic by the older generation. The automobile, by giving people mobility and privacy, was generally considered to have contributed to sexual license. Journalists wrote about "flappers," young women who were independent, assertive, and promiscuous. Birth control, though illegal, was promoted by Margaret Sanger and others, and was widely accepted. The sexual revolution occurred mostly among some urban dwellers, middle-class people, and students, who were an economically select group at the time. Many continued to adhere to the old ways. Compared with the period from 1960 to the present, it was a relatively conservative time.

Women

Many feminists believed that the passage of the Nineteenth Amendment in 1920 providing women suffrage would solve all problems for women. When it became apparent that women did not vote as a bloc,

March for Woman Suffrage

political leaders gave little additional attention to the special concerns of women. The sexual revolution brought some emancipation. Women adopted less bulky clothing with short skirts and bare arms and necks. They could smoke and socialize with men in public more freely than before. Birth control was more acceptable. Divorce laws were liberalized in many states at the insistence of women. In 1920 there was one divorce for every 7.5 marriages. By 1929 the ratio was 1 in 6. The number of employed women rose from 8.4 million in 1920 to 10.6 million in 1929, but the total workforce increased in about the same proportion. Black and foreign-born women comprised fifty-seven percent of the female workforce, and domestic service was the largest job category. Most other women workers were in traditional female occupations such as secretarial and clerical work, retail sales, teaching, and nursing. Rates of pay were below those for men. Most women still pursued the traditional role of housewife and mother, and society accepted that as the norm.

Blacks

The migration of Southern rural blacks to the cities continued, with about 1.5 million moving during the 1920s. By 1930 about twenty percent of blacks lived in the North, with the largest concentrations in New York, Chicago, and Philadelphia. While they were generally better off economically in the cities than they had been as tenant farmers, they tended to hold low-paying jobs and were confined to segregated areas of the cities. The Harlem section of New York City, with a black population of 73,000 in 1920 and 165,000 in 1930, was the largest black urban community, and became the center for black writers, musicians, and intellectuals. Blacks throughout the country developed jazz and blues as music forms, which enjoyed widespread popularity. W. E. B. DuBois, the editor of *The Crisis*, continued to call for integration and to attack segregation despite his disappointment with the lack of progress after World War I. The National Association for the Advancement of Colored People was a more conservative but active voice for civil rights, and the National Urban League concentrated on employment and economic advancement. Lynchings continued in the South, and the antiblack activities of the Ku Klux Klan is mentioned under Social Conflicts later in this chapter.

Marcus Garvey and the UNIA

A native of Jamaica, Marcus Garvey founded the Universal Negro Improvement Association there in 1914 and moved to New York in 1916. He advocated black racial pride and separatism rather than integration, and a return of blacks to Africa. Some of his ideas soon alienated the older black organizations. He developed a large following, especially among Southern blacks, but his claim of six million members in 1923 may be inflated. An advocate of black economic self-sufficiency, he urged his followers to buy only from blacks, and founded a chain of businesses, including grocery stores, restaurants, and laundries. In 1921 he proclaimed himself the provisional president of an African empire and sold stock in the Black Star Steamship Line that would take migrants to Africa. The line went bankrupt in 1923, Garvey was convicted and imprisoned for mail fraud in the sale of the line's stock, and was then deported. His legacy was an emphasis on black pride and self-respect.

Mexicans and Puerto Ricans

Mexicans had long migrated to the southwestern part of the United States as agricultural laborers, but in the 1920s they began to settle in cities such as Los Angeles, San Antonio, and Denver. Like other immigrants, they held low-paying jobs and lived in poor neighborhoods, which they called *barrios*. The 1920s also saw the first large migration of Puerto Ricans to the mainland, mostly to New York City. There they were employed in manufacturing, in service industries such as restaurants, and in domestic work. They lived in barrios in Brooklyn and Manhattan.

Education

Free elementary education was available to most students in 1920, except for many black children. Growth of elementary schools in the 1920s reflected population growth and the addition of kindergartens. High school education became more available, and the number of public secondary schools doubled from 2.2 million in 1920 to 4.4 million in 1930. High school instruction shifted from an emphasis on college preparation to include vocational education, which was funded in part by the Smith-Hughes Act of 1917 that gave federal funds for agricultural and technical studies. There was also a substantial growth in enrollment in higher education from 600,000 in 1920 to 1.1 million in 1930.

Religion

Church and synagogue membership increased more rapidly than the population during the 1920s, despite much religious tension and conflict. Most Protestants had been divided North and South since before the Civil War. By the 1920s, there was another major division between the modernists who accommodated their thinking with modern biblical criticism and evolution, and fundamentalists who stressed the literal truth of the Bible and creationism. There was also division on social issues such as support of labor. The only issue that united most Protestants, except Lutherans, was prohibition. The Roman Catholic Church and Jewish congregations were assimilating the large number of immigrants who had arrived prior to 1922. They also found themselves under attack from the Ku Klux Klan and the immigration restrictions.

Popular Culture

The trend whereby entertainment shifted from the home and small social groups to commercial profit-making activities had begun in the late-nineteenth century and reached maturity in the 1920s. Spending for entertainment in 1929 was $4.3 billion. The movies attracted the most consumer interest and generated the most money. Movie attendance averaged 40 million a week in 1922 and 90 million a week in 1929. Introduction of sound with *The Jazz Singer* in 1927 generated even more interest. Stars like Douglas Fairbanks, Gloria Swanson, Rudolph Valentino, Clara Bow, and Charlie Chaplin were tremendously popular. Americans spent ten times more on movies than on all sports, the next attraction in popularity. It was called the golden age of major-league baseball, with an attendance increase of over fifty percent during the decade. Millions followed the exploits of George Herman "Babe" Ruth and other stars. Boxing was popular and made Jack

Dempsey and others famous. College football began to attract attention with Knute Rockne coaching at Notre Dame and Harold "Red" Grange playing for the University of Illinois. When Grange signed with the Chicago Bears in 1926, professional football began to grow in popularity. Commercial radio began when station KDKA in Pittsburgh broadcasted the election results in November 1920. By 1929 over ten million families, over one-third of the total, had radios. National network broadcasting began when the National Broadcasting Company was organized in 1926, followed by the Columbia Broadcasting System in 1927. Radio was free entertainment, paid for by advertising. Despite the many new diversions, Americans continued to read, and millions of popular magazines were sold each week. Popular books of the period included the Tarzan series and Zane Grey's Westerns, as well as literary works, some of which are mentioned under Literary Trends.

Literary Trends

Many talented writers of the 1920s were disgusted with the hypocrisy and materialism of contemporary American society, and expressed their concern in their works. Often called the "Lost Generation," many of them, such as novelists Ernest Hemingway and F. Scott Fitzgerald and poets Ezra Pound and T.S. Eliot, moved to Europe. Typical authors and works include Ernest Hemingway's *The Sun Also Rises* (1926) and *A Farewell to Arms* (1929); Sinclair Lewis's *Babbitt* (1922), *Arrowsmith* (1925), and *Elmer Gantry* (1927); F. Scott Fitzgerald's *The Great Gatsby* (1925) and *Tender Is the Night* (1929); John Dos Passos' *Three Soldiers* (1921); and Thomas Wolfe's *Look Homeward, Angel* (1929). H. L. Mencken, a journalist who began publication of the *American Mercury* magazine in 1922, ceaselessly and vitriolicly attacked the "booboisie," as he called middle-class America, but his literary talent did not match that of the leaders of the period.

Social Conflicts

A Conflict of Values

The rapid technological changes represented by the automobile, the revolution in morals, and the rapid urbanization with many immigrants and blacks inhabiting the growing cities brought a strong reaction from white Protestant Americans of older stock who saw their traditional values gravely threatened. In many ways their concerns continued the emotions of wartime hysteria and the Red Scare. The traditionalists were largely residents of rural areas and small towns, and the clash of farm values with those of an industrial society of urban workers was evident. The conflict is often called a rural-urban conflict, and to a great extent it was, but some think the lines of division were not that neat. The traditionalist backlash against modern urban industrial society expressed itself primarily through intolerance.

The Ku Klux Klan

On Thanksgiving Day in 1915 the Knights of the Ku Klux Klan, modeled on the organization of the same name in the 1860s and 1870s, was founded near Atlanta by William J. Simmons. Its purpose was mainly to intimidate blacks, who were experiencing an apparent rise in status during World War I. The Klan remained small until 1920 when two advertising experts, Edward Y. Clark and Elizabeth Tyler, were hired by the leadership. Clark and Tyler used modern advertising to recruit members, charged a ten dollar initiation fee of which they received $2.50, and made additional money from the sale of regalia and emblems. By 1923 the Klan had about five million members throughout the nation. The largest concentrations of members were in the South, the Southwest, the Midwest, California, and Oregon. The use of white hoods, masks, and robes, and secret ritual and jargon seemed to appeal mostly to lower middle-class men in towns and small cities. The Klan stood for "100 percent pure Americanism" to preserve "native, white, Protestant supremacy." It opposed blacks and Catholics primarily. In addition, Jews and the foreign-born were often its targets. It also attacked bootleggers, drunkards, gamblers, and adulterers for violating moral standards. The Klan's methods of repression included cross burnings, tar and featherings, kidnappings, lynchings, and burnings. The Klan was not a political party, but it endorsed and opposed candidates, and exerted considerable control over elections and politicians in at least nine states. The Klan began to decline after 1925 when it was hit by scandals, especially the murder conviction of Indiana Grand

Dragon David Stephenson. The main reason for its decline was the staunch opposition of courageous editors, politicians, and other public figures who exposed its lawlessness and terrorism in the face of great personal danger of violence. Many historians see the Klan as the American expression of fascism, which was making headway in Italy, Germany, and other European nations during the twenties.

Immigration Restriction

There had been calls for immigration restriction since the late nineteenth century. Labor leaders believed that immigrants depressed wages and impeded unionization. Some progressives believed that they created social problems. In June 1917 Congress, over Wilson's veto, had imposed a literacy test for immigrants and excluded many Asian nationalities. During World War I and the Red Scare, almost all immigrants were considered radicals and communists, and the tradition was quickly picked up by the Klan. With bad economic conditions in postwar Europe, over 1.3 million came to the United States during the three years from 1919 through 1921. As in the period before the war, they were mostly from southern and eastern Europe and mostly Catholics and Jews, the groups most despised by nativist Americans. In 1921 Congress quickly passed the Emergency Quota Act, which limited immigration by nation to three percent of the number of foreign-born persons from that nation in the United States in 1910. In practice, the law admitted about as many as wanted to come from such nations as Britain, Ireland, and Germany, while severely restricting Italians, Greeks, Poles, and eastern European Jews. It became effective in 1922 and reduced the number of immigrants annually to about forty percent of the 1921 total. Congress then passed the National Origins Act of 1924, which set the quotas at two percent of the number of foreign-born persons of that nationality in the United States in 1890, excluded all Asians, and imposed an annual maximum of 164,000.

Immigration from Western Hemisphere nations, including Canada and Mexico, was not limited. The law further reduced the number of southern and eastern Europeans, and cut the annual immigration to twenty percent of the 1921 figure. In 1927 the annual maximum was reduced to 150,000. The quotas were not fully calculated and implemented until 1929. Objections to the law were not aimed at the idea of restriction, but at the designation of certain nationalities and religious groups as undesirable. The law was resented by such groups as Italian- and Polish-Americans.

Prohibition

The Eighteenth Amendment, which prohibited the manufacture, sale, or transportation of intoxicating liquors, took effect in January 1920. It was implemented by the Volstead Act of October 1919, which defined intoxicating beverages as containing one-half of one percent alcohol by volume and imposed criminal penalties for violations. Many states had authorized the sale of light beer, believing that it was not covered by the amendment, but Anti-Saloon League lobbyists pushed through the Volstead Act. Many historians believe that prohibition of hard liquor might have been successful if light wine and beer had been allowed. As things turned out, the inexpensive light beverages were less available while expensive illegal hard liquor was readily available. Prohibition was enforceable only if many people in the society accepted and supported it. Enforcement was reasonably effective in some rural Southern and Midwestern states that had been dry before the amendment. In urban areas where both foreign-born and native citizens often believed that their liberty had been infringed upon, neither the public nor their elected officials were interested in enforcement. Speakeasies, supposedly secret bars operated by bootleggers, replaced the saloons. Smuggled liquor flowed across the boundaries and coastlines of the nation, and the manufacture of "bathtub gin" and similar beverages was undertaken by thousands. Organized crime, which previously had been involved mainly with prostitution and gambling, grew tremendously to meet the demand. Al Capone of Chicago was perhaps the most famous of the bootlegging gangsters. The automobile was used both to transport liquor and to take customers to speakeasies. Women, who had not gone to saloons in the pre-prohibition period, frequented speakeasies and began to drink in public. By the mid-1920s, the nation was badly divided on the prohibition issue. Support continued from rural areas and almost all Republican officeholders. The Democrats were divided between the urban Northerners who advocated repeal, and rural, especially Southern, Democrats who supported prohibition. Some people who originally favored prohibition changed their views because of the public hypocrisy and criminal activity which it caused.

Creationism and the Scopes Trial

Fundamentalist Protestants, under the leadership of William Jennings Bryan, began a campaign in 1921 to prohibit the teaching of evolution in the schools, and thus protect belief in the literal Biblical account of creation. The idea was especially well-received in the South. In 1925 the Tennessee legislature passed a law that forbade any teacher in the state's schools or colleges to teach evolution. The American Civil Liberties Union found a young high school biology teacher, John Thomas Scopes, who was willing to bring about a test case by breaking the law. Scopes was tried in Dayton, Tennessee, in July 1925. Bryan came to assist the prosecution, and Chicago trial lawyer Clarence Darrow defended Scopes. The trial attracted national attention through newspaper and radio coverage. The judge refused to allow expert testimony, so the trial was a duel of words between Darrow and Bryan. As was expected, Scopes was convicted and fined one hundred dollars. Bryan died of exhaustion a few days after the trial. Both sides claimed a moral victory. The anti-evolution crusaders continued their efforts, and secured enactment of a statute in Mississippi in 1926. They failed after a bitter fight in North Carolina in 1927 and in several other states until Arkansas in 1928 passed an anti-evolution law by use of the initiative.

Sacco and Vanzetti

On April 15, 1920, two unidentified gunmen robbed a shoe factory and killed two men in South Braintree, Massachusetts. Nicola Sacco and Bartolomeo Vanzetti, Italian immigrants and admitted anarchists, were tried for murder. Judge Webster Thayer clearly favored the prosecution, which based its case on the political radicalism of the defendants. After they were convicted and sentenced to death in July 1921, there was much protest in the United States and in Europe that they had not received a fair trial. After six years of delays, they were executed on August 23, 1927. A debate on their innocence and the possible perversion of American justice continued long afterward. The men were ultimately vindicated by Governor Michael Dukakis in 1977.

Government and Politics in the 1920s: The Harding Administration

Warren G. Harding

Harding was a handsome and amiable man of limited intellectual and organizational abilities. He had spent much of his life as the publisher of a newspaper in the small city of Marion, Ohio. He recognized his limitations, but hoped to be a much-loved president. He showed compassion by pardoning socialist Eugene V. Debs for his conviction under the Espionage Act and inviting him to dinner at the White House. He also persuaded U.S. Steel to give workers the eight-hour day. A convivial man, he liked to drink and play poker with his friends, and kept the White House stocked with bootleg liquor despite prohibition. He was accused of keeping a mistress, Nan Britton. His economic philosophy was conservative.

Warren G. Harding

The Cabinet and Government Appointments

Harding appointed some outstanding persons to his Cabinet, including Secretary of State Charles Evans Hughes, a former Supreme Court justice and presidential candidate; Secretary of the Treasury Andrew Mellon, a Pittsburgh aluminum and banking magnate and reportedly the richest man in America; and Secretary of Commerce Herbert Hoover, a dynamic multimillionaire mine owner who was famous for wartime relief efforts. Less impressive was his appointment of his cronies Albert B. Fall as Secretary of the Interior and Harry M. Daugherty as Attorney General. Other cronies, some dishonest, were appointed to other government posts.

Tax Reduction

Mellon believed in low taxes and government economy to free the rich from "oppressive" taxes and thus encourage investment. The farm bloc of Midwestern Republicans and Southern Democrats in Congress prevented cuts in the higher tax brackets as great as Mellon recommended. The Revenue Acts of 1921 and 1924 cut the maximum tax rates to fifty percent and then to forty percent. Taxes in lower brackets were also reduced, but inheritance and corporate income taxes were retained. Despite the cuts, Mellon was able to reduce the federal debt by an average of $500 million a year.

The Fordney-McCumber Tariff

Mellon sought substantial increases in the tariffs, but again there was a compromise with the farm bloc. The Fordney-McCumber Tariff of September 1922 imposed high rates on farm products and protected such infant industries as rayon, china, toys, and chemicals. Most other items received moderate protection, and a few items including farm equipment, were duty-free. The president could raise or lower rates to a limit of fifty percent on recommendation of the Tariff Commission. The average rate was about thirty-three percent, compared with about twenty-six percent under the previous tariff.

The Budget

As a result of the Budget and Accounting Act of 1921, the federal government had a unified budget for the first time. The law also provided for a director of the budget to assist in its preparation and a comptroller general to audit government accounts.

The Harding Scandals

Harding apparently was completely honest, but several of his friends whom he appointed to office became involved in major financial scandals. Most of the information about the scandals did not become public knowledge until after Harding's death.

The "Teapot Dome" Scandal began when Secretary of the Interior Albert B. Fall in 1921 secured the transfer of several naval oil reserves to his jurisdiction. In 1922 he secretly leased reserves at Teapot Dome in Wyoming to Harry F. Sinclair of Monmouth Oil and at Elk Hills in California to Edward Doheny of Pan-American Petroleum. A Senate investigation later revealed that Sinclair had given Fall $305,000 in cash and bonds and a herd of cattle, while Doheny had given him a $100,000 unsecured loan. Sinclair and Doheny were acquitted in 1927 of charges of defrauding the government, but in 1929 Fall was convicted, fined, and imprisoned for bribery.

Another scandal involved Charles R. Forbes, appointed by Harding to head the new Veterans' Bureau. He seemed energetic and efficient in operating the new hospitals and services for veterans. It was later estimated that he had stolen or squandered about $250 million in bureau funds.

Scandal also tainted Attorney General Daugherty who, through his intimate friend Jesse Smith, took bribes from bootleggers, income tax evaders, and others in return for protection from prosecution. When the scandal began to come to light, Smith committed suicide in Daugherty's Washington apartment in May 1923. There was also evidence that Daugherty received money for using his influence in returning the American Metal Company, seized by the government during the war, to its German owners.

Harding's Death

Depressed by the first news of the scandals, Harding left in June 1923 for an extended trip that included a tour of Alaska. On his return to California, he died suddenly in San Francisco on August 2, 1923, apparently of a heart attack. Rumors of foul play or suicide persisted for years.

Coolidge Becomes President

Vice President Calvin Coolidge became president to complete Harding's term. As the scandals of the deceased president's administration came to light, Coolidge was able to avoid responsibility for them. He had a reputation for honesty, although he did not remove Daugherty from the Cabinet until March 1924.

The Election of 1924

The Republicans

Progressive insurgents failed to capture the convention. Calvin Coolidge was nominated on the first ballot with Charles G. Dawes as his running mate. The platform endorsed business development, low taxes, and rigid economy in government. The party stood on its record of economic growth and prosperity since 1922.

The Democrats

The party had an opportunity to draw farmers and labor into a new progressive coalition. An attractive Democratic candidate would have had a good chance against the bland Coolidge and the Harding scandals. Instead, two wings of the party battled to exhaustion at the convention. The Eastern wing, led by Governor Alfred E. Smith of New York, wanted the platform to favor repeal of prohibition and to condemn the Ku Klux Klan. Southern and Western delegates, led by William G. McAdoo and William Jennings Bryan, narrowly defeated both proposals. Smith and McAdoo contested for 103 ballots with neither receiving the two-thirds necessary for nomination. John W. Davis, a conservative Wall Street lawyer, was finally chosen as a dark horse with Charles W. Bryan, brother of William Jennings, as the vice presidential candidate. The platform favored a lower tariff, but otherwise was similar to the Republican document.

The Progressives

Robert M. LaFollette, after failing in a bid for the Republican nomination, formed a new Progressive Party with support from Midwest farm groups, socialists, and the American Federation of Labor. The platform attacked monopolies, and called for the nationalization of railroads, the direct election of the president, and other reforms.

The Campaign

Neither Coolidge nor Davis were active or effective campaigners. Republican publicity concentrated on attacking LaFollette as a communist. LaFollette campaigned vigorously, but he lacked money and was disliked by many for his 1917 opposition to entrance into World War I.

The Election

Coolidge received 15,725,016 votes and 382 electoral votes, more than his two opponents combined. Davis received 8,385,586 votes and 136 electoral votes, while LaFollette had 4,822,856 votes and 13 electoral votes from his home state of Wisconsin.

The Coolidge Administration

Calvin Coolidge

Coolidge was a dour and taciturn man. Born in Vermont, his adult life and political career were spent in Massachusetts. "The business of the United States is business," he proclaimed, and "the man who builds a factory builds a temple." His philosophy of life was stated in the remark that "four-fifths of all our troubles in this world would disappear if only we would sit down and keep still." Liberal political commentator Walter Lippmann wrote that "Mr. Coolidge's genius for inactivity is developed to a very high point." He intentionally provided no presidential leadership.

The McNary-Haugen Bill

In 1921 George Peek and Hugh S. Johnson, farm machinery manufacturers in Illinois, developed a plan to raise prices for basic farm products. The government would buy and resell in the domestic market a commodity such as wheat at the world price plus the tariff. The surplus would be sold abroad at the world price, and the difference made up by an equalization fee on all farmers in proportion to the amount of the commodity they had sold. When farm conditions did not improve, the idea was incorporated in the McNary-Haugen Bill, which passed Congress in 1927 and 1928, but was vetoed both times by Coolidge. The plan was a forerunner of the agricultural programs of the 1930s.

Muscle Shoals

During World War I the government had constructed a dam and two nitrate plants on the Tennessee River at Muscle Shoals, Alabama. In 1925 Senator George W. Norris of Nebraska led the defeat of a plan to lease the property to private business, but his proposal for government operation was vetoed by Coolidge in 1928. The facility was to become the nucleus of the Tennessee Valley Authority in the 1930s.

Veterans' Bonus

Legislation to give veterans of World War I twenty-year endowment policies with values based on their length of service was passed over Coolidge's veto in 1924.

The Revenue Act of 1926

Mellon's tax policies were finally implemented by this law which reduced the basic income tax, cut the surtax to a maximum of twenty percent, abolished the gift tax, and cut the estate tax in half.

The Election of 1928

The Republicans

Coolidge did not seek another term, and the convention quickly nominated Herbert Hoover, the secretary of commerce, for president and Charles Curtis as his running mate. The platform endorsed the policies of the Harding and Coolidge administrations.

The Democrats

Governor Alfred E. Smith of New York, a Catholic and an antiprohibitionist, controlled most of the non-Southern delegations. Southerners supported his nomination with the understanding that the platform would not advocate repeal of prohibition. Senator Joseph T. Robinson of Arkansas, a Protestant and a prohibitionist, was the vice presidential candidate. The platform differed little from the Republican, except in advocating lower tariffs.

The Campaign

Hoover asserted that Republican policies would end poverty in the country. Smith was also economically conservative, but he attacked prohibition and bigotry. He was met in the South by a massive campaign headed by Bishop James Cannon, Jr., of the Methodist Episcopal Church South, attacking him as a Catholic and an antiprohibitionist.

The Election

Hoover received 21,392,190 votes and 444 electoral votes, carrying all of the North except Massachusetts and Rhode Island, and seven states in the Solid South. Smith had 15,016,443 votes for 87 electoral votes in eight states.

Foreign Policy in the Twenties

The Washington Conference

At the invitation of Secretary of State Charles Evans Hughes, representatives of the United States, Great Britain, France, Japan, Italy,

China, the Netherlands, Belgium, and Portugal met in Washington in August 1921 to discuss naval limitations and Asian affairs. Three treaties resulted from the conference.

The Five Power Pact or Treaty, signed in February 1922, committed the United States, Britain, Japan, France, and Italy to end new construction of capital naval vessels, to scrap some ships, and to maintain a ratio of 5:5:3:1.67:1.67 for tonnage of capital or major ships in order of the nations listed. Hughes did not realize that the treaty gave Japan naval supremacy in the Pacific.

The Nine Power Pact or Treaty was signed by all of the participants at the conference. It upheld the Open Door in China by binding the nations to respect the sovereignty, independence, and integrity of China.

The Four Power Pact or Treaty bound the United States, Great Britain, Japan, and France to respect each other's possessions in the Pacific, and to confer in the event of disputes or aggression in the area.

War Debts, Reparations, and International Finance

The United States had loaned the Allies about $7 billion during World War I and about $3.25 billion in the postwar period, and insisted on full payment of the debts. Meanwhile, Germany was to pay reparations to the Allies, but by 1923 Germany was bankrupt. The Dawes Plan, proposed by American banker Charles G. Dawes, was accepted in 1924. Under it, American banks made loans of $2.5 billion to Germany by 1930. Germany paid reparations of over $2 billion to the Allies during the same period, and the Allies paid about $2.6 billion to the United States on their war debts. The whole cycle was based on loans from American banks.

The Kellogg-Briand Pact

A group of American citizens campaigned during the 1920s for a treaty that would outlaw war. In 1927 the French foreign minister, Aristide Briand, proposed such a treaty with the United States. Frank B. Kellogg, Coolidge's secretary of state, countered by proposing that other nations be invited to sign. At Paris, in August 1928, almost all major nations signed the treaty that renounced war as an instrument of national policy. It outlawed only aggression, not self-defense, and had no enforcement provisions.

Latin America

American investment in Latin America almost doubled during the 1920s to $5.4 billion, and relations with most nations in the region improved. Coolidge removed the marines from Nicaragua in 1925, but a revolution erupted and the marines were returned. Revolutionary General Augusto Sandino fought against the marines until they were replaced by an American-trained national guard under Anastasio Somoza. The Somoza family ruled Nicaragua until 1979 when they were overthrown by revolutionaries called the Sandinistas.

Herbert Hoover listens to a radio set in the 1920s.

The Great Depression: The Crash

Hoover Becomes President

Herbert Hoover, an Iowa farm boy and an orphan, graduated from Stanford University with a degree in mining engineering. He became a multimillionaire from mining and other investments around the world. After serving as the director of the Food Administration under Wilson, be became secretary of commerce under Harding and Coolidge. He believed that an associative economic system with voluntary cooperation of business and government would enable the United States to abolish poverty through continued economic growth.

The Stock Market Boom

Stock prices increased throughout the decade. The boom in prices and volume of sales was especially active after 1925, and was intensive during 1928–1929. The Dow-Jones Industrial Average for the year 1924 was 120; for the month of September 1929 it was 381; and for the year 1932 it dropped to 41. Stocks were selling for more than 16 times their earnings in 1929, well above the rule of thumb at the time of ten times their earnings.

The Stock Market Crash

Careful investors, realizing that stocks were overpriced, began to sell to take their profits. During October 1929, prices declined as more stock was sold. On "Black Thursday," October 24, 1929, almost 13 million shares were traded, a large number for that time, and prices fell precipitously. Investment banks tried to boost the market by buying, but on October 29, "Black Tuesday," the market fell about 40 points with 16.5 million shares traded. A long decline followed until early 1933, and with it, depression.

Quiz: Chapters 9 and 10

1. Which of the following was passed into law during the presidency of Woodrow Wilson?

    (A) The Pure Food and Drug Act

    (B) A progressive income tax

    (C) A high protective tariff

    (D) A national old-age pension

    (E) The Sherman Antitrust Act

2. All of the following were characteristic of the 1920s EXCEPT

    (A) voting rights for women.

    (B) prohibition and bootlegging.

    (C) consumerism and easy credit.

    (D) Progressivist reform and union growth.

    (E) Ku Klux Klan power and popularity.

3. Which of the following best describes the administrations of Warren Harding and Calvin Coolidge?

    (A) "The trusts must be broken!"

    (B) "The only thing we have to fear is fear itself!"

    (C) "The business of government is business!"

    (D) "The taste of empire is in the mouths of the people!"

    (E) "The world must be made safe for democracy!"

4.   The "Lost Generation" refers to

   (A)   those young adults whose lives and families were devastated by the Great Depression of the 1930s.

   (B)   the millions of young men killed in the senseless trench warfare of World War I.

   (C)   young writers disillusioned by the materialism, decadence, and conformity dominating 1920s America.

   (D)   the thousands of workers killed or injured in efforts to form and promote worker safety in turn-of-the-century America.

   (E)   the generation of young Americans caught up in the turmoil of war protests and moral collapse during the 1960s.

5.   Joseph Pulitzer was a pioneer in the development of

   (A)   news journals aimed exclusively at the upper class and social elites in America.

   (B)   weekly journals focusing exclusively on economic news.

   (C)   yellow journalism.

   (D)   ethics in journalism laws to prevent slanderous news stories that often ruined innocent peoples' lives.

   (E)   the nation's first national "wire service," UPI.

6.   Industrial committees that helped mobilize the country's war efforts during World War I were

   (A)   instrumental in preventing corruption and labor dissension from crippling the mobilization campaign.

   (B)   so dominated by greedy businessmen cashing in on

the war they were disbanded and replaced by the War Industries Board.

(C) the key to an efficient war effort following the collapse of the War Industries Board.

(D) ruled unconstitutional by the conservative Supreme Court and were forced to reorganize as unfunded private consulting groups.

(E) not formed until so late in the war effort that they had little impact other than to streamline the process for the transfer of men and equipment from the United States to France.

7. Black Americans during World War I, for the most part,

    (A) were treated with dignity in Europe.

    (B) suffered little discrimination at home.

    (C) believed integration was becoming a reality in American society.

    (D) refused to participate in the war effort.

    (E) endorsed the policy of nonviolent resistance.

8. The case of Nicola Sacco and Bartolomeo Vanzetti in the 1920s best illustrated

    (A) America's "Return to Normalcy."

    (B) the lack of compassion toward immigrants.

    (C) the treatment of Italians.

    (D) the reckless vigilante spirit that existed in the Southern states.

    (E) the extent of the "Red Scare."

9. The 1925 Scopes trial in Dayton, Tennessee,

   (A) concerned the struggle to tax church property in Tennessee.

   (B) was an effort by the state of Tennessee to ban the use of snakes in religious services.

   (C) focused on the efforts of the Protestant fundamentalists to impose prohibition on the state.

   (D) demonstrated the rural fundamentalist belief that the theory of evolution was a subversive attempt to destroy the meaning of the Bible.

   (E) supported the efforts of the Ku Klux Klan to prevent southern European immigrants from settling in the state.

10. The Nineteenth Amendment, added to the United States Constitution in 1920, did which of the following?

    (A) Limited the president to two terms

    (B) Created the federal income tax

    (C) Outlawed the sale and transportation of alcoholic beverages

    (D) Enfranchised women

    (E) Ended prohibition

ANSWER KEY

1.	(B)	6.	(B)
2.	(D)	7.	(A)
3.	(C)	8.	(E)
4.	(C)	9.	(D)
5.	(C)	10.	(D)

DETAILED ANSWERS

1. **(B)** The income tax became law under Wilson. The Pure Food and Drug Act (A) was passed under Taft, and the Sherman Antitrust Act (E) under Benjamin Harrison. The old-age pension (D) had to wait for Franklin Roosevelt. High protective tariffs (C) have existed at a number of times throughout U.S. history. The Underwood Tariff passed under Wilson represented a lowering of tariff rates.

2. **(D)** The 1920s were a mixture of both conservative and liberal trends. On the liberal side, women were granted the right to vote with ratification in 1920 of the Nineteenth Amendment to the Constitution. With new forms of credit and advertising, combined with increases in wages and productivity, consumerism became the new American ethic.

On the conservative side, prohibition was enacted with the passage of the Eighteenth Amendment to the Constitution in 1919. Its enforcement began on a large scale in 1920, opening the door for bootlegging and the rise of organized crime in America. The Ku Klux

Klan, using new advertising techniques to market itself, reached a peak membership of 5 million people in 1925, before sex scandals, corruption, poor leadership, and public revulsion at Klan activities broke its power base and discredited it as a major political force. Throughout the mid-1920s, however, the Klan was a force to be feared and accommodated, and Klan activities had a very intimidating effect on local and regional politics in the South, Midwest, and mid-Atlantic regions of the country.

The only choice not characteristic of the 1920s is choice (D). The Progressive movement, so forceful before World War I, was eclipsed by the pro-business economic growth philosophies of Harding, Coolidge, Hoover, and the Republicans. Progressivist reforms were rolled back throughout the 1920s, negating many gains previously made in regulating businesses and securing labor rights. These gains were sacrificed on the altars of economic growth and laissez-faire capitalism. Progressivism would not return to the fore until the enactment of Franklin Roosevelt's "New Deal" in the 1930s, where Progressivist principles were carried far beyond anything hoped for at the turn of the century.

3.   **(C)**   Both Harding and Coolidge promoted policies favorable to business. They firmly believed in an association between business and government that would help the nation prosper. Their policies reflected a repudiation of Progressivism and a philosophy that what is good for business is good for the country. In that sense, they truly felt that "The business of government IS business." They believed strong business growth would provide jobs and would improve the entire economy. Their policies helped spur the tremendous economic growth that drove the nation forward from 1922 through 1929. Unfortunately, these same antiregulatory, laissez-faire business policies permitted greed and abuses leading directly to the stock market crash of 1929 and the Great Depression that followed.

4.   **(C)**   Most Americans welcomed the economic growth and prosperity of the mid-1920s. However, some found the collapse of Progressivism, the subsequent dominance of materialistic consumerism, laissez-faire capitalism with its greed, corruption, and conspicuous consumption, as well as the emphasis on social conformity and dearth

of spirituality, to be morally repugnant. This repugnance and cynicism regarding America's social framework were captured most poignantly in the works of several young American authors. F. Scott Fitzgerald, H.L. Mencken, Ernest Hemingway, and Sinclair Lewis wrote stories of heroes as flawed as the villains they sought to conquer. Their works raised questions about traditional assumptions of right and wrong and often left those questions unanswered. They painted unsettling pictures of American society, frequently with a sharply critical, sometimes satirical, portrayal of American hypocrisy and decadence.

Their unsettling works, with the inherent crying out at the loss of ideals, values, and purpose, as well as the interwoven criticism of the current dominance of materialism, led critics and historians to label them the "Lost Generation." A whole generation of young writers faced what they believed to be a spiritually lost America desperately needing to find new and meaningful goals and values. These writers' works attempted to point out the folly of 1920s America and rekindle the idealism and sense of deeper purpose they felt necessary for America to live up to its potential for all its citizens.

5.   **(C)**   Pulitzer believed that newspapers should be targeted at the masses. In this vein, his newspaper, *New York World*, used a collection of sensationalist stories, muckraking, and a publishing style designed to make the news read like a soap opera, to popularize newspapers among the middle class and the poor. His tactics worked. Using banner headlines, emphasizing the most scandalous or gory aspects of a story, exaggerating stories or making up details designed to arouse the reader, all served to catch people's attention and bring them back for more. Since his paper used a cheap yellow ink in printing a popular comic strip of the time, the term "yellow journalism" came to symbolize this early form of "tabloid" style news reporting. Pulitzer's techniques were so effective in increasing his newspaper's readership that soon newspaper publishers throughout the nation were copying his style and "yellow journals" were springing up in nearly every major U.S. city.

6.   **(B)**   When the United States declared war on Germany and entered World War I, a massive mobilization effort was needed to prepare the nation for wartime requirements. Procedures for drafting, training,

and transporting soldiers had to be quickly organized. Industrial production had to be regeared for wartime production needs. At first, this mobilization effort was headed by a number of industrial committees that advised the government on selection and cost of equipment. However, it soon became apparent that many of the businessmen running these committees had more than the nation's interests at heart. Many were using the committees as vehicles to quick wartime riches. Press reports of the corruption quickly led to public demands for reform. Wilson responded by disbanding the various committees and replacing them in July 1917 with the War Industries Board (WIB). The WIB coordinated war production for the remainder of the war.

7.   **(A)**   Black Americans, both military and civilian, were treated better in Europe than in the United States. Generally, they were not subjected to the discrimination and segregation they experienced in the United States.

8.   **(E)**   Events in Europe as well as this country after World War I convinced many Americans that the Communists and their sympathizers were using the postwar bitterness to secure political power. The apparent success of the Communist revolution in Russia put state and federal law enforcement agencies on their guard against radical uprisings— the Red Scare. In one of the last episodes of the Red Scare, two philosophical anarchists, Nicola Sacco and Bartolomeo Vanzetti, were arrested for a robbery and murder that many believed they did not commit. Despite impassioned agitation for their release, Sacco and Vanzetti were executed in 1927.

9.   **(D)**   There was a resurgence of religious fundamentalism during the 1920s. Generally, fundamentalists believed in the literal truth of the Bible, including the story of Creation as set forth in the Book of Genesis. Therefore, they opposed the theory of evolution advanced by Charles Darwin in *The Origin of Species*. In Tennessee, fundamentalists won the adoption of a law prohibiting the teaching of evolution in the states' public schools and colleges. John T. Scopes, a biology teacher in Dayton, Tennessee, deliberately violated this law in 1925. The American Civil Liberties Union recruited Clarence Darrow to defend Scopes, and

William Jennings Bryan assisted the prosecution. Although Scopes was found guilty, the trial discredited Bryan and the anti-evolutionists.

10. **(D)** In 1890, the two major women's groups combined as the National American Women's Suffrage Association (NAWSA). NAWSA made women's suffrage its main objective and concentrated on a state-by-state approach. By 1896, Wyoming, Utah, Colorado, and Idaho had been won over to women's suffrage, and California voted for women's suffrage in 1911. The suffragists then shifted the campaign back to the national level. By 1920, three-quarters of the states had ratified the Nineteenth Amendment.

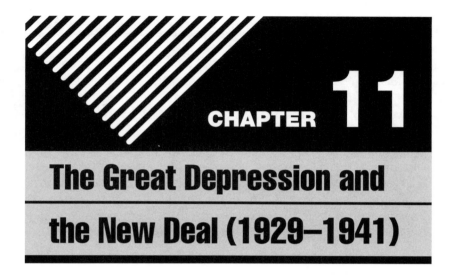

CHAPTER 11

The Great Depression and the New Deal (1929–1941)

Reasons for the Depression

A stock market crash does not mean that a depression must follow. A similar crash in October 1987 did not lead to a depression. In 1929 a complex interaction of many factors caused the decline of the economy.

Many people had bought stock on a margin of ten percent, meaning that they had borrowed ninety percent of the purchase through a broker's loan and put the stock as collateral. Broker's loans totaled $8.5 billion in 1929, compared with $3.5 billion in 1926. When the price of a stock fell more than ten percent, the lender sold the stock for whatever it would bring and thus further depressed prices. The forced sales brought great losses to the banks and businesses that had financed the broker's loans, as well as to the investors.

There were already signs of recession before the market crash in 1929. Because the gathering and processing of statistics was not as advanced then as now, some factors were not so obvious to people at the time. The farm economy, which involved almost twenty-five percent of the population, had been depressed throughout the decade. Coal, railroads, and New England textiles had not been prosperous. After 1927 new construction declined and auto sales began to sag. Many workers had been laid off before the crash of 1929.

Many scholars believe that there was a problem of underconsumption, meaning that ordinary workers and farmers, after using their consumer credit, did not have enough money to keep buying the products that were being produced. One estimate says that the income of the top one percent of the population increased at least seventy-five percent during the decade, while that of the bottom ninety-five percent increased only six percent. The process continued after the depression began. After the stock market crash, people were conservative and saved their money, thus reducing the demand for goods. As demand decreased, workers were laid off or had wage reductions, further reducing their purchasing power and bringing another decrease in demand.

With the decline in the economy, Americans had less money for foreign loans and bought fewer imported products. That meant that foreign governments and individuals were not able to pay their debts in the United States. The whole reparations and war debts structure collapsed. American exports dropped, further hurting the domestic economy. The depression eventually spread throughout the world.

Depression-era poster for a government program.

Economic Effects of the Depression

During the early months of the depression most people thought it was just an adjustment in the business cycle that would soon be over. Hoover repeatedly assured the public that prosperity was just around the corner. As time went on, the worst depression in American history set in, reaching its bottom point in early 1932. The gross national product fell from $104.6 billion in 1929 to $56.1 billion in 1933. Unemployment reached about 13 million in 1933, or about twenty-five percent of the labor force excluding farmers. National income dropped fifty-four percent from $87.8 billion to $40.2 billion. Labor income fell about forty-one percent, while farm income dropped fifty-five percent from $11.9 billion to $5.3 billion. Industrial production dropped about fifty-one percent. The banking system suffered as 5,761 banks, over twenty-two percent of the total, failed by the end of 1932.

**Destitute peapickers in California during the Great Depression.
A 32-year-old mother of seven children in February 1936.**

The Human Dimension of the Depression

As the depression grew worse, more and more people lost their jobs or had their wages reduced. Many were unable to continue credit payments on homes, automobiles, and other possessions, and lost them. Families doubled up in houses and apartments. Both the marriage rate and the birth rate declined as people put off family formation. Hundreds of thousands became homeless and lived in groups of makeshift shacks called Hoovervilles in empty spaces around cities. Others traveled the country by foot and boxcar seeking food and work. State and local government agencies and private charities were overwhelmed in their attempts to care for those in need, although public and private soup kitchens and soup lines were set up throughout the nation. Malnutrition was widespread but few died of starvation, perhaps because malnourished people are susceptible to many fatal diseases.

Hoover's Depression Policies

The Agricultural Marketing Act

Passed in June 1929 before the market crash, this law proposed by the president created the Federal Farm Board with a revolving fund of $500 million to lend the agricultural cooperatives to buy commodities, such as wheat and cotton, and hold them for higher prices. Until 1931 it did keep agricultural prices above the world level. Then world prices plummeted, the board's funds ran out, and there was no period of higher prices in which the cooperatives could sell their stored commodities.

The Hawley-Smoot Tariff

This law, passed in June 1930, raised duties on both agricultural and manufactured imports. It did nothing of significance to improve the economy, and historians argue over whether or not it contributed to the spread of the international depression.

Voluntarism

Hoover believed that voluntary cooperation would enable the country to weather the depression. He held meetings with business leaders at which he urged them to avoid layoffs of workers and wage cuts, and he secured no-strike pledges from labor leaders. He urged all citizens to contribute to charities to help alleviate the suffering. While people were generous, private charities could not begin to meet the needs.

Public Works

In 1930 Congress appropriated $750 million for public buildings, river and harbor improvements, and highway construction in an effort to stimulate employment.

The Reconstruction Finance Corporation

Chartered by Congress in 1932, the RFC had an appropriation of $500 million and authority to borrow $1.5 billion for loans to railroads, banks, and other financial institutions. It prevented the failure of basic firms on which many other elements of the economy depended, but was criticized by some as relief for the rich.

The Federal Home Loan Bank Act

This law, passed in July 1932, created home loan banks with a capital of $125 million to make loans to building and loan associations, savings banks, and insurance companies to help them avoid foreclosures on homes.

Relief

Hoover staunchly opposed the use of federal funds for relief for the needy. In July 1932 he vetoed the Garner-Wagner Bill that would have appropriated funds for relief. He did compromise by approving legislation authorizing the RFC to lend $300 million to the states for relief, and to make loans to states and cities for self-liquidating public works.

The Bonus Army

The Bonus Expeditionary Force, which took its name from the American Expeditionary Force of World War I, was a group of about

14,000 unemployed veterans who went to Washington in the summer of 1932 to lobby Congress for immediate payment of the bonus that had been approved in 1926 for payment in 1945. At Hoover's insistence, the Senate did not pass the bonus bill, and about half of the BEF accepted a congressional offer of transportation home. The remaining five or six thousand, many with wives and children, continued to live in shanties along the Anacostia River and to lobby for their cause. After two veterans were killed in a clash with the police, Hoover, calling them insurrectionists and communists, ordered the army to remove them. On July 28, 1932, General Douglas MacArthur, the army chief of staff, assisted by Majors Dwight D. Eisenhower and George S. Patton, personally commanded the removal operation. With machine guns, tanks, cavalry, infantry with fixed bayonets, and tear gas, MacArthur drove the veterans from Washington and burned their camp.

The Farm Holiday Association

Centered in Iowa, the association, headed by Milo Reno and others, called a farm strike in August 1932. They urged farmers not to take their products to market in an effort to raise farm prices. The picketing of markets led to violence, and the strike collapsed.

The Election of 1932

The Republicans

At the convention in Chicago, Hoover was nominated on the first ballot. The platform called for a continuation of his depression policies.

The Democrats

Franklin D. Roosevelt, the popular governor of New York, gained the support of many Southern and Western delegates through the efforts of his managers Louis Howe and James Farley. When the convention opened in Chicago, he had a majority of delegates, but not the necessary two-thirds for nomination. House speaker John Nance Garner, a favorite son candidate from Texas, threw support to Roosevelt, who was nominated on the fourth ballot. Garner then became the vice

presidential candidate. Roosevelt took the unprecedented step of flying to the convention to accept the nomination in person, declaring that
he pledged a "new deal" for the American people. The platform called
for the repeal of prohibition, government aid for the unemployed, and
a twenty-five percent cut in government spending.

The Campaign

Hoover declared that he would lead the nation to prosperity with
higher tariffs and the maintenance of the gold standard. He warned that
the election of Roosevelt would lead to grass growing in the streets of
the cities and towns of America. Roosevelt called for "bold, persistent
experimentation," and expressed his concern for the "forgotten man"
at the bottom of the economic heap, but he did not give a clear picture
of what he intended to do. Roosevelt had a broad smile and amiable
disposition that attracted many people, while Hoover was aloof and
cold in his personal style.

The Election

Roosevelt received 22,809,638 votes for 57.3 percent of the total
and 472 electoral votes, carrying all but six Northeastern states. Hoover
had 15,758,901 votes and 59 electoral votes. Despite the hard times,
Norman Thomas, the Socialist candidate, received only 881,951 votes.
The Democrats also captured the Senate and increased their majority
in the House.

The First New Deal

Franklin D. Roosevelt

The heir of a wealthy family and a fifth cousin of Theodore
Roosevelt, Franklin was born in 1882 on the family estate at Hyde
Park, New York. He graduated from Harvard and the Columbia Law
School, married his distant cousin Anna Eleanor Roosevelt in 1905,
and practiced law in New York City. He entered state politics, then
served as assistant secretary of the navy under Wilson, and was the
Democratic vice presidential candidate in 1920. In 1921 he suffered an

attack of polio that left him paralyzed for several years and on crutches or in a wheelchair for the rest of his life. In 1928 he was elected governor of New York to succeed Al Smith and was reelected in 1930. As governor, his depression programs for the unemployed, public works, aid to farmers, and conservation attracted national attention.

The Cabinet

Important cabinet appointments included Senator Cordell Hull of Tennessee as secretary of state; Henry A. Wallace as secretary of agriculture; Harold L. Ickes as secretary of the interior; Frances Perkins, a New York social worker, as secretary of labor and the first woman appointed to a Cabinet post; and James A. Farley, Roosevelt's political manager, as postmaster general.

The Brain Trust

Roosevelt's inner circle of unofficial advisers, first assembled during the campaign, was more influential than the cabinet. Prominent in it were agricultural economist Rexford G. Tugwell, political scientist Raymond Moley, lawyer Adolph A. Berle, Jr., the originators of the McNary-Haugen Bill—Hugh S. Johnson and George Peek—and Roosevelt's personal political advisor, Louis Howe.

The New Deal Program

Roosevelt did not have a developed plan of action when he took office. He intended to experiment and to find which worked. As a result, many programs overlapped or contradicted others, and were changed or dropped if they did not work.

Repeal of Prohibition

In February 1933, before Roosevelt took office, Congress passed the Twenty-first Amendment to repeal prohibition and sent it to the states. In March the new Congress legalized light (lower alcohol content) beer. The amendment was ratified by the states and took effect in December 1933.

The Banking Crisis

In February 1933, as the inauguration approached, a severe banking crisis developed. Banks could not collect their loans or meet the demands of their depositors for withdrawals, and runs occurred on many banks. Eventually banks in thirty-eight states were closed by the state governments, and the remainder were open for only limited operations. An additional 5,190 banks failed in 1933, bringing the depression total to 10,951.

The Inaugural Address

When Roosevelt was inaugurated on March 4, 1933, the American economic system seemed to be on the verge of collapse. Roosevelt assured the nation that "the only thing we have to fear is fear itself," called for a special session of Congress to convene on March 9, and asked for "broad executive powers to wage war against the emergency." Two days later, he closed all banks and forbade the export of gold or the redemption of currency in gold.

Legislation of the First New Deal

The Hundred Days and the First New Deal

The special session of Congress, from March 9 to June 16, 1933, passed a great body of legislation that has left a lasting mark on the nation, and the period has been referred to ever since as the "Hundred Days." Over the next two years, legislation was added, but the basic recovery plan of the Hundred Days remained in operation. Hence, the period from 1933 to 1935 is called the First New Deal. A new wave of programs beginning in 1935 is called the Second New Deal. The distinction was not known at the time, but is a device of historians to differentiate between two stages in Roosevelt's administration.

Economic Legislation of the Hundred Days

The banking crisis was the most immediate problem facing Roosevelt and the Congress. A series of laws were passed to deal with the crisis and to reform the American economic system.

The Emergency Banking Relief Act was passed on March 9, the first day of the special session. The law provided additional funds for banks from the RFC and the Federal Reserve, allowed the Treasury to open sound banks after ten days and to merge or liquidate unsound ones, and forbade the hoarding or exporting of gold. On March 12, Roosevelt assured the public of the soundness of the banks in the first of many "fireside chats," or radio addresses. People believed him and most banks were soon open with more deposits than withdrawals.

The Banking Act of 1933, or the Glass-Steagall Act, established the Federal Deposit Insurance Corporation (FDIC) to insure individual deposits in commercial banks and separated commercial banking from the more speculative activity of investment banking.

The Truth-in-Securities Act required that full information about stocks and bonds be provided by brokers and others to potential purchasers.

The Home Owners Loan Corporation (HOLC) had authority to borrow money to refinance home mortgages and thus prevent foreclosures. Eventually, it lent over three billion dollars to over one million home owners.

Gold was taken out of circulation following the president's order of March 6, and the nation went off the gold standard. Eventually, on January 31, 1934, the value of the dollar was set at $35 per ounce of gold, fifty-nine percent of its former value. The object of the devaluation was to raise prices and help American exports.

Later Economic Legislation of the First New Deal

The Securities and Exchange Commission was created in 1934 to supervise stock exchanges and to punish fraud in securities trading.

The Federal Housing Administration (FHA) was created by Congress in 1934 to insure long-term, low-interest mortgages for home construction and repair.

Relief and Employment Programs of the Hundred Days

These programs were intended to provide temporary relief for people in need, and were to be disbanded when the economy improved.

The Federal Emergency Relief Act appropriated $500 million for aid to the poor to be distributed by state and local governments. Half of the funds were to be distributed on a one to three matching basis with the states. It also established the Federal Emergency Relief Administration under Harry Hopkins. Additional appropriations were made many times later.

The Civilian Conservation Corps enrolled 250,000 young men ages 18 to 24 from families on relief to go to camps where they worked on flood control, soil conservation, and forest projects under the direction of the War Department. A small monthly payment was made to the family of each member. By the end of the decade, 2.75 million young men had served in the corps.

The Public Works Administration, under Secretary of the Interior Harold Ickes, had $3.3 billion to distribute to state and local governments for building projects such as schools, highways, and hospitals. The object was to "prime the pump" of the economy by creating construction jobs. Additional money was appropriated later.

Later Relief Efforts

After the Hundred Days, in November 1933, Roosevelt established the Civil Works Administration under Harry Hopkins with $400 million from the Public Works Administration to hire four million unemployed workers. The temporary and makeshift nature of the jobs, such as sweeping streets, brought much criticism, and the experiment was terminated in April 1934.

Agricultural Programs of the Hundred Days

The Agricultural Adjustment Act of 1933 created the Agricultural Adjustment Administration (AAA), which was headed by George Peek. It sought to return farm prices to parity with those of the 1909 to 1914 period. Farmers agreed to reduce production of principal farm commodities and were paid a subsidy in return. The money came from a tax on the processing of the commodities. Farm prices increased, but tenants and sharecroppers were hurt when owners took land out of cultivation. The law was declared unconstitutional in January 1936 on the grounds that the processing tax was not constitutional.

The Federal Farm Loan Act consolidated all farm credit programs into the Farm Credit Administration to make low-interest loans for farm mortgages and other agricultural purposes.

Later Agricultural Programs

The Commodity Credit was established in October 1933 by the AAA to make loans to corn and cotton farmers against their crops so they could hold them for higher prices.

The Frazier-Lemke Farm Bankruptcy Act of 1934 allowed farmers to defer foreclosure on their land while they obtained new financing and helped them to recover property already lost through easy financing.

The National Industrial Recovery Act

This law, passed on June 16, 1933, the last day of the Hundred Days, was viewed as the cornerstone of the recovery program. It sought to stabilize the economy by preventing extreme competition, labor-management conflicts, and overproduction. A board composed of industrial and labor leaders in each industry or business drew up a code for that industry that set minimum prices, minimum wages, maximum work hours, production limits, and quotas. The antitrust laws were temporarily suspended. The approach was based on the idea of many economists at the time; because a mature industrial economy produced more goods than could be consumed, it would be necessary to create a relative shortage of goods in order to raise prices and restore prosperity. The idea was proved wrong by the expansion of consumer goods after World War II. Section 7a of the law also provided that workers had the right to join unions and to bargain collectively. The National Recovery Administration (NRA) was created under the leadership of Hugh S. Johnson to enforce the law and generate public enthusiasm for it. In May 1935 the law was declared unconstitutional in the case of *Schechter v. United States*, on the grounds that Congress had delegated legislative authority to the code-makers, and that Schechter, who slaughtered chickens in New York, was not engaged in interstate commerce.

It was argued later that the NRA had unintentionally aided big firms to the detriment of smaller ones because the representatives of the larger firms tended to dominate the code-making process. It was generally unsuccessful in stabilizing small businesses such as retail stores and was on the point of collapse when it was declared unconstitutional.

The Tennessee Valley Authority

Different from the other legislation of the Hundred Days that addressed immediate problems of the depression, the TVA, a public corporation under a three-member board, was proposed by Roosevelt as the first major experiment in regional public planning. Starting from the nucleus of the government's Muscle Shoals property on the Tennessee River, the TVA built 20 dams in an area of 40,000 square miles to stop flooding and soil erosion, improve navigation, and generate hydroelectric power. It also manufactured nitrates for fertilizer, conducted demonstration projects for farmers, engaged in reforestation, and attempted to rehabilitate the whole area. It was fought unsuccessfully in the courts by private power companies. Roosevelt believed that it would serve as a yardstick to measure the true cost of providing electric power.

Effects of the First New Deal

The economy improved but remained far from recovered between 1933 and 1935. The gross national product rose from $74.2 billion in 1933 to $91.4 billion in 1935. Manufacturing salaries and wages increased from $6.24 billion in 1933 to over $9.5 billion in 1935, with average weekly earnings going from $16.73 to $20.13. Farm income rose from $1.9 billion in 1933 to $4.6 billion in 1935. The money supply, as currency and demand deposits, grew from $19.2 billion to $25.2 billion. Unemployment dropped from about 25 percent of nonfarm workers in 1933 to about 20.1 percent, or 10.6 million, in 1935. While the figure had improved, it was a long way from the 3.2 percent of predepression 1929, and suffering as a result of unemployment was still a major problem.

The Second New Deal: Opposition from the Right and Left

Criticism of the New Deal

The partial economic recovery brought about by the first New Deal provoked criticism from the right for doing too much and from the left for doing too little. Conservatives and businessmen criticized the deficit financing, which accounted for about half of the federal budget, federal spending for relief, and government regulation of business. They frequently charged that the New Deal was socialist or communist in form, and some conservative writers labeled the wealthy Roosevelt "a traitor to his class." People on the lower end of the economic scale thought that the New Deal, especially the NRA, was too favorable to big business. Small businesspeople and union members complained that the NRA codes gave control of industry to the big firms, while farmers complained that the NRA set prices too high. The elderly thought that nothing had been done to help them. Several million people who were or had been tenant farmers or sharecroppers were badly hurt. When the AAA paid farmers to take land out of production, the landowners took the money while the tenants and sharecroppers lost their livelihood. Several opposition organizations and persons were particularly active in opposing Roosevelt's policies.

The American Liberty League was formed in 1934 by conservatives to defend business interests and promote the open shop. While many of its members were Republicans and it was financed primarily by the Du Pont family, it also attracted conservative Democrats like Alfred E. Smith and John W. Davis. It supported conservative congressional candidates of both parties in the election of 1934 with little success.

The Old Age Revolving Pension Plan was advanced by Dr. Francis E. Townsend, a retired California physician. The plan proposed that every retired person over sixty receive a pension of $200 a month, about double the average worker's salary, with the requirement that the money be spent within the month. The plan would be funded by a national gross sales tax. Townsend claimed that it would end the depression by putting money into circulation, but economists thought it fiscally impossible. Some three to five million older Americans joined Townsend Clubs.

The Share Our Wealth Society was founded in 1934 by Senator Huey "The Kingfish" Long of Louisiana. Long was a populist demagogue who was elected governor of Louisiana in 1928, established a practical dictatorship over the state, and moved to the United States Senate in 1930. He supported Roosevelt in 1932, but then broke with him, calling him a tool of Wall Street for not doing more to combat the depression. Long called for the confiscation of all fortunes over five million dollars and a tax of 100 percent on annual incomes over one million dollars. With the money the government would provide subsidies so that every family would have a "homestead" of house, car, and furnishings worth at least $5,000, a minimum annual income of $2,000, and free college education for those who wanted it. His slogan was "Every Man a King." Long talked of running for president in 1936, and published a book entitled *My First Days in the White House*. His society had over five million members when he was assassinated on the steps of the Louisiana Capitol on September 8, 1935. The Reverend Gerald L.K. Smith appointed himself Long's successor as head of the society, but he lacked Long's ability.

The National Union for Social Justice was headed by Father Charles E. Coughlin, a Catholic priest in Royal Oak, Michigan, who had a weekly radio program. Beginning as a religious broadcast in 1926, Coughlin turned to politics and finance, and attracted an audience of millions of many faiths. He supported Roosevelt in 1932, but then turned against him. He advocated an inflationary currency and was anti-Semitic, but beyond that his fascist-like program was not clearly defined.

The Second New Deal Begins

Roosevelt's Position

With millions of Democratic voters under the sway of Townsend, Long, and Coughlin, with the destruction of the NRA by the Supreme Court imminent, and with the election of 1936 approaching the next year, Roosevelt began to push through a series of new programs in the spring of 1935. Much of the legislation was passed during the summer of 1935, a period sometimes called the Second Hundred Days.

Legislation and Programs of the Second New Deal

The Works Progress Administration (WPA) was started in May 1935 following the passage of the Emergency Relief Appropriations Act of April 1935. Headed by Harry Hopkins, the WPA employed people from the relief rolls for thirty hours of work a week at pay double the relief payment but less than private employment. There was not enough money to hire all of the unemployed, and the numbers varied from time to time, but an average of 2.1 million people per month were employed. By the end of the program in 1941, 8.5 million people had worked at some time for the WPA at a total cost of $11.4 billion. Most of the projects undertaken were in construction. The WPA built hundreds of thousands of miles of streets and roads, and thousands of schools, hospitals, parks, airports, playgrounds, and other facilities. Hand work was emphasized so that the money would go for pay rather than equipment,

The WPA sought to build pride in America by putting people to work.

provoking much criticism for inefficiency. Unemployed artists painted murals in public buildings; actors, musicians, and dancers performed in poor neighborhoods; and writers compiled guide books and local histories.

The National Youth Administration (NYA) was established as part of the WPA in June 1935 to provide part-time jobs for high school and college students to enable them to stay in school and to help young adults not in school to find jobs.

The Rural Electrification Administration (REA) was created in May 1935 to provide loans and WPA labor to electric cooperatives to build lines into rural areas not served by private companies.

The Resettlement Administration (RA) was created in the Agriculture Department in May 1935 under Rexford Tugwell. It relocated destitute families from seemingly hopeless situations to new rural homestead communities or to suburban greenbelt towns.

The National Labor Relations or Wagner Act was passed in May 1935 to replace the provisions of Section 7a of the NIRA. It reaffirmed labor's right to unionize, prohibited unfair labor practices, and created the National Labor Relations Board (NLRB) to oversee and insure fairness in labor-management relations.

The Social Security Act was passed in August 1935. It established a retirement plan for persons over age sixty-five funded by a tax on wages paid equally by employee and employer. The first benefits, ranging from $10 to $85 per month, were paid in 1942. Another provision of the act had the effect of forcing the states to initiate unemployment insurance programs. It imposed a payroll tax on employers that went to the state if it had an insurance program and to the federal government if it did not. The act also provided matching funds to the states for aid to the blind, handicapped, and dependent children, and for public health services. The American Social Security system was limited compared with those of other industrialized nations, and millions of workers were not covered by it. Nonetheless, it marked a major change in American policy.

The Banking Act of 1935 created a strong central board of governors of the Federal Reserve System with broad powers over the operations of the regional banks.

The Public Utility Holding Company or Wheeler-Rayburn Act of 1935 empowered the Securities and Exchange Commission to restrict public utility holding companies to one natural region and to eliminate duplicate holding companies. The Federal Power Commission was created to regulate interstate electrical power rates and activities, and the Federal Trade Commission received the same kind of power over the natural gas companies.

The Revenue Act of 1935 increased income taxes on higher incomes, and also inheritance, large gift, and capital gains taxes.

The Motor Carrier Act of 1935 extended the regulatory authority of the Interstate Commerce Commission to cover interstate trucking lines.

The Election of 1936

The Democrats

At the convention in Philadelphia in June, Roosevelt and Garner were renominated by acclamation on the first ballot. The convention also ended the requirement for a two-thirds vote for nomination. The platform promised an expanded farm program, labor legislation, more rural electrification and public housing, and enforcement of the antitrust laws. In his acceptance speech, Roosevelt declared that "this generation of Americans has a rendezvous with destiny." He further proclaimed that he and the American people were fighting for democracy and capitalism against the "economic royalists," businesspeople he charged with seeking only their own power and wealth, and opposing the New Deal.

The Republicans

Governor Alfred M. Landon of Kansas, a former progressive supporter of Theodore Roosevelt, was nominated on the first ballot at the convention in Cleveland in June. Frank Knox, a Chicago newspaper publisher, was chosen as his running mate. The platform criticized the New Deal for operating under unconstitutional laws, and called for a balanced budget, higher tariffs, and lower corporate taxes. It did not call for the repeal of all New Deal legislation, and promised better and less expensive relief, farm, and labor programs. In effect, Landon and the Republicans were saying that they would do about the same thing, but do it better.

The Union Party

Dr. Francis Townsend, Father Charles Coughlin, and the Reverend Gerald L. K. Smith, Long's successor in the Share Our Wealth Society, organized the Union Party to oppose Roosevelt. The nominee was Congressman William Lemke of North Dakota, an advocate of radical farm legislation but a bland campaigner. Vicious attacks by Smith and Coughlin on Roosevelt brought a backlash against them, and American Catholic leaders denounced Coughlin.

The Election

Roosevelt carried all of the states except Maine and Vermont with 27,757,333 votes, or 60.8 percent of the total, and 523 electoral votes. Landon received 16,684,231 votes and 8 electoral votes. Lemke had 891,858 votes for 1.9 percent of the total. Norman Thomas, the Socialist candidate, received 187,000 votes, only 21 percent of the 881,951 votes he received in 1932.

The New Deal Coalition

Roosevelt had put together a coalition of followers who made the Democratic Party the majority party in the nation for the first time since the Civil War. While retaining the Democratic base in the Solid South and among white ethnics in the big cities, Roosevelt also received strong support from Midwestern farmers. Two groups that made a dramatic shift into the Democratic ranks were union workers and blacks. Unions took an active political role for the first time since 1924, providing both campaign funds and votes. Blacks had traditionally been

Republican since emancipation, but by 1936 about three-fourths of the black voters, who lived mainly in the Northern cities, had shifted into the Democratic Party.

The Last Years of the New Deal

Court Packing

Frustrated by a conservative Supreme Court that had overturned much of his New Deal legislation, Roosevelt, after receiving his overwhelming mandate in the election of 1936, decided to curb the power of the court. In doing so, he overestimated his own political power and underestimated the force of tradition. In February 1937 he proposed to Congress the Judicial Reorganization Bill that would allow the president to name a new federal judge for each judge who did not retire by the age of 70 $1/2$. The appointments would be limited to a maximum of fifty, with no more than six added to the Supreme Court. At the time, six justices were over the proposed age limit. Roosevelt cited a slowing of the judicial process due to the infirmity of the incumbents and the need for a modern outlook. The president was astonished by the wave of opposition from Democrats and Republicans alike, and uncharacteristically refused to compromise. In doing so, he not only lost the bill but he lost control of the Democratic Congress, which he had dominated since 1933. Nonetheless, the court changed its position as Chief Justice Charles Evans Hughes and Justice Owen Roberts began to vote with the more liberal members. The National Labor Relations Act was upheld in March 1937 and the Social Security Act in April. In June a conservative justice retired, and Roosevelt had the opportunity to make an appointment.

The Recession of 1937–1938

Most economic indicators rose sharply between 1935 and 1937. The gross national product had recovered to the 1930 level, and unemployment, if WPA workers were considered employed, had fallen to 9.2 percent. Average yearly earnings of the employed had risen from $1,195 in 1935 to $1,341 in 1937, and average hourly manufacturing earnings from 55 cents to 62 cents. During the same period, there were huge federal deficits. In fiscal 1936, for example, there was a deficit of $4.4 billion in a budget of $8.5 billion. Roosevelt decided that the recovery was sufficient to warrant a reduction in relief programs and a move toward a balanced budget. The budget for fiscal 1938, from July 1937 to June 1938, was reduced to $6.8 billion, with the WPA experiencing the largest cut. During the winter of 1937–1938, the economy slipped rapidly and unemployment rose to 12.5 percent. In April 1938 Roosevelt requested and received from Congress an emergency appropriation of about $3 billion for the WPA, as well as increases for public works and other programs. In July 1938 the economy began to recover, and it regained the 1937 levels in 1939.

Legislation of the Late New Deal

With the threat of adverse Supreme Court rulings removed, Roosevelt rounded out his program during the late 1930s.

The Bankhead-Jones Farm Tenancy Act, passed in July 1937, created the Farm Security Administration (FSA) to replace the Resettlement Administration. The FSA continued the homestead projects and loaned money to farmers to purchase farms, lease land, and buy equip-

Poster showing a man with WPA shovel attacking a wolf named Rumor.

ment. It also set up camps for migrant workers and established rural health care programs.

The National Housing, or Wagner-Steagall Act, passed in September 1937, established the United States Housing Authority (USHA), which could borrow money to lend to local agencies for public housing projects. By 1941 it had loaned $750 million for 511 projects.

The Second Agricultural Adjustment Act of February 1938 appropriated funds for soil conservation payments to farmers who would remove land from production. The law also empowered the Agriculture Department to impose market quotas to prevent surpluses in cotton, wheat, corn, tobacco, and rice if two-thirds of the farmers producing that commodity agreed.

The Fair Labor Standards Act, popularly called the minimum wage law, was passed in June 1938. It provided for a minimum wage of 25 cents an hour, which would gradually rise to 40 cents, and a gradual reduction to a workweek of forty hours, with time and a half for overtime. Workers in small businesses and in public and nonprofit employment were not covered. The law also prohibited the interstate shipment commerce manufactured using children under 16 years old.

Social Dimensions of the New Deal Era

Blacks and the New Deal

Blacks suffered more than other people from the depression. Unemployment rates were much higher than for the general population, and before 1933 they were often excluded from state and local relief efforts. Blacks did benefit from many New Deal relief programs, but about forty percent of black workers were sharecroppers or tenants who suffered from the provisions of the first Agricultural Adjustment Act. Roosevelt seems to have given little thought to the special problems of black people, and he was afraid to endorse legislation such as an antilynching bill for fear of alienating the southern wing of the Democratic Party. Eleanor Roosevelt and Harold Ickes strongly supported civil rights, and a "Black Cabinet" of advisors was assembled in the

Interior Department. More blacks were appointed to government positions by Roosevelt than ever before, but the number was still small. When government military contracts began to flow in 1941, A. Philip Randolph, the president of the Brotherhood of Sleeping Car Porters, proposed a black march on Washington to demand equal access to defense jobs. To forestall such an action, Roosevelt issued an executive order on June 25, 1941, establishing the Fair Employment Practices Committee to insure consideration for minorities in defense employment.

Native Americans and the New Deal

John Collier, the commissioner of the Bureau of Indian Affairs, persuaded Congress to repeal the Dawes Act of 1887 by passing the Indian Reorganization Act of 1934. The law restored tribal ownership of lands, recognized tribal constitutions and government, and provided loans to tribes for economic development. Collier also secured the creation of the Indian Emergency Conservation Program, a Native American CCC for projects on the reservations. In addition, he helped Native Americans secure entry into the WPA, NYA, and other programs.

Mexican Americans and the New Deal

Mexican Americans benefitted the least from the New Deal, for few programs covered them. Farm owners turned against them as farm workers after they attempted to form a union between 1933 and 1936. By 1940 most had been replaced by whites dispossessed by the depression. Many returned to Mexico, and the Mexican American population dropped almost forty percent from 1930 to 1940.

Women During the New Deal

The burden of the depression fell on women as much or more as it did on men. Wives and mothers found themselves responsible for stretching meager budgets by preparing inexpensive meals, patching old clothing, and the like. "Making do" became a slogan of the period. In addition, more women had to supplement or provide the family income by going to work. In 1930 there were 10.5 million working women comprising twenty-nine percent of the workforce. By 1940 the figures had grown to over 13 million and thirty-five percent. There was much criticism of working women based on the idea that they deprived men of jobs. Male job losses were greatest in heavy industry such as factories and mills, while areas of female employment such as retail sales were not hit as hard. Unemployed men seldom sought jobs in the traditional women's fields.

Labor Unions

Unions During the First New Deal

Labor unions had lost members and influence during the twenties, and slipped further during the economic decline of 1929 to 1933. The National Industrial Recovery Act gave them new hope when Section 7a guaranteed the right to unionize, and during 1933 about 1.5 million new members joined unions. It soon became clear that enforcement of the industrial codes by the NRA was ineffective, and labor leaders began to call it the "National Run Around." As a result, in 1934 there were many strikes, sometimes violent, including a general strike in San Francisco involving about 125,000 workers.

Craft versus Industrial Unions

The passage of the National Labor Relations or Wagner Act in 1935 resulted in a massive growth of union membership, but only at the expense of bitter conflict within the labor movement. The American Federation of Labor was made up primarily of craft unions. Some leaders, especially John L. Lewis, the dynamic president of the United Mine Workers, wanted to unionize the mass production industries, such as automobiles and rubber, with industrial unions. In 1934 the AFL convention authorized such unions, but the older unions continued to try to organize workers in those industries by crafts. In November 1935 Lewis and others established the Committee for Industrial Organization to unionize basic industries, presumably within the AFL. President William Green of the AFL ordered the CIO to disband in January

1936. When the rebels refused, they were expelled by the AFL executive council in March 1937. The insurgents then reorganized the CIO as the independent Congress of Industrial Organizations to be composed of industrial unions.

The Growth of the CIO

During its organizational period, the CIO sought to initiate several industrial unions, particularly in the steel, auto, rubber, and radio industries. In late 1936 and early 1937 it used a tactic called the sit-down strike, with the strikers occupying the workplace to prevent any production. There were 477 sit-down strikes involving about 400,000 workers. The largest was in the General Motors plant in Flint, Michigan, as the union sought recognition by that firm. In February 1937 General Motors recognized the United Auto Workers as the bargaining agent for its 400,000 workers. When the CIO established its independence in March 1937, it already had 1.8 million members, and it reached a membership of 3.75 million six months later. The AFL had about 3.4 million members at that time. By the end of 1941, the CIO had about 5 million members, the AFL about 4.6 million, and other unions about one million. Union members comprised about 11.5 percent of the workforce in 1933 and 28.2 percent in 1941.

Cultural Trends of the 1930s

Literary Developments

The writers and intellectuals who had expressed disdain for the middle-class materialism of the 1920s found it even more difficult to deal with the meaning of the crushing poverty in America and the rise of fascism in Europe during the 1930s. Some turned to communism, including the fifty-three writers who signed an open letter endorsing the Communist presidential candidate in 1932. Some turned to proletarian novels, such as Jack Conroy in *The Disinherited* (1933) and Robert Cantwell in *The Land of Plenty* (1934). Ernest Hemingway seemed to have lost his direction in *Winner Take All* (1933) and *The Green Hills of Africa* (1935), but in *To Have and Have Not* (1937), a strike novel, he turned to social realism, and *For Whom the Bell Tolls* (1941) expressed his concern about fascism. Sinclair Lewis also dealt with fascism in *It Can't Happen Here* (1935) but did not show the power of his works of the 1920s. John Dos Passos depicted what he saw as the disintegration of American life from 1900 to 1929 in his trilogy *U.S.A.* (1930–1936). William Faulkner sought values in Southern life in *Light in August* (1932), *Absalom! Absalom!* (1936), and *The Unvanquished* (1938). The endurance of the human spirit and personal survival were depicted in James T. Farrell's trilogy *Studs Lonigan* (1936) about the struggles of lower-middle-class Irish Catholics in Chicago, while Erskine Caldwell's *Tobacco Road* (1932) dealt with impoverished Georgia sharecroppers, and John Steinbeck's *The Grapes of Wrath* (1939) depicted "Okies" migrating from the dust bowl to California in the midst of the depression.

Popular Culture

The depression greatly reduced the amount of money available for recreation and entertainment. There was an increase in games and sports among family groups and friends. The WPA and the CCC constructed thousands of playgrounds, playing fields, picnic areas, and the like for public use. Roosevelt and Harry Hopkins, the director of the WPA, hoped to develop a mass appreciation of culture through the WPA murals in public buildings, with traveling plays, concerts, and exhibits, and with community arts centers. Beyond some revival of handicrafts, it is doubtful that the program had much effect. There were, however, several popular forms of entertainment.

Radio was the favorite form of daily entertainment during the depression because, after the initial cost of the instrument, it was free. There were about forty million radios in the United States by 1938. It provided comedy and mystery shows, music, sports, and news. A study at the time indicated that radio tended to make Americans more uniform in their attitudes, taste, speech, and humor.

While radio was the form of entertainment most used, the movies were the most popular. By 1939 about sixty-five percent of the people went to the movies at least once a week. The movie industry was one of the few that did not suffer financially from the depression. Movies were the great means of escape, providing release from the pressures of the depression by transporting people to a make-believe world of beauty, mystery, or excitement. Spectacular musicals with dozens of dancers and singers, such as *Broadway Melody of 1936*, were popular. The dance team of Fred Astaire and Ginger Rogers thrilled millions in *Flying Down to Rio* and *Shall We Dance?* Shirley Temple charmed the public as their favorite child star. Judy Garland rose to stardom in *The Wizard of Oz*, while animated films like *Snow White* appealed to children of all ages. People enjoyed the triumph of justice and decency in *Mr. Smith Goes to Washington* and *You Can't Take It With You* with Jimmy Stewart. Dozens of light comedies starred such favorites as Cary Grant, Katharine Hepburn, Clark Gable, and Rosalind Russell, while Errol Flynn played in such larger-than-life roles as Robin Hood. A different kind of escape was found in gangster movies with Edward G. Robinson, James Cagney, or George Raft. Near the end of the decade, *Gone With The Wind*, released in 1939 starring Clark Gable and Vivien Leigh, became a timeless classic, while *The Grapes of Wrath* in 1940 commented on the depression itself.

The popular music of the decade was swing, and the big bands of Duke Ellington, Benny Goodman, Glenn Miller, Tommy Dorsey, and Harry James vied for public favor. The leading popular singer was Bing Crosby. City African Americans refined the country blues to city blues, and interracial audiences enjoyed both city blues and jazz. African American musicians were increasingly accepted by white audiences.

Comic strips existed before the thirties, but they became a standard newspaper feature as well as a source of comic books during the decade. "Dick Tracy" began his war on crime in 1931 and was assisted by "Superman" after 1938. "Tarzan" began to swing through the cartoon jungles in 1929, and "Buck Rogers" began the exploration of space in 1930.

New Deal Diplomacy and the Road to War

The Good Neighbor Policy

Roosevelt and Secretary of State Cordell Hull continued the policies of their predecessors in endeavoring to improve relations with Latin American nations, and formalized their position by calling it the Good Neighbor Policy.

Nonintervention

At the Montevideo Conference of American Nations in December 1933, the United States renounced the right of intervention in the internal affairs of Latin American countries. In 1936, at the Buenos Aires Convention, the United States further agreed to submit all American disputes to arbitration. Accordingly, the marines were removed from Haiti, Nicaragua, and the Dominican Republic by 1934. The Haitian protectorate treaty was allowed to expire in 1936, the right of intervention in Panama was ended by treaty in 1936, and the receivership of the finances of the Dominican Republic ended in 1941.

Cuba

The United States did not intervene in the Cuban revolution in the spring of 1933, but it did back a coup by Fulgencio Batista to overthrow the liberal regime of Ramon Grau San Martín in 1934. Batista was given a favorable sugar import status for Cuba in return for establishing a conservative administration. In May 1934 the United States abrogated its Platt Amendment rights in Cuba except for control of the Guantanamo Naval Base.

Mexico

The Mexican government of Lazaro Cardenas began to expropriate American property, including oil holdings, in 1934. Despite calls for intervention, Roosevelt insisted only on compensation. A joint commission worked out a settlement that was formally concluded on November 19, 1941.

The London Economic Conference

An international conference in London in June 1933 tried to obtain tariff reduction and currency stabilization for the industrialized nations. Roosevelt would not agree to peg the value of the dollar to other currencies because he feared that it might impede his recovery efforts. The conference failed for lack of American cooperation.

Recognition of Russia

The United States had not had diplomatic relations with the Union of Soviet Socialist Republics since it was established after the 1917 revolution. In an effort to open trade with Russia, mutual recognition was negotiated in November 1933. The financial results were disappointing.

Philippine Independence

The Tydings-McDuffie Act of March 1934 forced the Philippines to become independent on July 4, 1946, rather than granting the dominion status that the Filipinos had requested.

The Reciprocal Trade Agreement Act

This law, the idea of Cordell Hull, was passed in June 1934. It allowed the president to negotiate agreements that could vary from the rates of the Hawley-Smoot Tariff up to fifty percent. By 1936 lower rates had been negotiated with 13 nations, and by 1941 almost two-thirds of all American foreign trade was covered by agreements.

United States Neutrality Legislation

Isolationism

Belief that the United States should stay out of foreign wars and problems began in the 1920s and grew in the 1930s. It was fed by House and Senate investigations of arms traffic and the munitions industry in 1933 and 1934, especially an examination of profiteering by bankers and munitions makers in drawing the United States into World War I by Senator Gerald Nye of North Dakota. Books of revisionist history that asserted that Germany had not been responsible for World War I and that the United States had been misled were also influential during the 1930s. A Gallup poll in April 1937 showed that almost two-thirds of those responding thought that American entry into World War I had been a mistake. Such feelings were strongest in the Midwest and among Republicans, but were found in all areas and across the political spectrum. Leading isolationists included Congressman Hamilton Fish of New York, Senator William Borah of Idaho, and Senator George Norris of Nebraska, all Republicans. Pacifist movements, such as the Fellowship of Christian Reconciliation, were influential among college and high school students and the clergy.

The Johnson Act of 1934

When European nations stopped payment on World War I debts to the United States, this law prohibited any nation in default from selling securities to any American citizen or corporation.

The Neutrality Acts of 1935

Isolationist sentiment prompted Senator Key Pittman, a Nevada Democrat to propose these laws. Roosevelt would have preferred more presidential flexibility, but Congress wanted to avoid flexibility and the mistakes of World War I. The laws provided that, on outbreak of war between foreign nations, all exports of American arms and munitions to them would be embargoed for six months. In addition, American ships were prohibited from carrying arms to any belligerent, and the president was to warn American citizens not to travel on belligerent ships.

The Neutrality Acts of 1936

The laws gave the president authority to determine when a state of war existed, and prohibited any loans or credits to belligerents.

The Neutrality Acts of 1937

The laws gave the president authority to determine if a civil war was a threat to world peace and covered by the Neutrality Acts, prohibited all arms sales to belligerents, and allowed the cash-and-carry sale of nonmilitary goods to belligerents.

Threats to World Order

The Manchurian Crisis

In September 1931 the Japanese army invaded and seized the Chinese province of Manchuria. The action violated the Nine Power Pact and the Kellogg-Briand Pact. When the League of Nations sought consideration of some action against Japan, Hoover refused to consider either economic or military sanctions. The only American action was to refuse recognition of the action or the puppet state of Manchukuo which the Japanese created.

Ethiopia

Following a border skirmish between Italian and Ethiopian troops, the Italian army of Fascist dictator Benito Mussolini invaded Ethiopia from neighboring Italian colonies in October 1935. The League of Nations failed to take effective action, the United States looked on, and Ethiopia fell in May 1936.

Occupation of the Rhineland

In defiance of the Versailles Treaty, Nazi dictator Adolph Hitler sent his German army into the demilitarized Rhineland in March 1936.

The Rome-Berlin Axis

Germany and Italy, under Hitler and Mussolini, formed an alliance called the Rome-Berlin Axis on October 25, 1936.

The Sino-Japanese War

The Japanese launched a full-scale invasion of China in July 1937. When Japanese planes sank the American Gunboat *Panay* and three Standard Oil tankers on the Yangtze River in December 1937, the United States accepted a Japanese apology and damage payments while the American public called for the withdrawal of all American forces from China.

The "Quarantine the Aggressor" Speech

In a speech in Chicago in October 1937, Roosevelt proposed that the democracies unite to quarantine the aggressor nations. When public opinion did not pick up the idea, he did not press the issue.

German Expansion

Hitler brought about a union of Germany and Austria in March 1938, took the German-speaking Sudetenland from Czechoslovakia in September 1938, and occupied the rest of Czechoslovakia in March 1939.

The Invasion of Poland and the Beginning of World War II

On August 24, 1939, Germany signed a nonaggression pact with Russia that contained a secret provision to divide Poland between them. German forces then invaded Poland on September 1, 1939. Britain and France declared war on Germany on September 3 because of their treaties with Poland. By the end of September, Poland had been dismembered by Germany and Russia, but the war continued in the west along the French-German border.

The American Response to the War in Europe

Preparedness

Even before the outbreak of World War II, Roosevelt began a preparedness program to improve American defenses. In May 1938 he requested and received a naval construction appropriation of about one billion dollars. In October, Congress provided an additional $300 million for defense, and in January 1939 a regular defense appropriation of $1.3 billion with an added $525 million for equipment, especially airplanes. Defense spending increased after the outbreak of war. In August 1939, Roosevelt created the War Resources Board to develop a plan for industrial mobilization in the event of war. The next month he established the Office of Emergency Management in the White House to centralize mobilization activities.

The Neutrality Act of 1939

Roosevelt officially proclaimed the neutrality of the United States on September 5, 1939. He then called Congress into special session on September 21 and urged it to allow the cash-and-carry sale of arms. Despite opposition from isolationists, the Democratic Congress, in a vote that followed party lines, passed a new Neutrality Act in November. It allowed the cash-and-carry sale of arms and short-term loans to belligerents, but forbade American ships to trade with belligerents or Americans to travel on belligerent ships. The new law was helpful to the Allies because they controlled the Atlantic.

Changing American Attitudes

Hitler's armies invaded and quickly conquered Denmark and Norway in April 1940. In May, German forces swept through the Netherlands, Belgium, Luxembourg, and France. The British were driven from the continent, and France surrendered on June 22. Almost all Americans recognized Germany as a threat. They divided on whether to aid Britain or to concentrate on the defense of America. The Committee to Defend America by Aiding the Allies was formed in May 1940, and the America First Committee, which opposed involvement, was incorporated in September 1940.

Greenland

In April 1940 Roosevelt declared that Greenland, a possession of conquered Denmark, was covered by the Monroe Doctrine, and he supplied military assistance to set up a coastal patrol there.

Defense Mobilization

In May 1940 Roosevelt appointed a Council of National Defense chaired by William S. Knudson, the president of General Motors, to direct defense production and especially to build 50,000 planes. The Council was soon awarding defense contracts at the rate of $1.5 billion a month. The Office of Production Management was created to allocate scarce materials, and the Office of Price Administration was established to prevent inflation and protect consumers. In June, Roosevelt made Republicans Henry L. Stimson and Frank Knox secretaries of war and the navy, respectively, partly as an attempt to secure bipartisan support.

Selective Service

Congress approved the nation's first peacetime draft, the Selective Service and Training Act, in September 1940. Men twenty-one to thirty-five were registered, and many were called for one year of military training.

Destroyers for Bases

Roosevelt had determined that to aid Britain in every way possible was the best way to avoid war with Germany. He ordered the army and navy to turn over all available weapons and munitions to private dealers for resale to Britain. In September 1940 he signed an agreement to give Britain fifty American destroyers in return for a ninety-nine-year lease on air and naval bases in British territories in Newfoundland, Bermuda, and the Caribbean.

The Election of 1940

The Republicans

Passing over their isolationist front-runners, Senator Robert A. Taft of Ohio and New York attorney Thomas E. Dewey, the Republicans nominated Wendell L. Willkie of Indiana, a dark horse candidate. Willkie was a liberal Republican who had been a Democrat most of his life and the head of an electric utility holding company that had fought against the TVA. The platform supported a strong defense program, but severely criticized the New Deal domestic policies.

The Democrats

Roosevelt did not reveal his intentions regarding a third term, but he neither endorsed another candidate nor discouraged his supporters. When the convention came in July, he sent a message to the Democratic National Committee implying that he would accept the nomination for a third time if it were offered. He was then nominated on the first ballot, breaking a tradition that had existed since the time of Washington. Only with difficulty did Roosevelt's managers persuade the delegates to accept his choice of vice president, Secretary of Agriculture Henry A. Wallace, to succeed Garner. The platform endorsed the foreign and domestic policies of the administration.

The Campaign

Willkie's basic agreement with Roosevelt's foreign policy made it difficult for him to campaign. Willkie had a folksy approach that appealed to many voters, but he first attacked Roosevelt for the slowness of the defense program, and then, late in the campaign, called him a warmonger. Roosevelt, who lost the support of many Democrats, including his adviser James Farley, over the third term issue, campaigned very little. When Willkie began to gain on the warmongering issue, Roosevelt declared on October 30 that "your boys are not going to be sent into any foreign wars."

The Election

Roosevelt won by a much narrower margin than in 1936, with 27,243,466 votes, 54.7 percent, and 449 electoral votes. Willkie received 22,304,755 votes and 82 electoral votes. Socialist Norman Thomas had 100,264 votes, and Communist Earl Browder received 48,579.

American Involvement with the European War

The Lend-Lease Act

The British were rapidly exhausting their cash reserves with which to buy American goods. In January 1941, Roosevelt proposed that the United States provide supplies to be paid for in goods and services after the war. The Lend-Lease Act was passed by Congress and signed on March 11, 1941, and the first appropriation of $7 billion was provided. In effect, the law changed the United States from a neutral to a nonbelligerent on the Allied side.

The Patrol of the Western Atlantic

The Germans stepped up their submarine warfare in the Atlantic to prevent the flow of American supplies to Britain. In April 1941 Roosevelt started the American Neutrality Patrol. The American navy would search out but not attack German submarines in the western half of the Atlantic, and warn British vessels of their location.

Greenland

In April 1941, United States forces occupied Greenland, and in May the president declared a state of unlimited national emergency.

Occupation of Iceland

American marines occupied Iceland, a Danish possession, in July 1941 to protect it from seizure by Germany. The American navy began to convoy American and Icelandic ships between the United States and Iceland.

The Atlantic Charter

On August 9, 1941, Roosevelt and Winston Churchill, the British prime minister, met for the first time on a British battleship off Newfoundland. They issued the Atlantic Charter which described a postwar world based on self-determination for all nations. It also endorsed the principles of freedom of speech and religion and freedom from want and fear, which Roosevelt had proposed as the Four Freedoms earlier that year.

Aid to Russia

Germany invaded Russia in June 1941, and in November the United States extended lend-lease assistance to the Russians.

The Shoot-on-Sight Order

The American destroyer *Greer* was attacked by a German submarine near Iceland on September 4, 1941. Roosevelt ordered the American military forces to shoot on sight at any German or Italian vessel in the patrol zone. An undeclared naval war had begun. The American destroyer *Kearny* was attacked by a submarine on October 16, and the destroyer *Reuben James* was sunk on October 30, with 115 lives lost. In November, Congress authorized the arming of merchant ships.

The Road to Pearl Harbor

A Japanese Empire

Following their invasion of China in 1937, the Japanese began to speak of the Greater East Asia Co-Prosperity Sphere, a Japanese empire of undefined boundaries in east Asia and the western Pacific. Accordingly, they forced out American and other business interests from occupied China, declaring that the Open Door policy had ended. Roosevelt responded by lending money to China and requesting American aircraft manufacturers not to sell to Japan.

The Embargo of 1940

Following the fall of France, a new and more militant Japanese government in July 1940 obtained from the German-controlled Vichy French government the right to build air bases and to station troops in northern French Indochina. The United States, fearing that the step would lead to further expansion, responded in late July by placing an embargo on the export of aviation gasoline, lubricants, and scrap iron and steel to Japan, and by granting an additional loan to China. In December the embargo was extended to include iron ore and pig iron, some chemicals, machine tools, and other products.

The Tripartite Pact

Japan joined with Germany and Italy to form the Rome-Berlin-Tokyo Axis on September 27, 1940, when it signed the Tripartite Pact or Triple Alliance with the other Axis powers.

The Embargo of 1941

In July 1941, Japan extracted a new concession from Vichy France by obtaining military control of southern Indochina. Roosevelt reacted by freezing Japanese funds in the United States, closing the Panama Canal to Japan, activating the Philippine militia, and placing an embargo on the export of oil and other vital products to Japan.

Japanese-American Negotiations

Negotiations to end the impasse between the United States and Japan were conducted in Washington between Secretary Hull and Japanese Ambassador Kichisaburo Nomura. Hull demanded that Japan withdraw from Indochina and China, promise not to attack any other area in the western Pacific, and withdraw from the Tripartite Pact in return for the reopening of American trade. The Japanese offered to withdraw from Indochina when the Chinese war was satisfactorily settled, to promise no further expansion, and to agree to ignore any obligation under the Tripartite Pact to go to war if the United States entered a defensive war with Germany. Hull refused to compromise.

A Summit Conference Proposed

The Japanese proposed in August 1941 that Roosevelt meet personally with the Japanese prime minister, Prince Konoye, in an effort to resolve their differences. Such an action might have strengthened the position of Japanese moderates, but Roosevelt replied in September that he would do so only if Japan agreed to leave China. No meeting was held.

Final Negotiations

In October 1941, a new military cabinet headed by General Hideki Tojo took control of Japan. The Japanese secretly decided to make a final effort to negotiate and to go to war if no solution was found by November 25. A new round of talks followed in Washington, but neither side would make a substantive change in its position, and on November 26, Hull repeated the American demand that the Japanese remove all their forces from China and Indochina immediately. The Japanese gave final approval on December 1 for an attack on the United States.

Japanese Attack Plans

The Japanese planned a major offensive to take the Dutch East Indies, Malaya, and the Philippines in order to obtain the oil, metals, and other raw materials that they needed. At the same time, they would attack Pearl Harbor in Hawaii to destroy the American Pacific fleet to keep it from interfering with their plans.

American Awareness of Japanese Plans

The United States had broken the Japanese diplomatic codes and knew that trouble was imminent. Between December 1 and December 6, 1941, it became clear to administration leaders that Japanese task forces were being ordered into battle. American commanders in the Pacific were warned of possible aggressive action there, but not forcefully. Apparently, most American leaders thought that Japan would attack the Dutch East Indies and Malaya, but would avoid American territory so as not to provoke action by the United States. Some argue that Roosevelt wanted to let the Japanese attack so that the American people would be squarely behind the war.

The forward magazine of USS Shaw explodes during the second Japanese attack wave on Pearl Harbor, Dec. 7, 1941.

The Pearl Harbor Attack

At 7:55 A.M. on Sunday, December 7, 1941, the first wave of Japanese carrier-based planes attacked the American fleet in Pearl Harbor. A second wave followed at 8:50 A.M. American defensive action was almost nil, but by the second wave a few anti-aircraft batteries were operating and a few army planes from another base in Hawaii engaged the enemy. The United States suffered the loss of two battleships sunk, six damaged and out of action, three cruisers and three destroyers sunk or damaged, and a number of lesser vessels destroyed or damaged. All of the 150 aircraft at Pearl Harbor were destroyed on the ground. Worst of all, 2,323 American servicemen were killed and about 1,100 wounded. The Japanese lost 29 planes, five midget submarines, and one fleet submarine.

The Declaration of War

On December 8, 1941, Roosevelt told a joint session of Congress that the day before had been a "date that would live in infamy." Congress declared war on Japan with one dissenting vote. On December 11, Germany and Italy declared war on the United States.

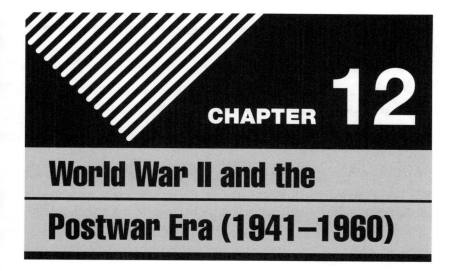

CHAPTER **12**

World War II and the
Postwar Era (1941–1960)

Declared War Begins

Declaration of War

On December 8, Congress declared war on Japan. Three days later the Axis powers, Germany and Italy, declared war on the United States. Great Britain and the United States then established the Combined Chiefs of Staff, headquartered in Washington, to direct Anglo-American military operations.

Declaration of the United Nations

On January 1, 1942, representatives of 26 nations met in Washington, D.C., and signed the Declaration of the United Nations, pledging themselves to the principles of the Atlantic Charter and promising not to make a separate peace with their common enemies.

The Home Front

War Production Board

The WPB was established in 1942 by President Franklin D. Roosevelt for the purpose of regulating the use of raw materials.

Wage and Price Controls

In April 1942 the General Maximum Price Regulation Act froze prices and extended rationing. In April 1943, prices, wages, and salaries were all frozen.

Revenue Act of 1942

The Revenue Act of 1942 extended the income tax to the majority of the population. Payroll deduction for the income tax began in 1944.

Social Changes

Rural areas lost population while coastal areas increased rapidly. Women entered the workforce in increasing numbers. Blacks moved from the rural South to Northern and Western cities with racial tensions often resulting, most notably in the June 1943, racial riot in Detroit.

Smith-Connolly Act

Passed in 1943, the Smith-Connolly Antistrike Act authorized government seizure of a plant or mine idled by a strike if the war effort was impeded. It expired in 1947.

Korematsu v. United States

In 1944 the Supreme Court upheld President Roosevelt's 1942 order that Issei (Japanese Americans who had emigrated from Japan) and Nisei (native-born Japanese Americans) be relocated to concentration camps. The camps were closed in March 1946.

Smith v. Allwright

In 1944 the Supreme Court struck down the Texas primary elections, which were restricted to whites, for violating the Fifteenth Amendment.

Presidential Election of 1944

President Franklin D. Roosevelt, together with new vice presidential candidate Harry S. Truman of Missouri, defeated his Republican opponent, Governor Thomas Dewey of New York.

Death of Roosevelt

Roosevelt died on April 12, 1945, at Warm Springs, Georgia. Harry S. Truman became president.

The North African and European Theaters

Nearly 400 ships were lost in American waters of the Atlantic to German submarines between January and June 1942.

The United States joined in the bombing of the European continent in July 1942. Bombing increased during 1943 and 1944 and lasted to the end of the war.

The Allied army under Dwight D. Eisenhower attacked French North Africa in November 1942. The French surrendered.

In February 1943, during the Battle of Kassarine Pass, North Africa, the Allied army met General Erwin Rommel's Africa Korps. Although the battle is variously interpreted as a standoff or a defeat for the U.S., Rommel's forces were soon trapped by the British moving in from Egypt. In May 1943, Rommel's Africa Korps surrendered.

Allied armies under George S. Patton invaded Sicily from Africa in July 1943 and gained control by mid-August. Moving from Sicily, the Allied armies invaded the Italian mainland in September. Benito Mussolini had already fallen from power and his successor, Marshal Pietro Badoglio, surrendered. The Germans, however, put up a stiff resistance with the result that Rome did not fall until June 1944.

In March 1944, the Soviet Union began pushing into Eastern Europe.

On "D-Day," June 6, 1944, Allied armies under Dwight D. Eisenhower, now commander-in-chief of Supreme Headquarters, Allied Expeditionary Forces, began an invasion of Normandy, France.

D-Day Landing at Normandy

Allied armies under General Omar Bradley took the transportation hub of St. Lo, France in July.

Allied armies liberated Paris in August. By mid-September, they had arrived at the Rhine, on the edge of Germany.

Beginning December 16, 1944, at the Battle of the Bulge, the Germans counterattacked, driving the Allies back about fifty miles into Belgium. By January the Allies were once more advancing toward Germany.

The Allies crossed the Rhine in March 1945. In the last week of April, Eisenhower's forces met the Soviet army at the Elbe.

On May 7, 1945, Germany surrendered.

The Pacific Theater

By the end of December 1941, Guam, Wake Island, the Gilbert Islands, and Hong Kong had fallen to the Japanese. In January 1942, Raboul, New Britain fell, followed in February by Singapore and Java, and in March by Rangoon, Burma.

The U.S. air raids on Tokyo in April 1942 were militarily inconsequential, but they raised Allied morale.

U.S. forces surrendered at Corregidor, Philippines, on May 6, 1942.

In the Battle of the Coral Sea, May 7–8, 1942 (northeast of Australia, south of New Guinea and the Solomon Islands), planes from the American carriers *Lexington* and *Yorktown* forced Japanese troop transports to turn back from attacking Port Moresby. The battle stopped the Japanese advance on Australia.

At the Battle of Midway, June 4–7, 1942, American air power destroyed four Japanese carriers and about 300 planes while the U.S. lost the carrier *Yorktown* and one destroyer. The battle proved to be the turning point in the Pacific.

A series of land, sea, and air battles took place around Guadalcanal in the Solomon Islands from August 1942 to February 1943, stopping the Japanese.

The Allied strategy of island hopping, begun in 1943, sought to neutralize Japanese strongholds with air and sea power and then move on. General Douglas MacArthur commanded the land forces moving from New Guinea toward the Philippines, while Admiral Chester W. Nimitz directed the naval attack on important Japanese islands in the central Pacific.

U.S. forces advanced into the Gilberts (November 1943), the Marshalls (January 1944), and the Marianas Islands (June 1944).

In the Battle of the Philippine Sea, June 19–20, 1944, the Japanese lost three carriers, two submarines, and over 300 planes while the Americans lost 17 planes. After the American capture of the Marianas Islands, General Tojo resigned as premier of Japan.

The Battle of Leyte Gulf, October 25, 1944, involved three major engagements that resulted in Japan's loss of most of its remaining naval power. It also brought the first use of the Japanese kamikaze, or suicide, attacks by Japanese pilots who crashed into American carriers.

Forces under General Douglas MacArthur liberated Manila in March 1945.

Between April and June 1945 in the battle for Okinawa, nearly 50,000 American casualties resulted from the fierce fighting that virtually destroyed Japan's remaining defenses.

The Atomic Bomb

The Manhattan Engineering District was established by the army engineers in August 1942 for the purpose of developing an atomic bomb. The mission eventually became known as the Manhattan Project. J. Robert Oppenheimer directed the design and construction of a transportable atomic bomb at Los Alamos, New Mexico.

On December 2, 1942, Enrico Fermi and his colleagues at the University of Chicago produced the first atomic chain reaction.

On July 16, 1945, the first atomic bomb was exploded at Alamogordo, New Mexico.

The *Enola Gay* dropped an atomic bomb on Hiroshima, Japan, on August 6, 1945, killing about 78,000 people and injuring 100,000 more. On August 9, a second bomb was dropped on Nagasaki, Japan. Some 40,000 people were killed in the explosion. Thousands more died later from burns, injuries, and radiation exposure.

On August 8, 1945, the Soviet Union entered the war against Japan.

Japan surrendered on August 15, 1945. The formal surrender was signed on September 2.

Diplomacy

Casablanca Conference

On January 14–25, 1943, Franklin D. Roosevelt and Winston Churchill, prime minister of Great Britain, declared a policy of unconditional surrender for "all enemies."

Moscow Conference

In October 1943, Secretary of State Cordell Hull obtained the Soviet's agreement to enter the war against Japan after Germany was defeated and to participate in a world organization after the war was over.

World War II Ends

Declaration of Cairo

Issued on December 1, 1943, after Roosevelt met with General Chiang Kai-shek in Cairo from November 22 to 26, the Declaration of Cairo called for Japan's unconditional surrender and stated that all Chinese territories occupied by Japan would be returned to China and that Korea would be free and independent.

Teheran Conference

The first "Big Three" (Roosevelt, Churchill, and Stalin) conference, met at Teheran from November 28 to December 1, 1943. Stalin reaffirmed the Soviet commitment to enter the war against Japan and discussed coordination of the Soviet offensive with the Allied invasion of France.

Yalta Conference

On February 4–11, 1945, the "Big Three" met to discuss postwar Europe. Stalin said that the Soviet Union would enter the Pacific war within three months after Germany surrendered and agreed to the "Declaration of Liberated Europe" which called for free elections. They called

Yalta Conference: Churchill, Roosevelt, and Stalin (l-r).

for a conference on world organization, to meet in the U.S. beginning on April 25, 1945, and agreed that the Soviets would have three votes in the General Assembly and that the U.S., Great Britain, the Soviet Union, France, and China would be permanent members of the Security Council. Germany was divided into occupation zones, and a coalition government of communists and noncommunists was agreed to for Poland. Roosevelt accepted Soviet control of Outer Mongolia, the Kurile Islands, the southern half of Sakhalin Island, Port Arthur (Darien), and participation in the operation of the Manchurian railroads.

Potsdam Conference

From July 17 to August 2, 1945, Truman, Stalin, and Clement Atlee (who during the conference replaced Churchill as prime minister of Great Britain) met at Potsdam. During the conference, Truman ordered the dropping of the atomic bomb on Japan. The conference disagreed on most major issues but did establish a Council of Foreign Ministers to draft peace treaties for the Balkans. Approval was also given to the concept of war-crimes trials and the demilitarization and denazification of Germany.

The Emergence of the Cold War and Containment

Failure of U.S.–Soviet Cooperation

By the end of 1945, the Soviet Union controlled most of Eastern Europe, Outer Mongolia, parts of Manchuria, Northern Korea, the Kurile Islands, and Sakhalin Island. In 1946–1947 the Soviet Union took over Poland, Hungary, Rumania, and Bulgaria.

Iron Curtain

In a speech in Fulton, Missouri, in 1946, Winston Churchill stated that an Iron Curtain had been spread across Europe separating the democratic from the authoritarian communist states.

Containment

In 1946, career diplomat and Soviet expert George F. Kennan warned that the Soviet Union had no intention of living peacefully with the United States. The next year, in July 1947, he wrote an anonymous article for Foreign Affairs in which he called for a counterforce to Soviet pressures for the purpose of "containing" communism.

Truman Doctrine

In February 1947 Great Britain notified the United States that it could no longer aid the Greek government in its war against communist insurgents. The next month President Harry S. Truman asked Congress for $400 million in military and economic aid for Greece and Turkey. He argued in what became known as the "Truman Doctrine" that the United States must support free peoples who were resisting communist domination.

Marshall Plan

Secretary of State George C. Marshall proposed in June 1947 that the United States provide economic aid to help rebuild Europe. Meeting in July, representatives of the European nations agreed on a recovery program jointly financed by the United States and the European countries. The following March, Congress passed the European Recovery Program, popularly known as the Marshall Plan, providing more than $12 billion in aid.

Czechoslovakia

In February 1948, the Soviets sponsored a coup d'état in Czechoslovakia, thereby extending communism in Europe.

Berlin Crisis

After the United States, France, and Great Britain announced plans to create a West German Republic out of their German zones, the Soviet Union in June 1948 blocked surface access to Berlin. The U.S. then instituted an airlift to transport supplies to the city until the Soviets lifted their blockade in May 1949.

NATO

In April 1949, the North Atlantic Treaty Organization was signed by the United States, Great Britain, France, Italy, Belgium, the Netherlands, Luxembourg, Denmark, Norway, Portugal, Iceland, and Canada. The signatories pledged that an attack against one would be considered an attack against all. Greece and Turkey joined the alliance in 1952 and West Germany in 1954. The Soviets formed the Warsaw Treaty Organization in 1955 to counteract NATO.

Atomic Bomb

The Soviet Union exploded an atomic device in September 1949.

International Cooperation

Bretton Woods, New Hampshire

At a conference held July 1–22, 1944, representatives from Europe and the United States signed agreements for an international bank and a world monetary fund to stabilize international currencies and rebuild the economies of war-torn nations.

Yalta Conference

In February 1945, Roosevelt, Churchill, and Stalin called for a conference on world organization to meet in April 1945 in the United States.

United Nations

From April to June 1945, representatives from 50 countries met in San Francisco to establish the United Nations. The U.N. charter created a General Assembly composed of all member nations that would act as the ultimate policy-making body. A Security Council, made up of 11 members, including the United States, Great Britain, France, the Soviet Union, and China as permanent members and six additional nations elected by the General Assembly for two-year terms, would be responsible for settling disputes among U.N. member nations.

Containment in Asia

Japan

General Douglas MacArthur headed a four-power Allied Control Council that governed Japan, allowing it to develop economically and politically.

China

Between 1945 and 1948, the United States gave over $2 billion in aid to the Nationalist Chinese under Chiang Kai-shek and sent George C. Marshall to settle the conflict between Chiang's Nationalists and Mao Tse-tung's Communists. In 1949, however, Mao defeated Chiang and forced the Nationalists to flee to Formosa (Taiwan). Mao established the People's Republic of China on the mainland.

General Douglas MacArthur

Korean War

On June 25, 1950, North Korea invaded South Korea. President Truman committed U.S. forces commanded by General MacArthur but under United Nations auspices. By October, the U.N. (mostly American) had driven north of the 38th parallel that divided North and South Korea. Chinese troops attacked MacArthur's forces on November 26, pushing them south of the 38th parallel, but by spring 1951, the U.N. forces had recovered their offensive. MacArthur called for a naval blockade of China and bombing north of the Yalu River, criticizing the president for fighting a limited war. In April 1951, Truman removed MacArthur from command.

Armistice

Armistice talks began with North Korea in the summer of 1951. In June 1953, an armistice was signed leaving Korea divided along virtually the same boundary that had existed prior to the war.

Troops During the Korean War

Eisenhower-Dulles Foreign Policy

John Foster Dulles

Dwight D. Eisenhower, elected president in 1952, chose John Foster Dulles as secretary of state. Dulles talked of a more aggressive foreign policy, calling for "massive retaliation" and "liberation" rather than containment. He wished to emphasize nuclear deterrents rather than conventional armed forces. Dulles served as secretary of state until ill health forced him to resign in April 1959. Christian A. Herter took his place.

Hydrogen Bomb

The U.S. exploded its first hydrogen bomb in November 1952 while the Soviets followed with theirs in August 1953.

Soviet Change of Power

Josef Stalin died in March 1953. After an internal power struggle that lasted until 1955, Nikita Khrushchev emerged as the Soviet leader. He talked of both "burying" capitalism and "peaceful coexistence."

Dwight D. Eisenhower

Asia

In 1954 the French asked the U.S. to commit air forces to rescue French forces at Dien Bien Phu, Vietnam, as they were besieged by the nationalist forces led by Ho Chi Minh, but Eisenhower refused. In May 1954 Dien Bien Phu surrendered.

Geneva Accords

France, Great Britain, the Soviet Union, and China signed the Geneva Accords in July 1954, dividing Vietnam along the 17th parallel. The North would be under Ho Chi Minh and the South under Emperor Bao Dai. Elections were scheduled for 1956 to unify the country, but Ngo Dinh Diem overthrew Bao Dai and prevented the elections from taking place. The United States supplied economic aid to South Vietnam.

Southeast Asia Treaty Organization

Dulles attempted to establish a Southeast Asia Treaty Organization parallel to NATO but was able to obtain only the Philippine Republic, Thailand, and Pakistan as signatories in September 1954.

Quemoy and Matsu

The small islands of Quemoy and Matsu off the coast of China were occupied by the Nationalist Chinese under Chiang Kai-shek but claimed by the People's Republic of China. In 1955, after the mainland Chinese began shelling these islands, Eisenhower obtained authorization from Congress to defend Formosa (Taiwan) and related areas.

Middle East—The Suez Canal Crisis

The United States had agreed to lend money to Egypt, under the leadership of Colonel Gamal Abdul Nasser, to build the Aswan Dam but refused to give arms. Nasser then drifted toward the Soviet Union and in 1956 established diplomatic relations with the People's Republic of China. In July 1956 the U.S. withdrew its loan to Egypt. In response, Nasser nationalized the Suez Canal. France, Great Britain, and Israel then attacked Egypt, but Eisenhower demanded that they pull out. On November 6, a cease fire was announced.

Eisenhower Doctrine

President Eisenhower announced in January 1957 that the U.S. was prepared to use armed force in the Middle East against communist aggression. Under this doctrine, U.S. marines entered Beirut, Lebanon, in July 1958 to promote political stability during a change of government. The marines left in October.

Summit Conference with the Soviet Union

In July 1955, President Eisenhower met in Geneva with Anthony Eden, prime minister of Great Britain, Edgar Faure, premier of France, and Nikita Khrushchev and Nikolai Bulganin, at the time co-leaders of the Soviet Union. They discussed disarmament and reunification of Germany but made no agreements.

Atomic Weapons Test Suspension

In October 1958, Eisenhower and Khrushchev voluntarily suspended atmospheric tests of atomic weapons.

Soviet-American Visitations

Vice President Richard M. Nixon visited the Soviet Union, and Soviet Vice-Premier Anastas I. Mikoyan came to the United States in the summer of 1959. In September Premier Khrushchev toured the United States and agreed to another summit meeting.

U-2 Incident

On May 1, 1960, an American U-2 spy plane was shot down over the Soviet Union and pilot Francis Gary Powers was captured. Eisenhower ultimately took responsibility for the spy plane and Khrushchev angrily called off the Paris summit conference, which was to take place in a few days.

Latin America

The U.S. supported the overthrow of President Jacobo Arbenz Guzman of Guatemala in 1954, because he began accepting arms from the Soviet Union.

Vice President Nixon had to call off an eight nation goodwill tour of Latin America after meeting hostile mobs in Venezuela and Peru in 1958.

In January 1959, Fidel Castro overthrew Fulgencio Batista, dictator of Cuba. Castro soon began criticizing the United States and moved closer to the Soviet Union, signing a trade agreement with the Soviets in February 1960. The United States prohibited the importation of Cuban sugar in October 1960 and broke off diplomatic relations in January 1961.

The Politics of Affluence: Demobilization and Domestic Policy

Truman Becomes President

Harry S. Truman, formerly a senator from Missouri and vice president of the United States, became president on April 12, 1945. In September 1945, he proposed a liberal legislative program, including expansion of unemployment insurance, extension of the Employment Service, a higher minimum wage, a permanent Fair Employment Practices Commission, slum clearance, low-rent housing, regional TVA-type programs, and a public works program, but was unable to put it through Congress.

Employment Act of 1946

This act established a three-member Council of Economic Advisors to evaluate the economy, advise the president, and set up a Congressional Joint Committee on the Economic Report. The act declared that the government was committed to maintaining maximum employment.

Atomic Energy

Congress created the Atomic Energy Commission in 1946, establishing civilian control over nuclear development and giving the president sole authority over the use of atomic weapons in warfare.

Price Controls

Truman vetoed a weak price control bill passed by Congress, thereby ending the wartime price control program. When prices quickly increased about 6%, Congress passed another bill in July 1946. Although Truman signed this bill, he used its powers inconsistently, especially when—bowing to pressure—he ended price controls on beef. In late 1946, he lifted controls on all items except rents, sugar, and rice.

Harry S. Truman

Labor

In early 1946, the United Auto Workers, under Walter Reuther, struck General Motors, and steelworkers, under Philip Murray, struck U.S. Steel, demanding wage increases. Truman suggested an eighteen cent-per-hour wage increase and in February allowed U.S. Steel to raise prices to cover the increase. This formula became the basis for settlements in other industries. After John L. Lewis's United Mine Workers struck in April 1946, Truman ordered the government to take over the mines and then accepted the union's demands, which included safety and health and welfare benefits. The president averted a railway strike by seizing the railroads and threatening to draft strikers into the army.

Demobilization

By 1947 the total armed forces had been cut to 1.5 million. The army fell to 600,000 from a WWII peak of 8 million. The Serviceman's Readjustment Act (G.I. Bill of Rights) of 1944 provided $13 billion in aid ranging from education to housing.

Taft-Hartley Act

The Republicans, who had gained control of Congress as a result of the 1946 elections, sought to control the power of the unions through the Taft-Hartley Act, passed in 1947. This act made the "closed-shop" illegal; labor unions could no longer force employers to hire only union members although it allowed the "union-shop" in which newly hired employees were required to join the union. It established an eighty-day cooling-off period for strikers in key industries; ended the practice of employers collecting dues for unions; forbade such actions as secondary boycotts, jurisdictional strikes, featherbedding, and contributing to political campaigns; and required an anticommunist oath of union officials. The act slowed down efforts to unionize the South and by 1954 fifteen states had passed "right to work" laws, forbidding the "union-shop."

Reorganization of the Armed Forces

In 1947 Congress passed the National Security Act creating a National Military Establishment, National Security Council, Joint Chiefs of Staff, and Central Intelligence Agency (CIA). Together these organizations were intended to coordinate the armed forces and intelligence services.

Government Reorganization

Truman in 1947 appointed former President Herbert Hoover to head a Commission on Organization of the Executive Branch. The Commission's 1949 report led to the Organization Act of 1949 that allowed the president to make organizational changes subject to congressional veto.

Civil Rights

In 1946 Truman appointed the President's Committee on Civil Rights, which a year later produced its report *To Secure These Rights*. The report called for the elimination of all aspects of segregation. In 1948 the president banned racial discrimination in federal hiring practices and ordered desegregation of the armed forces.

Presidential Succession

The Presidential Succession Act of 1947 placed the speaker of the House and the president pro tempore of the Senate ahead of the secretary of state and after the vice president in the line of succession. The Twenty-second Amendment to the Constitution, ratified in 1951, limited the president to two terms.

Election of 1948

Truman was the Democratic nominee, but the Democrats were split by the States' Rights Democratic Party (Dixiecrats), which nominated Governor Strom Thurmond of South Carolina, and the Progressive Party, which nominated former Vice President Henry Wallace. The Republicans nominated Governor Thomas E. Dewey of New York. After traveling widely and attacking the "do-nothing Congress," Truman won a surprise victory.

The Fair Deal

The Fair Deal Program

Truman sought to enlarge and extend the New Deal. He proposed increasing the minimum wage, extending Social Security to more people, maintaining rent controls, clearing slums and building public housing, and providing more money to TVA, rural electrification, and farm housing. He also introduced bills dealing with civil rights, national health insurance, federal aid to education, and repeal of the Taft-Hartley Act. A coalition of Republicans and Southern Democrats prevented little more than the maintenance of existing programs.

Farm Policy

Because of improvements in agriculture, overproduction continued to be a problem. Secretary of Agriculture Charles F. Brannan proposed a program of continued price supports for storable crops and guaranteed minimum incomes to farmers of perishable crops. It was defeated in Congress and surpluses continued to pile up.

Anticommunism

Smith Act

The Smith Act of 1940, which made it illegal to advocate the overthrow of the government by force or to belong to an organization advocating such a position, was used by the Truman administration to jail leaders of the American Communist Party.

Loyalty Review Board

In response to criticism, particularly from the House Committee on Un-American Activities, that his administration was "soft on communism," Truman established this board in 1947 to review government employees.

The Hiss Case

In 1948 Whittaker Chambers, formerly a communist and then an editor of *Time*, charged Alger Hiss, a former State Department official and then president of the Carnegie Endowment for International Peace, with having been a communist who supplied classified American documents to the Soviet Union. In 1950 Hiss was convicted of perjury, the statute of limitations on his alleged spying having run out.

McCarran Internal Security Act

Passed in 1950, this act required communist-front organizations to register with the attorney general and prevented their members from defense work and travel abroad. It was passed over Truman's veto.

Rosenberg Case

In 1950 Julius and Ethel Rosenberg, as well as Harry Gold, were charged with giving atomic secrets to the Soviet Union. The Rosenbergs were convicted and executed in 1953.

Joseph McCarthy

On February 9, 1950, Senator Joseph R. McCarthy of Wisconsin stated that he had a list of known communists who were working in the State Department. He later expanded his attacks to diplomats and scholars and contributed to the electoral defeat of two senators. After making charges against the army, he was censured and discredited by the Senate in 1954 and died in 1957.

Eisenhower's Dynamic Conservatism

1952 Election

The Republicans nominated Dwight D. Eisenhower, most recently NATO commander, for the presidency and Richard M. Nixon, senator from California, for the vice presidency. The Democrats nominated Governor Adlai E. Stevenson of Illinois for president. Eisenhower won by a landslide; for the first time since Reconstruction, the Republicans won some Southern states.

Conservatism

Eisenhower sought to balance the budget and lower taxes but did not attempt to roll back existing social and economic legislation. Eisenhower first described his policy as "dynamic conservatism" and then as "progressive moderation." The administration abolished the Reconstruction Finance Corporation, ended wage and price controls, and reduced farm price supports. It cut the budget and in 1954 lowered tax rates for corporations and individuals with high incomes; an economic slump, however, made balancing the budget difficult.

Social Legislation

Social Security was extended in 1954 and 1956 to an additional 10 million people, including professionals, domestic and clerical workers, farm workers, and members of the armed services. In 1959 benefits were increased 7%. In 1955 the minimum wage was raised from 75 cents to $1.00 an hour.

Public Power

Opposed to the expansion of the TVA, the Eisenhower administration supported a plan to have a privately owned power plant (called Dixon-Yates) built to supply electricity to Memphis, Tennessee. After two years of controversy and discovery that the government consultant would financially benefit from Dixon-Yates, the administration turned to a municipally owned power plant. The Idaho Power Company won the right to build three small dams on the Snake River rather than the federal government establishing a single large dam at Hell's Canyon. The Atomic Energy Act of 1954 allowed the construction of private nuclear power plants under Atomic Energy Commission license and oversight.

Farm Policy

The Rural Electrification Administration announced in 1960 that ninety-seven percent of American farms had electricity. In 1954 the government began financing the export of farm surpluses in exchange for foreign currencies and later provided surpluses free to needy nations, including milk to school children and to the poor in exchange for governmental issued food stamps.

Public Works

In 1954 Eisenhower obtained congressional approval for joint Canadian-U.S. construction of the St. Lawrence Seaway, giving ocean-going vessels access to the Great Lakes. In 1956 Congress authorized construction of the Interstate Highway System, with the federal government supplying ninety percent of the cost and the states ten percent. The program further undermined the American railroad system.

Supreme Court

Eisenhower appointed Earl Warren, formerly governor of California, chief justice of the Supreme Court in 1953. That same year he appointed William J. Brennan associate justice. Although originally perceived as conservatives, both justices used the court as an agency of social and political change.

Election of 1956

The 1956 election once again pitted Eisenhower against Stevenson. The president won easily, carrying all but seven states.

Space and Technology

The launching of the Soviet space satellite *Sputnik* on October 4, 1957, created fear that America was falling behind technologically. Although the U.S. launched *Explorer I* on January 31, 1958, the concern continued. In 1958 Congress established the National Aeronautics and Space Administration (NASA) to coordinate research and development and the National Defense Education Act to provide grants and loans for education.

Sherman Adams Scandal

In 1958 the White House chief of staff resigned after it was revealed that he had received a fur coat and an oriental rug in return for helping a Boston industrialist deal with the federal bureaucracy. This became known as the Sherman Adams Scandal.

Labor

The Landrum-Griffen Labor-Management Act of 1959 sought to control unfair union practices by establishing rules such as penalties for misuse of funds.

New States

On January 3, 1959, Alaska became the 49th state and on August 21, 1959, Hawaii became the 50th.

Civil Rights

Initial Eisenhower Actions

Eisenhower completed the formal integration of the armed forces, desegregated public services in Washington, D.C., naval yards, and veteran's hospitals, and appointed a Civil Rights Commission.

Legal Background to Brown

In *Ada Lois Sipuel v. Board of Regents* (1948) and *Sweatt v. Painter* (1950) the Supreme Court ruled that African Americans must be allowed to attend integrated law schools in Oklahoma and Texas.

Brown v. Board of Education of Topeka

In *Brown v. Board of Education of Topeka*, a 1954 case, NAACP lawyer Thurgood Marshall challenged the doctrine of "separate but equal" (*Plessy v. Ferguson*, 1896). The court declared that separate educational facilities were inherently unequal. In 1955 the court ordered states to integrate "with all deliberate speed."

Southern Reaction

Although at first the South reacted cautiously, by 1955 there were calls for "massive resistance," and White Citizens Councils emerged to spearhead the resistance. State legislatures used a number of tactics to get around *Brown*. By the end of 1956, desegregation of the schools had advanced very little.

Little Rock

Although he did not personally support the Supreme Court decision, Eisenhower sent 10,000 National Guardsmen and 1,000 paratroopers to Little Rock, Arkansas, to control mobs and enable blacks to enroll at Central High in September 1957. A small force of soldiers was stationed at the school throughout the year.

Emergence of Nonviolence

On December 11, 1955, in Montgomery, Alabama, Rosa Parks, a black woman, refused to give up her seat on a city bus to a white and was arrested. Under the leadership of Martin Luther King, Jr., a black pastor, blacks of Montgomery organized a bus boycott that lasted for a year, until in December 1956 the Supreme Court refused to review a lower court ruling that stated that separate but equal was no longer legal.

Civil Rights Acts

Eisenhower proposed the Civil Rights Act of 1957 that established a permanent Civil Rights Commission and a Civil Rights Division of the Justice Department, which was empowered to prevent interference with the right to vote. The Civil Rights Act of 1960 gave the federal courts power to register African American voters.

Ending "Massive Resistance"

In 1959 state and federal courts nullified Virginia laws which prevented state funds from going to integrated schools. This proved to be the beginning of the end for "massive resistance."

Sit-Ins

In February 1960, four black students who had been denied service staged a sit-in at a segregated Woolworth lunch counter in Greensboro, North Carolina. This inspired sit-ins elsewhere in the South and led to the formation of the Student Nonviolent Coordinating Committee (SNCC). SNCC's primary aims included the end of segregation in public accommodations and winning voting rights.

The Election of 1960

The Nominations

Vice President Richard M. Nixon won the Republican presidential nomination while the Democrats nominated Senator John F. Kennedy for the presidency with Lyndon B. Johnson, majority leader of the Senate, as his running mate.

Catholicism

Kennedy's Catholicism was a major issue until, on September 12, he told a gathering of Protestant ministers that he accepted the separation of church and state and that he would not allow Catholic leaders to tell him how to act as president.

Debates

A series of televised debates between Kennedy and Nixon helped create a positive image of Kennedy and may have been a turning point in the election.

Kennedy's Victory

Kennedy won the election by slightly over 100,000 popular votes and 94 electoral votes, based on majorities in New England, the Middle Atlantic, and the South.

Society and Culture

Gross National Product (GNP)

The GNP almost doubled between 1945 and 1960, growing at an annual rate of 3.2% from 1950 to 1960. Inflation, meanwhile, remained under 2% annually throughout the 1950s. Defense spending was the most important stimulant, and military-related research helped create or expand the new industries of chemicals, electronics, and aviation. The U.S. had a virtual monopoly over international trade, because of the devastation of the World War. Technological innovations contributed to productivity, which jumped 35% between 1945 and 1955. After depression and war, Americans had a great desire to consume. Between 1945 and 1960, the American population grew by nearly 30%, which contributed greatly to consumer demand.

Consumption Patterns

Home ownership grew by 50% between 1945 and 1960. These new homes required such appliances as refrigerators and washing machines, but the most popular product was television, which increased from 7,000 sets in 1946 to 50 million sets in 1960. *TV Guide* became the fastest growing magazine, and advertising found the TV medium especially powerful. Consumer credit increased 800% between 1945 and 1957 while the rate of savings dropped to about 5% of income. The number of shopping centers rose from eight in 1945 to 3,840 in 1960. Teenagers became an increasingly important consumer group, making—among other things—a major industry of rock 'n' roll music, with Elvis Presley as its first star, by the mid-1950s.

Demographic Trends

Population Growth

In the 1950s population grew by over 28 million, 97% of which was in urban and suburban areas. The average life expectancy increased from 66 in 1955 to 71 in 1970. Dr. Benjamin Spock's *The Commonsense Book of Baby and Child Care* sold an average of one million copies a year between 1946 and 1960.

The Sun Belt

Aided by the use of air conditioning, Florida, the Southwest, and California grew rapidly, with California becoming the most populous state by 1963. The Northeast, however, remained the most densely populated area.

Suburbs

The suburbs grew six times faster than the cities in the 1950s. William Levitt pioneered the mass-produced housing development when he built 10,600 houses (Levittown) on Long Island in 1947, a pattern followed widely elsewhere in the country. The Federal Housing Administration helped builders by insuring up to 95% of a loan and buyers by insuring their mortgages. Thanks in part to the development of the interstate highway system during the Eisenhower administration, auto production increased from 2 million in 1946 to 8 million in 1955, which further encouraged the development of suburbia. As increasing numbers of African Americans moved into the Northern and Midwestern cities, whites moved to the suburbs, a process dubbed "white flight." About twenty percent of the population moved their residence each year.

Middle Class

The number of American families that were classified as middle class changed from 5.7 million in 1947 to more than 12 million by the early 1960s.

Jobs

The number of farm workers dropped from 9 million to 5.2 million between 1940 and 1960. By 1960 more Americans held white-collar than blue-collar jobs.

Conformity and Security

Corporate Employment

Employees tended to work for larger organizations. By 1960, thirty-eight of the workforce was employed by organizations with over 500 employees. Such environments encouraged the managerial personality and corporate cooperation rather than individualism.

Homogeneity

Observers found the expansion of the middle class an explanation for the emphasis on conformity. David Riesman argued in *The Lonely Crowd* (1950) that Americans were moving from an inner-directed to an outer-directed orientation. William Whyte's *The Organization Man* (1956) saw corporate culture as emphasizing the group rather than the individual. Sloan Wilson's *The Man in the Grey Flannel Suit* (1955) expressed similar concerns in fictional form.

Leisure

The standard workweek shrank from six to five days. Television became the dominant cultural medium, with over 530 stations by 1961. Books, especially as paperbacks, increased in sales annually.

Women

A cult of feminine domesticity re-emerged after World War II. Marynia Farnham and Ferdinand Lundberg published *Modern Woman: The Lost Sex* in 1947; Farnham suggested that science supported the idea that women could find fulfillment only in domesticity. Countless magazine articles also promoted the notion that a woman's place was in the home.

Religion

From 1940, when less than half the population belonged to a church, membership rose to more than sixty-five percent by 1960. Catholic Bishop Fulton J. Sheen had a popular weekly television show, "Life Worth Living," while Baptist evangelist Billy Graham held huge crusades. Norman Vincent Peale best represented the tendency of religion to emphasize reassurance with his best-seller *The Power of Positive Thinking* (1952). Critics noted the shallowness of this religion. Will

Herberg in *Protestant-Catholic-Jew* (1955) said that popular religiosity lacked conviction and commitment. Reinhold Niebuhr, the leading neo-orthodox theologian, criticized the self-centeredness of popular religion and its failure to recognize the reality of sin.

Seeds of Rebellion

Intellectuals

Intellectuals became increasingly critical of American life. John Kenneth Galbraith in *The Affluent Society* (1958) argued that the public sector was underfunded. John Keats's *The Crack in the Picture Window* (1956) criticized the homogeneity of suburban life in the new mass-produced communities. The adequacy of American education was questioned by James B. Conant in *The American High School Today* (1959).

Theater and Fiction

Arthur Miller's *Death of a Salesman* (1949) explored the theme of the loneliness of the other-directed person. Novels also took up the conflict between the individual and mass society. Notable works included J.D. Salinger's *The Catcher in the Rye* (1951), James Jones's *From Here to Eternity* (1951), Joseph Heller's *Catch-22* (1955), Saul Bellow's *The Adventures of Augie March* (1953), and John Updike's *Rabbit, Run* (1960).

Art

Painter Edward Hopper portrayed isolated, anonymous individuals. Jackson Pollock, Robert Motherwell, Willem de Kooning, Arshile Gorky, and Mark Rothko were among the leaders in abstract expressionism, in which they attempted spontaneous expression of their subjectivity.

The Beats

The Beats were a group of young men alienated by twentieth-century life. Their movement began in Greenwich Village, New York, with the friendship of Allen Ginsburg, Jack Kerouac, William Burroughs, and Neal Cassady. They emphasized alcohol, drugs, sex, jazz, Buddhism, and a restless vagabond life, all of which were vehicles for their subjectivity. Ginsberg's long poem *Howl* (1956) and Kerouac's novel *On the Road* (1957) were among the more important literary works to emerge from the Beat movement.

Quiz: Chapters 11 and 12

1. Which of the following was not one of Hoover's responses to the Great Depression?

   (A) He at first stressed the desirability of localism and private initiative rather than government intervention.

   (B) He saw the Depression as akin to an act of nature, about which nothing could be done except to ride it out.

   (C) He urged the nation's business leaders to maintain wages and full employment.

   (D) His strategy for ending the Depression was a failure.

   (E) He was not able to avoid increasing unpopularity.

2. Franklin D. Roosevelt's New Deal program attempted or achieved all of the following EXCEPT

   (A) raised farm prices by paying farmers not to plant.

   (B) encouraged cooperation within industries so as to raise prices generally.

(C) supported the creation of the Reconstruction Finance Corporation.

(D) invigorated the economy by lowering tariff barriers.

(E) restored confidence in the banking system.

3. In order to deal with the crisis in banking at the time of his inauguration, Franklin Roosevelt

(A) drastically curtailed government spending and cut taxes.

(B) declared a four-day "banking holiday" and prohibited the export of money.

(C) urged Congress to pass legislation banning fractional reserve banking and holding bank trustees responsible for all deposits.

(D) announced a multi-billion dollar federal bailout package.

(E) announced the nationalization of all banks with over $100 million in total assets.

4. The 1932 demonstration known as the "Bonus March" involved

(A) farmers disgruntled about low prices for meat, grain, and dairy products.

(B) homeless persons building shantytowns near Washington, D.C.

(C) Japanese-Americans protesting forced relocation from the West Coast.

(D) World War I veterans demanding financial aid from the federal government.

(E)   migrant farm workers seeking employment in California.

5.   All of the following statements about the Taft-Hartley Act are true EXCEPT

(A)   it had long been the goal of a number of large labor unions.

(B)   it allowed the president to call an eight-day cooling-off period to delay any strike that might endanger national safety or health.

(C)   it outlawed the closed shop.

(D)   it was backed by congressional Republicans.

(E)   it was vetoed by President Truman.

6.   The underlying issue that led to the outbreak of war between the United States and Japan in 1941 was

(A)   Japanese aid to the Germans in their war against Britain.

(B)   U.S. desire to annex various Pacific islands held by Japan.

(C)   Japanese desire to annex the Aleutian Islands.

(D)   Japanese desire to annex large portions of China.

(E)   American resentment of Japanese trading policies and trade surpluses.

7.   The Marshall Plan was

(A)   a strategy for defeating Germany.

(B)   a strategy for defeating Japan.

(C)   an American economic aid program for Europe.

(D)   an American commitment to give military and economic aid to any nation resisting Communist aggression.

(E)   a civil-defense plan for surviving a Soviet nuclear strike.

8.   The thrust of Roosevelt's "Good Neighbor" policy was to

(A)   retreat from the military interventionism and blatant economic domination that had characterized previous American policy toward Latin America.

(B)   guarantee the protection of Latin America and South America from European aggression by permanently stationing U.S. forces in the region.

(C)   promote "Good Samaritanism" in the United States by encouraging people who still owned their own homes to provide temporary housing for their neighbors who had become homeless because of the Great Depression.

(D)   force Latin American countries to cooperate peacefully with each other and end their petty border disputes or face United States military intervention.

(E)   supply Britain with the food and nonmilitary essentials they needed to maintain their struggle against Nazi Germany.

9.   Senator Joseph McCarthy was known for

(A)   leading a "witch hunt" to expose communists in the U.S.

(B)   recommending large-scale American intervention in Vietnam.

(C)   helping to formulate a major economic aid plan for Western Europe in the late 1940s.

(D)   leading the peace faction of the Democratic Party in the 1968 presidential campaign.

(E)   being the first American Senator convicted of spying for the Soviet Union (in 1956).

10.   What event, in 1957, caused a near panic among U.S. leaders and led to a massive increase in spending for science programs, etc. in U.S. schools and research institutions?

(A)   The revelation of huge Soviet stockpiles of deadly chemical weapons to be used in any future confrontation with the United States

(B)   The launching of *Sputnik* by the Soviet Union

(C)   The detonation of a hydrogen bomb by the Soviet Union

(D)   The development of the microprocessor by the Soviet Union

(E)   Soviet Premier Nikita Khrushchev's promise to "bury" the West

ANSWER KEY

1.	(B)	6.	(D)
2.	(C)	7.	(C)
3.	(B)	8.	(A)
4.	(D)	9.	(A)
5.	(A)	10.	(B)

DETAILED ANSWERS

1.   **(B)**   Hoover did NOT see the Depression as akin to an act of nature, about which nothing could be done. He did stress the desirability of localism and private initiative (A) and urged the nation's business leaders to maintain wages and full employment (C), but his efforts ended in failure (D), and he was the target of growing unpopularity (E).

2.   **(C)**   It was FDR's predecessor, Herbert Hoover, who in 1932 established the Reconstruction Finance Corporation. In doing so, he broke with many leaders in the Republican Party, including Secretary of the Treasury Andrew Mellon, who believed the government had no choice but to let the business cycle run its course. Roosevelt's New Deal contained every other element listed.

3.   **(B)**   Roosevelt declared a banking holiday, closing all banks to prevent anxious depositors from demanding their money and causing the banks to default. Curtailing government spending and taxes (A)

was the last thing Roosevelt wanted to do and would probably have had little effect on the immediate banking crisis at the time of Roosevelt's inauguration. Nationalizing banks (E), on the other hand, would have been rather extreme and was probably seen by Roosevelt as politically inadvisable. Banning fractional reserve banking (C) would at least have addressed the root problem but was as extreme in another direction and was not suggested by anyone in government at that time. A multi-billion dollar federal bailout (D) has been the federal government's response to the savings and loan crisis of the late 1980s and early 1990s.

4. **(D)** The "Bonus March" involved World War I veterans demanding financial aid from the federal government during the Depression. A few of the Bonus Marchers did build shacks near Washington, D.C. (B). Many farmers—and others—were disgruntled in 1932 (A), but the means of expressing it was generally by voting for Franklin D. Roosevelt for president.Also during this time there were a number of farm workers seeking employment in California (E). Later, during the Second World War, Japanese-Americans were relocated (C), but they could hardly have protested by marching on Washington.

5. **(A)** The Taft-Hartley Act was definitely not sought but rather vehemently opposed by the labor unions. It did allow the president to call a cooling-off period (B), and it outlawed the closed shop (C). It was backed by Congressional Republicans (D), vetoed by President Truman (E), and passed over his veto.

6. **(D)** The basic issue in the coming of war between the U.S. and Japan in 1941 was Japan's desire to annex large portions of China. The Japanese were not yet aiding the Germans in their war against Britain (A) and did not desire to annex the Aleutians (C)—although during the course of the war they did attack and occupy a couple of them. The U.S. did not desire the Japanese-held islands in the Pacific (B)—though during the war the U.S. wound up taking a great many of them. American resentment of Japanese trading policies (E) characterizes more the last quarter of the twentieth century.

7. **(C)** The Marshall Plan was an American economic aid program for Europe. The Truman Doctrine was the American commitment to help countries threatened by Communism (C).

8. **(A)** The "Good Neighbor" policy sought to smooth over relations between the United States and Latin America by retreating from the blatant interventionism that dominated U.S. policy into the 1930s. The effects of interventionism had become increasingly costly to the point that the benefits derived were not worth the expense. In 1933, Franklin Roosevelt officially consolidated many changes already under way in U.S. policy toward Latin America under the heading of the "Good Neighbor" policy. Under this plan, the United States would pull back from the nearly constant use of military intervention to control Latin American nations. The United States government would cease acting unilaterally in Latin American affairs and would attempt to consult with and seek the approval of Latin American governments before intervening in the region. In addition, the United States would support Latin American governments headed by strong, independent leaders and would help train Latin American military forces so they could defend themselves. United States banks would also provide loans and other economic assistance to help stabilize fragile Latin American economies.

While the United States still dominated many aspects of Latin American life, with the enactment of the "Good Neighbor" policy that domination was handled more diplomatically, with somewhat more respect for local authorities. Many of the leaders who emerged at this time were military dictators who were trained by American military personnel as part of the effort to train Latin American military forces. These dictators owed their power to the United States and often stayed in power only as a result of U.S. backing. So, while the days of the "Big Stick" effectively ended with the "Good Neighbor" policy, U.S. domination of the region continued, albeit at a somewhat reduced level of visibility.

9. **(A)** Joseph McCarthy, the junior senator from Wisconsin, set the tone for the early 1950s in America with his relentless attacks on the "Communist menace" in America. McCarthy used American fears

of Communist subversion to catapult himself out of obscurity in the United States Senate and into national prominence. He made his initial charges in a Lincoln's Birthday speech in Wheeling, West Virginia, claiming that the U.S. State Department was infested with Communists. Although he was lying, his charges struck a chord in the national psyche and within days people were clamoring for the ouster of the alleged Communists. He used these charges to build a political base of support from which he went on to blame virtually all of America's failures since World War II on wealthy intellectuals supposedly selling out the country to the Communists. His attacks played upon latent bigotry, racism, and anti-Semitism, but the Korean War and the arrest of alleged spies such as the Rosenbergs convinced enough people that he was probably correct in his allegations that few attempted to stop him. President Eisenhower tried to ignore McCarthy and hoped he would undercut himself with his reckless allegations and unfounded charges.

Eventually, McCarthy did ruin his own career. His charges became more and more spectacular and more and more unprovable. Finally, when he charged that the army officer corps was a hotbed of Communist activity, Eisenhower decided enough was enough. Senate hearings were called in 1954 to investigate McCarthy's charges, and they were nationally televised. McCarthy was as bullying and overbearing as ever, attempting to ruin the reputation of virtually anyone who stood up to him. In the end, these tactics disgusted the American public and fellow senators. McCarthy's popularity plummeted and the Senate condemned him. He remained a senator but finished his career a broken man. He died of alcohol-related causes in 1957.

10. **(B)** The launching of *Sputnik* reverberated across the United States like nothing had since Pearl Harbor. After World War II Americans were taught to fear the Soviet Union through the glasses of the Cold War. However, one area of American-Soviet relations in which nearly all Americans felt more than secure was the superiority of American technology and American scientific know-how. Sure, the Russians had developed an atomic bomb and later a hydrogen bomb, but only after their spies had managed to steal plans from America. The inferiority of Soviet weapons was well known and widely joked about. Then came *Sputnik*, a little metal sphere which, when placed in orbit around the

earth making it the world's first man-made orbital satellite, shook the world.

Suddenly, Soviet technological ineptitude was no longer a laughing matter. It became increasingly unhumorous when repeated American attempts to duplicate *Sputnik* failed miserably. American self-confidence was badly shaken. The quality of American science education was questioned, as was the moral fiber of the country. For the military, a new term suddenly blossomed into existence: Intercontinental Ballistic Missile (ICBM). If the Soviets could put a satellite into orbit, then it was no great leap for them to place a nuclear warhead on top of a missile and drop it right down Washington's collective throat. American Cold War fears intensified.

Using *Sputnik* as an excuse, Washington demanded and got increased funding for the military, particularly funding for missile research, as well as increased funding for education. Most of the education money was directed at colleges and universities and focused on mathematics and science education. It roused America from its complacency and led to a new wave of technical advances related to the influx of science-related funding.

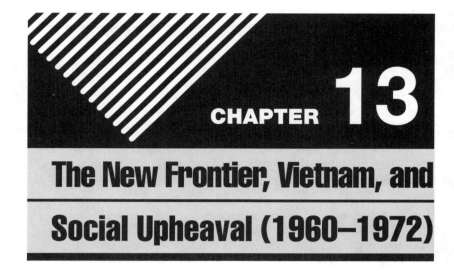

CHAPTER 13

The New Frontier, Vietnam, and Social Upheaval (1960–1972)

Kennedy's "New Frontier" and the Liberal Revival

Legislative Failures

Kennedy was unable to get much of his program through Congress because of an alliance of Republicans and southern Democrats. He proposed plans for federal aid to education, urban renewal, medical care for the aged, reductions in personal and corporate income taxes, and the creation of a Department of Urban Affairs. None of these proposals passed.

Kennedy did gain congressional approval for raising the minimum wage from $1.00 to $1.25 an hour and extending it to 3 million more workers.

Housing Act

The 1961 Housing Act provided nearly $5 billion over four years for the preservation of open urban spaces, development of mass transit, and the construction of middle-class housing.

Civil Rights

Freedom Riders

In May 1961, blacks and whites, sponsored by the Congress on Racial Equality, boarded buses in Washington, D.C., and traveled across the South to New Orleans to test federal enforcement of regulations prohibiting discrimination. They met violence in Alabama but continued to New Orleans. Others came into the South to test the segregation laws.

Justice Department

The Justice Department, under Attorney General Robert F. Kennedy (1925–1968), the president's brother, began to push for civil rights, including desegregation of interstate transportation in the South, integration of schools, and supervision of elections.

Mississippi

In the fall of 1962, President Kennedy called the Mississippi National Guard to federal duty to enable an African American, James Meredith, to enroll at the University of Mississippi.

Mercury astronaut John Glenn shows President Kennedy the Friendship 7 Space Capsule at Cape Canaveral, Fla., Feb. 23, 1962.

John F. Kennedy

March on Washington

Kennedy presented a comprehensive civil rights bill to Congress in 1963. It banned racial discrimination in public accommodations, gave the attorney general power to bring suits on behalf of individuals for school integration, and withheld federal funds from state-administered programs that practiced discrimination. While the bill was held up in Congress, 200,000 people marched on August 28, 1963, in Washington, D.C. During their demonstration, Martin Luther King, Jr., gave his "I Have a Dream" speech.

The Cold War Continues

Bay of Pigs

Under Eisenhower, the Central Intelligence Agency had begun training some 2,000 men for an invasion of Cuba to overthrow Fidel Castro, the left-leaning revolutionary who had taken power in 1959. On April 19, 1961, this force invaded at the Bay of Pigs, but was pinned down and forced to surrender. Some 1,200 men were captured.

Berlin Wall

After a confrontation between Kennedy and Khrushchev in Berlin, Kennedy called up reserve and National Guard units and asked for an increase in defense funds. In August 1961, Khrushchev responded by closing the border between East and West Berlin and ordering the erection of the Berlin Wall.

Nuclear Testing

The Soviet Union began the testing of nuclear weapons in September 1961. Kennedy then authorized resumption of underground testing by the United States.

Cuban Missile Crisis

On October 14, 1962, a U-2 reconnaissance plane brought photographic evidence that missile sites were being built in Cuba. On October 22, Kennedy announced a blockade of Cuba and called on Khrushchev to dismantle the missile bases and remove from Cuba all

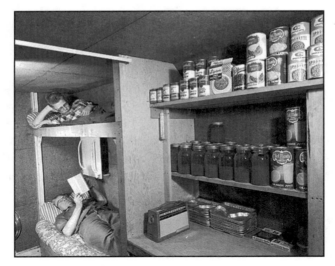

A Cold War-era fallout shelter

weapons capable of attacking the United States. Six days later, Khrushchev backed down, withdrew the missiles, and Kennedy lifted the blockade. The United States promised not to invade Cuba and removed missiles from bases in Turkey, claiming they had planned to do so anyway.

Afterwards, a "hot line" telephone connection was established between the White House and the Kremlin to effect quick communication in threatening situations.

Nuclear Test Ban

In July 1963, a treaty banning the atmospheric testing of nuclear weapons was signed by all the major powers except France and China.

Alliance for Progress

In 1961, Kennedy announced the Alliance for Progress, which would provide $20 million in aid to Latin America.

Peace Corps

The Peace Corps, established in 1961, sent young volunteers to Third World countries to contribute their skills in locally sponsored projects.

Johnson and the Great Society

Kennedy Assassination

On November 22, 1963, Kennedy was assassinated by Lee Harvey Oswald in Dallas, Texas. Jack Ruby, a nightclub owner, killed Oswald two days later. Conspiracy theories emerged. Chief Justice Earl Warren led an investigation of the murder and concluded that Oswald had acted alone, but questions remain.

Following President Kennedy's assassination, Lyndon B. Johnson takes the oath of office aboard Air Force One.

Lyndon Johnson

Succeeding Kennedy, Johnson had extensive experience in both the House and Senate, and as a Texan, was the first southerner to serve as president since Woodrow Wilson. He pushed hard for Kennedy's programs, which were languishing in Congress.

A tax cut of more than $10 billion passed Congress in 1964, and an economic boom resulted.

Civil Rights Act

The 1964 Civil Rights Act outlawed racial discrimination by employers and unions, created the Equal Employment Opportunity Commission to enforce the law, and eliminated the remaining restrictions on African American voting.

Election of 1964

Lyndon Johnson was nominated for president by the Democrats, with Senator Hubert H. Humphrey of Minnesota for vice president. The Republicans nominated Senator Barry Goldwater, a conservative from Arizona. Johnson won more than sixty-one percent of the popular vote and could now launch his own "Great Society" program.

Johnson signs the Civil Rights Act of 1968.

Health Care

The Medicare Act of 1965 combined hospital insurance for retired people with a voluntary plan to cover physician's bills. Medicaid provided grants to states to help the poor below retirement age.

Education

In 1965, the Elementary and Secondary Education Act provided $1.5 billion to school districts to improve the education of poor people. Head Start prepared educationally disadvantaged children for elementary school.

Immigration

The Immigration Act of 1965 discontinued the national origin system, basing immigration instead on such things as skills and the need for political asylum.

Cities

The 1965 Housing and Urban Development Act provided 240,000 housing units and $2.9 billion for urban renewal. The Department of Housing and Urban Affairs was established in 1966, and rent supplements for low-income families also became available.

Apollo 11's Buzz Aldrin on the lunar surface.

Space

Fulfilling a goal established by Kennedy, Neil Armstrong and Edwin "Buzz" Aldrin became the first humans to walk on the moon, on July 20, 1969.

Emergence of Black Power

Voting Rights

In 1965, Martin Luther King, Jr., announced a voter registration drive. With help from the federal courts, he dramatized his effort by leading a march from Selma to Montgomery, Alabama, between March 21 and 25. The Voting Rights Act of 1965 authorized the attorney general to appoint officials to register voters.

Racial Riots

Seventy percent of African Americans lived in city ghettos across the country. It did not appear that the tactics used in the South would help them. Frustration built up. In August 1965, Watts, an area of Los Angeles, erupted in a riot. More than 15,000 National Guardsmen were brought in; 34 people were killed, 850 wounded, and 3,100 arrested. Property damage reached nearly $200 million. In 1966, New York and

Chicago experienced riots, and the following year there were riots in Newark and Detroit. The Kerner Commission, appointed to investigate the riots, concluded that they were directed at a social system that prevented African Americans from getting good jobs and crowded them into ghettos.

Black Power

Stokely Carmichael, chairman of SNCC, was by 1964 unwilling to work with white civil-rights activists. In 1966, he called for the civil rights movements to be "black-staffed, black-controlled, and black-financed." Later, he moved on to the Black Panthers, self-styled urban revolutionaries based in Oakland, California. Other leaders such as H. Rap Brown also called for Black Power.

King Assassination

On April 4, 1968, Martin Luther King, Jr., was assassinated in Memphis. James Earl Ray pleaded guilty and was convicted of the murder. Riots in more than 100 cities followed. Ray died in prison in 1998.

Black Officials

Despite the rising tide of violence, the number of African Americans achieving elected and appointed office increased. Among the more prominent were Associate Justice of the Supreme Court Thurgood Marshall, Secretary of Housing and Urban Affairs Robert Weaver, and Senator Edward W. Brooke.

Ethnic Activism

United Farm Workers

Cesar Chávez founded the United Farm Workers' Organizing Committee to unionize Mexican-American farm laborers. He turned a grape pickers strike in Delano, California, into a national campaign by attacking the structure of the migrant labor system through a boycott of grapes.

Native Americans

The American Indian Movement (AIM) was founded in 1968. At first it staged sit-ins to bring attention to Native American demands. By the early 1970s, it was turning to the courts.

The New Left

Demographic Origins

By the mid-1960s, the majority of Americans were under age 30. College enrollments increased fourfold between 1945 and 1970.

Students for a Democratic Society

SDS was organized by Tom Hayden and Al Haber of the University of Michigan in 1960. Hayden's Port Huron Statement (1962) called for "participatory democracy." SDS drew much of its ideology from the writings of C. Wright Mills, Paul Goodman, and Herbert Marcuse.

Free-Speech Movement

Students at the University of California, Berkeley, staged sit-ins in 1964 to protest the prohibition of political canvassing on campus. Led by Mario Savio, the movement changed from emphasizing student's rights to criticizing the bureaucracy of American society. In December, police broke up a sit-in; protests spread to other campuses around the nation.

Vietnam

Student protests began focusing on the Vietnam War. In the spring of 1967, 500,000 gathered in Central Park in New York City to protest the war, many burning their draft cards. SDS became more militant and willing to use violence. It turned to Lenin for its ideology.

1968

More than 200 large campus demonstrations took place in the spring, culminating in the occupation of buildings at Columbia University to protest the university's involvement in military research and its poor relations with minority groups. Police wielding clubs eventually broke up the demonstration. In August, thousands gathered in Chicago to protest the war during the Democratic convention. Although police violence against the demonstrators aroused anger, the antiwar movement began to split between those favoring violence and those opposed to it.

Decline

Beginning in 1968, SDS began breaking up into rival factions. After the more radical factions began using bombs, Tom Hayden left the group. By the early 1970s, the New Left had lost political influence, having abandoned its original commitment to democracy and nonviolence.

The Counterculture

Origins

Like the New Left, the founders of the counterculture were alienated by bureaucracy, materialism, and the Vietnam War, but they turned away from politics in favor of an alternative society. In many respects, they were heirs of the Beats.

Counterculture Expression

Many young people formed communes in such places as San Francisco's Haight-Ashbury district or in rural areas. "Hippies," as they were called, experimented with Eastern religions, drugs, and sex, but most were unable to establish a self-sustaining lifestyle. Leading spokesmen included Timothy Leary, Theodore Roszak, and Charles Reich.

Women's Liberation

Betty Friedan

In *The Feminine Mystique* (1963), Betty Friedan argued that middle-class society stifled women and did not allow them to use their individual talents. She attacked the cult of domesticity.

National Organization for Women

Friedan and other feminists founded the National Organization for Women (NOW) in 1966, calling for equal employment opportunities and equal pay.

Problems

The women's movement was largely limited to the middle class. The Equal Rights Amendment failed to pass. Abortion rights stirred up a counter "right-to-life" movement.

Vietnam

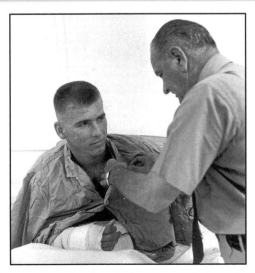

President Johnson awards a medal to a wounded serviceman in Cam Rahn Bay, South Vietnam (1966).

Background

After the French defeat in 1954, the United States sent military advisors to South Vietnam to aid the government of Ngo Dinh Diem. The pro-Communist Vietcong forces gradually grew in strength, partly because Diem failed to follow through on promised reforms. They received support from North Vietnam, the Soviet Union, and China. The U.S. government supported a successful military coup against Diem in the fall of 1963.

Escalation

In August 1964—after claiming that North Vietnamese gunboats had fired on American destroyers in the Gulf of Tonkin—Lyndon Johnson pushed the Gulf of Tonkin resolution through Congress, authorizing him to use military force in Vietnam. After a February 1965 attack by the Vietcong on Pleiku, Johnson ordered operation "Rolling Thunder," the first sustained bombing of North Vietnam. Johnson then sent combat troops to South Vietnam; under the leadership of General William C. Westmoreland, they conducted search and destroy operations. The number of troops increased to 184,000 in 1965, 385,000 in 1966, 485,000 in 1967, and 538,000 in 1968.

Defense of American Policy

"Hawks" defended the president's policy and, drawing on containment theory, said that the nation had the responsibility to resist aggression. Secretary of State Dean Rusk became a major spokesman for the domino theory, which justified government policy by analogy with England's and France's failure to stop Hitler prior to 1939. If Vietnam should fall, it was said, all Southeast Asia would eventually go. The administration stressed its willingness to negotiate the withdrawal of all "foreign" forces from the war.

Tet Offensive

On January 31, 1968, the first day of the Vietnamese new year (Tet), the Vietcong attacked numerous cities and towns, American bases, and even Saigon. Although they suffered large losses, the Vietcong won a psychological victory, as American opinion began turning against the war.

Election of 1968

Eugene McCarthy

In November 1967, Senator Eugene McCarthy of Minnesota announced his candidacy for the 1968 Democratic presidential nomination, running on the issue of opposition to the war.

New Hampshire

In February, McCarthy won forty-two percent of the Democratic vote in the New Hampshire primary, compared with Johnson's forty-eight percent. Robert F. Kennedy then announced his candidacy for the Democratic presidential nomination.

Johnson's Withdrawal

Lyndon Johnson withdrew his candidacy on March 31, 1968, and Vice President Hubert H. Humphrey took his place as a candidate for the Democratic nomination.

Kennedy Assassination

After winning the California primary over McCarthy, Robert Kennedy was assassinated by Sirhan Sirhan, a young Palestinian. This event assured Humphrey's nomination.

The Nominees

The Republicans nominated Richard M. Nixon, who chose Spiro T. Agnew, governor of Maryland, as his running mate in order to appeal to southern voters. Governor George C. Wallace of Alabama ran for the presidency under the banner of the American Independent party, appealing to fears generated by left-wing protestors and big government.

Nixon's Victory

Johnson suspended air attacks on North Vietnam shortly before the election. Nonetheless, Nixon, who emphasized stability and order, defeated Humphrey by a margin of 1 percent. Wallace's 13.5 percent was the best showing by a third-party candidate since 1924.

The Nixon Conservative Reaction

Civil Rights

The Nixon administration sought to block renewal of the Voting Rights Act and delay implementation of court-ordered school desegregation in Mississippi. After the Supreme Court ordered busing of students in 1971 to achieve school desegregation, the administration proposed an antibusing bill, which was blocked in Congress.

Supreme Court

In 1969, Nixon appointed Warren E. Burger, a conservative, as chief justice, but ran into opposition with the nomination of southerners Clement F. Haynesworth, Jr., and G. Harrold Carswell. After these nominations were defeated, he nominated Harry A. Blackmun, who received Senate approval. He later appointed Lewis F. Powell, Jr., and William Rehnquist as associate justices. Although more conservative than the Warren court, the Burger court did declare the death penalty, as used at the time, unconstitutional in 1972 and struck down state anti-abortion legislation in 1973.

Revenue Sharing

The heart of Nixon's "New Federalism," passed by Congress in 1972, was a five-year plan to distribute $30 billion of federal revenues to the states.

Congressional Legislation

Congress passed bills giving 18-year-olds the right to vote (1970), increasing Social Security benefits and funding for food stamps (1970), as well as establishing the Occupational Safety and Health Act (1970), the Clean Air Act (1970), laws to control water pollution (1970, 1972), and the Federal Election Campaign Act (1972). None was supported by the Nixon administration.

Economic Problems and Policy

Unemployment climbed to six percent in 1970, real gross national product declined in 1970, and in 1971 the United States experienced a trade deficit. Inflation reached twelve percent by 1974. These problems resulted from federal deficits in the 1960s, growing international competition, and rising energy costs.

In 1969, Nixon cut spending and raised taxes. He encouraged the Federal Reserve Board to raise interest rates. The economy worsened. In 1970, Congress gave the president the power to regulate prices and wages. Nixon used this power in August 1971 by declaring a ninety-day price and wage freeze and taking the United States off the gold standard. At the end of the ninety days, he established mandatory guidelines for wage and price increases. Finally, in 1973, he turned to voluntary wage and price controls, except on health care, food, and construction. When inflation increased rapidly, Nixon cut back on government expenditures, impounding funds already appropriated by Congress.

Vietnamization

Nixon proposed that all non-South Vietnamese troops be withdrawn in phases, and that an internationally supervised election be held in South Vietnam. The North Vietnamese rejected this plan.

The president then turned to "Vietnamization," the effort to build up South Vietnamese forces while withdrawing American troops. In 1969, Nixon reduced American troop strength by 60,000, but at the same time ordered the bombing of Cambodia, a neutral country, in the interests of flushing out Vietcong.

Protests

Two Moratorium Days in 1969 brought out several hundred thousand protesters, and reports of an American massacre of Vietnamese at My Lai reignited controversy over the nature of the war, but Nixon continued to defend his policy. Troop withdrawals continued, and a lottery system was instituted in 1970 to make the draft more equitable. In 1973, Nixon abolished the draft and established an all-volunteer army.

Cambodia

In April 1970, Nixon announced that Vietnamization was succeeding and that another 150,000 American troops would be out of Vietnam by the end of the year. A few days later, he sent troops into Cambodia to clear out Vietcong sanctuaries and resumed bombing of North Vietnam.

Kent State

Protests against escalation of the war were especially strong on college campuses. During a May 1970 demonstration at Kent State University in Ohio, National Guardsmen opened fire on protestors, killing four students. Soon after, two black students were killed by a Mississippi state policeman at Jackson State University. Several hundred colleges were soon closed down by student strikes, as moderates joined the radicals. Congress repealed the Gulf of Tonkin Resolution.

Pentagon Papers

The publication in 1971 of "the Pentagon Papers," classified Defense Department documents that were leaked to the press, revealed that the government had misled the Congress and the American people about its intentions in Vietnam during the mid-1960s.

End of U.S. Involvement

In the summer of 1972, negotiations between the United States and North Vietnam began in Paris. By October, a draft agreement was developed that included provisions for a cease-fire, the return of American prisoners of war, and the withdrawal of U.S. forces from Vietnam. A few days before the 1972 presidential election, Henry Kissinger, the president's national security advisor, declared that "peace was at hand."

Resumption of Bombing

Nixon resumed bombing of North Vietnam in December 1972, claiming that the North Vietnamese were not bargaining in good faith. In January 1973, the opponents reached a settlement in which the North Vietnamese retained control over large areas of the South and agreed to release American prisoners of war within sixty days. After the prisoners were released, the United States would withdraw its remaining troops. On March 29, 1973, the last American combat troops left South Vietnam. Nearly 60,000 Americans had been killed and 300,000 more wounded; the war's financial cost to the United States was $109 billion.

War Powers Act

Later in 1973, the War Powers Act was passed. It required congressional approval of any commitment of combat troops beyond ninety days.

Foreign Policy

China

With his national security advisor, Henry Kissinger, Nixon took some bold diplomatic initiatives. Kissinger traveled to China and the Soviet Union for secret sessions to plan summit meetings with the Communists. In February 1972, Nixon and Kissinger went to China to meet with Mao Tse-tung and his associates. The United States agreed to support China's admission to the United Nations and to pursue economic and cultural exchanges.

Soviet Union

At a May 1972 meeting with the Soviets, the Strategic Arms Limitation Treaty (SALT) was signed. The signatories agreed to stop making nuclear ballistic missiles and to reduce the number of antiballistic missiles to 200 for each power.

Middle East

Following the Arab-Israeli war of 1973, Arab states staged an oil boycott to push the Western nations into forcing Israel to withdraw from lands controlled since the Six-Day War of 1967. Kissinger, now secretary of state, negotiated the withdrawal of Israel from some of the lands, and the Arabs lifted their boycott. The five-member Organization of Petroleum Exporting Countries (OPEC)—composed of Venezuela, Saudi Arabia, Kuwait, Iraq, and Iran—then raised the price of oil from about $3.00 to $11.65 a barrel. U.S. gas prices doubled and inflation shot above ten percent.

Election of 1972

George McGovern

The Democrats nominated Senator George McGovern of South Dakota for president and Senator Thomas Eagleton for vice president. After the press revealed that Eagleton had been treated for psychological problems, McGovern eventually forced him off the ticket, replacing him with Sargent Shriver.

George Wallace

George Wallace, a longtime segregationist, ran once again as the American Independent party candidate. While campaigning at a Maryland shopping center on May 15, 1972, he became the victim of an assassination attempt that left him paralyzed below the waist. Arthur Bremer, 21, was sentenced to 63 years for shooting Wallace and three others.

Richard M. Nixon

Richard M. Nixon and Spiro T. Agnew, who had been renominated by the Republicans, won a landslide victory, receiving 521 electoral votes to McGovern's 17.

CHAPTER 14

Watergate, Carter, and the

New Conservatism

(1972–2009)

The Watergate Scandal

The Break-In

What became known as the Watergate crisis began during the 1972 presidential campaign. Early on the morning of June 17, James McCord, a security officer for the Committee for the Re-election of the President, and four other men broke into Democratic headquarters at the Watergate apartment complex in Washington, D.C., and were caught while going through files and installing electronic eavesdropping devices. On June 22, Nixon announced that the administration was in no way involved in the burglary attempt.

James McCord

The trial of the burglars began in early 1973, with all but McCord (who was convicted) pleading guilty. Before sentencing, McCord wrote a letter to U.S. District Court Judge John J. Sirica arguing that high Republican officials had known in advance about the burglary and that perjury had been committed at the trial.

Further Revelations

Soon Jeb Stuart Magruder, head of the Nixon re-election committee, and John W. Dean, Nixon's attorney, revealed that they had been involved. Dean testified before a Senate Watergate committee that Nixon had been involved in covering up the incident. Over the next several months, extensive involvement of the White House administration, including payment of "hush" money to the burglars, destruction of FBI records, forgery of documents, and wiretapping, was revealed. Dean was fired and H.R. Haldeman and John Ehrlichman, who headed the White House staff, and Attorney General Richard Kleindienst, resigned. Nixon claimed that he had not personally been involved in the cover-up but refused, on the grounds of executive privilege, to allow investigation of White House documents.

White House Tapes

Under considerable pressure, Nixon agreed to the appointment of a special prosecutor, Archibald Cox of Harvard Law School. When Cox obtained a subpoena for tape recordings of White House conversations (their existence had been revealed in testimony during the Senate hearings)—and the administration lost an appeal in the appellate court—Nixon ordered Elliot Richardson, the attorney general, to fire Cox. Both Richardson and his subordinate, William Ruckelshaus, resigned, leaving Robert Bork, the solicitor general, to carry out the order. This "Saturday Night Massacre," which took place on October 20, 1973, caused a storm of controversy. The House Judiciary Committee, headed by Peter Rodino of New Jersey, began looking into the possibility of impeachment. Nixon agreed to turn the tapes over to Judge Sirica and named Leon Jaworski as the new special prosecutor. But it soon became known that some of the tapes were missing and that a portion of another had been erased.

The Vice Presidency

Vice President Spiro Agnew was accused of income tax fraud and having accepted bribes when he was a local official in Maryland. He

Nixon departing from the White House after resigning Aug. 9, 1973.

resigned the vice presidency in October 1973 and was replaced by Congressman Gerald R. Ford of Michigan under provisions of the new Twenty-fifth Amendment.

Nixon's Taxes

Nixon was accused of paying almost no income taxes between 1969 and 1972, and of using public funds for improvements to his private residences in California and Florida. The IRS reviewed the president's tax return and assessed him nearly $500,000 in back taxes and interest.

Indictments

In March 1974, a grand jury indicted Haldeman, Ehrlichman, former Attorney General John Mitchell, and four other White House aides, and named Nixon as an unindicted coconspirator.

Calls for Resignation

In April, Nixon released edited transcripts of the White House tapes, the contents of which led to further calls for his resignation. Jaworski subpoenaed sixty-four additional tapes, which Nixon refused to turn over, and the case went to the Supreme Court.

Impeachment Debate

Meanwhile, the House Judiciary Committee televised its debate over impeachment, adopting three articles of impeachment. It charged the president with obstructing justice, misusing presidential power, and failing to obey the committee's subpoenas.

Resignation

Before the House began to debate the impeachment, the Supreme Court ordered the president to release the subpoenaed tapes to the special prosecutor. On August 5, Nixon, under pressure from his advisors, made public the tape of June 23, 1972. This tape, recorded less than a week after the break-in, revealed that Nixon had used the CIA to keep the FBI from investigating the case. Nixon announced his resignation on August 8, 1973, to take effect at noon the following day. Gerald Ford then became president.

Legislative Response

Congress responded to the Vietnam War and Watergate by enacting legislation intended to prevent such situations. In 1974 Congress limited the amounts of contributions and expenditures in presidential campaigns. It also strengthened the 1966 Freedom of Information Act by requiring the government to act promptly when asked for information and to prove its case for classification when attempting to withhold information on grounds of national security.

The Ford Presidency

Gerald Ford

Gerald Ford was in many respects the opposite of Nixon. Although a partisan Republican, he was well liked and free from any hint of scandal. Ford almost immediately encountered controversy when, in September 1974, he offered to pardon Nixon. Nixon accepted the offer, although he admitted no wrongdoing and had not yet been charged with a crime.

The Economy

Ford also faced major economic problems, which he approached somewhat inconsistently. Saying that inflation was the major problem, he called for voluntary restraints and asked citizens to wear "Whip Inflation Now," or WIN, buttons. The economy went into decline. Ford asked for tax cuts to stimulate business and argued against spending for social programs.

When New York City teetered on the verge of bankruptcy in 1975, Ford at first opposed federal aid but changed his mind when the Senate and House Banking Committees guaranteed the loans.

Vietnam

As North Vietnamese forces pushed back the South Vietnamese, Ford asked Congress to provide more arms for the South. Congress rejected the request, and in April 1975, Saigon fell to the North Vietnamese.

Election of 1976

Ronald Reagan, formerly a movie actor and governor of California, opposed Ford for the Republican nomination, but Ford won by a slim margin. The Democrats nominated James Earl Carter, formerly governor of Georgia, who ran on the basis of his integrity and lack of Washington connections. Carter, with Senator Walter Mondale of Minnesota as his vice presidential candidate, narrowly defeated Ford.

Carter's Moderate Liberalism

Policy Orientation in the Carter Administration

Carter sought to conduct the presidency on democratic and moral principles. The former peanut farmer, however, often misread political sentiment on Capitol Hill: the administration typically proposed complex programs but failed to support them through the legislative process.

The Economy

Carter approached economic problems inconsistently. In 1978, he proposed voluntary wage and price guidelines. Although somewhat successful, the guidelines did not apply to oil, housing, and food. Carter then named Paul A. Volcker as chairman of the Federal Reserve Board. Volcker tightened the money supply in order to reduce inflation, but this action caused interest rates to go even higher. High interest rates depressed sales of automobiles and houses, which in turn increased unemployment. By 1980, unemployment stood at 7.5 percent, interest at 20 percent, and inflation at 12 percent.

Domestic Achievements

Carter offered amnesty to Americans who had fled the draft and gone to other countries during the Vietnam War. He established the Departments of Energy and Education and placed the civil service on a merit basis. He created a "superfund" for cleanup of chemical waste dumps, established controls over strip mining, and protected 100 million acres of Alaskan wilderness from development.

Carter's Foreign Policy

Human Rights

Carter sought to base foreign policy on human rights, but was criticized for inconsistency and lack of attention to American interests.

President Jimmy Carter, 1977.

Panama Canal

Carter negotiated a controversial treaty with Panama, affirmed by the Senate in 1978, that provided for the transfer of ownership of the canal to Panama in 1999 and guaranteed its neutrality.

China

Carter ended official recognition of Taiwan and in 1979 recognized the People's Republic of China. Conservatives called the decision a "sell-out."

SALT II

In 1979, Carter signed the Strategic Arms Limitation Treaty II with the Soviet Union. The treaty set a ceiling of 2,250 bombers and missiles for each side, and set limits on warheads and new weapons systems. It never reached the Senate floor.

Camp David Accords

In 1978, Carter negotiated the Camp David Accords between Israel and Egypt. Bringing Anwar Sadat, president of Egypt, and Menachem Begin, prime minister of Israel, to Camp David, Maryland, for two weeks in September 1978, Carter sought to end the state of war that existed between the two countries. Israel promised to return occupied land in the Sinai to Egypt in exchange for Egyptian recognition, a process completed in 1982. An agreement to negotiate the Palestinian refugee problem proved ineffective.

Afghanistan

The policy of detente went into decline. Carter criticized Soviet restrictions on political freedom and reluctance to allow dissidents and Jews to emigrate. In December 1979, the Soviet Union invaded Afghanistan. In response, Carter stopped shipments of grain and technology to the Soviets, withdrew his support for SALT II, and barred Americans from competing in the 1980 Moscow Summer Olympics.

The Iranian Crisis

The Iranian Revolution

In 1978 a revolution forced the shah of Iran to flee the country, replacing him with a religious leader Ayatollah Ruhollah Khomeini. Because the United States had supported the shah with arms and money, the revolutionaries were strongly anti-American, calling the United States the "Great Satan."

Hostages

After Carter allowed the exiled shah to come to the United States for medical treatment in October 1979, some 400 Iranians broke into the American embassy in Teheran on November 4, taking the occupants captive. They demanded that the shah be returned to Iran for trial and that his wealth be confiscated and given to Iran. Carter rejected these demands; instead, he froze Iranian assets in the United States and established a trade embargo against Iran. He also appealed to the United Nations and the World Court. The Iranians eventually freed the African-American and women hostages, but kept fifty-two others.

In April 1980, Carter ordered a marine rescue attempt, but it collapsed after several helicopters broke down and another crashed, killing eight men. Secretary of State Cyrus Vance resigned in protest before the raid began, and Carter was widely criticized for its failure.

The Election of 1980

The Democrats

Carter, whose approval rating in public opinion polls had dropped to about twenty-five percent in 1979, successfully withstood a challenge from Senator Edward M. Kennedy of Massachusetts for the Democratic presidential nomination.

The Republicans

The Republicans nominated Ronald Reagan of California, who had narrowly lost the 1976 nomination and was the leading spokesman for American conservatism. Reagan chose George Bush, a New Englander transplanted to Texas and former CIA director, as his vice presidential candidate. One of Reagan's opponents, Congressman John Anderson of Illinois, continued his presidential campaign on a third-party ticket.

The Campaign

While Carter defended his record, Reagan heavily favored increased defense spending, but also called for reductions in government spending and taxes. Reagan talked of granting more power to the states. He advocated what were coming to be called traditional values—family, religion, hard work, and patriotism.

Reagan's Victory

Reagan won by a large electoral majority, and the Republicans gained control of the Senate and increased their representation in the House.

American Hostages

After extensive negotiations with Iran, in which Algeria acted as an intermediary, Carter released Iranian assets and the hostages were freed on January 20, 1981—the day of Reagan's inaugural. It had been 444 days since they had been taken captive.

The Reagan Presidency: Attacking Big Government

Tax Policy

An ideological though pragmatic conservative, Ronald Reagan acted quickly and forcefully to change the direction of government policy.

President Ronald Reagan at a political rally (1982).

He placed priority on cutting taxes. His approach was based on "supply-side" economics, the idea that if government left more money in the hands of the people, they would invest rather than spend the excess on consumer goods. The results would be greater production, more jobs, and greater prosperity, and thus more income for the government despite lower tax rates.

Economic Recovery Tax Act

Reagan asked for a thirty percent tax cut, and despite fears of inflation on the part of Congress, in August 1983 obtained a twenty-five percent cut, spread over three years. The percentage was the same for everyone; hence, high-income people received greater savings than middle- and low-income individuals. To encourage investment, capital gains, gift, and inheritance taxes were reduced and business taxes liberalized. Anyone with earned income was also allowed to invest up to $2,000 a year in an Individual Retirement Account (IRA), deferring all taxes on both the principal and its earnings until retirement.

Government Spending

Congress passed the Budget Reconciliation Act in 1981, cutting $39 billion from domestic programs, including education, food stamps, public housing, and the National Endowments for the Arts and Humanities. While cutting domestic programs, Reagan increased the defense budget by $12 billion.

SDI

Reagan concentrated on obtaining funding for the development of a computer-controlled Strategic Defense Initiative (SDI) system, dubbed by the press "Star Wars" after the movie of that name. SDI would destroy incoming enemy missiles from outer space. Skeptical about its technological feasibility and fearful of enormous costs, Congress balked and scaled back the proposal during Reagan's second term.

Increasing Revenue

Because of rising deficits, Reagan and Congress increased taxes in various ways. The 1982 Tax Equity and Fiscal Responsibility Act reversed some concessions made to business in 1981. Social Security benefits became taxable income in 1983. In 1984, the Deficit Reduction Act increased taxes by another $50 billion. But the deficit continued to increase.

Assassination Attempt

John W. Hinckley shot Reagan in the chest on March 30, 1981. The president was wounded but made a swift recovery. His popularity increased, possibly helping his legislative program.

Antitrust

Reagan ended ongoing antitrust suits against IBM and AT&T, thereby fulfilling his promise to reduce government interference with business.

Women and Minorities

Although Reagan appointed Sandra Day O'Connor to the Supreme Court, his administration gave fewer of its appointments to women and minorities than had the Carter administration. The Reagan administration also opposed "equal pay for equal work" and renewal of the Voting Rights Act of 1965.

Problems with Appointed Officials

A number of Reagan appointees were accused of conflict of interest, including Anne Gorsuch Burford and Rita Lavelle of the Environmental Protection Agency, Edwin Meese, presidential advisor and later attorney general, and Michael Deaver, the deputy chief of staff. Ray Donovan, secretary of labor, was indicted but later acquitted of charges that he had made payoffs to government officials while he was in private business. By the end of Reagan's term, more than 100 of his officials had been accused of questionable activities.

Asserting American Power

Soviet Union

Reagan took a hard line against the Soviet Union, calling it an "evil empire." He placed new cruise missiles in Europe, despite considerable opposition from Europeans.

Election of 1984

The Democrats

Walter Mondale, a former senator from Minnesota and vice president under Carter, won the Democratic nomination over Senator Gary Hart and Jesse Jackson, an African American civil-rights leader. Mondale chose Geraldine Ferraro, a congresswoman from New York, as his running mate. Mondale criticized Reagan for his budget deficits, high unemployment and interest rates, and reduction of spending on social services.

The Reagan Victory

The Republicans renominated Ronald Reagan and George Bush. Reagan drew support from groups such as the Moral Majority, founded by Fundamentalist evangelist Jerry Falwell. (The Fundamentalists had become a major political presence, voicing opposition to abortion, advocating an amendment to allow prayer in public schools, and identifying with the cause of Israel and a strong military defense budget.) Reagan's appeal also derived from an in-your-face anti-Soviet stance and decreased inflation, interest rates, and unemployment during his watch. He defeated Mondale handily, gaining nearly sixty percent of the vote by breaking apart the Democratic coalition of industrial workers, farmers, and the poor that had existed since FDR's time. Yet, his coattails proved short: the GOP lost two seats in the Senate and gained little in the House.

Second-Term Foreign Concerns

Libya

Reagan challenged Mu'ammar al-Qadhafi, the anti-American leader of Libya, by sending Sixth Fleet ships within the Gulf of Sidra, which Qadhafi claimed. When Libyan gunboats challenged the American ships, American planes destroyed the gunboats and bombed installations on the Libyan shoreline. Soon after, a West German night club popular among American servicemen was bombed, killing a soldier and a civilian. Reagan, believing the bombing was ordered directly by Qadhafi, launched an air strike from Great Britain against Libyan bases in April 1986.

Soviet Union

After Mikhail S. Gorbachev became the premier of the Soviet Union in March 1985 and took a more flexible approach toward both domestic and foreign affairs, Reagan softened his anti-Soviet stance. But despite the Soviets' assurances that they would honor the unratified SALT II agreement, Reagan argued that they in fact had not adhered to the pact; as a result, he sought to expand and modernize the American defense system.

Arms Control

Reagan and Gorbachev had difficulty reaching an agreement on arms limitations at summit talks in 1985 and 1986. Finally, in December 1987, they signed an agreement eliminating medium-range missiles from Europe.

Iran-Contra

Near the end of 1986, a scandal arose involving William Casey, head of the CIA, Lieutenant Colonel Oliver North of the National Security Council, Admiral John Poindexter, national security advisor, and Robert McFarlane, former national security advisor. In 1985 and 1986, they had sold arms to the Iranians in hopes of encouraging them to use their influence in getting American hostages in Lebanon released. The profits from these sales were then diverted to the Nicaraguan *Contras* in an attempt to get around congressional restrictions on funding the *Contras*. The president was forced to appoint a special prosecutor, and Congress held hearings on the affair in May 1987.

Nicaragua

The Reagan administration did not support a peace plan signed by five Central American nations in 1987, but the following year the *Sandinistas* and the *Contras* agreed on a cease-fire.

Second-Term Domestic Affairs

Tax Reform

The Tax Reform Act of 1986 lowered tax rates, changing the highest rate on personal income from fifty percent to twenty-eight percent and on corporate taxes from forty-six percent to thirty-four percent. At the same time, it removed many tax shelters and tax credits. The law did away with the concept of progressive taxation, the requirement that the percentage of income taxed increased as income increased. Instead, over a two-year period, it established two rates, fifteen percent on incomes below $17,850 for individuals and $29,750 for families and twenty-eight percent on incomes above these amounts. The tax system would no longer be used as an instrument of social policy.

Economic Patterns

Unemployment declined, reaching 6.6 percent in 1986, while inflation fell as low as 2.2 percent during the first quarter of that year. The stock market was bullish through mid-1987.

Agriculture

With the general slowing of inflation and the decline of world agricultural prices, many American farmers began to descend into bankruptcy in the mid-1980s, often dragging the rural banks that had made them the loans into bankruptcy as well. Although it lifted the ban on wheat exports to the Soviet Union, the Reagan administration reduced price supports and opposed debt relief passed by Congress.

Deficits

The federal deficit reached $179 billion in 1985. At about the same time, the United States experienced trade deficits of more than $100 billion annually, partly because management and engineering skills had fallen behind Japan and Germany, and partly because the United States provided an open market to foreign businesses. In the mid-1980s, the United States became a debtor nation for the first time since World War I. Consumer debt also rose from $300 billion in 1980 to $500 billion in 1986.

Black Monday

On October 19, 1987, labeled "Black Monday" on Wall Street, the Dow Jones Industrial Average dropped more than 500 points, or over twenty percent. Between August 25 and October 20, the market lost over a trillion dollars in paper value. Fearing a recession, Congress in November 1987 reduced 1988 taxes by $30 billion.

NASA Tragedy

The explosion of the space shuttle *Challenger* soon after liftoff on January 28, 1986, damaged NASA's credibility and reinforced doubts about the complex technology required to implement the Strategic Defense Initiative. All aboard perished, including a New Hampshire teacher who was the first private citizen to go into space.

Supreme Court

Reagan reshaped the court. In 1986, he replaced Chief Justice Warren C. Burger with Associate Justice William H. Rehnquist, probably the most conservative member of the court. Although failing in his nomination of Robert Bork for associate justice, Reagan successfully appointed other conservatives to the court: Sandra Day O'Connor, Antonin Scalia, and Anthony Kennedy.

Election of 1988

The Candidates

After a sex scandal eliminated Senator Gary Hart from the race for the Democratic presidential nomination, Governor Michael Dukakis of Massachusetts emerged as the victor over his major challenger, Jesse Jackson (see below). He chose Senator Lloyd Bentsen of Texas as his vice presidential running mate. Vice President George Bush, after a slow start in the primaries, won the Republican nomination. He chose Senator Dan Quayle of Indiana as his running mate. Bush easily defeated Dukakis, but the Republicans were unable to make any inroads in Congress.

For African Americans in Politics, Progress Hits a Glass Ceiling

Civil-rights leader, Baptist minister, and politician Jesse Jackson was the first black man to make a serious bid for the U.S. presidency—in the Democratic Party's nomination races in 1983–1984 and 1987–1988. Before him, Shirley Chisholm, who in 1968 had become the first black woman elected to the U.S. Congress, made a bid for the Democratic nomination for U.S. president in 1972, winning 152 delegates before withdrawing from the race. After taking up residency in Washington, D.C., Jackson attained elective office when, in 1990, the Washington City Council created two unpaid offices of "statehood senator"—better known as "shadow senator"—to lobby Congress for statehood for the District of Columbia. Fusing the church pulpit with the bully pulpit, he has been effective not just in articulating the needs of blacks but of the underprivileged class in general. An associate of the Rev. Dr. Martin Luther King, Jr., Jackson went on to found Operation PUSH (People United to Save Humanity), a Chicago-based organization that advocated black self-help and gave him a platform for his liberal views. A Jackson-led voter-registration drive was key to the election of Harold Washington as Chicago's first black mayor in April 1983. New York, Los Angeles, Cleveland, Baltimore, Atlanta, and Washington, D.C., also elected black mayors in the last two decades of the twentieth century. Overall, as the century wound down, more blacks were gaining local office, but seldom were they winning statewide elections. According to the Joint Center for Political and Economic Studies, a Washington, D.C., think tank that researches the political and economic conditions of black Americans, the U.S. had 8,868 black elected officials (including Jackson's own son, Rep. Jesse L. Jackson, Jr., of Illinois) in 1998, up 212 from the year before. That number, however, accounted for only 1.7% of all officials holding elective office in the U.S. Some states, such as Colorado, Georgia, Illinois, and Ohio, have elected black lieutenant governors and state attorneys general, but none has had a black governor since L. Douglas Wilder, the grandson of slaves, left the governor's mansion in Virginia in January 1994. His victory in that state's 1989 gubernatorial election made him the first elected black governor in the United States.

Bush Abandons Reaganomics

Budget Deficit

Soon after George Bush took office as president on January 20, 1989, the budget deficit for 1990 was estimated at $143 billion. With deficit estimates continuing to grow, Bush held a "budget summit" with congressional leaders in May 1990, and his administration continued talks throughout the summer. In September, the administration and Congress agreed to increase taxes on gasoline, tobacco, and alcohol, establish an excise tax on luxury items, and raise Medicare taxes. Cuts were also to be made in Medicare and other domestic programs. The 1991 deficit was now estimated to be over $290 billion. The following month, Congress approved the plan, hoping to cut a cumulative amount of $500 billion from the deficit over the next five years. In a straight party vote—Republicans voting against and Democrats voting in favor—Congress in December gave the power to decide whether new tax and spending proposals violated the deficit-cutting agreement to the Congressional Budget office. This power had been in the hands of the White House Office of Management and Budget.

Savings and Loan Debacle

With the savings and loan industry in financial trouble in February 1989, largely because of bad real-estate loans, Bush proposed to close or sell 350 institutions, to be paid for by the sale of government bonds. In July he signed a bill that created the Resolution Trust Corporation to oversee the closure and merging of savings and loans, and that provided $166 billion over ten years to cover the bad debts. Estimates of the total cost of the debacle ran upward of $300 billion.

Scandals in the Financial Markets

Charges of insider trading, stock manipulation, and falsification of records resulted in Drexel Burnham Lambert, a major securities firm, pleading guilty in December 1988 to six violations of federal law. The company filed for bankruptcy and Michael Milken, its "junk bond king" (junk bonds are bonds below an investment grade of BB or Bb, which because of their risk carry a two- to three-point interest advantage), pleaded guilty to conspiracy, among other charges, in 1990. Meanwhile, in July 1989, forty-six futures traders at the Chicago Mercantile Exchange were charged with racketeering.

Economic Slowdown

The gross national product slowed from 4.4 percent in 1988 to 2.9 percent in 1989. Unemployment gradually began to increase, reaching 6.8 percent in March 1991, a three-year high. Every sector of the economy except for medical services and all geographical areas experienced the slowdown. The "Big Three" automakers posted record losses and Pan American World Airways and Eastern Airlines entered bankruptcy proceedings. In September 1991, the Federal Reserve lowered the interest rate.

Other Domestic Issues Under Bush

Exxon Valdez

After the *Exxon Valdez* spilled more than 240,000 barrels of oil into Alaska's Prince William Sound in March 1989, the federal government ordered Exxon Corporation to develop a clean-up plan, which it carried out until the weather prevented it from continuing in September. The *Valdez* captain, Joseph Hazelwood, was found guilty of negligence the following year. Exxon, the state of Alaska, and the U.S. Justice Department reached a settlement in October 1991 requiring Exxon to pay $1.025 billion in fines and restitution through 2001.

Congressional Ethics Violations

After the House Ethics Committee released a report charging that Speaker Jim Wright had violated rules regulating acceptance of gifts and outside income, Wright resigned in May 1989. A short time later, the Democratic whip Tony Coelho resigned because of alleged improper use of campaign funds.

Pollution

The Clean Air Act, passed in October 1990 and updating the 1970 law, mandated that the level of emissions was to be reduced fifty percent by the year 2000. Cleaner gasolines were to be developed, cities were to reduce ozone (an ingredient in photo-chemical smog), and nitrogen oxide emissions were to be cut by one-third.

Civil Rights

The Americans with Disabilities Act, passed in July 1990, barred discrimination against people with physical or mental disabilities. In October 1990, Bush vetoed the Civil Rights Act on the grounds that it established quotas, but a year later he accepted a slightly revised version that, among other things, required that employers in discrimination suits prove that their hiring practices are not discriminatory.

Supreme Court Appointments

Bush continued to reshape the Supreme Court in a conservative direction when, upon the retirement of Justice William J. Brennan, he successfully nominated Judge David Souter of the U.S. Court of Appeals in 1989. Two years later, Bush nominated a conservative African American, Judge Clarence Thomas, also of the U.S. Court of Appeals, upon the retirement of Justice Thurgood Marshall. Thomas's nomination stirred up opposition from the NAACP and other liberal groups, which supported affirmative action and abortion rights. Dramatic charges of sexual harassment against Thomas from Anita Hill, a University of Oklahoma law professor, were revealed only days before the nomination was to go to the Senate. The charges provoked a reopening of Judiciary Committee hearings, which were nationally televised. Nonetheless, Thomas narrowly won confirmation in October 1991.

Bush's Activist Foreign Policy

Panama

Since coming to office, the Bush administration had been concerned with Panamanian dictator Manuel Noriega because he allegedly provided an important link in the drug traffic between South America and the United States. After economic sanctions, diplomatic efforts, and an October 1989 coup failed to oust Noriega, Bush ordered 12,000 troops into Panama on December 20. The Americans installed a new government headed by Guillermo Endara, who had earlier won a presidential election that was then nullified by Noriega. On January 3, 1990, Noriega surrendered to the Americans and was taken to the United States to stand trial on drug-trafficking charges, a trial that began in September 1991. Found guilty in 1992, he was sentenced to forty years' imprisonment. Twenty-three United States soldiers and three American civilians were killed in the Panamanian operation. The Panamanians lost nearly 300 soldiers and more than 500 civilians.

China

After the death in April 1989 of reformer Hu Yaobang, formerly general secretary and chairman of the Chinese Communist Party, students began prodemocracy marches in Beijing. By the middle of May, more than one million people were gathering in Beijing's Tiananmen Square and elsewhere in China, calling for political reform. Martial law was imposed and in early June the army fired on the demonstrators. Estimates of the death toll in the wake of the nationwide crackdown on demonstrators ranged between 500 and 7,000. In July 1989, U.S. National Security Advisor Brent Scowcroft and Deputy Secretary of State Lawrence Eagleburger secretly met with Chinese leaders. When they again met the Chinese in December and revealed their earlier meeting, the Bush administration faced a storm of criticism for its policy of "constructive engagement" from opponents arguing that sanctions were needed. Although establishing sanctions on China in 1991 on high-technology satellite-part exports, Bush continued to support renewal of China's Most Favored Nation trading status.

Collapse of East European Communism

Bush-Gorbachev Summits

Amid the collapse of communism in Eastern Europe, Bush met with Mikhail Gorbachev in Malta from December 1 through 3, 1989; the two leaders appeared to agree that the Cold War was over. On May 30 and 31, 1990, Bush and Gorbachev met in Washington to discuss the possible reunification of Germany and signed a trade treaty between the United States and the Soviet Union. The meeting of the two leaders in Helsinki on September 9 addressed strategies for the developing Persian Gulf crisis. At the meeting of the "Group of 7" nations (Canada, France, Germany, Italy, Japan, the United Kingdom, and the United States) in July 1991, Gorbachev requested economic aid from the West. A short time later, on July 30 and 31, Bush met Gorbachev in Moscow, where they signed the Strategic Arms Reduction Treaty (START), which cut United States and Soviet nuclear arsenals by thirty percent, and pushed for Middle Eastern talks.

President George H.W. Bush with troops in the Gulf War.

Persian Gulf Crisis

July 1990: Saddam Hussein of Iraq charged that Kuwait had conspired with the United States to keep oil prices low and began massing troops at the Iraq-Kuwait border.

August 1990: On August 2, Iraq invaded Kuwait, an act that Bush denounced as "naked aggression." One day later, 100,000 Iraqi soldiers were poised south of Kuwait City, near the Saudi Arabian border. The United States quickly banned most trade with Iraq, froze Iraq's and Kuwait's assets in the United States, and sent aircraft carriers to the Persian Gulf. After the U.N. Security Council condemned the invasion, Bush on August 6 ordered the deployment of air, sea, and land forces to Saudi Arabia, dubbing the operation "Desert Shield." At the end of August, there were 100,000 American soldiers in Saudi Arabia.

September 1990: Bush encouraged Egypt to support American policy by forgiving Egypt its debt to the United States. He also obtained pledges of financial support from Saudi Arabia, Kuwait, and Japan, among other nations, to help pay for the operation.

October 1990: On October 29, the Security Council warned Hussein that further actions might be taken if he did not withdraw from Kuwait.

November 1990: In November, Bush ordered that U.S. forces be increased to more than 400,000. On November 29, the United Nations set January 15, 1991, as the deadline for Iraqi withdrawal from Kuwait.

January 1991: On January 9, Iraq's foreign minister, Tariq Aziz, rejected a letter written by Bush to Hussein. Three days later, after an extensive debate, Congress authorized the use of force in the Gulf. On January 17 an international force that included the U.S., Great Britain, France, Italy, Saudi Arabia, and Kuwait launched an air and missile attack on Iraq and occupied Kuwait. The United States called the effort "Operation Desert Storm." Under the overall command of the army's General H. Norman Schwarzkopf, the military effort emphasized high-technology weapons, including F-15E fighter bombers, F-117A stealth fighters, Tomahawk cruise missiles, and Patriot antimissile missiles. Beginning on January 17, Iraq sent SCUD missiles into Israel in an effort to draw that country into the war and hopefully break up the U.S.-Arabian coalition. On January 22 and 23, Hussein's forces set Kuwaiti oil fields on fire and spilled oil into the gulf.

February 1991: On February 23, the allied ground assault began. Four days later, Bush announced that Kuwait was liberated and ordered offensive operations to cease. The United Nations established the terms for the cease-fire: Iraqi annexation of Kuwait to be rescinded, Iraq to accept liability for damages and return Kuwaiti property, Iraq to end all military actions and identify mines and booby traps, and Iraq to release captives.

April 1991: On April 3, the Security Council approved a resolution to establish a permanent cease-fire; Iraq accepted U.N. terms on April 6. The next day the United States began airlifting food to Kurdish refugees on the Iraq-Turkey border who were fleeing the Kurdish rebellion against Hussein, a rebellion that was seemingly encouraged by Bush, who nonetheless refused to become militarily involved. The

United States estimated that 100,000 Iraqis had been killed during the war, while the Americans had lost about 115 lives.

Toward a Middle East Conference

On February 6, 1991, the United States had set out its postwar goals for the Middle East. These included regional arms control and security arrangements, international aid for reconstruction of Iraq and Kuwait, and resolution of the Israeli-Palestinian conflict. Immediately after cessation of the conflict, Secretary of State James Baker toured the Middle East attempting to promote a conference to address the problems of the region. After several more negotiating sessions, Saudi Arabia, Syria, Jordan, and Lebanon had accepted the United States proposal for an Arab-Israeli peace conference by the middle of July; Israel conditionally accepted in early August. Despite continuing conflict with Iraq, including U.N. inspections of its nuclear capabilities, and new Israeli settlements in disputed territory which kept the conference agreement tenuous, the nations met in Madrid, Spain, at the end of October. Bilateral talks in early November between Israel and the Arabs concentrated on procedural issues.

Breakup of the Soviet Union

Collapse of Soviet Communism and the End of the Cold War

The Soviet Union began to break up in 1990, when Lithuania declared its independence. In the aftermath of an attemped coup by hardline Communists later that year, other Soviet republics followed suit. For the United States, the collapse of the U.S.S.R. meant that the Cold War, which had begun in 1945, was finally over. The United States was now the world's only superpower. In September 1991, President Bush announced that the U.S. would carry out the unilateral removal and destruction of ground-based tactical nuclear weapons in Europe and Asia, removal of nuclear-armed Tomahawk cruise missiles from surface ships and submarines, immediate destruction of intercontinental ballistic missiles covered by the START treaty, and an end to the twenty-four-hour alert for strategic bombers, which the United States had maintained for decades. Gorbachev responded the next month by announcing the immediate deactivation of intercontinental ballistic missiles covered by START, removal of all short-range missiles from Soviet ships, submarines, and aircraft, and destruction of all ground-based tactical nuclear weapons. He also said that the Soviet Union would reduce its forces by 700,000 troops, and he placed all long-range nuclear missiles under a single command.

New foreign policy challenges emerged, however. Yugoslavia broke up into several different nations, and the region was plunged into a brutal war. Conflict threatened other parts of the world as well. The disintegration of the Soviet Union meant more nations had nuclear weapons, as several of the former Soviet republics had access to them.

The Election of 1992

William Jefferson Clinton, governor of Arkansas, overcame several rivals and won the Democratic presidential nomination, choosing Senator Al Gore of Tennessee as his candidate for vice president. Clinton and Reform Party candidate H. Ross Perot emphasized jobs and the economy, as well as the debt. Bush stressed traditional values and his foreign policy accomplishments. In the general election, Clinton won forty-three percent of the popular vote and 370 electoral votes, thereby defeating George Bush, who received thirty-eight percent of the vote, and independent candidate Ross Perot, who took nineteen percent of the vote but no electoral votes.

Rocky Start: Upon taking office, Clinton created a storm of protest when he proposed lifting the ban on homosexuals in the military. In July 1993, a compromise "Don't ask, don't tell" policy was struck, requiring gays and lesbians to be discreet about their sexual orientation and not to engage in homosexual acts. On the legislative front, Clinton was strongly rebuffed in a first-term attempt, led by the First Lady, to comprehensively reform the nation's healthcare system. In the 1994 mid-term elections, in what Clinton himself considered a repudiation of his administration, the Republicans took both houses of Congress from the Democrats and voted in Newt Gingrich of Georgia as Speaker of the House. Gingrich had helped craft the Republican congressional campaign strategy to dramatically shrink the federal government and give more power to the states.

Clinton, however, was not without his successes, both on the legislative and diplomatic fronts. He signed a bill establishing a five-day waiting period for handgun purchases, and he signed an anticrime bill emphasizing community policing. He signed the Family and Medical Leave Act, which required large companies to provide up to twelve weeks' unpaid leave to workers for family and medical emergencies. He also championed welfare reform (a central theme of his campaign), but made it clear that the legislation he signed into law in August 1996 radically overhauling FDR's welfare system disturbed him on two counts—its exclusion of legal immigrants from getting most federal benefits and its deep cut in federal outlays for food stamps; Clinton said these flaws could be repaired with further legislation. In foreign affairs, Clinton signed the North American Free Trade Agreement (NAFTA), which, as of January 1994, lifted most trade barriers with Mexico and Canada. Clinton sought to ease tensions between Israelis and Palestinians, and he helped bring together Itzhak Rabin, prime minister of Israel, and Yasir Arafat, chairman of the Palestine Liberation Organization, for a White House summit. Ultimately, the two Middle East leaders signed a 1994 accord establishing Palestinian self-rule in the Gaza Strip and Jericho. In October 1994, Israel and Jordan signed a treaty to begin the process of establishing full diplomatic relations. Rabin was assassinated a year later by a radical, right-wing Israeli. The Clinton administration also played a key role in hammering out a peace agreement in 1995 in war-torn former Yugoslavia—where armed conflict had broken out in 1991 between Serbs, Croats, Bosnian Muslims, and other factions and groups.

Controversy Swirls Around the President: The president came to be dogged by a number of controversies, including his and his wife's role in a complex Arkansas real estate deal called Whitewater, the removal of employees from the White House travel office, the suicide of Deputy White House Counsel Vince Foster, and a sexual harassment suit (later settled out of court) brought against the president by Paula Jones, a former Arkansas state employee. Whitewater spawned the Jus-

President Clinton and Russian President Yeltsin at private dinner in Russia.

tice Department's appointment of an independent counsel, Robert B. Fiske, to look into it. Fiske's successor, Kenneth W. Starr, would expand the scope of the investigation. (Congress ultimately soured on the independent counsel law—enacted as a kind of coda to Watergate—and allowed it to expire in mid-1999.)

The Election of 1996

Clinton recaptured the Democratic nomination without a serious challenge, while longtime GOP Senator Robert Dole of Kansas, the Senate majority leader, had to overcome several opponents but orchestrated a harmonious nominating convention with running mate Jack Kemp, a former New York congressman and Cabinet member during the Bush administration. In November 1996, with most voters citing a healthy economy and the lack of an enticing alternative in Dole or the Reform Party's Perot, Clinton received forty-nine percent of the vote (47 million popular votes and 379 electoral votes), becoming the first Democrat to be returned to the White House since FDR, in 1936. Dole won forty-one percent (39 million popular votes, 159 electoral votes) and Perot polled eight percent of the total (8 million popular votes). The GOP retained control of both houses of Congress.

The Election of 1998: In the congressional elections of 1998, the Democrats gained seats in both the House and the Senate. Seldom does the president's party gain seats in a mid-term election, so it was widely believed that this—in part—might have been backlash to the continued Republican-led prosecution of Clinton for alleged perjury and obstruction of justice.

Domestic Policy: Clinton sought a legacy as a preservationist by signing executive orders that set aside vast expanses of public lands, especially in the West.

Foreign Policy: During his second term, Clinton faced continued political unrest and civil war in the Balkans. In 1999 the Serbian government attacked ethnic Albanians in Kosovo, a province of Serbia. In response, NATO forces, led by the United States, bombed Serbia. Several weeks of bombing forced Serbian forces to withdraw from Kosovo. Meanwhile, Clinton was instrumental in bringing about a historic peace agreement in Northern Ireland, while the land-for-peace accord he tried to broker between the Palestinians and Israel proved elusive. Clinton also continued to seek a policy of expanding international trade by relaxing or eliminating trade barriers.

Campaign Finance Reform Fails to Pass: Though the issue of the influence of money on politics was not new, increasingly high levels of campaign spending and the contributions necessary to make such spending possible began to receive significant attention. Several bills were proposed in Congress, and Clinton pledged to support reform; by the end of his presidency in January 2001, however, no bill had passed.

Historic Economic Boom Falters: As of February 1, 2000, the U.S. economy had enjoyed its longest stretch of uninterrupted growth in the nation's history. Much of this growth, which had begun in March 1991, was fueled by a new industry, electronic commerce on the Internet. Stock prices generally rose, but share prices for Internet companies rose especially fast, soaring to extraordinary heights. In 2000, investors came to see e-businesses' and high-tech stock prices as unreasonably high. A number of such stocks tumbled, with some losing as much as ninety percent of their value. Soon many formerly high-flying Internet companies were folding and by the close of 2000 the future of the surviving e-businesses, as well as the economy as a whole, was uncertain.

Impeachment and Acquittal: In December 1998, Clinton was impeached by the House and in January and February 1999, he was tried and acquitted by the Senate on charges that he had lied about an adulterous affair with a White House intern. The affair had been uncovered by Starr.

The Election of 2000

The Democrats nominated Vice President Al Gore for president and Senator Joseph Lieberman for vice president. The Republican Party nominated Texas Governor George W. Bush (son of President George Bush). After some conflict, the Reform Party nominated Patrick Buchanan. The Green Party ran Ralph Nader. After one of the tightest presidential elections ever, highlighted by a withdrawn initial concession by Gore, a recount in Florida, and several court challenges, Bush was declared the winner.

American Society at the Dawn of the Twenty-First Century

Terrorism Hits Home: Major symbols of U.S. economic and military might—the World Trade Center in New York and the Pentagon just outside Washington, D.C.—were attacked on September 11, 2001, when hijackers deliberately crashed commercial jetliners into the buildings, toppling the trade center's 110-story twin towers. Thousands died in the worst act of terrorism in American history. The prime suspect, said President Bush, was Saudi exile Osama bin Laden, the alleged mastermind of previous attacks on U.S. interests overseas. Terrorist attacks had continued to be a grim reality overseas through the 1980s and early 1990s, with Americans frequently targeted. Yet such incidents had come to be viewed as something the United States wouldn't have to face on its own soil—until February 26, 1993, when a terrorist bomb ripped through the underground parking garage of the World Trade Center in New York City, killing six people and injuring more than 1,000. Convicted and sentenced to 240 years each were four Islamic militants. On April 19, 1995, the Oklahoma City federal building was bombed, killing 168 people and injuring 500. Timothy James McVeigh, a member of the American militia movement who had expressed hatred toward the U.S. government and was aggrieved over its assault two years earlier on a self-proclaimed prophet's compound in Waco, Texas, was put to death for the crime in June 2001. A second defendant, Terry Nichols, was convicted on federal charges of conspiracy and involuntary manslaughter and sentenced to life in prison.

The Iraq War: Claiming that Saddam Hussein harbored weapons of mass destruction (WMDs) and was connected with al Qaeda, the George W. Bush administration launched a preemptive war against Iraq on March 20, 2003. Although about thirty nations joined what was often referred to as the "coalition forces," only the United States and Great Britain contributed substantial numbers of soldiers. Initial military victory was swift, with the Hussein regime falling by April 9; Bush declared an end to major combat operations on May 1. The military was unable to find the WMDs, however, and it was ultimately concluded that prewar intelligence had been wrong. Despite the apparent victory of the coalition forces, armed opposition appeared almost immediately. Using such methods as traditional warfare, suicide bombings, remote-controlled bombs, and kidnappings, the insurgents were particularly strong in the "Sunni Triangle," an area roughly defined as a triangle with points at Baghdad (to the east), Tikrit (to the north), and Ramadi (to the west). The city of Fallujah became a resistance stronghold under the leadership of Abu Musab al-Zarqawi, a Jordanian, until American forces drove the rebels out in November 2004. Meanwhile, the Bush administration's decision to go to war and its handling of the conflict became an issue in the 2004 presidential election.

The Presidential Election of 2004: After a series of primary victories, Senator John F. Kerry of Massachusetts won the Democratic nomination for president and chose a former rival, Senator John R. Edwards

**President George W. Bush and First Lady Laura Bush
observe a moment of silence after the 9/11 terrorist attacks.**

of South Carolina, as his vice presidential running mate. The Republicans renewed their nomination of President George W. Bush and Vice President Richard B. Cheney. Kerry challenged Bush's economic policy and his handling of the Iraq War. In turn, Bush described Kerry as a liberal who favored high taxes and as a "flip-flopper" who could not be trusted with the nation's security; Bush presented himself, in contrast, as one who would provide firm leadership against terrorism. As in 2000, Ralph Nader ran a third party campaign, but had little effect on the election's outcome. Bush won the popular vote with 51 percent (to Kerry's 48 percent). He carried all states except those on the Pacific Coast, in the upper Midwest, and in the Northeast, thereby gaining 286 electoral votes to Kerry's 252. Republicans increased their control of both houses of Congress (they had regained the Senate in 2002). Although international issues dominated the campaign, exit polls suggested that moral values played a significant role among those who supported George W. Bush, many of whom described themselves as evangelical Christians. Not surprisingly, referendums opposing gay marriages, which had emerged as an issue partly because of recent judicial decisions, passed in all eleven states where they appeared on the ballot.

A Modern Plague Descends on America: In 1981 scientists announced the discovery of Acquired Immune Deficiency Syndrome, or AIDS, which was especially prevalent among—but not confined to—homosexual males and intravenous drug users. Widespread fear resulted, with an upsurge in homophobia. The revelation that a Florida dentist, who died in 1990, had transmitted human immunodeficiency virus, or HIV, to six patients led to calls for mandatory testing of healthcare workers. There were calls as well for fast-tracking drug approvals. In 1998 the federal Centers for Disease Control and Prevention estimated that between 400,000 and 650,000 Americans were HIV-positive, meaning that they had the virus that causes AIDS.

Urban America Rebounds: America's cities showed renewed promise at the dawn of the new century—though much remained to be done to attack a host of social and economic ills. *The Economist* reported in January 1998 that unemployment in the fifty biggest cities had fallen by a third over the prior four years, to about six percent. Rates for serious crime fell to their lowest in a generation. Cities such as New York—which two decades before had nearly gone bankrupt—and Los Angeles, victim of race riots and an earthquake during the early and mid-'90s, were "growing in both population and confidence." There were also comebacks like that of New Brunswick, N.J. Moribund in the 1970s, it forged a public–private partnership that resulted in more than $1 billion in investments over twenty-five years. In 1999 this city of 42,000 boasted a vibrant downtown (with small-business loans awarded to city-based businesses topping $1.2 million), a jobless rate of 6.6% (down from as high as 11.8% in 1993), a 34% drop in crime since 1991 for which so-called community policing got much of the credit, and the U.S. Department of Education's coveted Blue Ribbon Award for one of its elementary schools.

Writers Explore the Kaleidoscope of U.S. Life: The 1980s and 1990s saw the emergence of writers who threw light on various, sometimes hidden, facets of national life—from the immigrant experience as told by Amy Tan in *The Joy-Luck Club* (1989) and Oscar Hijuelos in

The Mambo Kings Play Songs of Love (1990) to Tom Wolfe's satirical take on greed and class and racial tensions in New York City in *The Bonfire of the Vanities* (1987) and, later, his look behind the patina of Deep South gentility in *A Man in Full* (1998). Toni Morrison's *Beloved* (1987) dramatized the African-American slave experience.

The U.S. Counts Its People: The 2000 decennial census counted 281,421,906 Americans, a 13.2% increase since 1990. The most populous state was California (33,871,648), the least populous, Wyoming (493,782).

Election of 2008

Democrat Barack Obama's victory over his Republican challenger, fellow U.S. Senator John McCain, in the 2008 presidential election marked a milestone in a number of ways. It shattered the record of campaign contributions received by a candidate when the Obama campaign raised more than $640 million. It also brought to the White House the first president born after the civil rights protests and reforms of the 1960s.

In the end, however, the main message inevitably comes back to the racial barrier that was broken. Two hundred thirty-two years after the nation's founding and 143 years after the 15th Amendment to the United States Constitution extended voting rights to blacks, a black man ascended to the presidency.

In this first year in office, Obama at once faced dire economic woes as the nation sank into recession and continued to wage war in Iraq and Afghanistan, even as he pursued a historic plan for health insurance reform to create a safety net for the many Americans without adequate or any coverage.

Along the way, in October 2009, in only his tenth month in office, he was awarded the Nobel Peace Prize, which he said he preferred to view not "as a recognition of my own accomplishments, but rather as an affirmation of American leadership on behalf of aspirations held by people in all nations."

Quiz: Chapters 13 and 14

1. Which of the following is true of the Gulf of Tonkin incident?

    (A) It involved a clash of U.S. and Soviet warships.

    (B) In it, two North Vietnamese fighter-bombers were shot down as they neared U.S. Navy ships.

    (C) It involved the seizure by North Vietnam of a U.S. Navy intelligence ship in international waters.

    (D) It led to major U.S. involvement in the Vietnam War.

    (E) In it, a U.S. Navy destroyer was damaged by a guided missile fired by a North Vietnamese plane.

2. The Bay of Pigs incident involved

    (A) the presence of Soviet nuclear missiles in Cuba.

    (B) a CIA plot to overthrow Chilean leader Salvador Allende.

    (C) a confrontation between U.S. and Soviet troops in Europe.

    (D) a clash between a U.S. Navy destroyer and North Vietnamese patrol boats.

    (E) a U.S.-sponsored attempt by free Cubans to overthrow Communist dictator Fidel Castro.

3. Which of the following best describes the methods advocated by Malcolm X?

    (A) Nonviolent defiance of segregation

    (B)   Armed violence against police and troops

    (C)   Patience while developing the skills that would make blacks economically successful and gain them the respect of whites

    (D)   Gradual assimilation of the two races until they became indistinguishable

    (E)   Meek acceptance of "Jim Crowism" until increasingly enlightened Southern whites were prepared to change it

4.   The American Hostage Crisis in Iran was precipitated by

    (A)   the American government allowing the deposed Shah of Iran to come to the United States for cancer treatment.

    (B)   Jimmy Carter's involvement in arranging the Camp David accords between the Egyptians and the Israelis.

    (C)   American air strikes against Iran's ally, Libya.

    (D)   American support for Israel's 1980 invasion of southern Lebanon.

    (E)   American attempts to overthrow the newly emplaced government of Ayatollah Khomeini.

5.   Actions taken by the United States in response to Iraq's invasion of Kuwait in August 1990 included all of the following EXCEPT

    (A)   U.N. coordination.

    (B)   protection of Saudi Arabia.

    (C)   imposing economic sanctions.

    (D)   Operation Desert Shield.

    (E)   immediate military response.

6.   Reaganomics is most closely associated with

    (A)   the "trickle-down" theory.

    (B)   the "controlled growth" theory.

    (C)   the "bubble up" theory.

    (D)   New Deal reform economics.

    (E)   Fair Deal progressivist economics.

7.   The Watergate scandal led to Richard Nixon's downfall primarily because

    (A)   of his role in planning and coordinating the Watergate break-in and other illegal campaign activity.

    (B)   the press, the Democrats, and some liberal Republicans united to rid themselves of Nixon and his conservative philosophy.

    (C)   he was already so unpopular because of his Vietnam War policies that virtually anything he did wrong would have been used as an excuse to remove him from office.

    (D)   of his role in directing the cover-up of the Watergate Affair.

    (E)   of his involvement with organized crime in carrying out political "dirty tricks" against his Democratic opponent George McGovern.

8.   President Carter's administration had its greatest difficulties with its

    (A)   Central American policy.

    (B)   energy conservation policy.

    (C)   land conservation policy.

(D)   Middle East policy.

(E)   economic policy.

9.   The "War on Poverty" was an attempt by

(A)   President Richard Nixon to aid Latin American nations.

(B)   President Lyndon Johnson to end hunger and economic despair in America.

(C)   President John F. Kennedy to organize the Peace Corps.

(D)   George Marshall to feed the people of Europe after World War II.

(E)   President Dwight Eisenhower to reduce the number of people on public assistance.

10.   The first female justice named to the Supreme Court was

(A)   Ann Richards.

(B)   Ruth Bader Ginsberg.

(C)   Madeleine Albright.

(D)   Sandra Day O'Connor.

(E)   Dee Dee Meyers.

ANSWER KEY

1.	(D)	6.	(A)
2.	(E)	7.	(D)
3.	(B)	8.	(E)
4.	(A)	9.	(B)
5.	(E)	10.	(D)

DETAILED ANSWERS

1.　**(D)**　The Gulf of Tonkin Incident led to major U.S. involvement in the Vietnam War. In the Gulf of Sidra during the 1980s, two clashes occurred involving the shooting down of Libyan, not Vietnamese, jets approaching U.S. ships (B). Off the coast of North Korea in 1968, Korean, not Vietnamese, forces seized the U.S. Navy intelligence ship *Pueblo* (C). In an incident in the Persian Gulf in 1987, the U.S. Navy frigate, not destroyer, *Stark,* was struck by a guided missile fired by an Iraqi, not North Vietnamese, plane (E).

2.　**(E)**　The Bay of Pigs incident involved a U.S.-sponsored attempt by free Cubans to overthrow Communist dictator Fidel Castro. The presence of Soviet nuclear missiles in Cuba was at issue in the Cuban Missile Crisis (A). The CIA did, apparently, play a role in the 1973 overthrow of Chilean leader Salvador Allende (B) though this had no direct connection to the Bay of Pigs. The clash between a U.S. Navy destroyer and North Vietnamese patrol boats (D) was the Tonkin Gulf incident and related to the Vietnam War.

3. **(B)** Malcolm X advocated armed violence against police and troops. Nonviolent defiance of segregation (A) was the policy of Martin Luther King. Patience while developing the skills that would make blacks economically successful and gain them the respect of whites (C) and (E) was the policy of Booker T. Washington. Gradual assimilation of the two races (D) was exactly the opposite of what Malcolm X taught.

4. **(A)** After he was overthrown by revolutionary forces in 1978, the Shah of Iran, asked for permission to enter the United States to receive cancer treatment. President Carter was warned that admitting the shah to the United States, for any reason, would look to the Iranians like America still supported the shah's regime and would lead to trouble. However, other advisors told Carter that the United States owed the shah a large debt of gratitude for the favors he had done for America and also for the lack of decisive support from the U.S. when his government was overthrown. Carter had previously refused to grant the shah exile in the United States, but when he was told of the shah's need for cancer treatment, he decided to allow the shah to enter the U.S. on humanitarian grounds. As predicted, the Iranians were infuriated by this. On November 4, 1979, young Iranian males, backed by their government and claiming to be students, seized the American embassy compound and took seventy-six hostages, sixty-two of whom were held for more than a year. It was the beginning of one of the worst nightmares in American foreign policy, and it helped ruin Carter's presidency.

5. **(E)** Operation Desert Shield became Operation Desert Storm on January 16, 1991, when President George Bush announced, "The world could wait no longer...." U.S. air and sea forces together with U.N. coalition allies utilized the high-tech weapons of the U.S. Allied forces to free Kuwait and appeared to have crushed the Iraqi army in a 100-hour ground offensive. Immediate steps were taken to coordinate efforts with the U.N. (A), protect Saudi Arabia (B), impose economic sanctions (C), and designate these efforts Operation Desert Shield (D).

6. **(A)** "Reaganomics" was the term coined for President Ronald Reagan's supply-side economic policies. Reagan believed that the way

to repair the shattered economy he inherited from the Carter administration was to cut federal spending on domestic programs while at the same time cutting taxes for the wealthy and for corporations. The "supply-side" theory advocated by Reagan asserted that by cutting taxes to businesses and to the rich, money would be freed up for future investments and the creation of new jobs. This investment income would offset the initial loss of tax revenue caused by the tax cuts. Eventually, through the creation of new jobs and investments, the money freed up by tax cuts to the rich would "trickle down" to the middle classes and the poor. While this sounded good on paper, it never worked out quite as well in real life. Yes, the tax cuts did spur investment, but the investments often didn't translate into jobs that paid well. The "trickle-down" was uneven and often quite limited. Many wealthy people pocketed the money rather than investing it. Still, new jobs were created and the nation began an economic expansion that lasted into the 1990s.

7.   **(D)**   What got Nixon into trouble was his involvement in covering up White House involvement with the entire Watergate Affair. What began as a second-rate burglary by a group of unknowns became a national scandal when the burglars' connections with the White House became public. Nixon actively involved himself in trying to prevent White House involvement in Watergate from reaching the public, and it was this effort that ruined his presidency.

Had Nixon admitted White House involvement from the beginning, firing those involved, and making a public apology for the "excesses" of his underlings, he probably would have completed a successful second term. However, he and his advisors felt that the damage from Watergate could be contained if White House involvement was kept secret. Documents were shredded, records were changed, people were paid off, and Nixon was involved every step of the way. When the press finally began unravelling the mystery, Nixon continued to deny involvement and continued the coverup. When it was revealed that the White House had a taping system that had recorded Nixon's conversations during the period in question, Nixon refused to release the tapes. Eventually, in April 1974, under increasing pressure and surrounded by growing stacks of incriminating evidence, Nixon released edited versions of the tapes. This move sparked even more controversy because the edited portions of the tapes included suspicious gaps where crucial conversations should have been.

Finally, under Supreme Court order, Nixon handed over unedited tapes which, combined with the other evidence, confirmed Nixon's involvement in a massive, illegal coverup of the Watergate Affair. Nixon, facing impeachment, was forced to resign in disgrace. Later, he was pardoned before being brought to trial, by new President Gerald Ford.

8. **(E)** Many people would argue, because of the highly publicized hostage crisis, that Carter's greatest difficulties were with his Middle East policy; however, the Camp David Accords, which many consider Carter's greatest success, were a central part of those policies. Carter's Central American policies, while somewhat criticized at home, were considered successful by most Central American experts. The Panama Canal Treaty and other Carter policies focused on human rights, earning him tremendous respect among Central and South American leaders.

Domestically, Carter's greatest successes were in the areas of energy and land conservation. Carter was determined to develop new alternative sources of energy to free the United States from dependence on foreign oil. He was also a naturalist determined to protect the environment. His funding of alternative fuels research and of the Environmental Protection Agency were positive moves of which most Americans approved.

Carter's biggest failure was in economic policy. While it can be argued that many of the economic calamities that befell Carter were not entirely his fault, as many of the country's economic difficulties can be traced back to Nixon's and Johnson's policies, Carter still failed to effectively deal with them. Carter was determined to cut federal spending and reduce the federal deficit in an effort to control rising inflation. Unfortunately, his policies resulted in increasing unemployment, higher interest rates, and continued inflation. By 1979, the prime lending rate reached a historic high of twenty percent. Home mortgage rates reached sixteen percent in many areas, putting many people out of the home buying market and sending the housing industry into a tailspin. Unemployment rose to over 7.5 percent and inflation was approaching 14 percent annually.

Carter's political opponents created a new measuring standard called the "misery index" to rate how poorly the nation's economy was doing. None of Carter's efforts seemed to effect the downwardly spiraling economy. When the Iran hostage crisis hit, Carter's presidency was already in ruins. Carter's failure to free the Iran hostages simply added to the public perception of his ineptitude and was symbolic of the collapse of his leadership. While people remember the hostage crisis, had the nation's economy been relatively healthy, Carter's image would have probably been much different. People might have been more willing to see the hostage crisis as not being his fault. With the economy in shambles, it was easy to add the hostage crisis as one more thing to blame on Carter's incompetence.

9.   **(B)**   In his 1964 State of the Union message, President Lyndon Johnson called for a "War on Poverty." The Economic Opportunity Act of 1964 established the Office of Economic Opportunity to carry out antipoverty programs.

10.   **(D)**   President Reagan chose the conservative jurist Sandra Day O'Connor to be the first woman to sit on the Supreme Court. Ruth Bader Ginsberg (B) was the second woman to sit on the court. Madeleine Albright (C) became the first female Secretary of State, Ann Richards (A) was governor of Texas, and Dee Dee Meyers (E) was at one time the press secretary to Clinton.

INDEX